Behind The By-Line HU

Best Wishes!
May all the years
ahead be happy
for you.

BEHIND THE BY-LINE HU

A Fiesty Newsman's Memoirs

HU BLONK

Wenatchee, Wash.
1992

Copyright © 1992 by
HU BLONK

All rights reserved including the rights to
translate or reproduce this work or parts
thereof in any form or by any media

LIBRARY OF CONGRESS CATALOG CARD NUMBER 92-074440
ISBN 0-87062-221-8

Orders and Inquiries:
Hubert Blonk
505 15th N.E.
E. Wenatchee, WA 98802

COVER PAGE PHOTOS

*The Grand Coulee Dam spillway was a spectacle before power production
consumed most of the water.*

A most unusual photo — a doe on a floe floats down the Columbia River.

Volunteers build a house during "Farm-In-A-Day" in the Columbia Basin.

DEDICATION

This book is dedicated to my courageous mother and father who brought two small children to a strange land whose language they did not understand and thereby opened up a world of opportunity for them.

And to my loyal wife of 45 years who without complaint allowed me to move many times in the furtherance of my career and in other ways contributed to what success I achieved, and who in every way was a great mother doing a splendid job of raising a daughter and providing a fine family atmosphere.

Preface

Few small town newspaper editors have had as exciting and extraordinary a career as has the author.

This book relates the many colorful episodes that this fiesty, Dutch-born journalist was involved in.

He reveals in considerable detail the spectacular phases of the construction of the world's largest concrete dam — the Grand Coulee — and the all-night revelry, prostitutes, and other aspects of the honky-tonk town that sprung up.

The book relates the author being a sandhog in an underwater construction activity, and being present during a leak in a cofferdam that threatened to flood the construction area and at a huge earth slide that endangered the lives of workmen.

The author relates being suspended along with several other students from the University of Washington, with attendant great publicity, for insisting on the people's right to know through freedom of speech and later losing a high-paying federal job for the same reason.

Along that line the reader learns about the author receiving significant awards for helping get enacted the Freedom of Information Act which for the first time provided full public access to federal government records and for helping keep the legal profession from closing courtrooms throughout the country.

These memoirs are somewhat personal in nature for they were primarily written for the author's family. They are provided in book form because acquaintances wanted to read them and a number of them about the dam may be of historic value.

Acknowledgments

The author is greatly indebted to the following:

The U.S. Bureau of Reclamation and the Wenatchee World for offering him challenging opportunities to serve the people in exciting ways.

The Associated Managing Editors Association for allowing him to spend 25 years on its Freedom of Information Committee defending the people's right to know throughout the land, three years as its chairman.

The state's Bench-Bar-Press Committee for having him as a charter and long-time member as it sought to assure fair trial and free press.

The author is also indebted to the following people and sources in the publication of the book.

Helen Kensrud, a special friend without whose ideas, enthusiasm and computer work this book might never have been produced.

My daughter, Julie Yeager, who insisted I record my memories for the family to enjoy and who was a key figure throughout the preparation.

Jane Cartwright, a great newspaper person, who contributed tremendously to the editing.

Tammy Caldwell for her help with the final editing.

Bill McGaughey, the World composing room foreman, who came up with the title for the book and aided in numerous ways, and Rolf Wagner, a member of his staff, who aided in the final editing and prepared the material for the printer.

Craig Sprankle, Bureau of Reclamation information man at the Grand Coulee Dam, who provided vital facts and photographs.

Stan Pachosa of Grand Coulee Dam for offering photographs and colorful facts of early Grand Coulee.

"The Mightiest Of Them All — Memories of Grand Coulee Dam" by L. Vaughn Downs, the book "Pioneers to Power," issued by the Bicentennial Association, and the Grand Coulee News, edited by Sidney Jackson, whose clippings supplemented a large batch from the Wenatchee World which the author saved.

Contents

BOOK FOUR — *"World" Wonderful*

Illustrations

BOOK ONE

TO AMERICA

Off with the Wooden Shoes

It began near a little farm canal in Hazerswoude, Holland, on March 7, 1909, and it ended near the Columbia River, State of Washington, U.S.A.

I was 83 when this book was published. In between was an exciting life made possible by two courageous people, my parents, Leendert and Maartje Blonk. They had the gumption to leave their native land for a huge new country, whose language they could not speak, accompanied by their two small children. They left their friends and relatives, never to see them again, so there might be a life of opportunity for themselves and their son, Hubertus Cornelus, and their daughter, Adriana, that was not to be found in tiny Netherland.

We lived in a two-story brick house in Holland. Sleeping quarters were in the upper story. There I could clearly hear, if I woke early, the sounds of farmers going to their land to milk their cows. Their wooden shoes (klompen) loudly hit the cobblestone street as they walked in the darkness.

The little canal near our house and an adjacent dairy barn sticks in my memory. There was fishing to do in the canal with the bait being a piece of bread rolled up into a small ball. The fish caught were only six-inch size but they were fish! The canal provided wintertime recreation, too. It was an ideal place to learn to skate. You just brought a chair out of the house and pushed it ahead of you slowly as you tried to stay erect. The skates were steel runners clamped between two pieces of wood.

Once I learned to skate, I could go from town to town via the canals. There was some danger of breaking through the ice as it was thin under the many bridges that span Holland's waterways.

We would get two weeks off from school so that we could enjoy skating. No wonder tiny Holland has long had some of the finest skaters in the world. Children are taught early. During the festivals we skated all over the canals holding onto Mom and Dad. We could skate well that way.

Adults joined the fun, too. There were tents around the ponds where one could get cocoa and "moppen," a soft gingersnap. My folks, who were so graceful as they glided over the ice, no doubt were a bit disappointed in how their son was skating — all hunched up trying to make speed and sometimes falling down.

The upper story of our house played a special role at Santa Claus time. It was customary to have an adult drop tiny square cookies the size of dice through an opening in the upstairs corner to the living room below. This always occurred on December 5, when Santa came into the house wearing a crown on his head and holding a staff in his hand. Outside one could hear chains rattle. These were carried by a Negro helper.

Santa Claus was called Sinta Klaas (St. Nicholas) and his helper was Swarta Piet (Black Pete). If we had been good Santa would give us gifts, but we were told that Swarta Piet would take them away if we had been bad.

Before entering the house, we took off our wooden shoes and left them outside. The front room, a family bedroom, another bedroom and the kitchen were on the first floor. Across the hall on the left was a guest room, a small eating alcove and a summer living room.

The house was located next to a bridge over a "sloot", as canals were called. It had a backyard with a stoop where my mother sometimes washed clothes. Nearby was a garden with vegetables, gooseberries, currants and strawberries.

There was also a play area where we played a game of territory using a knife. We each had a piece of ground and would take turns flipping the knife into the other's territory. We would then take whatever sections the knife pointed to. Whoever could acquire the most land would win. My sister and I enjoyed playing this game.

Besides their skating skill, Mom and Dad had acting ability. I recall my sister, who lived to be 75, having nightmares and crying when we were put to bed in the bedroom next to the front room. This occasionally happened when our parents and others were rehearsing a play to raise money for school projects. My sister would be scolded for crying and bothering them.

I particularly remember mother acting out a story about a little boy who had to go to school with a hole in his pants and was teased by other children until he cried. Mother would make it all seem so real that my sister would cry because she felt so sorry for the little tot.

Sunday was memorable for me because I was allowed to smoke one cigarette at age 10. It was kept in a little, attractive silver box that I have to this day. I did not get the habit and never did smoke in America. Taking up long-distance running in high school helped induce me to forego tobacco.

Hazerswoude was a tiny dorp (village) so there was not much excitement. It was quite an event when a double-decker bus would discharge passengers on the main street. The bus emitted considerable exhaust. For decades afterward whenever I smelled exhaust like it my mind would immediately flash back to Holland.

I also remember a man driving a lorry wagon who would give us children a small toy if we brought him a good-sized bundle of rags.

Whenever my dad went to Leiden on business he would bring back things that he knew we children enjoyed. Particularly tasty was "drop" (licorice) and "stroopwaffle"(syrup waffle). The latter consisted of a two to three-inch thick, circular waffle with syrup between the layers.

A doctor and his family lived across the street from us. We played with their two boys. "The youngest one and I were going to get married when we grew up," my sister recalled, "But one day he stuck me with a pin, and I got mad and called it off."

Adriana remembered her first bicycle as having pedals built up with blocks of wood so that her legs could reach them.

Some of our rememberances of school included hearing World War I bombs go off in the distance, taking French as a second language (instead of English which would have served us much better it later developed), and my sister sometimes being punished for talking too much. She would have to sit on the teacher's lap or worse yet sit next to a boy at the double-seat desks. Adriana really hated that.

On Sundays our family would attend the Dutch Reform Church located nearby. To this day we have a carved foot-stool in which hot coals were put to keep our feet warm during the services.

I was a bit pugnacious, I guess, or just a boy with a typical Dutch temperament. I got into fights once in awhile.

In later years, I would often relate how handicapped I was in America in taking on another kid because I did not know how to box. Boys didn't fight that way in Holland. There they would wrestle and when one got the other down he would take off his wooden shoe and hit him on the head with it. If you got mad and couldn't catch the kid, you'd throw your shoe at him. This act would sometimes result in the shoe splitting and your getting a severe bawling out when you got home. Repair was done by placing a metal strip around the wood.

One of our young life's particular excitements was going to Scheveningen on the ocean. It featured wooden sidewalks and bathouses on wheels. The latter could be moved to the edge of the water wherever the tide was. They were used to dress and undress in. There were also hundreds of wicker chairs with high backs I recall.

A dreary scene greets us in Canada

My uncle, John Blonk, had preceded my parents across the vast ocean. He settled on the prairies of Canada near Calgary. My folks were headed that way when they boarded the ship.

The first part of the voyage involved us crossing the English Channel to England. I and my mother got seasick almost immediately. That prevailed all the way to the St. Lawrence River in distant Canada. Adriana and my dad were sick only two days. My father used to bribe the steward for soft-boiled eggs which was the only food that appealed to us when we were sick.

My strongest memory of the ship crossing was seeing all the lights on the shore as we moved along the St. Lawrence River. It was real thrilling.

After getting off the boat in Quebec my folks met with a problem. In going to a hotel they found it full. Luckily a man in the lobby heard of their plight and offered to let us have his room. We didn't know where he slept that night. The room had only one large bed so we had to sleep on it cross-wise, all four of us.

After the long train ride we Hollanders finally arrived at Helmsdale, Alberta, where my father's brother had land on which wheat was grown. The soil was very dry and rocky. My father, I'm sure, was disappointed being used to the lush fields of Holland, but he joined in and helped clear the land.

I suspect that Uncle John had painted a rosier picture than the one that existed for I doubt if my folks would have abandoned their homeland for something like that.

Uncle John's house was very small and there were not enough beds for all of us to sleep in. My mother turned a table upside down and made a bed in it for Adriana.

Adriana and I quickly adapted. One of the fun things to do was place a snare around a gopher hole and then try to catch it by pulling on a long string. I always found it hard to kill anything caught that way.

Bigger holes in the ground were those of badgers. We didn't bother them much. The sound of their hissing scared us off.

Of course, there was school to attend. I started the first grade at age 11. The school was situated about three miles away. We'd hook a ride in a buggy coming up the road from an adjacent farm. The girl driver must have been of a nasty temperament for I recall that once she made a neighbor boy, who also rode with her, place his hand on the wood of the buggy and then she struck it with her whip. I don't know if that scared me away from women, but it was not until college that I dated anyone. Even then, I felt uncomfortable around females.

My most vivid memory of going to the little schoolhouse was the teacher writing the letters "C A T" on the blackboard. I had been put in the first grade although I was in the sixth in Holland because I could not understand English. I couldn't understand what the word on the black-board meant so the teacher finally drew a cat. Later, in the U.S., I jumped to the fourth grade, then back up to the 6th.

It wasn't very long before my folks decided to depart the dry country near Oyen. Dad wrote a Dutch friend in Thomas, situated between Kent and Auburn near Seattle, Wash., seeking work. He was hired.

America here we come

We took a train to Vancouver, Canada, where my folks had trouble finding a room for us in the dark of night. They also had difficulty conversing. Somehow, a couple of Dutch origin took them in tow after they crossed the border. This kind act developed into many years of close friendship.

A small house awaited the family in Thomas. Dad arrived there to go to work with Ad Schuurman on his dairy ranch. Adriana and I were quickly put back in school while our folks learned English the best they could, mostly by conversing with Americans.

My mother recalled buying a ham. The butcher wanted her to say which part of the hog she wanted the ham from and illustrated by slapping himself on the hip and then the upperpart of his body. In later years, mother learned considerable English from working crossword puzzles. This was noticeable in her letters to me while I was in college.

She wrote rather poor English, but once in awhile you'd find a three-syllable word among the simple words that I knew she learned from the puzzles.

I also worked for Schuurman, at times. I'd pitch hay onto a wagon and then would distribute it in the hay mow when thrown to me from the wagon.

I went to school at Thomas and soon was moved back into the sixth grade. By that time my English was good enough to get by although my pronunciation was still Dutch-like.

Meanwhile my mother continued to learn English the hard way. She and Mrs. Schuurman would surely confuse the storekeeper whenever they ventured into his place. One time my mother wanted yarn to fix a sock. She would say "hole in sock" but the storekeeper, instead of bringing her yarn, showed her scissors, thinking she wanted something to cut a hole with.

The grocer turned the women over to a Japanese helper in the store. They confronted him once with the request for a certain spice. He couldn't understand them so he put all the spices on the table and told the women to smell and decide which one they wanted.

Another time the two women went to the store with a picture of a pig that they had drawn. On it they had marked what part of the pork they wanted.

Some of the food we consumed in that youthful period remain vivid in memory. One was "beest" which was the first milk from a cow after it had calved. By warming it just right it would become a sort of custard. "Oliebollen" cooked in deep fat also were very tasty as were "poffertjes."

In a short while my father and mother decided they wanted to strike out on their own so they rented a dairy farm on the outskirts of Auburn from a man named Lund, who was a state legislator. The place had an attractive house at the end of a road, a large barn and a milkshed where the milk fresh from the Holstein cows would be chilled by allowing it to run over piping cooled by water inside.

Of course, I assisted in milking the cows, some 40 of them. There was no milking machine at first. Not many farmers of the day had them. In the morning milking would start at 3 a.m. and in the afternoon at 3 p.m.

My Dad was always very punctual. If we had the hay spread out in front of the animals five minutes before milking time Dad would wait five minutes so as to start milking exactly on time. The punctuality so taught has stayed with me throughout my life.

In winter time, the old barn was a frigid place. As you milked the foam generated would freeze on the side of the pail. Creating foam was one of the fun things about milking. If you spurted the milk out of the tits in exactly the same place each time a sizable amount of foam would form.

My Dad milked quietly but I always sang loudly or whistled.

Milking cows was just part of our daily chore. The folks ran a milk route in Auburn. My mother, a hard-working woman, would pitch in running it.

19

As Dad drove an old pick-up, we kids would sit on the tailgate and run to various houses. Because delivery was made in glass bottles one could always see the creamline. I missed that when in later years cardboard cartons were used and the milk was homogenized. The folks' enterprise was called "Blonk's Pure Milk Dairy."

In summertime when back from college — the University of Washington — I would join in to do haying, milking and other farmwork. My wrists would kill me for several weeks until they became adjusted again to milking.

The work on the farm during my high school days prevented me from participating in sports or other after-school activities. So I was never a key figure in student activities. But I did participate in an operetta and a negro minstrel show.

I played the role of "Alexander Salamander John Henry Jones." The stage appearance led me later to engage in amateur theatricals in Boise and Wenatchee when I worked in those communities.

As a student I was a hit-and-miss one, getting good grades one semester and bad the next. The latter was the result of my having loafed after doing well. One time, knowing my mother would be furious about the low grades on my report card, I first told her about having won the school oratorical contest. She more or less brushed that aside and concentrated on giving me a good talking to about not doing better in school.

During my last year I was able to substitute journalism and public speaking for English courses. I did not particularly like the latter, perhaps because of having missed some schooling in English having come from another land. Because I took public speaking, I won the local Lincoln essay contest sponsored in high schools throughout the country by some national organization. I have kept that three-inch-diameter medallion all my life.

By high school time I had overcome my accent. Earlier I could not say "three" instead coming out with "tree." Kids sometimes laughed at the accent, but it did not give me an inferiority complex.

One other problem confronted me at first. My mother dressed me up in old country style, in Little Lord Fauntleroy outfits, instead of the knickers the American kids were wearing. So they thought I was a sissy. This resulted in a number of fights. I always lost, because I did not know how to box.

I often referred to my early school days in the many speeches that I gave in my lifetime. I would tell the audience, that surely they could have gotten a more qualified speaker for the one they had was still in the first grade at age 11. I would then, of course, explain my having come from Holland and not speaking English.

I participated in a number of activities in high school. The 1927 "Invader," the annual of my senior year, lists them as: Hi-jink, 3 (the number referring to the year in school) Hi-Jink, 3A; Senior Play; Athletic Editor-Invader, 4; Boys Sports Editor of Annual, 4; Glee Club, 4; Lincoln Essay Contest, 4; Operetta, 4. I also turned out for track, running the mile, but I never earned a letter.

The annual published, adjacent to my picture, these words: "If someone couldn't laugh and be jolly this world wouldn't be what it is by golly."

A full page was devoted to the Senior Class Poem I wrote. It was entitled "Parting" and read as follows:

The time has come when we must part
The saddening of the loving heart
But before we step into the world of strife
Let us turn back - that happy life.

Come think again of the happy days.
Before we leave, our parting ways
Those memories shall long remain
Of teaching which was not in vain.

Joyful times, those days of yore
Yes, they shall live forevermore
In the minds of all the time is here
We now must leave, shed we a tear.

We know not how the future read
Nor know we how our paths shall lead
Let God be with us through the fight
That we may tread, "The Path of Right."

Winning the high school oratorical contest is on my record but I did poorly in the interschool competition. Later I would take a course in public speaking which would stand me in good stead for I was to deliver 250 speeches more or less in my lifetime. Most of them were on "the people's right to know."

My closest school chums were Arnold Galli, whose dad, a Swiss, had a dairy ranch, and Russell Pulling. The latter had a "bug," a two-seated car that he'd built. We went scooting about on that all over the place. Russell was to become my roommate during my freshman year at the U.W.

Arnold and I used to play on a Lutheran Church basketball team. I also played solos on the saxaphone at church gatherings on occasion, but not very good. At church box socials, Arnold always bid on my sisters entry as he had a crush on her at that time. During my college days I used to amuse the postman by addressing letters to Arnold as "Bovine Extractor." He still remembers my getting itching powder on him for amusement.

Louie Smith is a character I should mention in these memoirs. He being of an adventurous spirit induced me to hitchhike with him to Tacoma, which was about 15 miles away. He had promised to get me back by the time school was over for the day so that my folks would not know that I had played "hooky," but we got back in the early evening, where upon my anxious folks ordered me straight to bed!

The dairy enterprise my folks ventured into was not profitable, not because they did not put in long hours or have good business sense, but because they had been sold cows with tuberculosis. This forced them to dispose of them at a considerable loss.

So they finally gave up and tried raising poultry and selling eggs on a route. The same misfortune struck them again. After they had bought the chickens, they found that the previous owner substituted culls that did not produce well. My father had a method of checking the chickens to determine if they were good layers. But before he could take over the ranch, the shift to poorer stock had been made.

Later Dad leased another dairy farm where hoeing thistles was a prime job for me.

Having become tremendously interested in journalism in my senior high school year, I decided that I wanted to attend college.

The folks had no money to pay for my education so during the summer preceding the fall term at the University I dug drainage ditches. I worked with an older worker and each day I would try to dig more ditch than the preceding day. I always liked a challenge and was considered a good worker. In later years I repeatedly told my grandsons that it pays to do more than you're expected to do. I did so in the government or wherever else I worked.

My folks were poor but we never were hungry. Once Adriana and I wanted to go to a show but there was no money for entertainment in the budget so we were allowed to sell a chicken, which we did by going door to door.

There was other recreation available during my growing-up days. Football in cow pastures was fun. I was generally the quarterback, hurtling the ball down field to a Virgil Swanson, who became a long-time friend. Turning out for high school track was enjoyable, although this ex-Hollander was never good at the long distances he chose to compete in. However, the sport led to my running intramural cross-country at the U. and one year making the varsity as the last, and slowest man picked.

When home from college going downtown, which was about a half mile away, was evening-time recreation for myself and a good friend, Henry Knickerbocker. We just walked around talking to other fellows. Neither of us was in search of female companionship. Fact is, I never dated in high school although I had a secret crush on a couple of pretty girls.

Even in college I shied away from girls. I didn't have either the money or the social graces or so I thought. Not until a year after I finished college did I take a girl seriously. I married her.

As long as I can remember, I was a jokester. On a hiking trip I put a sizable rock in the knapsack of a friend who was about to knock my block off when he found out what I had forced him to carry. In the years after that I played jokes on many people, including putting out phony front pages for special occasions. Sometimes I got paid back in kind.

The Auburn period of my life was a happy period despite all the hours I was required to work. I don't remember complaining although, among other things, I had to leave the old swimming hole in Green River at about 3 o'clock each day to get home in time to help with the milking. This was just about the time that the kids were starting to have a lot of fun.

On to College and Eating Beans

I was graduated from Auburn High School in 1927 and headed for the U.W., poor as I was.

In later years whenever I spoke on campus, I used to begin my speech by claiming I had eaten more beans than any other student in the history of the school. I could get a pot of beans at Sweitzer's Beanery on "the Avenue" for 15 cents. Sometimes by the weekend I would be "fed up" with beans and would indulge in bakery goods.

My living accomodations were equally spartan. Russell Pulling and I got an upstairs room in a preachers' big house on fraternity row. However, when Pulling had to leave for lack of funds, I moved into a basement room that was cheaper — $15 a month. It had pipes overhead, a narrow slit of a window, and was near a very noisy furnace.

I was able to pay my way through school by working summers, one year in a terra cotta plant and then digging ditches. At one time I had to borrow a whopping $500 from Pete Dykstra, a well-to-do Dutch farmer, for whom I had picked potatoes during the summer (at a speed that matched his). It took me about a year after graduating to repay the much appreciated loan.

Attending the U. was probably the most exciting period of my life. In my freshman year, I joined the University of Washington Daily as an ill-prepared sports writer, turned out for track — the two-mile and fall cross-country — attended pep rallies, and did all the other fun things that can accompany going to college.

On the paper, my duties escalated, I became sports editor and later associate editor. I failed to achieve the editorship. I felt that was because I was not a fraternity man and also had been accused of running an expose on athletes foot being rampant in Hec Edmundson Pavilion during the time of high school visitation to the campus. I ran for the job twice, always with the backing of the journalism faculty but not the support of the "frat" people.

Speaking of fraternities, we independents wanted to compete in cross-country intramurals so we had to form an organization. We called it "The Finish Club." In three years we retired the trophy. No wonder, said the"frat" runners, they're all a bunch of Finns, which we were not. These were the days of Paavo Nurmi, the famous Finland long-distance runner.

I used to start training for the fall term by running through my dad's pasture at Auburn and on to the highway and beyond. I was in good shape when competition started. I won many firsts, seconds and thirds, but never could take first in the Thanksgiving Turkey Run. This was the final event of the intramural season.

While writing on the Daily as associate editor, I was outspoken against ROTC. I sincerely felt that preparing for war would bring on war. In later years, I would not be so sure of this.

I spent a great deal of time in "The Daily Shack," which is what we called the place where we typed out our stuff.

Thus my grades suffered, although I got lots of B's, too many C's, and now and then an A in key subjects. We used to spend until two o'clock in the morning at the print shop.

One exciting time was traveling with the Husky basketball team to Oakland where they played California for the coast championship. I stowed away on the train that was carrying the athletes. Such stowing away was common for writers who went along with the football squad, because the conductor couldn't possibly count all the people aboard.

Basketball had a smaller number of players so stowing away was not done.

Enroute south, a player sat on the toilet and I stood behind the compartment door. When the conductor came he counted one person (the one on the toilet). On the trip back, the players hid me under papers spread out between the seats. While in Oakland, I sold their tickets outside the Oakland Auditorium and assisted Ira Blue on a coast radio broadcast with commentary at half-time. He later would become famous as the first talk show host of repute in the nation.

As a result of work on the Daily, I became campus correspondent for the Seattle Post-Intelligencer (P-I) at the staggering sum of $5 per week. I would have to go downtown to pound out my stories each day. In this capacity I learned the hard way about the importance of being accurate.

As I was about to leave the second story at the P-I building, City Editor Ed Stone stopped me to ask if the name of the student body president, Jerry Auchenbach, was spelled with a "k" or an "h." I said a "k." The next day the editor met me in the hall and shouted "Blonk, damn you, you said it was spelled with a "k" and it was an "h" and we had to replate!" I have never forgotten the early lesson.

One of the nice things about going to the P-I was that I could eat well once a week. A "Merry-Go-Round Cafe" had a rotating platform about 30 feet wide which was loaded with many delicious items, and for 35 cents I could eat all that I wanted. The huge stack of dirty dishes at my table allowed all to see my greed.

The campus correspondent assignment led the P-I to take me on as a full-time cub reporter. The job paid $10 a week. I covered a variety of news, and, in all candor, I must say that I did a lousy job. When the regular reporters got back from their summer vacations, I was let go.

Not having any cash reserve to tide me over until I could find something more suitable, I took a job as a newspaper carrier. My beat was First Avenue and the waterfront, an area of apartment houses, some of questionable repute, and the fisheries. I wrote up the experience in a somewhat liberal manner for the U.W. Columns, a humor magazine, and called the story "I Too Cover the Waterfront." (I have included the complete story further on in my college days rememberances). Max Millers' book, "I Cover the Waterfront," had just become a best seller. My story had a sour outlook on life, this being the days of the Depression.

It was from this humble carrier job that I went to Grand Coulee Dam. More about that later.

It was early in my Daily career that I shortened Hubert to "Hu" mainly because just about every sissy in the movies was named Hubert, and I didn't want to use "Hugh." I have continued to use the shortened version throughout my professional life.

When I wrote the sports column I used the corniest title "Blonkitis." It was popular, rating second only to Freddy Wyatt's gossip column which was printed a'la Walter Winchell.

It was my practice to never discuss any subject in the column for more than one paragraph. That policy of news by tid-bits was surely effective. Readers loved it.

Our class was a distinctive one, I believe. Rud Lawrence became vice-president of the New York Stock Exchange, Tom Griffith became senior editor of Life Magazine, Bob Trumbull was made Tokyo correspondent for the New York Times (he covered the war with Japan) and wrote a best seller, "The Raft." Harold Mansfield became public relations director for the Boeing Company. Others did almost equally well.

One worker on the Daily became famous in another way. Her name was Francis Farmer, a striking girl, who later became a movie star. Her life was depicted in a movie, and I felt that it sort of explained why later in life she committed suicide.

Some of us were pledged by Sigma Delta Chi, the national journalism fraternity. For the initiation we had to be on the campus a full day dressed in tuxedos. Despite the fancy dress we had to bend down periodically, hands on our ankles, to be hacked by a long paddle. Each fellow had a special assignment to complete. Mine was to sing at the luncheon in a sorority house. No doubt my shyness and blushing made me ideal for this. It really shook me up! Not to mention the sorority!

In my senior year the fraternity's local chapter named me recipient of the "Pa Kennedy" plaque which is given to the member having contributed most. Kennedy ran the University print shop and taught us typography. He was the member of the faculty advising our group.

While on the campus I was decidedly shy about girls. Art French and Slim Lynch, photographers at the P-I, knew this and loved to embarrass me. They'd come out to illustrate stories about the U., which meant that I was to provide a pretty girl for them to photograph. They'd drive down the avenue and see a classy gal across the street and then say "Blonk, that's the one we want." I'd have to cross the street and ask the girl to pose for them. I surmise that she probably thought that I was exercising a new way to pick her up.

So I asked a girl who worked on the Daily and who I knew quite well to agree to pose should I ever need someone for a photo. That resulted in embarrassment for me too, because it was customary in those days to ask the subject to raise her skirts so that her knees would show . . . real daring.

It was this atmosphere of modesty that later would cause By Fish, a friend, to be threatened with expulsion because he brought several girls onto the campus wearing bathing suits for a publicity picture. The loose-fitting suits covered everything but nevertheless U. officials said "No No," objecting to the publicity that resulted.

Knowing that I blushed prompted Fish and a fellow humor column writer, Emerson Daggett, to pound on a cafeteria tray while I was eating and then point to me. I turned red as a beet when a number of people stared at me. I got even with them later, when the two jokesters were eating near a cafe window on the Avenue. I started hollering, "Lookee,

lookee," and pointed to the two of them. Quite a crowd gathered and while they didn't blush, they were obviously uncomfortable.

I had a close association with Fish, who later was a humorist on the Seattle Times, and also with Daggett, who later became a communist. They wrote humorous sketches for the half-hour radio program that we staged for Radio Station KOL. I did short sport interviews.

I recall vividly two incidents during the broadcasts. One was a sketch that purported to advise listeners what television would be like when it came. The story had the announcer and his TV assistants entering the home of the University president, Hugo Winkenwerder. When he was not to be found at first, the announcer reported "There he is . . . in the bathroom." Then directly in front of the radio mike a glass of water was poured into another followed by the punchline "Why Dr. Winkenwerder!"

The second memory involves my having completed an interview with a sports dignitary and then Fish and Daggett reading a script for a sketch that supposedly took them below the surface of the ocean. To their surprise, page 7 of the script was missing. They kept talking about the various kinds of fish they were seeing etc. while I was down on the floor searching for the missing page. Someone else was looking around in the outer studio and found it. Then the broadcast was resumed. The ad-libbing required to keep the story moving while the search was on took real talent. Fish and Daggett had that talent in abundance.

My debut on radio was unique. At one time I blew directly into the microphone, in varying volumes, to provide the wind for a graveyard scene. Later, I contributed the sound of a turkey gobbling, something I am still able to do with a real degree of authenticity.

It was surprising that people were apprehensive about being on radio in those days. They were plainly scared, even rough, tough athletes like Paul Swegler, All-American football star from the university.

My radio experience led to my doing a 15-minute sports commentary on a Seattle station for free. It didn't last long, because I did not have time to prepare really good material.

An honor was bestowed on me during my senior year. I was made a member of the Oval Club that recognized students for having made major contributions in service to their Alma Mater.

Also as a senior I was awarded an "Honorary W" sweater. These were given to athletes who did not earn the more coveted "W." The former recognized continued devotion to the sport through having turned out for four consecutive years, in my case for track and cross-country.

Coach Hec Edmundsen put me on the Husky cross-country team. I was the final runner to be chosen for the seven-man squad. However, the Depression made it necessary to cut track expenses so a meet in Portland was cancelled. It was the only one on the schedule.

When U.W. track was over, I continued to stay in shape for a 10-mile run that was sponsored annually on the Fourth of July by the Seattle P-I. The route ran from Sixth and Pine in downtown Seattle to the U.W. stadium, where the runners would finish just before the fireworks display.

There were some 40 runners entered, including, according to the P-I, great runners from overseas. I took eighth, which was disappointing because another U.W. runner whom I had beaten before took third.

I must have been a pretty skinny guy in those days because as I ran down the course some kids hollered at me, "Keep going, Spareribs!" That was the name of a skeleton-like character in a popular comic strip.

In my junior year my interest in entering a 50-mile walking race around Green Lake was aroused. I thought I'd try to walk to my hometown of Auburn, which was about 25 miles distant, just to see what kind of time I could expect to make. Although I was in excellent shape, I soon found out that you use different muscles in walking than you do in running. The next day, I was stiff all over, not to mention having blisters that had broken and made bloody spots on my tennis shoes.

My running ended when I left college, only to return in later life, when I competed in road races with teen-agers and others. I ran up to the age of 70. School chum Arnold Galli recalled "You were always running, I could never keep up."

The students of the 1930 era were dressed in various manners, but cords and yellow slickers predominated. It was the custom to write initials or figures on the corduroys and many of them were quite dirty. There was actually a competition for the "dirtiest cords on campus" in which I won a top prize.

Not being a fraternity man, my socializing was confined to "mixers." Neither my schoolmate, Pulling, or myself could dance so we took dancing lessons at the old Trianon Ballroom. When my mother heard of my spending money for this purpose, she became very angry. She figured it was a waste of money.

I only dated once during my collegiate days and that was a blind date. It turned out to be a disaster. I was too timid to be a good companion to a girl that I had never met before, so she largely ignored me. I even ran out of money and had to borrow some from one of the fellows there so that I could take the gal to the restaurant that the group had decided to go to.

I never drank in college except for once. While out working on the P-I, I accompanied a bunch of the college kids to a party. They offered me a martini, and, knowing nothing about liquor, I proceeded to drink quite a few. In less than an hour they took me away. I awoke in someone else's house and saw the god-awfullest looking guy in the bed next to me. I soon discovered that I was looking into a mirror. Working on the police beat that day was a nightmare! I attempted to lie down most of the time.

Fuss on the Campus

In my senior year I got involved in an incident that would have a far-reaching impact on my career.

It resulted in my becoming the only person in the world who owns a chromium-plated crowbar. It now hangs framed against a background of black velvet in the hallway of my home.

It was awarded to me in the 1970's when I was with the Wenatchee World by the Allied Daily Newspapers of Washington for a rather long contribution to protection of the people's right to know through freedom of the press.

It all began on the University of Washington campus in 1933.

Before that I had been a fairly well behaved student in the institution's School of Journalism. Oh yes, I made caustic comments about sundry things in the University of Washington Daily, these included claiming that athlete's foot was rampant in an untidy Hec Edmundson Pavilion and that ROTC was unnecessary if we were to make any progress toward a peaceful world. But otherwise I had floated along peacefully toward a degree.

In my senior year I had joined the "Thursday Noon Club." "Joined" is actually not a good description of my becoming involved, because the club wasn't really a formal organization. It had no officers. Anyone could attend.

The objective of the group, while never formally stated, was to hear talks on both sides of controversial topics. It heard a militarist and a pacifist. In connection with a turbulent mayoralty campaign it listened to the fiery John Dore and a fluent individual who called himself "Radio Speaker Stevenson". He had a nightly, much-listened to program. Other opposing viewpoints were similarly heard.

The organization had for its members students of high scholastic standing (except myself) and numerous professors.

No one took exception to what the Thursday Noon Club was doing until the University administration learned that the next speaker was to be Mrs. Jesse London Wakefield, a former University student who gained much publicity through her imprisonment during the Kentucky coal fields strike several years earlier. The president of the U. called her an "asserted Communist" in the subsequent furor.

Mrs. Wakefield denied this. She said she'd addressed assemblies at many large Eastern colleges as a member of the International Labor Defense League and in doing so was not there "to preach or exalt Communism but to tell of her actual experiences in the Kentucky coal fields."

Butting your Head against an Anvil

When President Hugo Winkenwerder learned of the proposed Wakefield appearance, I immediately became involved, because I was the reporter covering the board of regents and the president's office. Winkenwerder called me to his office, and, there, he and the Dean of Students told me the club could not hold the meeting.

The exact conversation that took place is long forgotten but it was clear that the administration feared public reaction, or, more specifically, that of the legislature and downtown newspapers. I asked specifically why we couldn't have Mrs. Wakefield, and the president replied that it would make it more difficult for the school to get appropriations from the legislature.

This brought forth from me the caustic comment that any institution that wouldn't allow freedom of speech so that students could hear both sides of any issue shouldn't be entitled to appropriations.

President Winkenwerder ordered me to notify the officers of the Thursday Noon Club to cancel the appearance or else. I asked, "what if we proceeded anyway?" Then the Dean of Students made a remark I have never forgotten "Blonk, you'll be butting your head against an anvil."

Feeling strongly that the club was in no way communistic and had shown an admirable devotion to being open to all sides in a controversy, the leaders decided to ignore the Winkenwerder order and hear Mrs. Wakefield.

They were Vernon Withuhn, president; Emerson Daggett, vice-president; George Fahey, chairman of the speaker's bureau; and myself, chairman of the executive committee; and the following members of that committee: Miner Baker, Martin Iorns, John Clyde, Mervin Cole, Lawrence Kay, Seldon Menefee and Duane Robinson.

The University Daily came out with the headline, "Club Leaders Defy Faculty Censorship. Thursday Noon Luncheon Group Determined to Hear Speaker. Want Freedom. Winkenwerder Says All Political Speakers Banned."

The story said that the action was an "echo" to the ultimatum handed down by former President Lyle M. Spencer, in February, 1932, following a campus speech by Sherwood Eddy, who was called, in another story, "slightly pink."

The story went on "President Winkenwerder, questioned concerning the order, declared 'All talks of a political nature are necessarily banned from the campus; this includes all political propaganda which is likely to result in reduced appropriations from the legislature.'

"Pressure from the Seattle papers had already been brought to bear upon the University administration because of the liberal tendencies of the campus. The speaker is a confirmed propagandist although she isn't to talk on Communism.

"Vernon Withun, president of the club, stating he was unable to understand the action of the faculty committee or its censorship, insisted, 'The description of labor conditions in the Kentucky coal fields is not exceeding the definitions of free speech.'

"The Thursday Noon Club believes students have a right to know both sides of every question and with that aim in mind have been scheduling speakers to present all views of topical subjects.

"Hubert Blonk, student leader and prominent member of the luncheon club, voiced his opinions emphatically, "I am not a Communist, but I believe in freedom of speech above all. However, the speaker is to talk on Kentucky coal field labor relations and not on Communism. I feel it is about time that students stood up for their rights to gain a liberal education. (This was my first publicly quoted remark on the right of the people to know, which we defended through the years under the freedom of the press label).

The Daily story went on to say: "Asserting that speakers representing the Chamber of Commerce, religious groups, the American Legion and the faculty had been allowed to speak without first having secured permission, Emerson Daggett, one of the organizers of the club, said: "It seems strange that we have not been required to register our other speakers."

"George Fahey, who arranged the speech, declared 'The organization

29

has for its members, students of high scholastic standing. It is not a radical organization . . . We believe in hearing the truth and all the truth'."

The next day, the University of Washington Daily carried two more stories on developing events.

One said eleven student leaders of the Thursday Noon Club were to be arraigned before the faculty discipline committee, headed by Prof. R.W. Jones of Journalism, to explain why and, on what grounds, they chose to ignore President Winkenwerder's ultimatum that Mrs. Wakefield should not address yesterday's session of the club.

The paper said the committee has the authority to expel, suspend, warn or place students on probation.

Nearly 150 students and faculty members were present at the Wakefield talk, which club leaders had been urged to hold in Eagleson Hall, off campus, but had refused to do so because they felt the "description of labor conditions in Kentucky coal fields was not exceeding the definitions of free speech."

Mrs. Wakefield said she'd gone to the coal fields to arrange for food and lawyers for those in trouble. She said mine operators had a two-fold plan of winning the strike.

"They blacklisted all miners in their way, denying them food and taking away their living quarters," she said. And secondly, she continued, they allowed no relief agencies to operate. A soup kitchen was dynamited. Her car was also dynamited, and she was jailed for six weeks.

The university's discipline committee suspended, for six months, the students who'd allowed themselves to be called "officers" of the club. The total was nine. Two of the students, Mervin Cole and Lawrence Kay, were not affected for reasons I don't recall.

During the hearing we had stated that we understood that the rule against bringing in outside speakers without permission was applicable only when the speeches were of a political or controversial nature, and that we had contended that Mrs. Wakefield's address was actually a mild discourse.

At the time of the disciplinary action, Winkenwerder also ordered the club to be dissolved. And he "shortened somewhat the time in which the students could apply for re-instatement," according to a Seattle Times article of May 27. They could petition for readmittance less that a month later, which was June 12, to be exact. This meant graduating seniors could probably receive their degrees at the end of the summer quarter.

In fact, the U. President had some nice things to say about the trouble makers, while still defending his action. He said "Investigation shows that the Thursday Noon Club consists of students of good ability and apparently good character who meet for lunch and listen to speakers on various topics. Its organization is very loose, and the decision to go ahead with the meeting in question was reached simply by consultation among its members as they met one another on the campus.

"The issue was not free speech, but the disobedience of the rules and the express order of the president. As the university is an institution having as one of its purposes, the training of young men and women to become good citizens, the penalty imposed is felt to be adequate to make the offenders realize that constituted authorities of the university must not be disobeyed."

Editorially, we students were both supported and denounced. The Student Daily ran a couple of editorials. One was headed "Don't Muzzle 'Em — They Won't Bite" and the other "Red Headlines Scare Administration Into Throttling Free Speech."

On the other hand, The Seattle Times castigated the club's disposed leaders in an editorial and also in a column. In fact, we were called Communists.

It said: (in part) "This is not a new rule; in fact, it is almost . . . if not quite . . . as old as the University itself; so old, indeed, that for many years it has been recognized and accepted as a matter of course. Republicans and Democrats never attempt to hold campaign rallies on the campus as they do elsewhere; though there is nothing to prevent students — of voting age or less — from discussing the partisan slants of campaign issues as much as they please."

Then the Seattle Times focused on the students, saying "There is, then, no reason at all why this rule should be abrogated in favor of the only political group that now-a-days makes a point of asking for such consideration — the youthful Communistic enthusiasts . . .

"The University does not undertake to control their thoughts and their beliefs, but properly insists that they conform with the one rule that all other political groups respect without protest.

"If any young people wish to be Communists or to pose as such, that is their business. The business of the University authorities is to operate a school for the benefit of all students, including the considerable majority who are not and do not wish to be considered Communists. That business requires a few flat rules to apply to all concerned."

A May 26, 1933, University Daily editorial made this comment, in part "The action of the administration was certainly ill-advised. Had nothing been said of the affair, it would not have gained state and nation-wide publicity which resulted in a blackened name for the University, judging by the protests that were pouring in each day. Downtown newspapers, ready at every chance to play uphappenings at the University in bold red headlines, made the situation much worse. The University as a hot bed of communism, with be-whiskered agents from Moscow scurrying around to whisper in students ears. That's the picture they tried to paint of us.

"Perhaps the University administration will learn that no harm is ever done by letting the talkers talk themselves out. That's the way the English do in Hyde Park, London. With policemen there to guard the radicals who cry, "Down with the King!"

A May 31 editorial said this, in part "All this was the result of the students' desire to increase their knowledge beyond the limits provided by the University. Their cry against being treated like children with big ears . . . with nothing between them . . . is entirely legitimate. Their action was based on a principle, not on disrespect for the faculty rulings. It is unfortunate that to uphold that principle, they were obliged to cross the faculty . . .

"The issue between the students and faculty is not what it seems, Free speech against censored learning. The Daily believes it is not a desire to

31

plug student ears that prompted the administration's order, but the uncontrollable fear of criticism from the downtown press against campus political radicalism, and the consequent ill-will in Olympia, when the next University appropriations are sought . . ."

It is interesting to note, now, that the editor of the University, under whose authorization these editorials were published, was Rud Lawrence, who rose to become vice president of the New York Stock Exchange.

The controversy created a furor both on and off campus. Some instructors spent their entire lectures defending the action of the students, and one even urged them to openly defy the disciplinary ruling.

Petitions demanding the University administration to guarantee free speech were circulated in organized houses on the campus. Nearly 50 student leaders met and pledged themselves to fight for the right. The petition read "We, the undersigned students of the University of Washington, believing in our rights to hear both sides of controversial questions, petition the Board of Regents for an administration which will allow students free speech."

The battle to allow liberal speakers on the campus was to be carried to "taxpayers over the entire state," the Daily said, "and a committee has been formed to contact ministers to gather for students' constitutional rights . . . from the pulpit."

The Daily went on to say that "hundreds of influential persons in Seattle and adjoining cities are already planning letters protesting the administration's action."

A June 1, University Daily story said "the total number of signatures (on some 100 petitions being circulated) was steadily mounting toward the goal of 3,000."

A group of liberal students met personally with Governor Clarence D. Martin, requesting a liberal University administration that permitted free speech on the U. campus.

Throughout the rest of the summer of 1933, the issue was before the public. Numerous civic groups came to the support of those of us who had a genuine feeling that the public, in this case the students, had a right to know.

The turmoil came to a satisfying conclusion when the Board of Regents, under tremendous pressure, passed a resolution stating that from that day forward there would be "utmost freedom of speech on the campus of the University of Washington."

The next chapter in my fight for free speech would occur in the 1950's in the state of Idaho with dire consequences. That will be explained when my life in the Bureau of Reclamation is dealt with.

Other Campus Memories

Humorous incidents occured during my college days. I used to accompany Dick Romain, the reviewer for the U. of W. Daily, now and then as he visited various shows — from ballet to motion pictures. Enroute to one of these, he stopped at a "speak-easy" (where one knocked on a door, and if recognized, was admitted). While there, Dick bought a bottle of wine which he carried into the Fifth Avenue Theatre. Suddenly, in the quiet of the showhouse, there was a loud "pop!" I knew immediately what had caused the sound — the cork had blown off the bottle of wine when it had warmed up as Romain held it. I looked around each side of me and behind me to make it seem that the "pop" had happened elsewhere.

Only once did I try to work on the campus to help tide me over financially. I preferred to spend my time in the "Daily Shack," and to turn out for track. The job was waiting on tables in a rooming house. I was clumsy. I didn't last long there after cutting my finger while slicing bread.

My classmates pulled all sorts of stunts. Freddie Wyatt, who became a good newspaperman in the San Francisco area later, once sought to spend a week in a manhole on campus. Authorities stopped him, of course, but he got the junior prom the publicity he was seeking to bring it.

Once or twice a cadaver would appear in "Frosh Pond" in the center of the campus. It had been put there, I'm sure, by Daily Shack guys seeking to create a murder mystery. The cadavers were available at the medical school.

Students were welcomed each morning to the campus and bid goodbye each night by the chimes in a tall tower near Ravenna Boulevard. These were played by a blind man — George Bailey. It is an unforgettable memory of my happy college days.

One of the interesting personalities I encountered was Mike Foster. He was a pro who could dictate over the phone the most beautiful stories. He was a jokester, also. One time Mike called up the sports department of the P.I. from an adjacent room pretending to be a farmer who was complaining that there was no news in the paper about a "feller" who had just "swum" to Seattle from Vancouver, B.C. We, who were in on the joke, soon heard the sports editor arguing with the news editor whether the event was sports or straight news.

Mike also told us — and we could never tell when he was telling the truth — how once he had called up a number of residents along Alki Point to ask their help in spotting bodies from a shipwreck. He insisted that soon the beach was loaded with people, some of them pointing to "another body" when, in reality, it was nothing but drift wood.

Mike was a character. He would play the pipe organ during the wee hours of the morning. He used to bring "floozies" to the fraternity dances. His fraternity brothers got so annoyed with him one time that they threatened to kick him out. Mike got so mad that he took off his fratpin, flushed it down the toilet, and left.

I Too Cover the Waterfront

The following is the story I wrote for the monthly student humor magazine "Columns" in the fictional style of the popular "I Cover the Waterfront" about my experience delivering the P.I. on First Avenue, which I mentioned earlier.

"I have not been here long enough for the seagulls to recognize me. I hope never to be here long enough so that they can pass the word along about me from generation to generation, from egg to egg.

"Friends of mine, members of my University class, all strong and unwarrantedly hopeful in June, they too, now see their ambitions disappearing like the mists from the bay after the sun brings dawn and I reach customer Jones in his dumpy hole and throw a paper down his foul-smelling hallway. Few, if any, are yet on their way to becoming managers; few, if any, see any editors chair ahead; certainly none have become artists. They, too, like me, carrying papers in the ungodly hours before daybreak, are thinking now, something few of us did at the University.

"But then the sun comes up every day.

"The silvery color of early morn is never interesting to me unless I have reached customer Jones at the end of his hallway in one ramshackle shack on the Waterfront or at least the rusty mail slot of Sister McCarthy, whose only claim to distinction before God, is that she has read the paper without a miss for thirty years. Thirty years and five wonderful months now.

"It is indeed a gloriously, beautiful morning when I am through taking the paper apart so I can stuff it, piece by piece, through the too-narrow slit under the door of the Excelsior Fish Co. I used to soil my hands, even scratch my fingers on the rough boards at the Fish Co., but now I have learned to keep my hands clean. There is perfection even here. One must keep one's hands clean, my college days consistently remind.

" The Excelsior Fish Co. is the finish. I am through. Then I sit on the wharf. Maybe Joe will be there; he nearly always is. He gets any extra paper I may have and he reads carefully about the League of Nations, Wall Street, fine fashions and how to cook caviar.

"Maybe Joe will be there and we together sit and watch the dark and the lights, thousands of them, across the bay. Each light must have a different story. And Joe tells long stories about the old days. Joe always tells long stories. Joe talks too long, but practice makes his drone, a rhythm to your thoughts. One can think well, clearly and clanly in the cold winds off the bay, in the smell of rotten fish and musty wood, at the end of the world's long sleep. It is easy.

"Ole too, and John and the Silent One, they are my companions. We are four of a kind, but Ole and John and the Silent One don't get along. They only scowl when they meet. For business is bad, for there are just so many garbage cans to go through and four on that route is too many. John came last; he should move out. He isn't entitled to cut in on the pickings on First, Western and Waterfront. He has another route, a good route, Ole says, in the alleys between First and Second. Ole says that he should move out.

"I always stop to talk to Ole. Ole's job is a little cleaner. He only picks out the paper, cardboard and boxes from the cans. John and the Silent One are also after eatables, 'fruit.' Ole says they are lower level. 'They ain't got no respec' left.'

"Ole's job is a little cleaner, so I can talk more or less contentedly. I can't talk, looking at quarter rotten peaches, slimy bananas coming out of the darkness of garbage cans and disappearing into brown-spotted, wrinkled papersacks. I haven't been here long enough.

"Ole says there is too much competition. Two years ago he could make enough to live on, now 'it hardly reaches.' 'It ain't right,' Ole scowls, 'there's too many of us here.'

"Then he tells me, he tells me three or four times a month, he has to get it off his chest, of days long ago when he worked every day, before his wife died, how he nearly had his house paid for, how 'they' took it, how his rheumatism made it hard in the winter, how he hasn't worked the last three years, how 'this job is as good as any.'

"But no, sir, you ain't gonna ketch me livin' off the city, no sir.'

"And then with a haggard but determined, grim face and with an air of proudness, Ole walks off, he's 'got to get goin' otherwise John or the Silent One would get ahead of him.

"Most always I meet Ole near the telephone pole behind the 'big hotel.' When he walks away, I lumber up to Apartment 45 and I have never yet failed to think, never yet, of Prof. Carston and Prof. Antioch's long lectures at the University on 'rugged American indivisualism.'

"Strange places I go.

"At first I thought it was incense. Now I know it isn't. Always I wondered why such cheap lodging houses burned incense at 4 o'clock in the morning. It's wonderful how college training will set one to thinking. But I found out the incense was the 'sweet smell' of opium, cocaine, and the rest.

"Now it isn't such a sweet odor to me any more. Then I guess too, the police, the narcotics squad, must think it's incense or someone making candy in their room, because the rooms every morning have the same 'sweet' odor, and odor of rotten humanity, mixed with the smell of old-torn wallpaper and dumpiness. I am always glad when I am back on the street with the straggling sailors.

"Sailors. Uncle Sam's street posters, that swing in the morning winds, call them 'clean American youth.' They like the early morning. Always they go out for walks just before dawn. Sometimes alone, sometimes with weary, shabbily-clad young ladies on their arms. The Navy has a lot of singers. Sailors always sing. They make lots of noise. But they buy a paper a good many times, so they lighten up the morning. "University students, too, I see.

"Always they arrive in cars. They hurry even in the morning. Slamming the doors on their roadsters, they dash up creaky stairs, where happily I only have to give the paper a flip upwards. At first I didn't believe it, till I saw a classmate of mine. Now I've seen many of them. He was a member of the Square Club at the University and he thought no one ever walked First at that hour. But they always overlook the paper boy. He sees everything. Necking in the hallway stops not even momentarily as he passes by. Strange places these ever-lighted rooms with multi-colored bridge lamps at the windows. University students like bridge lamps.

"The cold dawn and the hours before are cruel to ideals.

"I mix with society, too. Walking on plush carpets, through beautifully lighted hallways on the 'exclusive' part of my route, I feel more in my element. I pray that it is. I have learned at college of the 'finer things of life,' of cozy sofas, nice books, radios and soft music, of the 'comforts of existence.' Here I find it. But I don't like the oak-paneled doors, the well-kept corridors, its inhabitants. To me they are cruel, mysterious. They cause me trouble. Complaints . . . they send in complaints. I make a noise, I put a paper in the wrong place. I am fifteen minutes late. Complaints ruin my 'profits,' fifteen cents is what I pay for their protest phone call to the office.

"I guess maybe my mind is warped, maybe I've the wrong view on things, maybe I'm not a clear-thinker. But always as I leave its soft rugs I compare Customer Jones' foul-smelling cellar and the 'exclusive.' It is inevitable. It is not pleasure.

"It is that way every morning. Sometimes I stop only for a moment; sometimes I sit down alone, or Joe will be there. I look over the bay. Fishing boats are going, many have gone, some are already back. But I prefer the quiet.

"It's easy to think in the morning. You see the picture clearer.

"But the sour smell. A sour smell comes from somewhere. Like life perhaps. It takes away from the glory of the silvery mist waving over the water. It strikes me in the face like a wet towel and straightens me up as I look for the beautiful. And somehow I can't think of the glory of the dawn without a combined thought of quarter-rotten peaches,slimy bananas coming out of the darkness of the garbage cans and disappearing into brown-spotted, wrinkled paper sacks.

"Professors who lecture on 'the beautiful' and the'good,' and the 'truth' in life, wouldn't like it here. Someday, I shall get one to come here. I wonder if they, too, would think of garbage cans or still only of 'ecstasy.'

"But I am not discouraged. Some day I shall get away. Away to the top, maybe.

"I worry-IS THERE A TOP!

"I have not been here long enough so that the seagulls recognize me. I hope never to be here long enough so that they can pass the word along about me from generation to generation, from egg to egg.

"I wonder . . ."

BOOK TWO

DAMSITE DAYS

Daily Hitch Hiking and Skimpy Meals

I landed in the little town of Almira in the Grand Coulee Dam area as the result of a phone call. It came as I was working as a newspaper carrier for the Seattle Post-Intelligencer.

I was advised by the University School of Journalism that there were a couple of job opportunities available. This was good news, because it was the time of the great Depression. The school said one job involved putting out a magazine of some sort for a Seattle woman and the other working for a man named Arthur Allen who was the publisher of a weekly covering the news of Grand Coulee Dam called the "Grand Coulee Record."

I remember asking: "Where's the Grand Coulee Dam?"

I accepted the latter job. At the outset, I worked in Allen's garage in Seattle. But soon he had me move to Almira where the Bureau of Reclamation, which was building the dam, had its headquarters.

On departing for Eastern Washington, Allen gave me a pair of boots so that I had footwear suitable for a construction job. I wore the boots for a good many years. They were so old and ill-fitting that they became identified with me. For a long-time after I left the job someone would mention them.

On arriving at Almira, I had little money in my pocket, so I picked the cheapest room in the Almira Hotel to stay in. It was situated on the third floor of a three-story building and had a magnificent view of a grubby window well.

I also skimped on meals. I always ate cinnamon toast for breakfast in the hotel's cafe, cheapest thing on the menu. For years afterwards some of the help would recall my repetitive breakfasts.

Each morning I'd venture forth on my reporting job via the hitchhiking method for I had no other means of travel. I had three principal areas to

37

cover — Wilbur, 12 miles away; Coulee City, 20 miles; and the dam site, 20 miles in another direction.

Getting to the dam and back was the easiest, because the activities at the damsite stimulated traffic. Coming back to Almira I often got a ride in a station wagon full of engineers. I often rode with Carl Haskin, who sold insurance, along with his partner, Otto Henning. Carl, a friendly man with a pleasant personality, would later become my father-in-law.

But waiting for a ride sometimes got quite tedious. Once in a while I would ask myself: "For this I went to college?" One night was particularly annoying. I got stuck 10 miles out of Almira after dark. I had to walk the whole distance. But I took the experience in stride, because I really was excited about the job.

My sojourn in Almira was made most pleasant after a while for when I was sitting in the lobby of the hotel I would note a very attractive girl coming down the street to her place of work. Later I learned it was a beauty shop and her name was Martha Haskin. She often wore a red, polka dot dress. In it, she was the prettiest thing I had ever seen. I often mentioned it to her later in our life. I liked her personality, she was soft-spoken, kind and considerate of others.

Her girl friend was a gal who dated nearly every young engineer about and was totally different from Martha Haskin. She went with me for a couple of weeks but I cut it off, so I could date her more reserved companion. But Martha was reluctant to go with me for fear of making her long-time friend angry. So it was to be two weeks before she'd date me. After that we went steady.

When I later moved to Grand Coulee Heights in 1934, I found it necessary to get some kind of transportation in order to go see Martha. I bought an old Studebaker for $75. It had its shortcomings. To get to Almira you had to go up a steep hill. At a certain spot the motor would stop. Something was wrong with the gas line. Anyway, I would take the cap off the gas tank and blow into it. After doing that the car would startup again and make it to the top of the hill.

Martha later took a beautician's job in Spokane, and I would go to see her there. For awhile she worked in Wenatchee. Because I had naturally wavy hair, I sometimes suspected that people thought that Martha had given me a "marcel" — something that wasn't done for men in those days.

I used to be embarrassed also during social events that the Haskins arranged. All holidays were spent with their close friends, the Dave Parrys, who were Welsh-born wheat farmers. The meals were always delicious, but the after-dinner period always involved Mrs. Parry reading "tea leaves." She would always predict, in an off-hand way, that Martha and I would be getting married, something that we had never discussed at that time.

My work with the weekly Grand Coulee Record continued until the summer of 1934 when it went broke. The publisher spend what money he took in from donations, banks and others interested in seeing the dam built for personal pleasures. The paper had no advertising of any kind.

I owed the Almira Hotel $60. I did not want to leave and have George McDonald, who owned the place and had become a personal friend, think

I was skipping out on the bill. So I wrote both the Wenatchee Daily World and the Spokane Chronicle a cocky letter, saying, in effect, that if they wanted the dam covered, there was only one guy who could do it and that was me. Both newspapers put me to work and I like to think I did such a good job for them that neither wanted to let me go even though I was writing for two afternoon newspapers competing for circulation at the damsite.

Both papers paid me space rate — so much per column inch. Because the publisher of the World, Rufus Woods, had been a key figure in bringing the project about I sent his newspaper more voluminous stories than I did the Chronicle. His paper took about everything I could write. However, I took no pictures for the World, for it did not furnish me a camera as did the Chronicle. I carried this camera, a Vollenda, in my hip pocket wherever I went. One time, while climbing up the face of the dam it fell out and went bouncing down the concrete incline and shattered.

I knew nothing about picture taking at the outset, but the Chronicle was most anxious to have me learn. So I sent in those I took for their opinion. The first one that was used appeared on the front page, much to my surprise and joy. It was a simple composition — three large pipes in a cofferdam discharging water. Later when I visited the office I made mention of the photo, being so proud of it. A couple of editors sort of grinned. Truth was, it had been so lousy that an artist had to virtually draw it in what I had photographed. They had gone to this trouble, because they wanted to inspire me to take more pictures for them.

I used to look forward to going to work everyday. I knew the workmen read my stuff, because the job was so big that a person on one part of the project wasn't likely to know what was going on across the river unless he read about it in the paper.

I followed the work religiously, particularly in regard to accidents or deaths. I kept a record of the number of men injured or killed so that when it happened again I was able to state the exact number. Some workers felt that I was suppressing these totals or that the company was hiding them.

This questioning of my honesty finally made me so mad I said "All right you sons of bitches, report those I haven't printed and I'll pay you $25 each!" No one ever claimed the money.

When I left the area the death total had reached 77.

The daily excitement of writing about the construction and boomtowns was accentuated with periodic visits to Spokane where Martha worked. She lived with her sister, Ollene, who had gone to Washington State for a while and was being courted by a dapper young fellow named Pat Patterson. They later married. Martha also had a second sister, Laura, who was a school teacher on the coast. She married George Hermes who was later a school principal at Shelton.

Martha and I were married October 2, 1935, in the parsonage of a church at Davenport. Our first home was a tiny place at the Cozy Apartments in Grand Coulee Center. It was little more than a one-room affair. My bride, a very tidy person, was kept busy fighting the dust that prevailed everywhere. Lots were being dug up for home and commercial buildings which added to the dust problem and it was aggravated by the fact that the apartment had cracks around the doors and windows.

After some months, we moved into a house that we bought in Electric City. We purchased it for $650. The price would make it sound like a shack, but actually it was one of the nicer homes at the damsite. We won the home-and-garden contest with it.

It contained a small dining room, a bathroom, kitchen, bedroom, and a small living room where I kept my typewriter in the corner.

Almira Cubbyhole to Damsite Shack

Before I got married, I had moved from my cubbyhole in the Almira Hotel to the damsite. My abode was not much better there. It consisted of a one-room shack about 12-by-12 feet in size that was situated in the sagebrush where the road to Almira and Wilbur took off from Grand Coulee Heights. It had no water or plumbing. An outhouse was situated 30 feet away.

The cabin was mighty chilly in wintertime. Ice would freeze in the pail that served as my water supply. Karl Stoffel, a Wenatchee Daily World writer, once spent a night with me and returned to tell the staff that ice was an inch thick in the pail — a bit of exaggeration.

I lived alone most of the time. For a while, Nelson Cheney, a U. W. classmate, lived with me. He represented the Spokesman-Review and later worked for Sid Jackson's weekly Grand Coulee News.

On my arrival in Grand Coulee, there were only scattered buildings to be seen between the two basalt walls of the coulee. Many were in various stages of construction and that included both homes and business structures. Coming down the hill from Almira, I could see springing up in the distance what later would become the well-known B Street with its great number of taverns, houses of prostitution and wooden sidewalks.

Being situated near the hubbub of activity instead of 20 miles away allowed me to step up news coverage. I estimate that I wrote about a thousand words a day for the World over the eight years I was there.

My news was taken in an envelope to Wenatchee by Washington Motor Coach. Once in a while, the driver would fail to deliver it, and I would shout my head off in complaint because that meant I lost a day's pay, because I was being paid space rates.

For short periods, I would be the entire daily press at the damsite. That occurred whenever the Spokesman-Review would lose its correspondent and ask me to fill in. That paper, like the Chronicle, was owned by the Cowles family. I also represented the Associated Press and Portland Oregonian and for a while wrote technical articles for the Pacific Builder and Engineer. The latter job was difficult, because its readers were engineers and construction people and the report had to be completely accurate. That meant tedious checking with the news sources. Luckily when the publisher said he had to reduce what he paid me for the articles, I had a good excuse to give up the job.

The first major news story that I wrote occurred in December 1933. It involved the excavation of the first cubic yard of overburden in the construction of the big dam by a Northwest steam shovel operated by

Goodfellow Bros. of Wenatchee. It had a subcontract with David H. Ryan of San Diego, Calif., which had the contract to excavate two million cubic yards of earth to expose some of the bedrock on which the big concrete structure was to sit.

The work had been preceded earlier by core drilling by Lynch Bros. of Seattle. The excavation and some other preliminary work was being paid for from a $377,000 appropriation by the State of Washington. It had also authorized the newly-formed Columbia Basin Commission to contract with the federal government to build the dam.

On July 16, 1933, there had been a sizable ground-breaking celebration before an exceptionally enthusiastic crowd of 3,000. The audience even applauded the benediction, according to a news story about the event published in the Wenatchee Daily World. The newspaper laughed about it, but said, "it all came from a feeling of enthusiastic gratitude in the knowledge that the big dam was on the way."

The crowd saw Governor Clarence D. Martin, armed with a heavy sledge, drive an engineering stake into the ground, and U.S. Senator C.C. Dill turned the first shovelful of earth.

The celebration was a two-pronged affair. Sponsored by the Almira and Grand Coulee chambers of commerce, it celebrated the opening of a road from Almira to the damsite, as well as the long-awaited start of engineering for the huge undertaking.

The Daily World reported that the day featured "heat and dust." People had come in a caravan from Wenatchee and by a special Northern Pacific train from Spokane connecting with busses and cars at Almira, and in individual automobiles.

The Wenatchee delegation was arranged by the late Irwin Jones, with Mayor John E. Mooney urging a large attendance because "construction of the Grand Coulee Dam is now a sure thing, and the biggest thing that has ever come to the state."

Additional enthusiasm was aroused by a Wenatchee Grand Coulee Dam committee, comprised of World publisher Rufus Woods; W.R. Prowell, president of the Columbia Basin Development League which was supported by 32 organizations; Mayor Mooney, Dr. E.J. Widby, former mayor of Wenatchee; and Ray Clark, treasurer of the development league and manager of the Cascadian Hotel.

The committee was happy, because a Washington, D.C., announcement had said that Dr. Elwood Mead, commissioner of the Federal Bureau of Reclamation, had signed a contract with the state Columbia Basin Commission for preliminary work for construction of the dam.

The World said of the significance of the ceremony that "the hopes and dreams of 15 long years were brought to realization."

A front-page headline over the article describing what happened in the sagebrush along the Columbia River where Sam Seaton ran a cable ferry read: "Cheapest Power in World to be Produced at Grand Coulee Dam." Sub-headlines said power would be generated for 1/20th of a cent per kilowatt.

The World described the impressive scene this way "It was a colorful day and a colorful crowd. Indians from the Colville reservation, in all their ceremonial finery, sat on the speakers' stand with high government dignitaries and project boosters.

"Shade was at a premium as the mercury touched 105 degrees, however a breeze sweeping up the river helped to alleviate the extreme heat. Hot dog and cold drink stands had blossomed in the sagebrush and the barkers lent a state fair aspect to the assemblage."

James O'Sullivan, a key figure in achieving the accomplishments, acted as chairman of the affair. He said "Completion of this project will mean more to the Pacific Northwest than anything ever before conceived."

Senator Dill said FDR had promised $60,000,000 to construct a dam 145 feet high, producing 250,000 kilowatts. (Later a higher dam was authorized).

"When the entire project is completed power will be manufactured for one-twentieth of a cent a kilowatt and delivered for one-quarter of a cent, the cheapest in the history of the world," Dill said.

The World editorialized a bit in the news story about the epic day. "The progress of consummation in the short space of 15 years has been astonishing," it said. "Significance of yesterday's dramatic event has been almost too stupendous for full realization."

On September 9, 1933, the first stake was driven in the sagebrush where the dam was to be situated.

The news of these events had been circulated widely, and, therefore, hundreds of job-hungry workers had started to flock to the damsite. During the Depression there were no other jobs to be found elsewhere. To take care of their needs, saloons and other business establishments had been opening up. The commercial activities were taking place in three principal areas being promoted by developers.

Paul Donaldson had purchased part of the Purtee property and had platted it. It was in this area named Grand Coulee that the later-famous B Street sprung up. A dapper retired Army officer named Fred Weil had acquired Si Buckley's land for the Continental Land Co. of Spokane. It became Grand Coulee Center. Adjacent to these land holdings, A. A. Elmore and Ida Fleischmann of Rock Island had gotten hold of land that became Grand Coulee Heights.

Earlier there had been nothing but sagebrush and settlers such as Charlie Osborne, the Laels, Kennedys and Nobles and Sam Seaton, who ran a cable ferry at the site of the dam.

The first business to arise on B Street was a restaurant run by two women — Miss A. E. "Johnny" Johnson and Mrs. B. G. Raymond. They called it the Grand Coulee Cafe. When the two ladies arrived at the damsite, they had put up a tent to live in while they built the restaurant. There were quite a few carpenters constructing various buildings. These men had no place to eat so they persuaded Miss Johnson to put up a table using two sawhorses and boards in front of her tent. She cooked meals inside the tent and served them outside.

At the same time commercial structures were going up at an ever-increasing tempo. Workers were driving up in their cars or other vehicles and unloading their worldly goods in the sagebrush. There was no housing to be obtained, except for 33 cabins Elmore and Fleischmann had brought from Rock Island.

The developers sold lots on which to build. It didn't take a lot of money to buy one in those days. On the Heights, prize view lots sold for the staggering sum of $250. You could buy any lot for $5 down and $5 a month. Developer Fleischmann reported, however, "You were lucky to get the $5."

Everyone who came to Grand Coulee was broke, period. So people would crawl into anything they could get for housing.

A couple by the name of Reed, who had a baby, dug a hole into a hillside and put a drum stove inside. Then they hung up a gunny sack across the front of the cave, and that kept them warm. They moved into a cabin Mrs. Fleischmann gave them later.

Another couple improvised in another way. All of the dance halls on B Street had upright pianos which were shipped in in a box. The couple got one of these, then added something to the front of it and that was their residence for a while.

Great Celebration When Bids Were Read

It was a big day for the project when finally bids were opened for the construction of the dam. It took place at Spokane, because there was no place at the damsite big enough to hold the crowd that was expected to attend the affair.

The date was June 18, 1934. I went to Spokane to participate in covering the historic event.

The Wenatchee World spared no ink to emphasize the importance of what happened.

A front-page headline the width of the page read:

$29,339,301 BID FOR GRAND COULEE DAM
Silas Mason of New York $5,216,280 Under Six Companies

There were two-column heads beneath that headline, they read:

Eyes Of Engineering World
Focused On Gigantic Project

Immediate Benefits To Industry Predicted
From Purchase Of Machinery, Material
Celebration Is Grant County Field Day

Opening Of Bids Heralded As Greatest Step
Since Building Of East-To-West Railway
Attended By Thousands

There was yet another big headline on the page, it read: **Nation's Oldest Contracting Firm Offers to Build Big Dam at 10 Million Under Estimate**

Frank A. Banks, construction engineer on the project for the Bureau of Reclamation, opened the bids.

He announced that a syndicate headed by the Silas H. Mason Co. of New York City, later called Mason-Walsh-Atkinson-Kier Company (MWAK)

43

had submitted the lowest offer at $29,339,301.50. Six Companies of Washington Inc., an affiliate of Six Companies Inc., the builder of the Boulder Dam on the Colorado River, submitted the only other acceptable bid. This was for $34,555,582.

A Mason company official reported that the company had been operating continuously for 106 years except for an interruption during the Civil War.

Nearly a thousand people, including dignitaries, contractors, engineers and interested spectators, jammed the Civic Auditorium for the formal opening of the bids.

Members of the Columbia Basin Commission, Governor Clarence D. Martin, consulting engineers for the reclamation bureau, Mr. Banks, Dr. Elwood Mead, U.S. Commissioner of Reclamation, R. F. Walter, chief bureau engineer, and other notables connected with the development sat at a long table below the platform where the bids were opened.

The bid opening had been proceded outside by the bursting of half a dozen bombs, the roar of army airplanes, music from the Fort George Wright band and the fluttering of flags in the morning breeze were signals that the long anticipated time had arrived. It was an occasion long to be remembered by a small group of loyal Columbia Basin boosters who were sitting in on the climax of their 16-year battle, including James O'Sullivan and Rufus Woods.

Following the reading of the totals on each of the two bids, Banks read the detailed bids on 85 separate construction items. First, the Mason offer the and the next of six companies. During this reading there were exclamations of surprise as some of the wide variances were made known.

The entire formality lasted less than half an hour, and, then, the entire group went outside for an informal introduction and an impressive Indian ceremony on a specially constructed grandstand in front of the Civic building.

It involved Dr. Mead, Mr. Walter and Mr. Banks being made "Big Chiefs" and crowned with the official head-dress of the Nez Perce tribe. Dr. Mead's title was "Chief Leknekus," meaning "Plenty Water;" Walter's name was "Chief Tueskbet," meaning "High Builder;" and Bank's name was "Chief Weatakio," meaning "High Mogul."

Short talks were given by the governor, Dr. Mead, Walter, Dr. Charles P. Berkey, noted geologist; E. F. Blaine, pioneer; Dr. F. W. Durand, Frank Bell, representing Senator C. C. Dill; Charles H. Paul, member of the Columbia Basin and Tennessee Valley consulting board; Joseph Jacobs, E. F. Banker, D. C. Henney, Earl F. Braden and Fred C. Jones of the Spokane Chamber of Commerce; and Horace C. Smith, state senator from Okanogan County.

Then an Indian rain dance was performed for the benefit of the drought-stricken Midwest.

It was a Spokane celebration but the mile-long parade made it look more like a Grant County field day. Residents from every town and hamlet in that county turned out almost 100 percent according to the Wenatchee World, and both the float and the county band were parade prize winners. Other North Central Washington communities were also represented including Okanogan, Nespelem, the new townsite of Osborne, White Bluffs, Almira, Grand Coulee and Wenatchee. The decorated car entered by the Wenatchee Chamber of Commerce was almost unanimously picked the most beautiful in the parade.

The Grant County band, led by T. E. Jenkins and followed by the county floats, drew steady plaudits from the thousands who lined the streets.

The largest daytime crowd in the history of the city was present for the parade and celebration.

There was a bit of humor associated with the serious business of opening the bids.

A bid was allegedly submitted by Mae West, the sexy movie star who was often in the news. Banks was obliged to announce it although he did not go into detail because, as he said, it was not accompanied by a bid bond as was required by the specifications. The "informal" bid, as Banks preferred to call the offer, was "stolen" from the press table by a souvenir hunter while eager newspaper reporters searched the building trying to locate the interesting, if not serious, offer to build the dam. I later found it had been written by Ed James, manager of the Roosevelt Theatre in Grand Coulee.

The poem read:

Gentlemen:

Now listen "big boys," I'm a builder
Too strong for Hollywood play.
If you "geeve it to me"
"Oh baby" you see
I will finish the dam in a day!

On page three to nine, I am seeing
Your specifications "so sweet;"
Let's go "Sweet Patootie"
Now please don't get snooty, but
Your Dammy has too many feet!

I can promise you "plenty diversion"
With foundation sufficient, "oh dear"
Now what do you say, "big commission"
Am I built well enough for a pier?

I can riprap your cofferdam penstocks,
Forty hours for stripping, "oh yeah!"
Master Dill, you're as grand as the Coulee
Some "nurtsies" for you N.R.A.

For a dollar I'd walk on your river;
I'll build your old dam for a dime;
And when I am through,
Old man river and you
Will be tickled to "see me sometime."

Yours without bond or vow,
Mae West

A Huge Job Ahead

It was a huge job the Bureau of Reclamation faced in 1933 when construction of the Grand Coulee Dam begun.

What was built was the largest concrete dam in the world and what, for a long time, was the biggest powerplant on earth.

Today it has an installed capacity of 6,494,000 kilowatts, which makes it the second largest power plant anywhere. It is exceeded only by the plant at Guri Dam on the Caroni River in Venezuela, which has an installed capacity of 10 million kilowatts.

Here are some of the statistics:

GRAND COULEE DAM

Total length of dam .... 5,223 ft.
Height above lowest bedrock .... 550 ft.
Height above downstream water level .... 350 ft.
Pump lift to feeder canal .... 280 ft.
Spillway width .... 1,650 ft.
Total concrete content .... 11,975,521 cu.yd.
    Original dam, power, and pumping plant .... 10,585,000 cu.yd
Total excavation, earth .... 38,574,503 cu.yd.
    Original dam and pumping plant..................... 20,535,422 cu.yd.
    Forebay dam and third power plant .... 18,039,081 cu.yd.
Total excavation, rock .... 7,062,629 cu.yd.
    Original dam, power and pumping plant .... 2,095,557 cu.yd.
    Forebay dam and third power plant .... 4,967,072 cu.yd.
Maximum concrete pour, 1 month .... 536,364 cu.yd.

Power Plants
    Left power plant — Main unit generators (9) .... 125,000 kw.
    Right power plant — Main unit generators (9) .... 125,000 kw.
    Third power plant — Main unit generators (3) .... 600,000 kw.
           Main unit generators (3) .... 700,000 kw.

Pumping-Generater Plants
    Pumps (6) .... 65,000 hp.
    Capacity (each pump) .... 1,600 cfs
    Reversible pump/generators (2) .... 67,500 hp.
                                                        50,000 kw.

Generating Capacity
    Pumping-Generating Plant .... 314,000 kw.
    Left Power plant .... 1,155,000 kw.
    Right Power plant .... 1,125,000 kw.
    Third Power plant .... 3,900,000 kw.
    Total generating capacity .... 6,494,000 kw.

Franklin D. Roosevelt Lake
    Length .... 151 mi.
    Total capacity .... 9,562,000 ac ft.
    Active capacity .... 5,232,000 ac ft.

Feeder Canal
    Length .... 1.6 mi.
    Capacity .... 16,000 cfs.

North Dam (earth fill)
    Length .... 1,450 ft.

Bank's Lake (equalizing reservoir)
    Length of reservoir .... 27 mi.
    Total capacity .... 1,275,000 ac ft.
    Active capacity .... 715,000 ac ft.

Dry Falls Dam
    Length .... 9,800 ft.

Irrigation
    Available for service .... 543,000 acres

Dam is Gargantuan Structure

George Sundborg in his book, "Hail Columbia" describes the magnitude of the Grand Coulee Dam in terms perhaps more meaningful than a mere set of statistics. He states:

"The Grand Coulee Dam is three times the size of the Great Pyramid of Giza which for seven thousand years held the title as man's largest structure.

"The Grand Coulee Dam occupies more space than 150 million people of the nation, and weighs twice as much, dwarfing all other concrete or masonry structures.

"The Grand Coulee Dam is so thick that four United States Capitols could be embedded in it.

"The Grand Coulee Dam contains more than ten million cubic yards of concrete, enough to build a sixteen-foot highway from Seattle to Boston and back to Los Angeles.

"The Grand Coulee Dam is fed from ice fields, glaciers, snow fields, springs and lakes, from sources in British Columbia, Montana, Idaho, Oregon, Washington, and even the edges of Wyoming, Nevada, and Utah.

"The Grand Coulee Dam is the biggest thing all in one piece ever built by man."

You Never Forgot The Mud

Grand Coulee looked like a movie set when construction of the big dam along the river below began.

Its B Street, where the beer parlors, upstairs places for entertainment by the girls, and other places of business sprung up was like a frontier town with many false-front buildings and muddy streets.

No one who lived in Grand Coulee during 1933 and 1934 will ever forget the mud!

Cars, such as they were in the Depression days, had great difficulty making their way through what was generally referred to as "gumbo." Trucks bringing in loads of lumber trying to keep up with the hectic construction taking place were particularly hard-pressed in getting about.

They met their Waterloo where the county road turned into B Street. Luckily for the drivers, an enterprising young man had a tractor parked near the Grand Coulee News to help them out. While he waited inside the office where he could keep warm, big trucks loaded with lumber would try to make the turn and back up and try again and again.

Finally this enterprising young man would sally forth at just the right psychological moment, and for $5, hook the tractor onto the truck and pull it over the steep pitch. The guy made a living that way all winter.

During the gumbo days of B Street, there was a popular story told by a Bob Mummy who was associated with a proposed electrical system.

He claimed that he was walking along where they had put down gravel for a sidewalk. He saw a man's hat and just thought he'd get that hat, a good-looking one.

When he picked it up there was a man's face looking up at him. Said the fellow "Think nothing of it there's a wagonload of hay and two horses under me."

One spring, the mud was knee-deep where the Eagles Club is now situated. Water came down a hill there and ran into the front door of a bakery.

When women tried to cross the street, the mud sucked off their galoshes. They'd come over in their stocking feet leaving their galoshes sticking in the mud.

One business woman was seen coming up to her house after dark carrying an arm load of groceries. She walked into a mud puddle in a low place. Suddenly her feet went out from under her. As she tried walking up the slick clay side of the low spot, she went down on her stomach. She was so mad, she just threw her groceries in the air and went home. She was muddy from head to foot.

I remember writing a story one day about a little child I saw on B Street. It read this way "A little fellow, hardly six years old and small for his age, cried about the condition of Grand Coulee streets yesterday.

"A team of horses had been at work with a scoop pulling the soupy mud, which looks ever so much like real soft, runny caramel candy, from out of the street to a vacant lot. The layer of soft 'goo' left a more solid foundation underneath. The whole main street of Grand Coulee town site looked much like a river of flowing lava.

"It happened that a little fellow, who cried too long and loud for the reporter to obtain his name, had unsuspectedly walked into the 'soup' which had been deposited along the slippery lane called a sidewalk. His little knee boots sank deeply into the mush and try as he would he was unable to move another step.

"Fastened solidly in the mud, the little man cried with all his might — about the condition of Grand Coulee streets yesterday.

"But the rest of the population just swishes through it all and thinks of the summertime when they'll be wiping this same mud (only in the form of dust) out of their eyes."

A lawyer named Bob Hunter, who later became a State Supreme Court Judge, had his trouble in the street, too. He was a nattily-clad individual who would become quite embarrassed when in crossing the street his rubbers would come off and there he'd be with gumbo all over his brightly shined shoes.

It was the practice of the day to strike a match across the sole of one's boots so some smokers attached sandpaper to the upper part of their boots because of the muddy conditions.

The dance halls had to call intermissions periodically so that the mud on the floor could be shoveled out.

In due time, a meeting was called to discuss the "gooey"predicament. Some 45 people attended. They took up a collection to have gravel put on the county road. The amount raised was $20 which was thought to be sufficient. However, it didn't prove to be enough. Before winter was over there were chuck holes three feet deep on B Street, the town's new weekly, the Grand Coulee News, reported.

In summertime, the gumbo became dust and a water wagon, paid for by volunteer donations, went up and down the street to settle it. The dance hall operators had intermissions to sweep the dust out.

The dust not only adversely affected the dance halls, it made living in the hurriedly thrown-up homes almost unbearable at times.

My wife was most annoyed about the dust. It would come under the doors and in other parts of the house where the walls did not fit tight.

The dust did not come from just off the roads. It blew off hundreds of lots which had been dug up to accomodate residences and commercial buildings.

Another source of dust were the frequent storms that occurred. They could be seen coming down the Coulee for miles. This would cause housewives to close all the windows and doors. With the temperature in the shade sometimes up to 114 degrees, the interiors of the houses would become suffocating. There was no air conditioning at that time.

These storms would sometimes last for hours. At times, one could not see across the street. After the wind had subsided, housewives would literally shovel the dirt out.

The dust situation was sometimes laughable. One man reported after one dust storm that he had been out digging post holes when the wind came up, so he took cover. When the wind died down, he found that it had blown the sand from around the holes that he had dug and left them six or eight inches above the ground.

49

They Whooped It Up on Payday

Friday was the big night on B Street. I told it to my readers about it this way . . .

"Long lines of working men, clad in every type of wearing apparel, stood waiting yesterday at several windows of the MWAK field office on the east shore. Swiftly the line moved past the windows but for an hour the line never lost its length because workmen kept joining it.

"Inside of the Mason City Bank, shorter lines waited impatiently in front of the tellers cages, the men holding in their hands a green colored paper. They crowded the bank until there was hardly room for any more people. As the workers passed out of the building, paper (also green colored) and silver coins passed into billfolds and pockets.

"Why all this? Because Friday's payday at the dam!

"On the outside of the big Coulee Trading Co. building, men congregated, talking of this and that. In the store itself, the grocery department was rushed and the soda fountain had nary an empty seat all morning. Everywhere men moved to and fro.

"In the big recreation hall, the bar was lined from one end to the other with thirsty workmen. The pool and billiard tables were surrounded by cue enthusiasts. The cigar and candy counters kept the cash register a-singing as supplies of stock were purchased. Happy smiles, more than usual, lined the many faces.

"Why? Because Friday's payday at the dam!

"Every card table in the hall was surrounded by chip-throwing, card-dealing laborers. The large light over each table showed the aura of blue smoke that filled the building. Shouts, loud talk and the shuffling of many hob-nail boots on the floor, mixed with the noise of more people coming into the building.

"In the morning, some workmen waited for the Grand Coulee bus to take them shopping, to beer parlors, or to the sporting houses to spend the afternoon and evening. Some cars, probably only a minority of those in camp, had been seen heading across the river.

"It was payday at the dam!

"Shopping in stores started early in the morning. The merchants got their advertising out early to generate the anticipated onrush. As in the lull before the storm, Thursday, when literally everybody was broke, was the deadest day of the week. Friday and Saturday were the peak business days of the private townsites. Post offices everywhere found workmen sending part of their paychecks home.

"During Friday evening, sidewalks along main street were lined with men. Loud music could be heard from the inside of buildings. Beer parlors did land-office business as money flowed freely. Not until late in the evening did over indulgence become noticeable.

"It was payday at the dam!

"The police blotter the next morning was well filled. The usual small group of disorderly drinkers found their way into the jail at Mason City, the contractors town.

"In the morning all was serene again. The party was over. "Where were you last night?" was an often asked question. Work rather than play, like business before pleasure, had replaced the spirit of yesterday.

"Friday's the most interesting day here . . . 'cause Friday's payday at the dam!"

In later years, as a result of my association with B Street, I was interviewed about paydays and other construction days goingson by public television in Seattle and The National Broadcasting System for its primary Sunday newscast with Jessica Savich.

All Kinds of Fun for the Workers

There were various types of entertainment available during early Grand Coulee days.

As explained earlier beer drinking was a popular pastime, particularly for those who didn't have their wives at the damsite during the early years — and that was nearly all the construction stiffs.

Stronger stuff was served upstairs, with or without the girls.

Card playing in the bars amused some, and others found taxi dancers to their liking. Dancing with your wife and friends in the bar amused some. There were also a couple of theatres, the Grand Coulee and the Roosevelt.

Since Friday was payday, as related before, B Street taverns were the hotspots that night as the workers let off steam after their hard week of labor. At one time there were some 8,800 employed on the project.

Places were jam-packed with the workers, dance hall girls, and tourists who flocked in to see the show, without realizing that they were a good part of it.

Some of the dance halls had taxi dancers, with whom you could dance for 10 cents.

During construction days at the dam, Richard Newberger, an Oregon writer, wrote "Our Promised Land," and in it, he declared that sin and salvation were doing business on the same street in the "piano box" town. He was referring to life on B Street.

Further he wrote: "In contrast to the dam which, rising block on block in the river canyon, appears as permanent as granite, the town of Grand Coulee seems as ephemeral as a one night circus stand. The buildings are of crude lumber or formed from tarpaper tacked to laths. Here and there is one of greater durability, but it is the exception. Some of the houses resemble big packing boxes. A piano would fill most of them to overflowing. Everything bespeaks haste, hurry and carelessness."

Further on in the book, he writes about conditions on B Street "It is likely there is nothing at Grand Coulee which does not exist in Seattle, Spokane, Portland or Denver or any other city. But it prevails in a highly concentrated form. So, Grand Coulee squats on its hills and is a definite social phase of a great engineering project in the wilderness. In it live wild and dissolute individuals and in it also live decent and respectable and upright Americans, who are trying to make a living on the country's last, great frontier."

Newberger once described B Street as having "saints on one side and sinners on the other."

One of the nicer places in town was the Grand Coulee Club, operated by Mr. and Mrs. John Pozar.

The first big celebration at the new town site occurred on New Year's Eve, 1933. Already there were a number of beer parlors and recreation spots in various areas.

The Columbia Cafe, the Wigwam and a place owned by Al Delducco, of Cle Elum, had opened for New Years.

The folks who were stuck at the damsite at the end of the year made the best of the facilities at hand to have fun. Touring beer parlors to toast in the New Year was popular.

One party ended around midnight at Al Meyer's beer dispensary, which was then located at the junction of the roads in Grand Coulee, having been moved up from its first location at the actual damsite.

There had been an earlier celebration on Thanksgiving. The group was so large that dinner couldn't be held in the one restaurant available, so the people moved on to Wallace's five-cent beer parlor, and the restaurant served the meal there. The cooks added "tators and stuff," so the crowd increased.

Things ended up in a party at the tavern that night. A man with an organ grinder came from somewhere, and he played music for the folks to dance to. Finally they had to stop him because the building, which was located on the edge of a cliff, had begun to sway.

Movie Theatres Popular Family Entertainment

Most of the families who came to the damsite after the early months when the father was there alone, were avid movie goers. They spent most of their money at the two theatres — the Roosevelt and the Grand Coulee. Pay on the dam, incidentally, was 50 cents an hour. With overtime the average paycheck was $20 to $25 a week.

The first thing families would buy was their week's groceries and they'd pay the rent on their cabin, usually due weekly. Then they spent whatever was left for other necessities and luxuries, such as going to a show.

People particularly enjoyed going to the Roosevelt which had been opened by Ed James, of Seattle, on November 3, 1934.

Andy Seresun was the first projectionist. For eight years, as a sideline, I handled the advertising and was on the stage once or twice a week as "MC" running "Bank Night" and "Keeno Night."

Seresun got a job doing the electrical work during construction of the building. He put in all the equipment and soon found that the power supply was inadequate to run the sound.

Electricity was provided by Three Engineers Inc. through diesel plants on the Columbia River. Because of an overload in trying to meet demands for power in the fast-growing dam site communities, the firm would have eight to ten outages a night. Seresun, therefore, built a gasoline-driven plant to run the sound system.

During a cold snap all the pipes in the place froze. There being no plumber in town, Seresun repaired the damage himself so that the show could go on.

The theatre seated 800, but, a number of times 1,300 people would come to the "Bank Night," there being two special showings. The special attraction involved people registering in a book. Over the months, the book would come to contain thousands of names, each name opposite a number. There was a weekly drawing and the person having the number drawn won a sizable cash prize if he or she was present. When no one won, the pot would increase by the amount not given away.

When the award rose to above $1,000, there'd be a thousand or more people outside the theatre. In order to comply with lottery laws, the name was always announced to the outside crowd. Once or twice the police had to stop traffic because main street was so jammed with humanity.

The quality of the motion pictures shown on "Bank Night" was always poor. The money aspect drew the people anyway.

"Keeno Night" followed "Bank Night". It consisted of a merchandise give-away through bingo cards. A large arrow would be spun on a 10-foot board to select the numbers.

It was lucky that the place had a large foyer and friendly firemen, for it would be packed on give-away nights with hundreds of people standing. James, a Seattle realtor who ran the theatre for a Mr. Grill of Seattle, made sure the fire department had lots of passes and, as an additional service, he'd have Seresun show a red line on the screen by means of a slide. It meant nothing to anyone other than the firemen who knew by the sign that there was a fire in the town.

James brought in frequent stage shows including units of "Major Bowes Amateur Hour," the radio rage of the nation at that time; the "Sons of the Pioneers" who made it to Hollywood; Virgil the Magician, Katherine Ellis, a psychic, and even a fan dancer.

Whenever questions to the psychic got dull, working with her on stage I would sometimes substitute questions of my own. One that always brought down the house was "Should I marry the man I'm living with?" Under present moral standards, it would hardly get a laugh.

The biggest laugh of all came when someone wrote out the question "What's in the mystery sandwich?" It referred to the food prepared by contractors for the lunch pails of men on the job who gave the sandwich that name. It was not a popular item, consisting mostly of leftovers.

The theatre operated a noisy sound truck to drum up business but got rid of it because its blaring advertising would disturb workers who were sleeping after or before a graveyard shift.

The showhouse was hit by fire a couple of times. Once the furnace flooded and set afire the soot in the chimney. A whole city block went up in flames another time, but theatre owner James had built a fire wall and that saved the building.

Later someone tried to set two fires outside the theatre in the early morning. A tourist going by called the fire department. In the afternoon another fire was found set near the projection booth. It was suspected that the man who operated a restaurant nearby wanted to collect insurance on his place.

The Roosevelt Theatre wasn't the first motion picture house at the damsite. The first was the Grand Coulee Theatre, started near B Street by a Mr. Johnson. It was showing pictures there before the roof was even on. Later you could watch the show through cracks in the building.

A familiar name associated with the Roosevelt theatre was Mickey Knox, a likeable fellow. He later replaced James. The Columbian theatre later offered damsite amusement. It was erected by James at Electric City. Seresun served as projectionist there for a short time. The system was run with power delivered by two diesel plants, which James put in because the power company wanted $800 for the loan of a transformer.

The diesel had a habit of running away when it got a little air in the fuel line. It burned up about $300 in lights over a short time.

The Columbian was eventually closed when it was found that it was drawing people away from the Roosevelt because of lower ticket prices.

After James departed the Roosevelt, Ollie Hartman, a veteran showman in Seattle and a most likeable man, took over management. He was there from 1936 to 1941. He later took over the management of the Mason City Theatre, also.

In the early days, motion pictures were suitable for the entire family — no sex, no swearing, and "hell" was never mentioned.

Kids sometimes caused the theatre trouble. They would slice seats or stick gum on them which at times would cause the theatre operator to get a cleaning bill from the next person using that seat. Any youngster found causing trouble at the Roosevelt would be shown to the cashier and she was told to never let the kid back in again. He would soon come begging to be allowed to return. It was a sure discipline.

Grand Coulee Gets A Band

"Pop" Wallis, who ran what would now be called a "deli", started a town band in 1937 It consisted of 11 members — 5 that could play, and 6 that couldn't. Included were Bill and Alden Wallis, Robert and Ronald Woods, Jerry and Bill Ford, to mention a few.

Wallis also organized an orchestra among the Sunday School members at the Community Church. Rod Hartman, later mayor of Coulee Dam, was one.

From a humble beginning, Wallis worked up a 40-piece band which went to the Apple Blossom Festival in Wenatchee. With the help of the Bureau of Reclamation uniforms were provided. These consisted of blue denim pants, white shirts with black ties, white safety belts and tin hats.

In the parade, Grand Coulee High School also cut quite a caper as did the Roosevelt Theatre's brand new sound truck. Bob Ross and seven other men used it to sing a song written by Wallis to the tune of the World War 1 "Caissons Go Marching Along" number. The words went like this:

"With a whang, with a bang, we will build Grand Coulee Dam
As the river goes rolling along.
There was Hill, there was Dill, who have swallowed bitter pills
In their battle to push it along.
So its heigh, heigh hee in the town of Grand Cou-lee
Our respects to Elwood Mead we want to pay
But where 'ere we go, we want the world to know
That we're building Grand Coulee Dam
While the river goes flowing along."

Whenever the Commercial Club wanted a band, they called the group of band members together. One night Bob Hunter staged a political rally and used the band. They made such a racket that manager James of the Roosevelt Theatre called the State Patrol to quell the disturbance. The whole town was upset over the interference by the law and eventually Wallis got a note of apology from the officers.

The Girls Entertained The Boys

There was one phase of B Street that I knew very little about, being a happily married man. It was the houses of prostitution that prevailed in the upstairs rooms above the many saloons.

I interviewed a Wenatchee doctor, who had been the health officer during the construction, when he retired years later. From him, I learned that there were a total of 55 whores in the towns. I don't suppose they were all there at one time but there were a lot of them.

The other girls on hand to entertain the workmen were taxi dancers. They charged 10 cents a dance in the beer joints. According to the fellows who were acquainted with them, they were a higher class of girls.

Because I knew so little about the behind-the-scene activities of these women, I interviewed a friend of mine who spent a lot of time in the joints and was sort of an authority on B Street night life. He went to the places nearly every night, but mainly because he liked to drink.

I was in the upstairs places only once, and, then only, because a half-drunk friend from out of town insisted on going in. I'd been asked to do that many times but always refused. This guy became very abusive with the girls. Finally the pimp told him to get out. My friend got real nasty about being thrown out. When we were at the bottom of the stairs, he was still cussing the fellow.

Suddenly the pimp came after us. We threw open the door and beat it down B Street, the guy not far behind. I remember thinking what a revolting development this was. Here I was perfectly innocent and I was about to get clobbered by a pimp. Luckily, he didn't catch us.

My friend, who understandably did not want his name mentioned in these memoirs, started as a laborer on the job and by the time he retired he had risen to a very responsible job with the Bureau of Reclamation.

Gus, as I shall call him, spoke rather highly of the taxi dancers. Besides dancing with the men they sold liquor for which they got paid a commission — so much a glass. The construction stiffs would, of course, buy the girls a drink, knowing they were charged hard liquor prices for colored water sold as loganberry wine. Gus knew this, because the girls could drink all night and never show it.

The three to five-piece orchestras would play dance numbers real fast. That way, the girls made a maximum amount of money. Gus said that sometimes one could hardly get around the dance floor once before the music ended.

When the downstairs places closed up at 2 a.m. — some were open all night — Gus would head for the upstairs to continue drinking moonshine that came from Seattle or Canada or some that was made by local bootleggers. When he got his weekly paycheck of $55, he'd pay his share of rent for the room where he lived and blow the rest drinking hard liquor at 25 cents a glass and beer at 10 cents a mug. Slot machines and juke boxes plus endless mugs of beer took a lot of his money.

The dance halls were extremely noisy with the orchestra playing, and the men in various stages of intoxication jabbering away amongst themselves. With all the noise, workers could hardly hear one another. To get a beer, sometimes there would be two men lined up behind each fellow sitting at the bar. One could hardly turn around if standing up.

The collective noise from the various places became so loud that Editor Sid Jackson ran an editorial in his weekly Grand Coulee News telling the proprietors to pipe down. He wrote that half a dozen places had loudspeakers over their doorways in an effort to attract passersby and they were making too much noise.

"The old pine tree" he stated "has been cut down and hauled to the mill a hundred times, Little Joe the Wrangler turns in his grave under the sod and the Lady on the Isle of Capri has her fingers and toes covered with rings, but the melody lingers on."

"Grand Coulee is probably the most colorful and musical city in the state. Our taste in music is far from high-brow. We too like mountain music. But have a heart! With the sourful tones of the dying cowboy seeping out over a half dozen loudspeakers far into the night, even mountain music gets stale."

The taxi dancers were not whores. Gus never was able to get a date from anyone of them, although he knew them well. Men never followed the girls home. They just left them alone. The girls would refuse to tell where they lived and would usually go home in pairs or triples. The dime-a-dance ladies were mostly from poor or broken families. Johnny Pozar's place, which had a sizable dance hall, housed the girls in tiny, individual rooms downstairs.

Gus described one of the whorehouses. It had a set of stairways leading up to it. There was a hallway, two big rooms with a couple of chairs and davenos, and individual rooms for each of the seven or eight girls working there; plus a kitchen with a lot of chairs around a table. Gus generally sat around the table to talk with the girls or the madam while consuming drinks. This was the case if he didn't want what the girls were otherwise paid to offer. He was a good customer money-wise.

With the men working various shifts there was activity from about noon till two or three o'clock in the morning.

Figuratively speaking, the turn-over in the houses was considerable. A Wenatchee businessman who had been on the bureau staff told me, when I was managing editor of the Wenatchee World, that he and a friend, for the fun of it, would park their car on B Street and watch men go upstairs and then time them as to how long it would be before they'd come back down. I asked what the average time was and he replied "About twenty minutes."

Gus listed a number of the houses — Spar, Pioneer, Gracie's, Model Rooms, Red Rooster, Frontier, Big Four, Seattle Rooms and Swanee Rooms. The latter two were the best known. Most of the places operated upstairs. Some had no names and called themselves "rooming houses." A few were apparently somewhat exclusive. They had to know you before they'd let you in.

One of the houses operated in a strange place — above the B Street fire station. Gus could not recall if the City of Grand Coulee owned the building or rented it.

The girls varied in age from probably 18 to 30, although the younger ones gave their age as 21. They charged $2 a "trick." Once a week they had to visit the county doctor for a health check-up. Gus maintains none was ever infected with venereal disease as far as he knew. If the joints needed more girls, they'd go to Seattle and bring in another load. While there were pimps about, they did not solicit. The demand was big enough they didn't need to. However, the girls turned their money over to them so that they could play cards and jukeboxes downstairs.

Every month or so, there would be raids on the places. That involved the girls being arrested and taken to the city police station to be booked. Then after the madam bailed them out, the girls would go right back to work.

Gus was present when one raid took place. He was drinking when officers opened the door. So he hid his glass in the cup of his hand and threw it out of the window when the officers were not looking. Gus was then told to "get the hell out of here," so he dashed down the stairway "10 steps at a time," as he put it. Once on the sidewalk he was told "Get back up there." But Gus made sure the law would not find him he mingled with the crowd.

There were juke boxes all over Grand Coulee. The Swanee Rooms had one in every room. Gus recalls the machines being emptied twice a day. The coins filled a 6 by 8-inch money box. There were juke boxes in all the beer parlors, plus slot machines and punchboards. The "slots" did not have handles on them as they do today. You pushed a button like you did on the juke box.

"B Street was a wild place in those early days," said Gus.

Was There Vice or Not?

Did Grand Coulee have a "deplorable" vice condition and a "vicious night life?"

A dispute over whether it did or did not raged for a week or more in the boom town, the argument becoming particularly vocal at two "slam-bang" city council meetings. Verbal pyrotechnic displays occurred then between Mayor Frank Tierney and some councilmen. Both sessions drew bumper crowds.

The Wenatchee Daily World reported that one doctor estimated 200 cases of social disease in the project area. That was not a great number to occur in an area with 10,000 population, according to a committee appointed by the mayor to refute the charges that vice was rampant.

Another committee, one appointed by local commercial clubs to offset the bad publicity out-of-town dailies were giving the area, reported there were only 69 cases of venereal disease being treated by physicians and hospitals.

The paper reported further that the MWAK, the main contractor, was anxious to curb the spread of the social disease as many of its workmen were infected. It said the general disability rate was higher than normal at the company's hospital.

The story read that so alarming had become the condition at the damsite that the outside possibility existed that the entire district would be put under quarantine, and the work at the damsite might actually be stopped.

Cleaning-up the situation, real or exaggerated, caused Dr. George Sparling, head of the local State Department of Health office, to say "We are going to send every afflicted person we find to Grant County jail in Ephrata and keep them there until they are cured." That would take six weeks, he said.

The state patrol, the policing agency at the damsite, announced that a new patrolman would be brought in to help curb vice and the Grant County sheriff said a new deputy would be sent. The latter agency also reported that a private station would be established to sell prophylactics.

People alarmed over the situation sent a telegram to Governor Clarence D. Martin asking for a clean-up. He replied that it was up to local authorities to handle the problem.

National publicity resulted from the fuss. A Chicago daily ran four photographs of beer hall scenes, a New York paper called Grand Coulee "the cesspool of the New Deal," and the New York Times assigned Richard Neuberger, who had authored a book on the Grand Coulee Dam, to thoroughly investigate conditions.

Throughout this turmoil Mayor Tierney kept protesting it was much to do about nothing. He challenged those making the accusations that vice was rampant to come to the police station and swear out warrants for places in which they had seen the law violated.

"Not one of them knew of particular cases," the mayor was quoted as saying.

An Affordable Boom Town

A boom town without boom town prices! That was Grand Coulee.

In days gone by, when towns sprang up for any number of reasons such as the finding of gold or striking oil, it was usual to find that prices skyrocketed. Many instances can be found when ham and eggs cost $3.50, smoking tobacco $5, a sack of flour $25, and so on.

This was not so at Coulee. There you found prices of household goods, groceries, and other daily necessities ranging very close to those in larger metropolitan centers. The boom-town spirit hadn't affected the cost of living in the slightest, a check-up of expenses revealed.

Bread at Grand Coulee cost 9 cents a loaf, eggs 15 cents a dozen, coffee from 25 to 30 cents a pound, canned milk 2 for 15 cents, canned corn or beans 2 for 25 cents, tomatoes 15 cents, cornflakes 15 cents, oranges 17 cents a dozen, cheese 16 cents a pound, pork 11 cents a pound, ham and bacon 15 cents a pound, and sugar 10 pounds for 49 cents.

Clothing prices were about the same as in the larger towns. Overalls sold for $1 a pair, blazers $2.95, underwear 89 cents, shirts $1. Miscellaneous prices were: toothpaste 19 cents, Kleenex 21 cents, alarm clocks $1.10, pocket watches $1, cod liver oil 75 cents a pint, to name a few.

The cost of building a home was also very reasonable. An average price of lumber was about $25 per thousand feet. This was slightly higher than "big town" lumber prices but taking into consideration the cost of transporting material to this far away area, you knew that there was no undue profiteering going on.

Most of the lumber came from Okanogan County and Spokane with some coming through Wenatchee from the coast. Seven lumber yards eventually supplied the Grand Coulee area. All of them did a thriving business.

It was estimated by one of the lumber dealers that $30,000 to $40,000 worth of lumber was sold there each month. It cost from $125 to $150 to build a fair-sized cabin. Like the lumber, the hardware materials were just as cheap in Grand Coulee as in the other towns.

Beer cost 10 cents a glass with one place offering it at 5 cents. Meals, and I mean meals like "mother used to serve," cost from 30 to 35 cents. This included soup, salad, meat, potatoes, vegetables and dessert.

A boom town without boom town prices — that was Grand Coulee.

Newspapers Compete in Growing Area

My competition consisted principally of two energetic editors who had come to the area realizing that with 2,000 people flocking into the upper Coulee, there was bound to be news and there would be a need for merchants to serve them. These, of course, would advertise.

The two weeklies in business in the fall of 1933 were the Grand Coulee News, which Sid Jackson of Mt. Angel, Oregon, started, and the Grand Coulee Booster, which was the brainchild of Mr. and Mrs. Bob Ross, of Richland. Jackson's paper was printed on B Street and Ross's was mimeographed using both sides of a single sheet of paper.

Jackson actually got out his first issue while workmen were completing his building. Early issues were of tabloid size. At that time, there was no electricity to run the press so power was provided by a small gas engine.

The Ross's began publishing about two weeks after Jackson did. They ran their business from a house trailer which also served as their home. They later brought in a printing plant and started a daily known as the Grand Coulee Times.

To meet the daily competition, Jackson's News went twice a week.

All the activity at the damsite brought in a third paper, a shopper run by Ben Rogoway, a Spokane advertising salesman. There were also some people who sought to produce a mimeographed daily without success.

Later, there were changes of ownerships involved in damsite newspapering, but it was Jackson and Ross who were the key figures in the field.

At the outset, the Grand Coulee News offered a couple of public services. It had the only telephone in the area, a pay one. Jackson got rid of the thing in about two months by having it moved across the street to a men's store because it had become an annoyance. People repeatedly rousted him and his employees out of bed after midnight because they wanted to take advantage of the cheaper rate then available elsewhere.

Because there was no post office in the fast-growing area, mail was brought in by whoever went to Almira or Coulee City. They brought it to the Grand Coulee News where Jackson's men would sort the mail and put it in the proper pigeon hole.

Later the mail was brought by a mailman on a Star Route running from Almira to Nespelem. He would leave the mail sack at the road junction at Grand Coulee Center where it was brought to B Street for sorting. That became quite a job, particularly at Christmas time. Seven sacks of mail arrived on Christmas Day, I was told. This required one of Jackson's ad men to spend most of the holiday sorting it all out.

Jackson finally was relieved of this "public service" when a woman agreed to run a private post office in one of the beer joints. There, you could rent a box for a nominal fee. Then finally the postal authorities recognized that mail service was badly needed and established an official post office.

It was tough going for the two editors coming to a town that had no water except for an old well at a homestead. There were no schools, no post office, no power and lights, no telephones and no churches.

Jackson, later a printer in Soap Lake and Grant County Treasurer, brought in printing equipment from Portland. He stored it in a tent until he could erect a building. Unlike the country at large today there was no thievery rampant at the damsite. Jackson left town and felt it perfectly safe to tie the front flap on the tent and leave his equipment inside.

Jackson's dad, Jimmy Jackson of Oroville, built the newspaper office with Jake (Dad) Kast of Loomis in charge. His assistant was F.T. Jasper of Oroville.

It was a historic moment when the first issue of the Grand Coulee News came out on November 3, 1933. The Waterville Empire Press plant set the type and the paper was printed, one page at a time, on a job press in the unfinished building at Grand Coulee.

Some years later the building went up in flames, burning Jackson's files, along with photographs of B Street and many other photos that made the news. (This is the principal reason that photographs of early day Grand Coulee town site are hard to come by).

Jackson and Ross lived the ups and downs of the construction days. They found that there is no place like a damsite for rumors. Business would decline sharply as rumors circulated about a drop in the available jobs. The constant threat that there would be a cut in Federal appropriations for the big dam also adversely affected cash registers in the new business houses.

The first work on the dam — the initial excavation — began in December 1933 and continued through early 1934. Then there followed a lull in construction, this to last until the bids for the first of two big contracts were opened in June 1934.

Things were pretty lean around the damsite at times and the newspaper reporters were hard pressed to get their daily share of news copy.

Some strange stories eminated from the damsite, usually with some basis of truth. Among these was one which involved the Three Engineers Co. It had brought the first diesel plant to the area to furnish light and power for preliminary work on the project and also for some of the damsite communities.

R. Claasen, vice president of the company, is believed to be the one who started the rumor about the firm being interested in forming a company that would, after the dam was completed and the upper Grand Coulee filled with water, establish a resort on Steamboat Rock.

According to the plan, boats would deliver customers to the rock, where they would be taken to the top by elevator. On top would be an elegant resort development including a restaurant, cocktail lounge, golf course and even an airplane landing strip (a plane actually did land on top of the rock at one time). Considering the fact that the state has now developed a park below Steamboat Rock, these boys were not so far off the beam after all in regard to the opportunities the area afforded.

There was spot news too of a type only Grand Coulee could generate, such as the arrival of the first bathtub in the Columbia Hotel, and the birth of the first baby in the area. The first one was a girl named Patricia Alene McMahn who was born in a cabin in Grand Coulee Heights. A Dr. Sorenson at Coulee Dam, the first physician on the project, delivered the child.

Mrs. Ida Fleishmann, who later married Sid Bartell, recalls the incident and also the arrival of the first boy baby. He belonged to the Butterfield family.

Front page news for Jackson and Ross and also for me, were the several big fires that hit the area. After each fire, the fire insurance companies would cancel their fire insurance. Later they would again issue policies, usually one or two in each block.

The coming of electricity to the towns was big news, too.

The three Engineers brought it to a little cabin where Ida Fleishmann's granddaughter was born. That was August 4, 1935, the day that President Roosevelt visited the damsite.

The power company later branched out to Grand Coulee Center and to the B Street area. The City of Grand Coulee ultimately bought the system. It has since been sold to Grant County Public Utility District.

Paul Bunyan Was There

Newsmen relaxed now and then, believe it or not, and just "chewed the fat." I wrote the following article about such a session:

The air was full of wind and the wind full of dust Saturday afternoon so the boys, the newspaper boys who day after day pound out this-and-that about the job, gathered around the pot-bellied stove in the back of Sid Jackson's Grand Coulee News office.

Words led to words, stories to stories, thoughts to ideas and ideas to stories as the guys exchanged pleasantries and moans of the day. Strange tales newspaper men can tell and, so it was no wonder, that soon an untouched yarn blossomed into being.

Minds in synchronization molded Chapter XXIV or such in the tales of Paul Bunyan. The combined idea went like this:

"Paul Bunyan, known far and near as the legendary woodsman who dug out Puget Sound and accomplished astonishing and unbelievable feats with his blue ox, Babe, came to pay a visit at Grand Coulee damsite. He was first noticed here as he stepped across the Columbia River, the water oozing just over the top of his shoes.

"After his trip from the woods, big Paul was thirsty so he took a drink out of the Columbia, lowering the river at Kettle Falls seven feet. Noticing the big, high 3,400-foot long suspension bridge, he tied it around his middle for a belt and used the longest section of rubber conveyor mat for a slingshot. He was about to flick the concrete mixing plant off the west abutment, when someone told him it would hold up the work, so he merely picked up a caterpillar tractor and used it for ammunition.

"The big 3,000 foot-long cofferdam attracted Paul's eye right off. He picked it up and said he would take it along to use as a many-link chain for his blue ox, Babe. People noticed Paul was limping and found out on inquiring that he had caught his ankle in the Grand Coulee, finally managing to free it after it had caught in between the walls.

"As it was about noon when Paul arrived, he was a little hungry. All the food prepared for 3,000 men was barely enough to whet his appetite. Flunkeys found it necessary to use ten miles of conveyor belt to bring him his food and they used the big 5,000-barrel cement silos for his coffee cup saucer.

"After dinner, Bunyan was heard to remark, 'Well, that ought to hold me until I can get a real dinner.' As a toothpick he used a 130-foot boom from one of the big cranes.

"Everybody was sorry Paul couldn't stay longer. On his way out, he scooped up a handful of earth from Rattlesnake Canyon leaving none there. There had been 12,000,000 yards in the gulch. He said he would use it in his ox's barnyard.

"Well, I guess I'll stay on the Columbia Basin lands near Quincy tonight,' he said on departing. That's about the only place I can stretch my legs around here.' Saying this, he picked up Steamboat Rock as he went by. 'This'll make a good pillow,' he said."

Job Stupefies Visitor

Many people are said to be unable to see the "forest for the trees," such was the case a lot of the time for those living in the area of the dam. They were left uninspired by the drama of one of the world's largest undertakings. But not one visiting newsman.

Art Gum (pen name), a traveling writer for the Oklahoma City Oklahoman, was overawed by the project and had this to say "I came, I saw, I am practically speechless!"

"It is the most ambitious, staggering, imagination-straining project for electrical generating and irrigation I ever saw or heard tell about. I'm telling you the truth, I was so astounded at the stupendous job that my lower jaw is still hanging weakly, and I don't think I'm going to get my mouth shut before the middle of next week."

Republicans Were Hard To Find

At the outset of construction, Grand Coulee Dam was noted for its predominance of Democrats.

That caused a problem during the first election. The law specified that in any election there should be a representative of the minority party on the election board. But nobody could be found who'd serve on behalf of the Republican Party, because nobody would admit he or she was a Republican.

Finally, a Mr. Elliot, who ran Elliot's Grocery, got into an argument one day about politics, and soon it became apparent that he was a Republican. He was immediately drafted to the election board, over his vigorous protests.

A couple of election results show how Democratic the damsite was. Roosevelt and Garner received 3,520 votes in six precincts at the dam, while Landon and Knox snagged only 259.

Roosevelt got 1,775 votes to 160 for Landon.

In the first of two elections, Governor Clarence Martin received 1,689 votes and his Republican opponent Roland H. Hartley won 218. In the second Martin got 3,332 and Hartley 274.

Among the strongest of the Democrats were Fleishmann and Elmore, the real estate developers on the Heights. So it was no surprise that some streets there were named after members of that party.

There was Garner St., after Vice President Garner; Hill St., after Congressman Sam B. Hill; Martin St., after Governor Clarence D. Martin; and Dill St., after U.S. Senator C. C. Dill.

There was also a street in Mason City named after President Franklin B. Roosevelt. The Republicans ribbed the Democrats about that, because for adjacent to the street sign, was one which read "Dead End Street."

I got involved in politics, something the Wenatchee World would not permit a reporter to do now. I was appointed precinct committeeman.

However, the truth is that I was not a legitimate precinct committeeman. I wasn't a U.S. citizen!

I figured I had become a citizen through my folks having received their papers. This was not so. Therefore, in June 1937, I was naturalized on my own in Ephrata. A friend of mine, Superior Court Judge Ed Schwellenbach, kept asking me questions. I had studied up and was well versed on the Constitution, so I answered them correctly for a while. However, Ed, as a joke, kept after me until he stumped me. Nevertheless, it was a proud day for me.

Getting a School Was a Problem

While most of the men seeking work on the dam or in the townsites left their families behind because of lack of lodging at the project, there grew a demand for schooling for those who had brought their youngsters.

At the outset, there were 19 children in the area but no school. However, there was a building that housed one where the North Dam is now located. It had no windows and no doors and a band of sheep had been walking through it. Of course, it was not usuable at the time, it was about ready to fall down.

To obtain a school, a Grand Coulee committee was selected in 1933 to contact the State Superintendent of Public Instruction. The committee called Olympia on the only telephone available. After a rather heated discussion during which the committee was told that no funds were available to provide the facilities, they were advised to contact the county superintendent of schools in Ephrata. The group met with her on a Thursday and was informed that if the community would furnish a building the county would furnish a teacher.

It was decided to do just that. The townsite promoter donated a lot and everyone tossed $25 in a hat to create a school fund. On a Friday, the committee made arrangements to buy lumber and hardware at cost, and on Saturday everyone who could drive a nail or saw a board showed up to build a one-room school with an addition to house the teacher.

On Sunday, it was plastered, and on Monday the committee notified the county superintendent that a school was ready to operate. Seats and a blackboard had been obtained from an abandoned schoolhouse which had been situated on the road to Bridgeport.

As Christmas was only a few days away the school opening was postponed until January 2. By that time the first teacher had arrived. He was a man who had been selected from the relief rolls. His salary was to be $69 per month. The enrollment by that time had already exceeded the school's seating capacity, so the children had to take turns sitting down at the desks. Enrollment totalled 109.

Early in 1934, Grand Coulee Center had developed in size so another school was needed. During the following summer, the state allocated $3,500 to District 55 and an 8-room school was built in the Center. When classes opened in September, the student count was over 400. There were 11 teachers plus a school superintendent and a high school principal. However, there were only enough credits from the previous year of state and county apportionments to pay for the first three hours of the first day with 180 school days ahead.

In March of 1935, a member one of the original group was elected to be a member of the School Board and shortly afterward the need for further expansion became evident. An architect was hired, and a Federal Grant for $45,000 was received, plus an allocation of $55,000 from Washington State, so the program was on the way.

Each day brought 15 or more new pupils from many different parts of the United States. Unemployment had been rampant for several years all over the country and the prospect of a job brought many families to the area. Many of them had to live temporarily in tents and some slept in their cars.

It then became apparent that it would be necessary to hire more teachers and run the original school on a double shift system from 8 a.m. to 12:30 p.m. and from 12:30 p.m. to 5 p.m., for some of the upper grades. In the lower grades there was an excess of absenteeism due to the fact that some families didn't have proper food to prepare lunches and the distances were too great for the children to walk back home for lunch, so they just stayed at home. It was decided to put on a school lunch program. Strenuous objections were voiced by the County Auditor and the Superintendent of Public Instruction, but the school group went ahead and did it anyway.

A contractor donated two large aluminum bowls, about two feet in diameter, to use to make lunches and the school organization went into debt (which was against the law) for an electric stove, a refrigerator, several typewriters and some sewing machines for the home economics department. Thus accreditation for the third year of operation was met.

The school lunch consisted of a large bowl of soup, crackers, and a large glass of milk at the cost of five cents. There were three categories of people involved in the lunch program: folks who could buy the tickets for the lunches, those who couldn't (they got help from the county), and the borderline ones whose tickets were paid for by the P.T.A. which had been organized early in the game and was doing a fine job. Also free books were obtained for the children. By getting them to attend school regularly, the school was able to collect about 25 cents a day from the state and five cents from the county to help pay for the cost of the operation.

When MWAK began work on the project it built Mason City to house workers and also a school building.

Engineers Town, as the Douglas County part of Coulee Dam was called, got its school through the Bureau of Reclamation.

Less Malnutrition

Nurses of the district health office in Grand Coulee who had been making physical examinations of hundreds of grade school pupils, reported nutrition amongst youngsters noticeably improved as wages went up and damsite layoffs were over.

Mrs. Marjorie Fager, a nurse, reported that children had suffered from malnutrition during the winter of 1937-38. "I saw children come to school last winter with nothing but cold potatoes in their lunches," she said.

Physical examinations were given so that parents could be told what problems their children might have and what remedies to take to improve them if necessary.

Incorporating City Brought On Disputes

In the fall of 1935, a great battle over the incorporation of the city of Grand Coulee took place. Land developers fought over it. Lawyer Joseph Wicks represented the old Grand Coulee area — the B Street group. Cabin-owner Al Roberts was also associated with it.

The battle started over the post office. Promotor Paul Donaldson had succeeded in having it located in Grand Coulee. Major Fred Weil then tried to get it. He had started the development of Grand Coulee Center, a townsite on land the Continental Land Co. had taken over on a mortgage foreclosure. The Major was a pretty shrewd operator. He was quite a promoter. He first sold a lot and induced a man to build a theater on it — the Roosevelt Theater. Then other places of business were built along his main street. He constructed the Continental Hotel and restaurant, and then persuaded the liquor board to place the liquor store in his hotel building.

The Major also persuaded the bus company to stop at a place near his hotel. The bus had previously stopped on B Street. He then went after the post office and had it moved to his hotel building.

All this caused the people of B Street to wake up to the fact that they were losing out. So to get the post office back, they sought to incorporate the Donaldson townsite as the town of Grand Coulee. This irritated the Major because if the town of Grand Coulee was incorporated, the post office would then have to move back to that area.

The original description in the petition to the Board of County Commissioners of the land that was to be included in the corporate limits of the town was found to be in error. The board, on the advice of Prosecuting Attorney Ed Schwellenbach, denied the petition. The Major then presented a petition to the board to incorporate the entire area, that is old Grand Coulee, Grand Coulee Center, and Grand Coulee Heights.

Things were going along pretty smoothly until the B Street people, under the leadership of Roberts and Judge Howard Russell, hired Wicks to stop the move.

The description of the corporate limits had to be stated on three different documents — first, in a petition presented by the property owners to the Board of County Commissioners; second, in the resolution of the board granting the petition; and third, in the notice of election of city officials.

Taking his cue from the action of the prosecuting attorney in having the county commissioners deny the first petition, Wicks examined the new petition. To his surprise, no two of these documents carried the same description. But to show this — that is to provide a valid description of the area to be included in the corporate limits — required the services of an engineer.

Wicks' clients had little money so the best he could do was to persuade a young engineer named Jed or Judd (I'm not certain of the name) to take the job. Jed was just out of school and was working for the Bureau of Reclamation. He prepared maps showing the descriptions in the three documents. The errors were obvious. With the election called by the county commissioners only a few days off, Wicks petitioned the Superior

Court to write up an injunction restraining the election board from holding the election. Superior Court Judge Jeffers granted the order.

Prior to this, Wicks, with the help of the engineer, prepared a corrected description of the land to be included by the incorporation. This was pending before the commissioners when Judge Jeffers granted the injunction.

That night there was a grand celebration on B Street. The next day Judge Russell came to Wicks and requested that he attend a meeting that evening to pick out the first group of city officials. Wicks declined telling him that he was a lawyer and the political aspects of the matter were in their department. Furthermore, he said he could have no part in the election because he didn't live in the area. He had bought his lot from Major Weil.

The lawyer told Judge Russell that his group should not be too certain that their petition would be granted eventhough it was the only one before the county commissioners. The statute provided that the commissioners could not act on the petition for a period of 30 days. About half of that time had expired since Wicks had filed the corrected petition, but his clients were so elated that they could see no reason why their petition would not be granted. They felt that the commissioners would be required to act upon it before "the Major" could file a corrected petition.

What Wicks suspected happened. The Major, through his attorney, Francis A. Klein of Ellensburg, petitioned the court for an injunction to restrain the commissioners from acting on the petition until a corrected petition for the incorporation of the entire area could be filed by the Major and his supporters. Judge Jeffers granted their petition. He held that the proper solution was to have the entire area included in the corporate limits, instead of a small segment.

This, of course, was a sensible and logical solution, but Wicks' clients would have none of it. They insisted he take the matter to the Supreme Court. Wicks worked all night preparing a petition that prohibited Judge Jeffers from signing the restraining order.

The hearing on this petition could not be held by the court for some six weeks. By the time the hearing came up, the question was mote for the Major's petition had then been filed for the statutory period of time that the commissioners had to act upon it. They did. They denied Wicks' petition and approved the Major's.

Then the question arose as to who should be city officials. Each side had a list of officers to present to the voters. The Major's people took the position that if anyone were to attempt to upset the election it would be Wicks. So to prevent him from taking such action they selected him as their candidate for city attorney. Wick's clients on B Street took the position that since they would need a friend in court after the incorporation Wicks should also be their candidate. Having no opposition Wicks was elected, notwithstanding the fact that he was county chairman of the Republican Party in a community that was 99.99 percent New Deal Democrats.

Thus the entire area became one incorporated city. The state examiner, a Mr. Bassett, came over to help set up the city government. He prepared the first eight or ten ordinances. The next 30 Wicks prepared. For that he received a salary of $50 a month.

It is interesting to note that Grand Coulee came into existence as a third class city. This had never before occurred in the state. Two other communities were incorporated that year — East Wenatchee and Nespelem as fourth class towns.

Howard Russell was appointed the first police judge. His pay was to be the total of the fines he could charge in justice of the peace cases. That was about $2.50 per case. Jake Meyers, who had been employed as a night merchants' patrolman for the business people in Grand Coulee Center, was appointed the first chief of police. Leonard Olive was appointed the first city clerk.

Money, of course, was the big problem for the town was starting from scratch. The first month Judge Russell took in the sum of $450 as his pay for police judge. It did not take the city council long to fix his salary at a flat $150 per month. Not bad because Wicks was only receiving just $50 a month as city attorney and he was doing all the work of preparing and prosecuting cases that were brought before Russell.

A few days after his becoming city attorney, one of the madams on B Street called at Wicks' office, either "Big Edna" or "Big Grace." At any rate, she was "big" and kept a couple of large German Shepherd dogs with her wherever she went. She came in and told Wicks that there was to be a meeting on B Street the next night and requested that he attend. He did not go.

A couple of days later she came back and wanted to know why he didn't attend the meeting. He told her he didn't know of any reason why he should have gone. She then became very frank, stating that what they wanted to know was what the pay-off was to be. Wicks told her very firmly that he had no knowledge of any pay-offs, and, that if he learned of any, he would make it his business to see that both the payer and the payee were prosecuted.

He further told her that he had never been in one of their joints and had no personal knowledge of what took place there, but that he had a good idea of what went on. However, so far as he was concerned as the city attorney, he would prosecute every case the law enforcement officers filed in police court.

He added that there were three rules that he would insist upon: first, there would be no soliciting by the girls from the upstairs windows; second, when the girls appeared on the street they would be dressed decently, and they would not solicit business; third, that if he ever heard of a man going in one of their places and being robbed, he would padlock every joint on B Street.

No further overtures were ever made to Wicks by any of these people on B Street. If the rules that he had laid down were ever violated, they were never brought to his attention.

Immediately after incorporation, two townsmen on B Street, Larry Massart, the plumber, and Val Airey, the druggist, requested that before winter Wicks prepare an ordinance to build concrete sidewalks to replace the board walks along B Street. The street, in the wintertime, was a loblolly of mud and a dust bowl in the summer. At the next council meeting the men inquired if he had prepared the ordinance. He told them that he had not, because, if he had, winter would be over before it could be acted upon under the municipal laws of the state.

Airey and Massart insisted that they must have these sidewalks in place before winter. Wicks told them that the only way they could do it was to figure out the cost, prorate it among the property owners, collect the money from them, deposit the money with city treasurer, a Dr. Cowen, who was with the Peerless Dentists, and instruct him to pay the bills as they were approved by the councilmen. They did so. Wicks always suspected that there had been considerable arm twisting. The sidewalks were in before the snow fell. A similar deal worked out for curbs at Grand Coulee Center.

Law Ignored In Getting The Sewer System

To provide a system to carry away overflow from the septic tanks (which at that time was flowing down the streets), the city contracted with a Yakima firm to build a sewer system. There was only one place to dump sewage and that was in Rattlesnake Canyon. The city limits came within about 30 feet of the canyon brink. Promotors Elmore and Fleischmann had contracted to buy the canyon.

Elmore proposed to the council that the city pay him 50 cents per month per user for the privilege of dumping sewage into the canyon. There were approximately a thousand occupied lots within the city limits. His proposal was promptly filed in the dead file.

The contractor and the city engineer, a Mr. Ferguson, proceeded with the construction of a sewerline until they were within about 30 or 40 feet of Elmore's line. Elmore told the engineer that they could not cross his line until the city made some agreement to compensate him for the use of his property. The engineer came to Wicks for advice.

Wicks asked him how long it would take to push the line over the brink. The engineer said three or four hours. That was a Friday afternoon so Wicks decided to gamble. He knew that Elmore could obtain an injunction to prevent them from proceeding with the line until some agreement was made with him. He knew, also, that Superior Court Judge Jeffers would be on the coast from Friday afternoon until Monday morning. Wicks told the engineer to go full speed ahead. Once the line was in, Elmore would have a damage suit against the city but the city would be disposing of its sewage properly.

Wicks later related what happened on Monday morning. Elmore came storming into the office with ruffled feathers and said, "Wicks, I thought that when a man owned a piece of land he owned it from the center of the earth to the heaven above." Wicks answered, "Yes, Mr. Elmore, I understand that to be the law." Elmore replied, "Then apparently the city of Grand Coulee has no respect for the law." Wicks said, "Oh, Mr. Elmore, we do. What do you mean?" Replied Elmore: "You know damn well what I mean. The city is dumping sewage on my land without any agreement for me to be compensated."

Wicks answered "We thought that your proposal was a little unreasonable." Elmore said, "You didn't even negotiate with me on the matter."

Wicks said, "You didn't ask us to negotiate." He said, "I'll sue the city," and Wicks answered, "Mr. Elmore, it is your right and privilege to do so."

And sue the city is what he did, claiming more in damages than the entire sewage system had cost. The case came on for trial before Judge Jeffers, sitting without a jury. Elmore went to great length to show how he had been damaged. In defense, Wicks introduced evidence to show how Mr. Elmore's property had been greatly improved by the city's building the sewage system. He showed that he had 20 occupied lots which would be increased in rental value by his paying the $20 hook-up charge and so would the value of the lots for sale.

Judge Jeffers, in summing up the case, went to great lengths to expound on the protection that the law gave to owners of property. He said that under the Constitution no governmental agency may take property for public use without just compensation. He said they had no alternative but to hold for the plaintiff. Elmore had been damaged and was entitled to judgment in the sum of $400. Thus, Elmore got his 20 occupied lots hooked up to the city sewer for free.

The Post Office Gets Kicked About

Business people worked under pioneering conditions in Grand Coulee during the early days, even government employees.

Two of them were my friends Postmaster Bob Ross and postal clerk Leo Cogeshall.

I recall seeing them at work in the winter of 1936-37. Sub-zero weather had been a daily occurrence and the Columbia River was frozen over from shore to shore.

I remember finding Leo wearing heavy woolen mittens, a stocking cap that came down over his face with holes cut into it for his eyes and mouth. He also wore several layers of underwear, sweaters and a mackinaw.

The post office, situated in the Center, had been built out of shiplap by Weil, the townsite promoter. The cracks between some boards were an inch wide.

Ross said that he found it difficult to do the bookkeeping and write legible figures while wearing wool gloves.

The two small oil heaters produced about as much heat as a candle in the Antarctic.

Earlier the Grand Coulee area found itself entangled in quite a fight as to where the post office should be located.

There had always been a lot of bickering, and it was very much in evidence during the fall of 1933 when the post office was the bone of contention.

Paul Donaldson, who was promoting the original townsite, better known as B Street, was of course anxious for the office to be established on his property, but he was not the only one.

Pompous ex-army officer Weil had arrived on the scene as a representative of the Continental Land Co. and immediately set to work laying out a townsite, soon to be known as Coulee Center. He graciously offered a suitable lot to the government as a location for the post office.

Also involved were Elmore and Fleischmann, who were developing Grand Coulee Heights.

In addition to the three at Grand Coulee there soon sprang up the communities of Delano, Electric City, Osborne and two small others located about halfway to Coulee City. One was called Rimrock.

At the time, the government engineers made their headquarters at the Almira Hotel but as soon as the winter weather was over, they leveled off some land and built a headquarters town on the west bank of the river.

Its unofficial name was Engineers Town. The Post Office Department decided that it was the proper place for the post office and that the name of the community would be Coulee Dam, Washington.

A young man from Ephrata, Harry Robbins, was named postmaster, but that did not settle the post office question because the residents of other towns wanted their own post offices.

The MWAK, prime contractors on the dam, decided they wanted their own post office in their construction camp on the east side of the river. The company named their community Mason City, Washington, and then persuaded the Post Office to establish an office there.

A postal employee from Chewelah moved to Mason City to take charge of the office. His name was Clarence Sears. He had to settle for the title of assistant postmaster because Mr. Kier, one of the contractors, decided that he should be postmaster, although his other duties kept him so busy that he had no time to sell stamps and distribute the mail.

In the meantime, a real hassle was in full swing between the three factions in the area that was later to consolidate into the one community known as Grand Coulee.

Congressman Hill proved himself to be a good politician by naming Charles Kinnune as acting postmaster because he had a small clothing store located on what was known as Lael's Addition. It was not in the original boundaries of the original town of Grand Coulee (B Street), nor was it in Grand Coulee Center, nor Coulee Heights.

That settled the issue for a short time, but wily old Major Weil remembered some of his former army training and built Mr. Kinnune a store that just happened to be big enough to house the Post Office as well as the clothing store. A partition was conveniently built down the middle of the building so the store and post office would not conflict with one another.

The winter of 1935-36 was a little more severe than the previous winter, and Charles Kinnune fell victim of pneumonia and died in March of 1936.

A number of persons applied for the vacant position and Bob Ross, who had just sold his newspaper to Bob and Howard Hilson (older brothers of Jack Hilson, the later owner of The Star), was the successful applicant. He served as postmaster from March 1936 until 1942 when he resigned to go into the clothing business at Coulee Dam.

It was the winter of 1936-37 that the severe cold hit, and postal employees worked all bundled up.

The druggist, Ed Johnson, took pity on them and built a nice concrete building to house the post office.

About 1938 business increased to a point where it was difficult to handle all the mail in one office, so the department agreed to establish a classified branch office on B Street. It was known as Station A.

This relieved the burden at the main office in Grand Coulee Center, and things ran smoothly for a couple of years.

But the disastrous fire that wiped out an entire block of business houses one summer put an end to Station A, for it too went up in smoke.

The fire started near the east end of the block so all the mail, stamps and some of the equipment were saved before the flames reached the sub-post office at the west end of the block.

About 65 percent of the incoming mail was handled through the general delivery windows, because the Postal Department would not recognize the fact that more boxes were needed. There was no mail delivered by carriers.

The general delivery window (two of them) were kept open from 8 a.m. until 6 p.m. six days a week, and there were very few moments during the day that there was not a lineup of people asking for mail.

Duplications of names was one of the biggest problems, because there might be three or four Bill Smiths or Tom Jones getting their mail at the general delivery window. It was very difficult to know which letter belonged to which person.

Occasionally there were some hostile customers who were sure someone else was getting their mail. One was a woman whose son was attending college. She was helping him out by doing his laundry at home each week. He would send the clothing to her in a suitcase and she would return it to him the same way. One week the suitcase became lost in the mail, and she was certain that someone in the Grand Coulee office was the rascal that stole her son's clothing. Ross never did know what happened to the missing suitcase, but for many weeks after that, the woman looked all the postal workers over very carefully to see if any of them were wearing any of her son's clothes.

Bill Kurth, the senior postal clerk, took over as postmaster when Ross resigned. He served the community from 1942 until Andy Pachosa took over the duties.

Area Short of Water and Electricity

Water was a problem when the sagebrush landscape was turned into a bustling community.

At the outset, the new townsite of Grand Coulee with its B Street obtained its water from a well on the Purtee homestead. That sufficed for a little while, because, at the beginning, most of the men there didn't drink water. They either drank coffee or beer.

But when the construction workers moved in their families, the demand became much greater, and, unfortunately, the well was found to be polluted. After that, water was hauled in by truck and sold at so much per gallon. It was removed from a 50-gallon barrel by means of a handpump. Each client carried home what he bought at the big tank.

Eventually, the Jannsen Water Co. of Seattle installed a water system involving several wells. The cost of hooking up was a constant gripe with townspeople. The charge was so high, because the company wanted to get its capital investment back that way. Monthly rates were to be the profit. After the city incorporated it acquired the system.

Grand Coulee Heights had its own water system, and residents were upset there, too. The supply, from a spring, was never adequate, so a community fight developed to get a better system. The way it was, people who wanted to beautify their yards found themselves without water in the middle of the summer, so lawns, plants and shrubs would die. It made the people very irate.

Several times the state's utilities department came in to investigate the complaints. It finally came up with a program that required that meters be installed to limit water usage. That didn't make people particularly happy, but it helped keep the demand down. Water cost $2.50 a month before the meters were installed, and the hookup charge was $15.

I got quite a water-related story one time. It involved the first bathtub reaching town. Eric Carlson installed it in the Columbia Hotel that he had constructed. People were lined up for long periods trying to take a bath via the new modern convenience.

Water was a vital element in another business that sprang up — the town's first beauty shop. It was situated in a tiny trailer. The beautician, if he might be called that, used a bowl and pitcher to wash your hair in. Mostly you just got your hair cut, and in the case of women, brushed back. No beauty work was done there. It was just a place to get cleaned up.

Besides water, electricity was a problem in the boom town. At the outset there was no power at the dam site. Then, as related earlier, an outfit called Three Engineers ran a powerline into Grand Coulee. But the demand was so great that the supply was soon exhausted. This caused at least three business houses to have trouble. The Grand Coulee News could not run its press at night because it would dim the projector in the nearby Grand Coulee Theater. The larger Roosevelt Theatre, situated in Grand Coulee Center, had a diesel plant ready to run when the voltage dropped so low projecting a picture was impossible.

Religion Comes to the Damsite

Church-goers had a few problems during the initial months of construction at the damsite. For one thing, there were no churches.

But worshippers solved that by ignoring separation of church and state. They held services in schoolhouses.

Mrs. Gladys Lee led services on the Heights, Rev. Black of Coulee City in Grand Coulee, and Rev. A. Farrelly of Wilbur in Mason City.

The first church building erected in the latter community was the Catholic Church. The contractor also erected a Community Church for the joint use of Protestants.

There being no Catholic church in Grand Coulee area, it was necessary, at first, for people there to depend on a very erratic ferry to cross the river to get to Sunday mass in Mason City. Several times the ferry broke down on a Sunday, so that worshippers either couldn't get to mass, or if they did get there, they couldn't get back. In case of the latter, the only way home was via Nespelem, then the Cache Creek Road, then the San Poil Road, then the Keller Ferry, and then on home to Grand Coulee.

That was a very round-about route over dirt and gravel roads. it took about five hours to make the trip.

Naturally, Grand Coulee wanted a Catholic Church of its own. So people there contacted Father Farrelly and told him "We want a church up on the hill."

A meeting was arranged in someone's home. The living room was full. Those present made it known that they wanted to buy Grand Coulee's original small schoolhouse and set it up in a central location.

The building was owned by the Pioneer's Club and had a value of $750. Jesse Zimmerman, a member of the Protestant group who had married a Catholic lady, agreed to pay the $100 that the club was willing to sell the structure for. The money was used by the club to have one last party.

As the meeting was going on, the good father who had come to the United States directly from Ireland and been assigned to the contractor's town, sat quietly. When agreement was reached, he spoke up and said "What a wonderful country this is, where people of different faiths can work together and build a church."

Soon a basement was dug under the old school building and later it was finished into a recreation room where many informal card parties were enjoyed by a lot of people. The church set up was subsequently enlarged and served its purpose for many years.

Preachers Argue

Under the heading: "Negro Populace is Rent Asunder," I later wrote about the internal strife that occurred amongst the colored people due to rival preachers.

The story is written in a style that nowadays would never be allowed. I tried to capture the dialect of the Blacks.

The story read:

A bit of internal strife — a miniature Civil War if you like — is smouldering among the Negro population at Coulee Dam.

One faction led by Reverend James R. Smartt, formerly of Yakima, has no liking for a group of so-called "outright sinners", who are said to be centered around Reverend Jefferson Doemus, formerly of Boulder Dam.

Reverend Smartt is located, with his congregation, in a big tent on the Coulee City highway where he feeds hungry transient workers and holds nightly meetings under the label "full gospel tabernacle and rescue mission."

Reverend Doemus holds no meetings, rescues nobody, but is working with the NRS (National Reemployment Service) and relief office at the damsite in an effort to put his friends to work on the dam.

Reverend Smartt leaves little doubt in one's mind that the Reverend Doemus is not a bona-fide preacher.

"He has lots of recommendations," Smartt said, "but none of them is signed. He came here from Boulder Dam with a man who is an outright sinnah. None of his people up theah (Doemus habitation — a sector of

Grand Coulee townsite) ah Christians. Doemus has no respec' or pride, and ah won't tie up wid him in no way, shape, fohm or fashion."

There are about 50 Negroes at the damsite now, with more coming from the South and Boulder Dam each week. Doemus has been conferring with the NRS office trying to get equal privilege in work rations here. Last week he had an encounter with one of the colored gentlemen, who as a result of the fracas, was fined in the Ephrata court.

Doemus, who sells homemade candy at the damsite for a living as he did in Las Vegas, near Boulder Dam, recently told the NRS office that "Reverend Smartt was a liah, das all he is." The two gentlemen visit the office on an average of twice a week and leave no doubt in the mind of C.C. Beery, representative, as to the qualifications of their rivals.

Reverend Smartt has even gone so far as to advertise for a congregation.

A recent issue of the Grand Coulee Daily Booster, contained this advertisement:

HELP WANTED — "One thousand skilled or unskilled laborers at the Legion Big Tent at the junction of the Grand Coulee Highway. We are beginning to build a spiritual dam and the work is so important we will have to put on day and night shifts.

"Our Plant is the Greatest in the World — Will supply light for the Whole Universe, and such equipment for irrigation that will produce from 30, 60 to 100-fold.

"We are going to Blast. Come and see the rocks fly!"

Lots of Business for The Law

When people came to the damsite in the early days of the construction, there was very little law enforcement.

But they soon saw the need for police, for the growing payroll attracted the usual compliment of undesirable characters typical of the Old West. Gamblers operated in many of the new beer parlors as soon as they opened up. Bootleggers purchased whiskey by the case in the nearby towns, cut it in half with water, put it into smaller bottles and sold it at double the price. Women came from Seattle and Spokane to ply their trade.

So law-abiding citizens sent a delegation to the county seat at Ephrata and got the promise that a deputy sheriff would be assigned to the area. With Grand Coulee being publicized as a wild place, a delegation was also sent to Olympia to see the governor.

He called in the attorney general, the head of the State Patrol, the head of the Department of Health and the chief of the State Liquor Board. Out of that meeting came a promise that there would be two state patrolmen, a state liquor store and a health office in the area. The state lawmen were important because four counties join at the damsite -Grant, Okanogan, Douglas and Lincoln.

So I soon became acquainted with the patrolman in charge. He was Francis McGinn out of Spokane. He had full police powers. Starting in

November, 1933, he faced some very trying times which he related to me as the construction progressed.

At first, McGinn had no office. Later, they built him a little frame building on a sand pile in the colored district off B Street. It had a cell and four bunks and a room for him to sleep in, plus a little added space for conducting police business.

Later, McGinn moved to Mason City because the quarters were better.

Traffic control wasn't much of a problem in those days. There was no speeding, because the roads were in such terrible shape.

McGinn was the only state officer at the damsite until 1934 when Deputy Sheriff Wilbur Anderson, son of an ex-Grant County sheriff, became a patrolman.

McGinn used to take warrants issued in one county and serve them in another. He later admitted that this wasn't legal but Grant County Prosecuting Attorney Ed Schwellenbach told him "it was all right." Nobody called him on it.

The young officer, who had done political work for the new governor, Clarence Martin, found Grand Coulee had a particularly annoying and unique problem.

With so many beer parlors on hand and the construction stiffs so thirsty after a hard day's work, McGinn found it necessary to make about a hundred arrests for urinating in the street.

He finally got people to cut it out, but he had some pretty good arguments about the charges. One guy said that if the state allows beer to be sold it ought to provide a place for nature to take its course.

McGinn didn't argue, he just said "Okay, I'll arrest you and you can take it to the Supreme Court."

Later, McGinn started to pick up drunk drivers. People were being injured and some killed, so he decided to put a stop to it.

McGinn was annoyed about the cases that he sometimes lost. He'd regularly get convictions in justice court, but the dozen times that an accused appealed and asked for a jury trial, the officer lost every time.

"I got reversed 12 times" he told me. "After it was all over, the jurors would admit that the guy was drunk but they said they hated to take away someone's drivers license."

While burglaries did occur, McGinn found it surprising that with 35 parolees reporting to his office, there had only been two stick-ups.

A lot of the "houses" with the girls were causing McGinn trouble.

Some of the joints were putting knockout drops in guy's drinks and then rolling them. McGinn would find them in the alley, unconscious and propped up against a building. He suspected that they were propped up against a different building. He'd wake them up and show them the joints in order to find out where they'd bought the drinks. But, said McGinn, the stairs leading to the second story in all the places were built alike, "so the guy who got slugged couldn't tell which joint he'd been in." He never got an identification in all the time that he was there.

McGinn and his officers made lots of raids because of the illegal sale of liquor, either by themselves or in company with the state Liquor Board's "flying squadron." In connection with most of the raids, someone tipped off the joints.

McGinn probably staged 50 to 100 raids.

B Street generally would know when a raid might be imminent. The bootleggers could see in the paper that the squadron had made arrests in some nearby town and figure that one was probably due in Grand Coulee.

The illegal sales occurred mostly in the "houses." Very little trouble was caused by the beer parlors, because owners didn't want to take a chance on losing their liquor license.

Arresting people on liquor charges raised a problem that the modern day policeman doesn't face.

They'd make a raid and "pinch" 10 to 15 people. They all wanted to put up bond right away, because they didn't want to go to jail. So they'd stand there with the bail money.

Jerry Jeremiah, chief of police for Grand Coulee, didn't want to be responsible for the money, and Judge Ben McMillan didn't want it, so McGinn would take the money, sometimes $3,000, and take it home. However, he made sure that someone else was around.

Some of the raids were exciting affairs.

One time, McGinn rushed into a bootleg joint, and the owner — a man named Henderson — dashed onto the roof through a window. There, patrolman "Wild Bill" Kellogg was waiting. He fired into the air. A scared Henderson plunged back into the room, through the open window, muttering "That Kellogg will kill somebody someday."

Another time, McGinn lost part of the seat of his pants, and his dignity along with it, when he went out a window after some bootlegger and his pants caught on a nail.

Some of the madams that McGinn had to deal with included Big Edna and Big Grace, who were whoppers; Patsy, a little gal, and Sandra, a college-educated woman.

One raid resulted in McGinn being sued and somewhat reprimanded by Grant County Superior Court Judge C.G. Jeffers.

He raided a Chinese joint in a basement several times. One time, a half hour after the arrest, someone called to say that the guy had just bought a drink in the same place again.

At the next raid, McGinn and fellow patrolmen took firemens hatchets and sledge hammers and just leveled the furniture and the bar. The only thing left was the piano. Kellogg wanted to smash that, but McGinn told him to lay off.

In the suit — for destruction of property — Judge Jeffers held for the defendants (the patrolmen), but he issued what McGinn later called "immortal words." Said the Judge "I appreciate your zeal as police officers, but I cannot sanction your Carrie Nation activities."

One liquor problem that McGinn faced, which was not of his own doing, caused him to feel that he didn't care if he stayed in the Grand Coulee area or not.

Grant County Prosecutor Ed Schwellenbach said the people of Grant County were coming to him to complain about failure to enforce the Sunday closing law. McGinn pointed out that there were three counties in the area, and that he couldn't say that you could drink in Mason City (Okanogan County) but not in Grand Coulee, which was in Grant County.

McGinn called prosecutors at Okanogan and Waterville but they didn't care to enforce the law despite McGinn's protest that it was a state law.

So he closed up the whole area. I wrote a story in the Wenatchee World about it. The headline said "Nespelem Has Beer, Why Can't We? Say Grand Coulee People."

The brewery people went to Governor Martin and tried to get McGinn moved out of there. The beer parlors stayed closed, but all hell broke loose, so he didn't care if he stayed at the dam or not.

When McGinn first came to Grand Coulee it was permissable to drink around the clock. Later a 2 a.m. closure was enforced.

McGinn was offered bribes "many times." He had many associations, of course, with justices of the peace. Some had little training. For instance, one asked McGinn if he could grant divorces.

At the outset, it was hard to get justices of the peace. When Grand Coulee people voted for the first time, Larry Edgerton, a big bartender in the Smoke Shop and a former sea captain, who had a smashed-in nose but was still considered a good looking guy, got one vote and was elected "judge."

Al Long, who ran the Smoke Shop, got mad as the dickens about his bouncer becoming a judge. However, he was told that Edgerton made a fine judge, that he just had to go easy and tone down his language a bit, for instance to say "illegitimate child" instead of "bastard."

He served a short while and then withdrew as the job interferred with his beer parlor occupation.

So McGinn would have to get someone else appointed judge, because he didn't have time to get them duly elected.

For years, McGinn prosecuted his own cases, because there were no prosecutors who had the time to handle the situations.

Bureau of Reclamation people once made things unpleasant for the patrol. The engineers didn't want to buy operators licenses, feeling they were driving on federal land. McGinn said they had to have them, and he was never reversed on this stand in court.

Lawyers Were a Busy Lot

Lawyers weren't doing any better financially during the Depression than were the workmen who had been drawn to the damsite seeking a means of livelihood. So a number of them came to the new townsites that had sprung up looking for clients.

The first one to arrive was Cliff Moe. He was soon joined by Robert Hunter. Joseph Wicks came early, too. He later took in Alan Spratlin as a partner. Also on the scene were Hugh Aitken and Lowell Vail. When the main contract was let, Tom Malott set up shop in Mason City as a local representative of the MWAK.

The most colorful of the lot were Hunter and Wicks. Each later rose to become a judge — Hunter as a member of the State Supreme Court, Wicks as a Superior Court judge in Okanogan County.

They and others practiced at the dam before justices of the peace.

These included Howard Russell, a carpenter and owner of several cabins on B Street, who was the only JP for a while; Ben McMillan, who ran a freight line; Tom Malott, a lawyer; Pete Schroeder, a safety engineer on the project; O. G. F. Marcus, a Bureau of Reclamation employee; and Ernest Nickel in Osborne.

Wicks' office was situated in a home he had built in Grand Coulee near a sand dune. It was only eight-by-eighteen feet in size. Wicks lived in the house with his wife and small daughter. There was no plumbing and no electricity. The family used an oil lamp for lighting and hauled water from a well in a garbage can. The "Chick Sale" they had to walk to for about a month was not of a classic art, but it served its purpose as a toilet.

All the lawyers advertised in the Grand Coulee News. Wicks' ad read: "Joseph Wicks, Attorney at Law and Notary Public. Located on the sand dune next to the Labor Temple. Services day and night."

All of the attorneys were pretty busy. There were no shifts for members of the legal profession. Frequently, some workmen coming off the swing shift would just have enough time to make it to a tavern and get a load on before it closed. Some of them would land in jail and call a lawyer to get them out. Others on the graveyard shift would make the "clink" earlier and would want to get out in time to work their shift. Those on the day shift would want out to make the 8 o'clock deadline for work the next morning.

The lawyers frequently appeared in justice courts to defend workers charged with drunken driving. Wicks once estimated he was involved in 40 to 50 cases during the two years he practiced in Grand Coulee — 1935 to 1937.

Hunter, who had come to the area in 1935 and lived in a tent for a while, tried a lot of cases involving drunkenness, too. Some people said that if it hadn't been for Hunter getting his clients out of jail, it would have taken a lot longer to build the dam.

One of Hunter's cases involved a man by the name of "Hard Rock" Davis who worked in the concrete mixing plant at the damsite. He had been arrested for drunken driving. Officers claimed that he had failed to respond over a two-mile distance to a siren and flashing lights.

His defense was that he was "hard of hearing" from working in the noisy concrete plant and did not hear the siren. Hunter was not too sure of that and it bothered his conscience a bit.

However, at the conclusion of the trial held in Okanogan, the judge read out loud the verdict of the jury "We find the defendant not guilty." "Hard Rock" turned to Hunter and asked: "What did he say?" That cleared Hunter's conscience immediately.

The state patrol, which was the policing agency for the area, found lawyers tough to deal with sometimes, particularly Wicks. For a while they would file their cases in the county seat at distant Ephrata to escape facing him in justice court. This procedure did not last long, however, because it was easier for Wicks to take a day off than for one or two of the officers to do so.

Some lawyers didn't like some of the verdicts that the "JP's" rendered and started to demand jury trials. But now and then it seemed to them that a justice of the peace had a favorite list of jurors, so there was considerable sparring during the selection process.

The "JPs" were not always as knowledgeable about the law as they should have been. One case comes to mind in that regard. A man had been convicted of drunkenness, but a friend claimed he didn't drink and must have been given knock-out drops. He had been circulating a petition to get the contract to water the streets that others wanted.

The job was to start in 15 days, so it was obvious that if the man was in jail he could hardly start the contract. Wicks was hired to defend him. He immediately asked for an appeal of the decision. He was told he could not appeal. Asked why not, the "JP" quoted from a statute in a book saying that a case not involving more than $20 could not be appealed, and that, in as much as he'd sentenced the young man to jail, there was no money involved and thus Wicks could not appeal the decision.

"It says so right here in this book," the judge said, confidently.

Wicks agreed that it did, but the judge was quoting civil proceedings and this was a criminal case.

The chagrined judge then fixed bond at $20 and the man was released.

The aftermath of the case is interesting, because it indicated that perhaps not all the newcomers in town were honorable and upstanding citizens.

Despite the favorable verdict, the young fellow decided not to try for the contract. It would cost him all the money he had, and he was sure that someone would put a stick of dynamite under his water wagon. Even when Wicks, making a non-legal gesture, offered to sleep under the wagon on alternate nights, the frustrated man decided not to pursue the venture because of the tough characters that were associated with some phases of B Street.

Sometimes people took matters into their own hand to settle disputes. One such case involved Charley Gibbs, who ran a lumberyard and moving outfit. He sold a man some lumber with which to construct a cabin. The man had bought a lot on contract, paying $5 down and the balance to be paid in monthly installments.

He built the cabin, then lost his job and left the area without leaving a forwarding address. Gibbs felt he was left holding the bag. He had paid Gibbs nothing on the lumber bill and paid nothing further on the contract for the lot. Gibbs figured the lumber in that cabin belonged to him.

So, Gibbs, using his house-moving outfit, picked up the cabin and hauled it back to his lumberyard.

The landowner hired lawyer Hunter to sue Gibbs for $99.99, the dollar-damage limit in a justice-of-the-peace jurisdiction. The landowner claimed Gibbs had stolen the cabin from him. Gibbs hired Wicks to represent him.

Of course, Hunter won the case, because, when a building is attached to real estate, it becomes part of it. Forfeiture of the contract to buy the lot passed the title of the building to the owner of the land.

A lady also tried to take matters into her own hands. She was inclined to over-indulge on occasions, and, on one of these, she ran into a car driven by a man on his way to work. She was obviously guilty, because she was driving on the wrong side of the road.

The woman insisted that the man pay her $25 which was the deductible amount of her insurance. She wanted that done, because her husband had told her that if her driving cost him anymore money he would ground her. Lawyer Wicks, who represented the man driver, saw no justice in that, and so he refused. The woman said that if the driver did not pay that amount, she would file drunken driving charges against him. But he still refused.

The annoyed male driver was getting increasingly agitated because he wanted to get away to make his shift at the dam. Patrolman Bill Kellogg, after having had the two cars moved off the traveled portion of the road, took his paddy wagon and drove the worker to his job.

The woman sought to induce Kellogg to file the drunken driving charge, but Kellogg refused. So she filed the suit herself. When it went to trial, the officer testified for the defense saying he did not smell liquor on the man's breath while he sat with him in his paddy wagon.

This prompted Wicks to assume a pose he seldom took in court. He praised a member of the state patrol. He referred to him as a dedicated, efficient and hard-working officer who belonged to one of the greatest law enforcement organizations in the state, and yes, even in the entire country and doubtless anywhere in the world.

In rebuttal, Prosecuting Attorney Ed Schwellenbach said "Gentlemen of the jury, these criminal cases are extremely serious matters even though they are minor, such as this case is. It is a serious matter for the prosecution to come before you and ask you to deprive this man of his freedom and send him to jail, or to ask you to take his hard-earned money in the nature of a fine that he may need to feed his children.

"Indeed it is serious for the state, serious for the defendant and all concerned. But serious as these matters are occasionally something funny occurs at these trials.

"Something unbelievably funny has happened here tonight. When Joe Wicks comes before the court and jury and praises the state patrol, gentlemen of the jury that is indeed funny!"

Schwellenbach got a good laugh but Wicks got the verdict.

Merchants Had It Tough

The businessmen or would-be businessmen lured to the damsite by all the publicity the prospective start of the dam was getting had a variety of experiences, many difficult, some humorous, all typical of what happens in a boom town.

Gus Thue was an early merchant in Grand Coulee. He described what happened to him and the atmosphere that prevailed in a letter to a friend and business associate, Oscar Skaar.

Having been told about a dam being built in Eastern Washington he had quit a job in St. Paul and with $1,000 in his pocket headed west.

A major portion of his story follows:

"In January, 1934, I made a trip to this 'Dam Site' everyone was talking about. It was to be an employment baby of the Roosevelt administration — to hire lots of men as unemployment was a problem.

"The location of the dam-to-be was in a spot on the Columbia called

Seaton's Ferry. The roads from Spokane were okay until we got to Wilbur or Almira. At that time, the road from Wilbur was impassable, so the 'gateway' to Coulee Dam was through Almira.

"The gateway was disputed and a glorious fight (ensued) between the two towns, to the point that the road signs erected as you approached either town indicating that one or the other town was the gateway were frequently chopped down by the other side. As soon as a sign was repaired, the other side would arrive in darkness of night with axes and saws and flatten it.

"That January, the road from Almira was passable (just barely), and with axle-deep mud in places we arrived to inspect the site. Shacks and tents were all over the hillsides. The promoters had staked out their spots to build a town and surveyed land up to that part reserved by government.

"Lots 25x120 feet sold at $200, but the Department of Interior was leasing lots just across the road at $5 a space, equal in size to the lots on private property. That's where I started, and staked out my claim to a piece of ground with a 30-day clause in the lease requiring us to move out in that length of time if the Department needed the land.

"My friends Bill Rosholt and Ernie Betz had a grocery store across the road, built on a four-wheel trailer and titled 'The Biggest Little Store By A Damsite.'' They lived (slept) behind it and were glad to share that with us until we could arrange space of our own.

"The ground where my building was to be built was on a hillside and some excavating was needed before we could set up a tent or lean-to of some sort. Needless to say, the first emergency shelter was the outhouse!

"When I first set foot in the area, there were no modern conveniences-no water, no lights, no post office, no bank, no insurance, and no police protection. However, there was no shortage of labor, nor of beer parlors, of which a new one opened on the famous B Street of boomtown Grand Coulee every Saturday night.

"In March our building job was finished and two counters were installed with $300 worth of variety goods thereon. We expected to sell at least half on the Grand Opening of the only store of its kind in the area, as it was advertised in the local presses. Well, business that day was not brisk at any time. Our store appeared as if we had two stretched-out breakfast tables with a one-by-four rim around them, loaded with merchandise, as if we had gone to town and bought some necessities for a trip. It must have struck our customers as a pretty skimpy start.

"The day's receipts were just as skimpy. When the cash drawer was emptied that first evening and the money counted — and we counted it over several times to be sure we had found it all — the grand total was $12.50! Not exactly hilarious, and a 'little less' than one-half of our opening stock. Still it was a start.

"That's about the way it went for about six months. The store grossed around $300 per month. All the business people were optimistic to a point, but nobody got rich quick. In the fall, news finally arrived — money had been appropriated by Congress for the low dam and, within days, the population began increasing. For the very first time we became worried about needing more space.

"Just about this time, Mrs. Clara Bohan appeared on the scene. She had leased a lot around the corner on some of the government land and was beginning to build a store that would measure 36x75 feet. In comparison to our present store it looked like a skating rink but there was a hitch. It would cost me $75 a month with the first and last months rent paid in advance. So far, I was only putting out $5 per month rent, how was I ever going to be able to pay 15 times that much?

"The decision was made for me by the arrival of a man who was willing to take my place and on making the deal gave me four one-hundred dollar bills.

"Soon after I got into Clara Bohan's building, Lucian Wray, who had a little five-and-ten cent store at Coulee City came in as a partner, and we opened our second store at Coulee City (on Main Street).

"We moved his $300 worth of stock up to that store and we prepared to buy more. One day, when we had been opened about five weeks, the dry cleaning plant across the alley exploded and blew cleaning solution all over the side of my building. It caught fire and in a very short time the rest of the block, our business and two others, were in ashes.

"We salvaged quite a bit of merchandise, but had no insurance. We figured the loss at around $1,400.

"At the time, I was president of the Eastside Improvement Club which built the first fire truck. It was based across the street from our Grand Coulee store and used for the first time on my fire at Grand Coulee Center. A drilling company had built a small water tank on the Grand Coulee side, with water mains in both town sites. When the Coulee Center fire was out, the water tank was empty.

"After this fire, I organized a fire insurance pool with two partners. Merchants put up $100 each until the pool was $1,000. Then, when someone had a fire, he got the money. We did have fires and reorganized the pool three times. After that, outside insurance companies began writing reasonable rated insurances. I paid $134 per $1,000 of coverage; later it was reduced to $35, if I remember correctly.

"Another time, we had a fire scare when I went to Portland on business. The Portland papers reported the news, one morning, about a fire at Grand Coulee, mentioning the stores that burned, but not mentioning ours. We called home and learned our store was saved. My partner had come from the other store and helped soak sacks, rugs, and whatever was available to beat out flying embers on the roof. It's a wonder it was saved!

"Within a week of our fire, we were open for business in half of a building which had been erected for a beer parlor. The place was 12 feet wide and 60 feet long. In the meantime we had attracted a competitor down the street who gave us a bad time for awhile, but finally went broke and we bought out his remaining stock at a discount.

"About four months later when we counted our cash receipts on Christmas Eve, we had taken in almost $1,000. The crisis had passed and from then on, financial problems leveled off for the time being."

Lots of Businesses on B Street

A sign that stands on B Street gives the following description of the street as it was in the early days.

Donated by the Grand Coulee Area Chamber of Commerce it reads:

"In 1933 the construction of the Grand Coulee Dam was begun. The first lodgings were tents and cabins as lots were being sold on B Street. Businesses were built as lumber was hauled in. From hotels and cafes, to dancehalls and ladies of the evening, B Street was one of the most exciting boomtown streets that ever existed."

The sign also listed the businesses and other buildings that existed on or near the street in the 1933-39 era. They were:

Grand Coulee Club
Peerless
Swanee Rooms
Smoke Shop
Workman's Club
Dam Site Cafe
Bungalow Hotel
Pryors Dry Good Store
Jess Lewis Grocery
Electric Supply Co.
La James Beauty Shoppe
Grayce's Dress Shop
Vic & Val Drug Store
Three Engineers
Columbia Club & Hotel
Deluxe Hotel
Bickle Hotel
Carstens Grocery
North Star Grocery
Coley's Barber Shop
Casino Gardens Dance Hall
Best Little Store by a Damsite
Hub Clothiers
Ted Atwaters Drug Store
Sam Bernstein's Clothing Store
Frontier Rooms
Thue's Dime Store
Grand Coulee Fire Station
Rawe's Hardware
Pioneer Credit Jewelers
Harry Wongs Chinese Noodle Parlor
Shooting Gallery
E. Ewing's Jewelers
Singer Sewing Machine Shop
Taxi-Workmen's Club
Richfield Service
Shoe Repair Shop

Silver Dollar
Peerless Painless Dentists
Pioneer
Big Three
Wagon Wheel Restaurant
Red Rooster
Blanche's Dress Shop
Al Roberts Cabins
Goldfoot Grocery
Hi Dam
Martin Dress Shop
Modern Bakery
Grand Coulee Theatre
Janssen Water Co.
Little Club
Bigalow Hotel
Wigwam
Seattle Rooms
Dog House Cafe
Station B.G.C. Post Office
Hod Carriers Hall
Plumbing Shop
Rogaway & Wilson Furniture
Butcher Shop & Grocery
Ice Cream Shop
Small School House
Grocery (near Division)
Star Hotel
Baker's Cabins
Shackelfords Studios
Hot Tamale Man
The Star
Grand Coulee Times
Spokane Chronicle
Grand Coulee News
Purple Sage
Ross Clothing

The sign says that the list, prepared in 1983, "was compiled by Elmer Rauch, Frank "Bud" Sanford, Cecil Scott, George and Edith Alling, and a 1939 phone book."

Last Roundup Adds Excitement

The construction of the world's largest concrete dam wasn't the only thing worthy of news coverage.

I also wrote about another exciting event. It involved what I called one of the last roundups.

I wrote it this way:

This is the saga of "The Last of the Wild Horses." It is the story of the latest and probably one of the last wild horse hunts held in the timbered region about 15 miles northwest of the site of the Grand Coulee dam.

For the end of the "wild horse" is near at hand in this section of the country. At the most, only 150 or maybe 200 remain of the thousands who once called the hilly forest areas near Nespelem their home range.

The recent wild-horse chase proved that only a few truly magnificent specimens of quivering horse flesh continue to prance defiantly from high slopes. Two herds were stirred up in Cull White's roundup, 45 horses in one lot and about 18 in the other. Of all these, most were puny, in-bred animals, 600 to 700 pounds in weight, with broomtails, knotted manes and shaggy appearances. Only one was the real stallion type you read about in stories of the wild horse days.

To begin at the beginning:

About fifteen cowboys were sent out into the distant hills and forests to form a fan-shaped line around what horses they might find. Slowly the drive toward the center of the fan starts, and grazing herds are pushed inward to a large plateau in the corner of which is located a corral.

This particular drive started Saturday and the stallion was not caught until Monday. In true western fashion, the familiar "chuck wagon" is brought into use, cowboys are garbed in regular uniform, ropes twirl as of old, everything is a revival of the old West.

Witnesses in the plateau can see the herds appear on the high slopes. The sun and shadows playing on the animals give off a black and white dot-dash effect to those watching from a distance. The stallion, who leads the herd and at other times pushes it ahead of him, is driven on and on away from his home to the dreaded corral.

He sets the pace. Eighteen horses in this particular group, made no move unless led by the stallion, who pranced, plumed his tail, pounded his hoofs and reared like the wild leaders shown in the movies. With head erect he gazed at the men following him, a snort would send his herd on, his stopping would slow them down. He was a true leader with the instincts of the wild.

On and on the horses were driven forward until they found themselves trapped in the plateau. A closer look at the stallion, who the riders wanted to use as an "outlaw" horse at the Pendleton Round Up, showed him to be a good-sized horse, with shiny coat and plenty of spirit. Once in the closed-in area, all that remained to do was to rope him. Without their leader the rest of the horses were panic-stricken, and ran about without apparent "horse sense."

In the roundup rush colts are left behind by their mothers and these are later picked up to be made into good range horses.

The area covered in Cull White's roundup is about 50 square miles. It is beautiful country for one who has lived in the dust of the dam for a few months. White plans to build a dude ranch and should draw plenty of people from all indications.

Cowboys tell of what might be called "the love life of a wild horse." When a young colt reaches the age of about two years, the old stallion literally kicks him out of the herd fearing the new male might cause him to lose some personal prestige with the "ladies."

Out of the herd the young stallion soon becomes a lonesome creature. In time he lures a mare from this herd and that herd and so on until he has a family of his own. Until that time however, he is one of the most lonesome animals in existence. So lonesome in fact that you could bring any mare around him and the stallion, so head over heels into romance, would simply follow her anywhere. Which at times was into a corral.

Thousands See FDR on Two Visits

The visits of President Franklin D. Roosevelt were newsworthy times for me.

He spoke, in his usual eloquent fashion, to an audience of about 25,000 people in Grand Coulee during his initial visit to the dam on August 4, 1934.

He came again on October 2, 1937, when another big crowd greeted him.

Both occasions were days of tremendous excitement. The fuss about the forthcoming visit started several weeks before it took place. It was a hectic period for the U.S. Bureau of Reclamation and damsite people doing the planning.

In 1934, they faced having to handle what I said in the Wenatchee Daily World would be "100,000" people, quoting some no-longer-remembered source. Later someone else cut the figure to a predicted "40,000."

As plans were announced and followed out, I flooded the paper daily with all sorts of pre-celebration stories. I kept the busline that took my envelopes to Wenatchee real busy.

One article said a grandstand capable of holding 200 distinguished guests was being built in a natural amphitheater in Grand Coulee (now the site of Safeway and other stores).

A special waterline was laid to provide 12 drinking fountains, said another story.

Other articles said 60 toilets were brought in. Food concessionaires were enlisted to feed the big mob expected, their profits to go to a school fund.

Parking was a huge undertaking with Wenatchee area motorists to be parked in one place, those from the Spokane region in another.

For the first time, the State Patrol was to use a mobile radio broadcasting system in handling traffic.

Ten doctors and 15 nurses were to staff small tent hospitals with 100 cots. Rough damsite roads were scraped smooth and watered to keep down the ever-present dust in the area.

I was to be engulfed with reporters from all over the nation. The influx required special phones for NBC and CBC (now CBS) and for writers of other news media. Six planes stood by at Ephrata airport to take photos to various wire services and major newspapers.

Communication arrangements were made "so that the crowd can be told exactly what the president was doing five or six miles away," one of my stories said.

Soon the great day arrived.

FDR came to the Coulee country by special train from Spokane. He left the train at Ephrata to ride in a convertible up the Grand Coulee highway from which other traffic was barred for a while. Enroute, at Soap Lake, his attention was drawn to a 100-foot-long table displaying Columbia Basin agricultural products. Elsewhere he saw a sign advocating a high dam. Only a low dam was planned at the time.

Traveling with him in the caravan were Mrs. Roosevelt, Washington Governor Clarence D. Martin, U.S. Senator C.C. Dill, and also Interior Secretary Harold Ickes and two other cabinet members.

Every kind of precaution was taken to assure a successful visit. A truck carrying additional water, oil and gasoline accompanied the motorcade.

President Roosevelt, seated alongside construction engineer Banks, smiled broadly as he was driven through a huge, enthusiastic throng awaiting his speech at Grand Coulee. At the damsite, despite objections of the Secret Service, he crossed the river on a ferry. When back in Grand Coulee for a short talk, he walked up a ramp that had been provided in back of the grandstand so that he could reach the microphone on his own. He had been crippled by polio. All the while the famous Roosevelt smile hardly disappeared and it was obvious that the crowd took an instant liking to him.

The President was introduced by Senator Dill. FDR spoke only a short time but he was impressive with that voice his fireside chats had made famous. Loudest cheers and applause occurred when he said that if his hopes were justified, the high dam would be built upon the 153-foot-high structure now underway. That's what the local folks and long-time project promoters wanted to hear.

The President was to be presented with several gifts but the Secret Service said there wasn't time. So those carrying them met FDR as he reached his car in back of the grandstand, out of view of the crowd.

The Young Men's Democratic Club gave him some Indian relics through Chief of the San Poils, Jim James.

It was expected the President would ask questions and the impressive-looking chief did not speak English fluently, so it was arranged that I would be there to help, being the precinct committeeman.

The velvet-lined case the president was given held four arrowheads, three hide scrapers, Indian money and a primitive drill. As expected, the President was inquisitive.

"What's this?" he asked, pointing to the arrowheads. I told him what they were.

"So this is a drill," he said. "Yes", I answered.

"And what's this?" was another question he voiced as he pointed to the hide scrapers. Again he was told.

The case the President took with him carried these words "Just a little more than 100 years ago the best engineering talent at Grand Coulee was represented by these simple Indian tools. We are contrasting these with the engineering you have made possible at Grand Coulee - a fitting monument to your faith in America. May this faith in your countrymen bring America forward as far as Coulee Dam is ahead of this simple token."

Back in his car, FDR was driven off. Later that day, I learned that just a mile or so out of town he felt hungry. He had ordered the Secret Service to stop the car so that he could get a hamburger or hot dog. They'd been real edgy about what he ate. Earlier they had ordered that his drinking water be tested for purity and that it contain no ice, a possible contaminant.

A few days after FDR departed I wrote a story that said a new sign had gone up over the roadside business that served FDR. It read "The President's Choice."

People were real happy over the visitation of such an important figure.

My day-after story carried the headline "Whoopee Lasts All Night at Dam Towns after FDR Visit."

The 1937 visit aroused excitement, too. The President again came by train to Ephrata and was driven in an auto caravan to the damsite.

The new towns had sprung up and advertised themselves along the travel route.

Osborne folks, near Electric City, erected a sign reading "Heart of the Grand Coulee."

Delano, near Grand Coulee, called attention to the fact that the community had chosen the President's middle name as its town name.

On the project, Mr. Roosevelt was driven to the vista house, near the site where the Green Hut Cafe once sat. He spent considerable time in a model room, where Construction Engineer Banks explained how the project was being built.

That done, FDR was taken in the caravan to the opposite side of the river. He passed the noisy concrete mixing plant where he could see four-cubic-yard buckets loaded on trains pulled onto the dam by diesel-electric locomotives. Then he was taken to a construction viewpoint.

My assignment there was to listen to what the President was asking Banks. I practically leaned on the President's shoulder in order to hear, being pushed gently back from the convertible by Secret Service personnel several times. After a short while the President was driven off.

I had been ordered to rush to a telephone to report to the Spokane Chronicle what the conversation had consisted of. Much to my disgust, I found I had locked the car keys inside my old Studebaker. But having been absent-minded like this several times before, I was able quickly to open the door with a wire found nearby.

After inspecting the project, the President was driven to a ramp in Mead Circle of Mason City, now the east side of Coulee Dam, whereon his chauffeur could drive his car. There he told a lively crowd that the project was a "national undertaking doing a national good."

The Associated Press said "Thirty thousand heard him." I doubt if there were that many there.

Later, the President ate lunch off a tray fastened to the side of his convertible near the home of Guy F. Atkinson, president of one of the firms in the construction group of contractors building the dam. He remained in a pleasant mood but did say to photographers: "Now you boys take all the pictures you want, then leave. I can't eat while I'm being photographed."

Local people and visitors showed the same enthusiasm for the President that they had showed on his previous visit.

I said in the Wenatchee World: "The greeting which the thousands in Mason City gave the president, still smiling, was nothing short of tumultuous."

Some four years later, I became an information officer for the Bureau of Reclamation. While in the Washington, D. C., office, I was assigned to write wording for nameplates to be put on for a monument to be erected to FDR and one on the dam itself.

Much to my pleasure the wording, except for three or four small changes, was used as I had written it.

The one on the dam reads:

Begun in time of adversity it stood in war as a sentinel of strength safeguarding the nation. Forever a monument to those who shared in its conception and its construction in peace it is the key to new American frontiers of opportunity in agriculture and industry."

I sort of think the late President Roosevelt, in light of his role in bringing the great structure about, would have liked the words.

The wording on the plaque at Franklin D. Roosevelt Lake read:

"To Franklin Delano Roosevelt, thirty-first president of the United States, whose vision and unswerving devotion to the cause of conservation and development of the natural resources of the west for national security and the permanent enrichment of the american people, brought about the construction of the Grand Coulee Dam, this reservoir is dedicated."

"Chick Sale" Asked For Advice Re FDR's Visit

In connection with the visit of the president, a committee purportedly wired the famous toilet consultant, Chick "The Specialist" Sale, for technical advice on "outside facilities."

The telegram, signed by "Elmer Woodhouse" and approved by Frank A. Banks, read as follows:

"Chick, are you coming to Grand Coulee to hear President Roosevelt? Boys here sure wish you would. Town's just gettin' started and ain't set to specialize for big crowds like we're expectin' Speakin' will be from big bowl, central like, meadow bottom and slopin' sides.

"Soil good, grow anything when get water from high dam but ain't no

89

natural settin's now, no apple trees, no wood-piles. We can't camouflage 'em so most of the boys feel we should make 'em beautiful and put 'em right out on the hillsides with flying pennants that sorta' say, 'Here I am.'

"Be nice feeling satisfaction just to have 'em located. And we can't agree on how many. There's 50,000 people comin' and some of 'em are gonna' need comfortin' mighty bad and mighty quick by the time they get here.

"Should ladies have one end and gents the other or should we keep 'em separate? Be bad gettin' lost on day like this. The boys agree that farmers should bring last years calalogs and for ventilation, this being presidents day, we won't use 'crescents or stars' but NRA letters instead.

"Everybody worryin'
Chick. Please wire."

Later President Harry Truman visited the dam. That trip and another incident involving Truman are related in another section of this book.

The Construction Was a Spectacle

While the many activities just described were happening on the hill, the construction stiffs were also busy on the river, and exciting things were developing.

A cross-section of humanity could be seen any day at the damsite. Every type of person, some with a past and many with a future, could be found in this hurriedly gathered together mass of workmen.

On the payroll there were former white collar workers alongside those who prided themselves on having the largest bunch of "cuss words" you could list. A big official of MWAK could supposedly cuss for three minutes straight without repeating himself.

Grand Coulee was surely the melting pot of the West. All types gathered there. Bootleggers, petty crooks, dope dealers, card and pool sharks, loud mouths and soft-spoken men all mixed with one another.

Many jobs warranted news attention for a couple of reasons. One, because of their interest to the reader, and the second, because I was being paid space rate (so much a column-inch).

A River of Dirt Flows

A tremendous excavation job confronted the first major contractor — MWAK Co.

All earth material was transported to spoil banks by belt conveyors. It was dug up by large electric shovels, then hauled by 8 to 10 cubic yard trucks and 12 to 20-yard buggies drawn by tractors to grizzlies, grate-like structures on the ground. There, boulders over 13 inches in diameter and other material were broken up and forced through the grizzlies by bulldozers.

Feeders under the grizzlies delivered the material over 60-inch belt conveyors to a surge feeder on the main-line conveyor. It carried it away into Rattlesnake Canyon and dumped it there at an elevation 500 to 600 feet above the point of origin.

A part of the material excavated on the east side of the river was carried by belts 4,000 feet across the stream and into the canyon.

The main-line conveyor was made up of sections, both long and short, depending on the grade at any point. Each section was driven by a 200-horsepower motor.

More than 5,000 horsepower of energy was used to drive the system. The average daily capacity was 40,000 yards and the maximum was 50,839 a day. The record monthly amount moved totaled more than a million yards. MWAK moved 15 million cubic yards of "common" (earth).

My good friend, L. Vaughn Downs, a Bureau of Reclamation engineer, who authored the excellent book, "The Mightiest of Them All — Memories of Grand Coulee Dam," said the conveyor system carried "a river of dirt." Aptly put.

The second contractor, Consolidated Builders Inc. also moved quantities of material from the damsite and adjacent areas. The combined amount moved by the contractors exceeded 21 million cubic yard.

How They Controlled The River

Bedrock under the entire damsite, including the river channel, was covered with a deep deposit of sand, clay, and boulders. In order to remove such material on the west side of the river, a 60-acre area was enclosed in a cofferdam. It was formed of timber cribs faced with steel piles and a 3,000-foot chain of cells of steel sheet piling along the river. They averaged 110 feet in height. The cells were approximately cylindrical in shape and about 50 feet in diameter. Seventeen thousand tons — 127 miles — of steel sheet piling were used in the west cofferdam.

From the enclosure area, 10,000,000 yards of clay and boulders were removed to expose bedrock, create a diversion channel, and provide a tailrace for the powerhouse; and within the enclosure, the west end on the foundation of the dam was built.

After the west end of the foundation, with its diversion channels, was completed, the flow of the river in its natural channel was stopped by a downstream cross-river cofferdam. It was comprised of timber cribs, built to fit the contour of the river bottom, floated into place, sunk by loading with gravel, and protected with a facing of steel sheet piles.

A second cross-river cofferdam, upstream, and the end of the west side concrete structure (blocks 39 and 40) completed the enclosure of a 55-acre area, which included that part of the river channel to be occupied by the dam.

The Big Slide Made Headlines

I was having my old boots repaired in a small shop along the highway in Grand Coulee early in the construction when one of the biggest news stories of my days at the damsite broke.

A fellow came rushing into the place to shout "Hu, you better get down the hill. They've had a 'helluva' slide down there!"

Immediately I hollered to the shoe repairman "Put that heel back on, hurry!" He did and I was out of there in a minute or so.

I raced afoot, as fast as I could, to the area on the west side where the slide was supposed to have occurred. It was in mid-morning, so I felt I could possibly still write a story to make that day's Spokane Chronicle. In the area where the highway now curves below the dam on the west side of the river a huge mass of earth, that someone estimated to be a million cubic yards in size, had slipped down a steep slope.

I found a lot of people milling around particularly near a large mound of earth at the bottom of the slide. Apparently, some sort of gulfing action set in motion by Goodfellow Bros' excavation caused the earth to pile up.

The slide had buried two tractors and lifted a 50-ton power shovel about thirty-five feet in the air on top of the mound. Miraculously, no one had been killed or injured.

The entire episode lasted less than two minutes. The whole mass of material moved 90 feet in that time. Telephone lines to the damsite were broken and powerlines carrying current to the townsites were snapped. Eight engineers, three diamond drillers and a line crew were working about 250 feet above the top level of the excavation area when the slide started.

One of the diamond drillers, W. A. Dibble, related his experience to me. He said "All at once we felt the ground starting to move. We started to run. Cracks opened up all around us. We jumped the cracks to keep from falling in. We weren't fast enough though and were carried down the hill on top of the slide."

Carl Fox, a man running the steam shovel in the excavation area near the slide, told me this "I had just taken another scoop when I felt myself going up in the air. Oscar Peterson on the shovel with me also rode up with me. The motion felt like an earthquake. Our shovel was lifted twenty or thirty feet higher than where we had been working."

Joe Meehan of the Columbia Basin Commission staff, which maintained an office at the damsite, immediately posted guards around the area to prevent accidents.

Once I got a substantial number of facts I started to dash up to the road leading to Grand Coulee where the only phone in the area was located. I wanted to get there ahead of Sid Jackson, editor of the Grand Coulee News and representative of the United Press. I wanted the Associated Press, which I represented at the damsite, and my own paper to have the story ahead of the rival wire service and the papers it served.

Luckily, I was able to hitch a ride with a fellow in a touring car which had a running board on it so I reached the phone first.

The Spokane Chronicle ran an extra on the slide. It was the last extra it ever published.

There was an interesting sidelight to this construction episode which I explained in my news stories. Jackson had complained many times about the dailies beating him to good stories because he published a weekly. In this instance, he was most happy because the slide, the biggest story to occur since construction had started, happened on his press day.

He typed out the copy, but, later, found that he was unable to publish the paper because the slide had wiped out his power line.

Some months after the mishap, the reason for the big cave-in was learned. Engineers working near the top of the slide area for Crick and

Kuney, which had the railway and highway contract, had found numerous chunks of hard clay there. They were of such formation as to leave no doubt as to the cause of the almost disastrous mishap.

The clay possessed seams. They were called soap seams and were just about as slippery.

The whole area where the Goodfellow shovels were working was riddled with these slippery seams some running hundreds of feet down.

The slide occurred when the "plug," or mass of earth which held the upper portions of the area in place, was removed by the excavators. Once taken away the entire million yards of overburden slid like a toboggan over the slippery seams. It was as though a cork had been taken out of the bottom of a funnel.

I found that when the soap seams were broken open and exposed to the sunlight, they shined like a mirror and a person could easily see himself in the reflection. When the two strata of the clay were rubbed against one another, the effect was like a bar of soap sliding down the side of a bathtub.

It was later found that much of the area in which the slide occurred had to be excavated.

Shovel Operator Brags About His Job

A shovel runner named John McDowell allegedly wrote a letter to his friend, Oscar, telling him how the excavation for the dam was carried out (his remarks were checked out and found to be accurate). The following is what he wrote. No corrections or editing of the copy was done.

Dear Oscar,

It seems like ages since I've written you but gosh we have been so darn busy out here building the dam that a fellow just ain't got no time to keep up on his correspondance. It sure is some job down here and I'm right in the middle of the whole darn works. Yeh, I got my job running one of those big shovels all right. Aimie says to say hello to Alice and that the kids are all good and healthy.

Course I know you're interested in the work I'm doing out here so I won't take any more time telling you that Aimie got a new dress or the radiator on my old Hupmobile froze up during that dawgone cold spell last week.

Honest, Oscar this job is the biggest darn thing in the whole world. I ain't seen nothing to compare with it. Just take my shovel for instance it moved 5,000 yards of dirt in one shift. We work seven hours here. I guess maybe you don't know how much that 5,000 yards is, well it's as much a 20,000 wheelbarrows full.

One day here, that was the record day of them all we moved 63,900 yards according to some figures I see in the paper. About 51,000 of that was moved by a belt converyor system we have, and it sure is some system. It has a series of rubber belts run by 200 horsepower motors, one belt dumping on the other and so on up a steep grade to a big canyon, one and a half miles away. During the average day of good operations that darn old belt dumped more than a ton a second, or a ton every time your watch ticked. Think of it.

We have moved more than 12,000,000 cubic yards of earth here already and now we're sure flying into the east side of the river, that is across the river from where we live in Grand Coulee. We ain't got the best accommodations but we kinda like Grand Coulee, it's a lively town, all right.

We've got about two to three million yards more to move, then we'll be all finished. A guy by the name of Ryan moved 3,000,000 a couple of summers ago so all in all we've taken out 15,000,000 yards. The MWAK, that's the name of the company here, stands for Mason-Walsh-Atkinson-Kier, a bunch of big shots. They get a $1 a yard so I guess they don't feel the depression.

The way we move this here dirt is this. I dump my stuff in a trailer which holds 12 yards. It takes about two dippers-full for me to fill one bucket as my shovel is a five-yard one but when heaping full will hold six or seven. Then the cat-man takes the muck to a place where there is a sort of a grid and dumps it. If there are lumps in the stuff, mostly clay here, a dozer smashes it through. The big belt, 60 inches wide, then picks up the muck from underneath and takes it to Rattlesnake Canyon. That's where we dump our stuff. I haven't seen any rattlesnakes yet.

This belt moves 620 feet per minute or eight miles an hour. I know Oscar you was a swell runner in your day but you sure would a had to travel to keep up with this belt. They say the conveyor system here is the biggest they ever built in the world. It takes just 5,000 horsepower to run the darn thing, think of that, you and Alice.

Right now we're working on the east side, across the river. A belt has been built across the Columbia, some stream it is too, and it takes the dirt away to the west side system which carries it to the dump pile. We are averaging about 20,000 yards a day over there.

There is little or no excavation on the west side now. Instead of five laterals a-working we have only one, that one takes the dirt now being taken out by two clamshells from block 40 which is a rectangular hole just behind the cofferdam, where they will move the first concrete. The laterals when they were all running looked just like arms on an actupos (I mean a devilfish, if I didn't spell it right) reaching out into the pit.

But this belt, that's the thing that would get you, Oscar and you too Alice. When you come out here at your first chance you sure wanta' look at that. There is about 11 miles of belt here all in all, the rest of it being used for moving sand and gravel from the pit to the concrete mixing plants. One section of it, I see by the paper, is 4,300 feet long, longer than from your house in Seattle to where Joe Pialaco lives from you, ain't that about four-fifths of a mile?

We sure are moving dirt out here all right, never heard the like of it. One reporter fellow last week figured out that it would take about 32,000 men with wheelbarrows and hand shovels to keep up the way we're doing out here. If one man did it all he wouda had to start when Andrew Jackson became president, about 107 years ago. That is if the fellow worked eight hours a day; if he worked 24 hours a day, just say like, he would be done in about 29 years.

We had at one time during the peak of excavation five-yard electric shovels. (Yeh, did you ever hear the like of it, they run 'em here by electricity, four-yard ones, and a half dozen smaller ones. We had cats and trailers working and bulldozers.)

I bet you wonder Oscar how we distribute the dirt on the end of the line. We have what we call a stacker, which is a belt which moves on a swinging arm. It is built on a caterpillar tread and moves wherever they want to go.

To get back to that belt again, for several months in a row we moved more than a million yards per month, once more than a million an a quarter. Think of that will ya.

I don't remember if you still know Art Brandson, he's running a jackhammer here. You remember he was the fellow who broke his leg on the Rock Island job. Well, he and his wife was over the other night and Art says that they have moved about 200,000 yards of rock in all, his boss told him.

They have about 800,000 to drill in all and the company gets $2 a yard.

There will have been drilled about 4,000,000 feet of holes by the time they get all through here. The good old powder monkeys follow Art and his gang of jackhammer men and blast the stuff loose. They will use about 300 tons of dynamite here for the blasting, Art says. Most of the stuff is 25 percent and delayed so that when they shoot, three times a day, at noon, at 8 p.m. and in the morning, it sounds just like a string of fire crackers going off on the Fourth.

Well, the kid is crying so better close and try and get him to sleep before he wakes the other two. Write me soon Oscar and say hello to Alice.

John

Cofferdam Leak Threatens Work

Deep sea diving, or as close to it as the Columbia River would allow, played an important role in the building of the cross-river cofferdams and the ultimate diversion of the river.

The main task of three divers was to see how the bottoms of the cofferdam cribs fit the floor of the river. They had to make certain that the fit was snug.

Cutting steel piling under water and placing dynamite on large rocks to remove them were other jobs the divers did.

The average diver ready to settle down in the river tipped the scales at nearly 500 pounds. His helmet equipment weighed about 80 pounds, a lead belt, if used, about the same, each shoe 25 pounds and the suit 40 pounds. Whenever needed, he had a 1,000 candle-power light encased in metal to radiate heat. This weighed more than his suit. The rays of the encased globe could cut through about 15 feet of water.

The diver had two men helping him don his sea-going outfit and to take it off. The one-piece suit fit high on the neck. The diver coated his hands with soap in order to get them through the rubber sleeve cuffs which were only 2 ½ inches in diameter.

Shoes of the suit were six inches wide and 18 inches long, with lead soles ¾ inches thick. The suit itself was made of five layers of material, three of canvas and two of rubber.

When the diver in his suit disappeared beneath the water, the gurgle of air bubbles rising to the top continued unceasingly. The rate of air escape is arranged for by a valve in the side of the helmet that could be pressed by the divers cheek.

The air pump on the barge, oiled only with a high grade olive oil, kept up a pressure of fresh air. The diver could control the air pressure within the suit through the use of two valves. Air pressure inside a suit was to be about equal to the water pressure outside.

The diver kept in constant contact with the deck via a telephone line. He also had a lifeline attached to the waist and head of the diving suit, and of course, had the all-important air line.

Keeping the Columbia River, the most powerful stream on the American continent, under control was no easy task. The contractor was ever cognizant of the danger that the big stream could overpower man as he attempted to confine it in the building of the dam.

The biggest risk was that the Columbia would break through one of the steel, sheet-piling cofferdams behind which excavation and concrete pouring was taking place. In mid-March of 1937, it did.

The mishap occurred at one of the clusters of cells of the cofferdam keeping the water out of the work area on the Okanogan side of the river. The break started slowly. It began with seepage coming through an earth-filled cell comprised of long sheets of interlocking piling driven to bedrock.

Knowing the cells could never be made watertight, MWAK had installed pumps at strategic points. But, in this instance, these were found unable to keep up with the flow of water pouring into the weakened cofferdam. Even installing additional pumps did not help. On March 17, MWAK began to fear a break was imminent.

I started writing stories about the threat and what was being done. An early headline in The Wenatchee World read "Man and Machine Battling Mighty River to Save Coffer." To stop the flow, which reached a peak of 29,000 gallons a minute as compared to the normal seepage of 2,000 a minute, all sorts of things were tried.

Sand, rock, gravel and clay by the truckloads were being dumped into the river at the point where the water was coming through. That didn't work, nor did adding brush and hay to the mixture.

My readers got the real impact of what was happening when I reported that Christmas trees and mattresses were being dumped at the point of the dangerous leak.

While this hectic activity was taking place it was felt safe to allow workmen to continue excavation and concrete pouring in the area made dry by the cofferdam. But on the morning of March 18th, the sheetpiling of one of the cofferdam cells split, so the contractor hustled his men out in a hurry.

What saved the day was forcing Bentonite into the gravel, sand and clay stratas by means of grouting machines. That material is a volcanic dust that expands to seven times its normal size when it gets wet. Five drill rigs bored holes into the material so the Bentonite could be inserted under high pressure to form a water-tight curtain.

The entire cluster of cells away from the leak were treated also. Sawdust, cement, wood shavings and other material were added while the grouting was done in the location of the large seepage.

Finally, after several days of around-the-clock activities, the leak was plugged and work went on as usual.

I reported that "mountains of material" had been forced into the broken cofferdam. The company said it was 1,250,000 pounds of cement, 150,000 pounds of Bentonite, 4,700 cubic feet of sawdust, 7,000 cubic feet of shavings and large quantities of sand.

Harvey Slocum, the colorful construction boss for MWAK (whom I shall describe in detail elsewhere) was in charge of the cofferdam-saving effort. I was told that he came down in his red pajamas at the outset of the break to take charge. I cannot personally testify to that, but I wouldn't be surprised that he did.

It cost an estimated $400,000 to subdue the Columbia River.

To prevent a reoccurrence of the mishap, several additional cells of sheet piling filled with gravel were constructed next to the troubled cell.

It was believed that the rupture may have been caused by some piling being pulled during the removal of the shore arms of the cofferdam. Also, the excavation of the riverbed nearby may have disturbed the main cell cluster, or it could have exposed a layer of sand within the clay.

I remember that there was also talk that the sheet piling had not been driven all the way to bedrock due to an obstruction of some kind.

Dirtiest Job and Scary One

Under that heading I wrote:

FOUND — The dirtiest job at Grand Coulee Dam. It's so dirty that you have to throw your work clothes away every two weeks and your overalls will actually stand up by themselves in a corner after a day's labor.

The job consists of applying "CA5" to steel beams, steel racks, steel linings of the trashracks, and outlet tubes on the dam. To let the cat out of the gunnysack, CA5 is a mixture closely resembling tar.

No matter how careful workmen are, the gooey stuff gets all over them and they actually look like they might have fallen into the tar barrel. In applying the tar-like substance to the steel outlet tubes, each 8 ½ feet in diameter, gobs of it fall on their heads and shoulders, with "marked" effect.

About 210 beams, each weighing 800 pounds, and 300 racks are to be painted with the black mix. There is 80 square feet of surface on each of the beams, 300 feet each on the racks and 900 in each of the 20 steel liners.

The mixture is applied to protect the steel against water. As it is to remain in place forever on the upstream face of the dam to keep logs and debris from passing through the tubes running through the spillway section every precaution is taken to administer the water-proof substance perfectly.

Every inch of the vast area to be covered must not be over 1/16 of an inch or less than 1/32 of an inch thick. It takes a gallon of tar to cover about 40 feet of surface.

So sticky is the "goo", that it takes two men to put one man's clothes on at the start of a shift and two to take them off. It is impossible to clean the clothes so the workmen simply buy new ones. To stand close to a fire to warm up has an unforeseen effect as the tar shields the legs from the heat but when made hot it stays hot and burns the skin.

The "CA5" is administered under a canvas tent which is hurriedly closed by workmen when a wind blows up dust that might settle in the tar. The bureau overlooks nothing.

The crew dressed in Klu-Klux-Klan-like hoods and armed with air hoses, clean every bit of steel before it is painted. Sand is injected into the air hose and when blown out gives up an emery-wheel effect. The hoods, with ising-glass fronts protect the workmen from the sand blasting.

Riveters Throw Hot Slugs

In the improvement of construction methods over the years, one spectacular job that featured the building of the dam has disappeared.

No longer does the assembly of structures or the erection of equipment involve rivets. But it did then. And how!

This was my story about it:

At Grand Coulee damsite white-hot rivets are flying through the air like bullets.

Grimy, sweating steel workers threw and fastened 7,000 of the hard pellets in building just one of the big hammerhead cranes on the high trestle deck. The uncanny accuracy of the heaters aiming at a funnel 50 to 75 feet away was a source of bewilderment to all but the accustomed.

George Ingle, who had been a steel worker since he was 14, was one of those who heaved the hot rivets to a catcher up on the steel girders of one of the hammerheads. He took the work as a matter of course and appeared surprised when you acted startled at his accuracy.

"Throwing rivets is nothing on this job," he'd say between spells when the rivet gun wasn't creating a bedlam, "the rivets here are only about three-quarter inch thick by 2 inches long, some 4 inches.

"Why at the Bay job (San Fransisco - Oakland Bay) we threw rivets 1 ½ inches thick and as long as 14 inches. Most of the men here worked for Bethlehem Steel on the Bay or Golden Gate job."

Ingle would turn the crank of his heating forge to quicken the heating of the rivets imbedded in the hot coals. It took about a minute to turn them white hot. How does a fellow learn this job? "Oh, he just practices, throwing a short way at first and then farther and farther," he'd say.

Ingle was throwing the rivets about 25 feet from the main trestle deck to the first cross-beam. He would point to a fellow heater, up 100 feet in the air, who was throwing his wares through a network of steel beams and cross-beams to a catcher 65 feet away.

Older, experienced heaters did their work very methodically. The younger ones liked to throw them around girders and through a maze of steel just to show they could.

The steel worker's job at the dam and elsewhere appeared scary. To workmen themselves it was "nothing." They would say "just look where you're walking, never think of falling because when you do fall it will be your last one."

Steel working men didn't mind height but they'd cuss when they noticed someone working below them because of the danger of hitting them with the falling hot rivets.

The men seemed to have a fatalistic attitude toward life, they were a bunch of loud-talking, swearing men, their faces generally rough appearing, and they liked their beer. When I think of the word "construction stiffs", the steel workers come to mind first.

Crane Men Up High

Of all the guys who took pride in doing their part in the building of the Columbia River's mighty dam, the operators of the big hammerhead cranes and whirleys towering high over the blocks of concrete must have enjoyed the greatest thrill.

Take a hammerhead crane operator for instance. He sat in a tiny four-by-four cab held by a few steel beams out over the edge of the dam 200 feet below. He was a kingpin in the concrete pouring program and a king sitting on a high throne overlooking a mighty construction domain.

This "ultra-ultra" of construction jobs, paying $1.65 an hour, gave the men a sense of power, like the fellow who pushed the lever that dynamites asunder a mighty mountain of once impregnable rock. The operator's efficiency made speed records possible.

The hammerhead operator used all four limbs to manipulate the giant crane. With the aid of a signalman stationed on the concrete below and hooked up to him by phone, he could drop a concrete bucket on a dime. The machine could lift 11 tons at the far end of the crane and 15 tons closer in.

In his left hand, he would hold the "rack control" lever, which moved the bucket back and forth on the crane runway (as a counter-balance moved in the opposite direction).

Some Jobs Shaky or Dangerous

I became a jackhammer man during the early rock excavation. I tried to be clever writing up the experience. The story went like this:

"There's a new kind of ailment at the damsite; no, it's not quite an epidemic but it's worth writing about.

"It's something like hay fever, and because it hasn't been given a Latin name, we'll call it 'granite fever.'

"Jackhammer men are the workmen most generally affected. To the uninitiated, who runs a jackhammer for the first time at a high altitude, such as the west side abutment, the ailment is accompanied by severe shaking and a dizzy feeling. The granite dust, emitted as the hammers drill into the rock, supplies the irritant which clogs the windpipes somewhat and gives the driller a feeling similar to a cold in the chest.

"This hanging on the edge of the cliff or standing on a narrow ledge, 300 feet from the bedrock below, and holding a rambling, vibrating hammer run by compressed air is no child's play. Eventhough a safety belt is fastened to one's middle and tied to steel fastened in the rock, working on the steep rock wall takes nerve.

"There are three shifts during which 50 men at a time work at this hazardous job. Looking up from the bottom of the pit they appear as mere ants on the high cliffs above. The noise of the drill rigs at work as it echos through the air is really the voice of Grand Coulee Dam - modern construction at work.

"When you hold one of the big hammers it seems to shake every muscle of your body. If you're leaning on the hammer and peering down it makes you feel mighty insignificant. In about five minutes you feel like a milk-shake and good and tired. Experienced drillers change position to prevent this tiring-out. They rest a foot on the hammer or even sit on it.

"Generally about 200 holes are drilled before the dynamite is set off, which occurs three times a day. When the drillers have finished the first row down the slope, they move up and the powder monkeys fill in the holes with sticks of dynamite. It's much like planting potatoes, row after row, only much more dangerous.

"Wires are strung over the granite bluff like aerials. These copper wires are connected with side wires leading to each of the holes. When the entire set-up is hooked up, the signal to 'shoot' is given.

"The first row goes off instantaneously. The next row is delayed a fraction of a second, the row higher up another fraction of a second and so on. The delay is to prevent the blast from taking place all at once, which might crack too much granite.

"It's quite a beehive, the west side drilling. When you're handling a jackhammer on that mighty rock face against which someday the big dam will be anchored, it makes you feel, as it must to the regular workmen, that your share in the building of the dam is perhaps no small thing after all."

A Risky Job

Many of the jobs at the dam were considered dangerous, and it was generally agreed that the "primer men" held one of them.

Three of these men were A. A. Dunn, Cecil Triplett and Riley Summers. Their task was to stick electric blasting caps into the thousands of sticks of dynamite that were to blow the granite for the pumping plant asunder.

The job was simple enough, but a slip might easily have blown any or all to Kingdom Come.

The "cap" was the shape of a slim fountain pen. The stick of dynamite was about the size of a large peppermint stick. The cap was inserted into a long opening in the stick and a wire attached to the cap was wound around the dynamite.

The men worked in a small shack far removed from the construction area. No electric light wires ran to the building - a precaution against explosion.

The men felt safe enough, they said. They would even throw the stick, each time they prepared one, into a box three to four feet away.

Hanging Over The Columbia River

One day I felt reckless and accompanied a geological survey expert on an expedition.

I wrote about the trip and put the following head over the story:

"If one really wishes to find out how insignificant he is, try hanging over the Columbia River as it swirls by at flood stage from a frail looking two-by-four board hanging from a long thin cable at the U.S. Geological Survey river gauging station.

"H. C. Woster was measuring the depth and velocity of the stream to determine the volume of water passing the damsite. A trip with him over the Columbia gives a person the feeling that maybe the world would be able to get along all right without him.

"The local station has a cable stretched from shore to shore and running on it is a steel-frame container large enough to hold two people.

"In strong winds and a small rainstorm the box swings back and forth with reckless abandon — much to the discomfort of the uninitiated.

"The river is measured at about 40 different places from river edge to river edge. At each point the depth is taken and velocity of the stream is measured. This cross-section allows mathmaticians to calculate the amount of water passing by.

"Woster was particularly checking the possible back-water effect of the three piers of the MWAK railroad bridge upstream from where the cable is located. Any obstruction in the river might raise its elevation and perhaps slow it up.

"Near the bridge, Woster found the river about 80 feet deep and traveling about 12 miles an hour.

"The local station was built in 1928 with an eye to the possible construction of a dam here. After the dam is finished, the apparatus will be needed more than ever as river control will be available from the dam and it can be accurately checked by this method.

"This 'swinging along with the breeze' business of Woster's is an all-day job, but long experience has made him feel as free as the 'man on the flying trapeze.' Not so for this reporter."

Salt Pills, Pack Horses and Things

The high walls of the damsite made it an oven in the heat of the summer. As a precaution against heat exhaustion and sunstroke, the workers consumed about 15,000 salt pills a day.

They were placed near water fountains in glass containers and in automatic vending machines.

I wrote about the use in the following:

"Grand Coulee damsite people looked hopefully toward the sky in search of a cloud as the mercury passed the hundred mark for the second day.

"Every attempt to keep cool was resorted to by the residents who live in temporary homes — from tar-paper shacks to well-built houses.

"The sprinkling system on top of the dormitories in Mason City threw down a cold spray constantly, lowering the temperature in the single mens' rooms from eight to ten degrees. The system has proved of value for the last four years.

"In the various towns surrounding the work project, many residents have built home-made air conditioners.

"The damsite is located between walls of metallic rock which creates an oven-like effect. It is always one of the hottest spots in the state according to mercury readings.

"On the project itself, salt pills disappear like ice cream cones at a school picnic. Their beneficial aid in helping the body retain fluids which is lost in the perspiration process is a proven fact."

Nature In The Raw Featured Some Engineering

Regular Alaskan sledges, pack horses, night camp fires, mountain-scaling, wading through five feet of snow and other hardships of life in the raw featured work in connection with the dam and the Columbia Basin project.

Coming back to the damsite from the mountain areas near the Canadian border where he had charge of a crew of 17 engineers doing triangulation work, Carl Berry described a picture of real backwoods life.

Berry had been summoned to the dam area to reset Alpha station of the coordinate system. The station, which was the so-called survey starting point of land associated with the Columbia Basin project, was shifted when excavators in Mason City cut down a small hill.

Berry and two other engineers had been working off Copper Butte at an elevation of 7,142 feet.

With the use of a directional theodolite pointing to each of eight lights kept in operation by eight engineers stationed at various mountain peaks over a 35-mile area, Berry measured distances with an accuracy of two feet in 100 miles.

The party was equipped with four packhorses, five trucks, and a boat. At one time, the group found it necessary to come down a steep mountain in one trip using the horses and equipment. But it was impossible to return to the top with the animals for a second load. So, an Alaskan sledge was fashioned out of materials available.

It took from five to six days to move the equipment from one station to another.

The watchers on each of the high peaks cooked their own meals, slept in tents and suffered a few of the hardships of outdoor life during the fall and winter.

Berry, a hunter by hobby, found deer and other game extremely plentiful in the region where he worked.

Two other engineers — Fred Berry and Ross Tiffany — had charge of engineering groups along the river doing replacement work; that is, reestablishing section corners. This was necessary to later determine how much land must be condemned after the water of the Columbia was backed up by the low or high dam. The 1310-foot traverse for the high dam had been run back as far as Hunter.

Long Rubber Belt Brought Sand and Gravel

The world's largest plant of its kind furnished sand and gravel for the concrete on this project. In a pit a mile and a half downstream from the dam, and 900 feet above the river on the east side, power shovels transfer material from the bank directly to a belt-conveyor system, which supplied it to the washing and screening plant. A belt conveyor, 5,965 feet long, moved the sand and the four sizes of gravel to storage piles at the damsite, and other conveyors supplied the concrete-mixing plants, that are on the west side via a suspension bridge.

The first cubic yards of the millions that flowed like a small river from the Brett gravel pit high on the skyline made a roaring debut as they tumbled down from a high airplane tripper. It marked the end of the journey from the grading plant to the storage piles.

Like all mechanical devices perfected for speedy operation, the gravel and sand transporting equipment was as nearly automatic as possible. All operations were controlled electrically from the end of the belt system.

In the control booth at the top of the airplane tripper, an operator set the 42-inch wide conveyor into action. The tripper raised the aggregate by belt some 30 feet and then from arms shooting out at right angles dropped the material on to stockpiles. Other belts then took it across a high suspension bridge over the river to the concrete plant 4,000 feet away.

They were fed by tunnels underneath the storage piles. The operator opening the tunnels also started the belt system at the far end and controlled it at all of the five belt stations enroute. Whenever a certain grade of gravel or sand was needed, he simply switched a lever and the material was there.

It took 12 minutes for the belt to bring its load from the gravel plant to the storage bins. It traveled from 350 to 400 feet per minute.

Being a Sandhog a Bit Frightening

I covered many exciting news events on the construction front during my eight years with pencil and pad.

The most scary one involved the sinking of a pneumatic caisson. It was used to keep water out of a work area deep in the river so that a concrete pier for the highway bridge that crossed the stream below the dam could be built.

I became a sandhog.

Other people may enjoy being sandhogs, but this reporter prefers other professions. I went through the process of "going down" under pressure in company with Will F. McKay, a USBR engineer. The stars never looked quite so bright as when I returned from the river depths.

Here's the procedure: One climbs into what is known as the manlock (a cylindrical can five feet wide and nine feet high). Twelve to fifteen men can be packed into this container. It has an opening in the top and a like lid in the bottom. The top is closed and the lock tender, in this case an expert by the name of Al Dowd who has worked at this for 16 years, starts letting air into the cylinder.

When you are packed in, one man tight against the other, it is easy to sympathize with the lowly sardine. As the air becomes more compressed, you notice your ears plugging up. By holding my nose, keeping my mouth closed, and blowing outward, I was able to open them up. This procedure is continued until 26 pounds per square inch pressure is reached. If your ears do not "pop" a severe pain sets in. The feeling is like your head is being pulled off. Then the person affected has to be let out.

Finally, after eight minutes of swallowing and nose blowing, the pressure below, where the men are working is equal to that in the cylinder so the bottom lid can be opened. Then you descend to bedrock by climbing down a 75-foot goo-covered ladder which is fastened to the inside wall of a two-foot diameter tube.

Out of the tube, I found myself in a 56-by-26-foot opening 62 feet below the river's surface. Twelve men were digging into the hard clay and loading buckets which were sent to the top through mudlocks. These locks contain compressed air that prevents any escape of air from the main working chamber.

The huge pier mass of concrete, 6,000 tons to be exact, was held up by the compressed air. The pier had a "cutting edge" six inches all around the four sides. Men remove the clay beneath this cutting edge and when the signal is given all the air is released and the 6,000 tons sink another distance, generally a foot at a time. This procedure is repeated until the concrete reaches bedrock.

First the bedrock is cleaned as spic and span as the kitchen sink of an industrious housewife. The chamber in which the men are working will later be filled with concrete. Then the major part of the pier building is over.

Sandhogs work two hours, then come up and rest two hours. They take hot showers, drink coffee, and then go back down for another two hours. These laborers get paid according to the amount of pressure they are subjected to, in this case $1.63 an hour. It takes them six minutes to enter the caisson via the compressed air manlock and 18 minutes to come out.

There is great danger for the men doing this work. Insurance companies generally refuse to insure them. Sandhogs can also suffer from an ailment known as the "bends." It is caused by the compression forcing nitrogen into the blood. This is very painful, sometimes causing hardened workmen to scream in pain. To recover, the worker is put into another cylinder known as the hospital lock wherein more pressure than that under which he worked is applied and then slowly decreased until he is cured.

I wasn't exactly at ease in the sandhog process. This anxiety was increased inside the cylinder once when some wise-acre stuck a finger in my ribs and let out a hissing sound. I thought for a split second that I was exploding.

But it made a good story, and that was the pay-off.

First Railroad Train Toots Into Town

In December of 1934, another significant milestone in the building of the dam was reached.

The last rail was laid and a golden spike was hammered into place for the 30-mile long railroad through the Grand Coulee from the connecting Northern Pacific line at Coulee City.

The line was built by David H. Ryan of San Diego and when the ballasting was finished, it was ready to handle the thousands of tons of supplies and machinery due. It was estimated that 50 carloads of material would be transported daily over the line during the life of the project.

A celebration marked the occasion. The dam builders, MWAK Co., were co-hosts with the Coulee Dam Legion post in entertaining a celebration queen and princesses at Mason City. "King" Ryan was host at a reception in Veterans Hall following the spike driving.

U.S. Senator Dill made what he said was his last public utterance as an office holder. He assailed as "pessimists" those who doubted that the power and irrigation project involving construction of a high dam would ever be completed. At the time only a low dam was being built.

"We are going to get the high dam," he declared. "This is the power house of America, the greatest undeveloped resource the nation has."

Governor Clarence D. Martin spoke at the Roosevelt Theatre and was given a standing ovation when he addressed the hundreds of people jammed into the place. He said that his chief aim in making the Grand Coulee visit was to see that Senator Dill properly crowned the queen. The governor saluted Miss Turner in the approved Martin manner.

Banks, the Cheney Cowles of Spokane, Dave Ryan and Homer Jones, state American Legion commander, also made brief speeches on the stage of the theatre. Major Fred Weil of Coulee Center was master of ceremonies.

After an hour of speaking, officials and visitors moved down the railroad track where the final rail was hoisted into place and the golden spike battered home. Whistles wheezed and the crowd cheered as the connecting link was dropped into place.

The railroad was later connected to a switchback to reach the damsite itself.

Grant County old-timers attending the festivities probably remembered stories of the famous railroad controversy in their county.

There were hand-to-hand battles and court fights, cracked heads and bitter words. A ribbon of steel to the Pacific Coast was the objective.

It was in 1889 that the trouble started. The Seattle-Lakeshore and Eastern was racing across the state from Spokane to Seattle with the Northern Pacific. Grading crews and track layers were following close on the heels of surveyors. Rails had been laid as far as Davenport and the grades were finished, closely paralleling each other, to within a few miles of Coulee City.

The big blow-up came when rival crews converged at a point a half-mile west of Coulee City, at that time a wide open cattle town. Surveys for each of the roads had led through a narrow rock cut. The country surrounding it

105

was of such a rocky and broken nature that the cut provided the only suitable outlet.

Every day as the 500 men on each grading crew pushed closer to this cut the tenseness and bitterness grew. Officials of the two roads had already taken the issue to court, but it was not settled, and often it was a case of first come, first served. There were fist fights at night in many of Coulee City's saloons. Picks, shovels and rocks were changed from construction aids to weapons.

One crew would set off a dynamite blast without warning the other and there would be a wild scramble for safety in a hail of boulders and dirt. A free-for-all would follow.

The grades pushed ahead, and there came a day in the fall of '89 when the men on one side were throwing dirt at the guys on the other side, and dodging as it came back. An impossible deadlock existed. Men were too busy fighting to get any work done.

When the Northern Pacific and the Seattle Lakeshore and Eastern fight was the hottest, Great Northern scouts were interested spectators. That line had already reached Spokane and was also seeking a route to the coast. Almost at the same time that the courts reached a decision and ordered the combatants to make the cut wide enough for two roads, Great Northern engineers found a better route, eliminating Coulee City and the Grand Coulee altogether. Taking advantage of the others' delay, Jim Hill's rail crews pushed on across to the Columbia toward Wenatchee.

The hard winter of 1889 tied up railroad building of any kind in Grant County, and it wasn't until 1890 that the Northern Pacific was built into Coulee City. The Seattle-Lakeshore and Eastern Company went broke after running its grade a few miles past there.

A Poet Lauds the Railroad

W. A. "Pop" Wallis, a Grand Coulee Center merchant, composed a literary gem about the railroad track which divided the Center, Heights and B Street. It was read at several civic affairs and drew much applause.

> Grand Coulee has a railroad track, the darned thing splits the town,
> The train goes "toot-toot" up one day, the next day "toot-toot" down.
> This train it hauls no wood or coal to keep our kiddies warm.
> But that darn track makes up for that in the households of this town.
> A stranger wanders into town, he wants to buy a lot; Paul gets the scent of that bank roll,
> And, say, does he get hot.
> The stranger sneaks and takes a stroll; he to the south doth go.
> The Major meets him at the track and they around do go.
> He, too, that roll of bills does spy, and a gleam comes into his innocent eye.

*He shows the wonders of his town, and offers a lot for a dollar
down.*

*Then Ida, she comes tripping in; she eyes that sucker with a
grin.*

*She takes him up the hill with her, and Paul and the Major
say, "Oh, brrr!"*

*At last the stranger gets away, confused and muddled all the
day.*

*He stretches comfy on his back, but all he can see is a
railroad track.*

*Now we hope our friends from over the way, have had their
money's worth today.*

*And tonight as they lay upon their backs, they will forget we
have those railroad tracks.*

The "Paul" referred to is Paul Donaldson, developer of the B Street region; the "Major," Major Fred M. Weil of the Center, and the "Ida," Mrs. Ida Fleischmann of the Elmore-Fleischmann interests from the Heights.

The First Concrete is Poured

I entered the world of concrete in a harsh manner.

And what a world it was for I was about to observe the pouring of more than 10 million cubic yards of mud in the building of the world's largest concrete structure. That was more than any reporter had ever seen.

I knew little about concrete except that it was grayish in color and that you walked on it. I learned quickly, for after having written several stories about the pouring of "cement" I was bombarded by engineers coming up to me and saying, in effect "You lunkhead, don't you know that cement is the powdery stuff that they make concrete with, not the finished product?"

I never made that mistake again. In fact, it became a fettish with me after I departed the dam to point out to numerous editors, including those of Time Magazine, that they were making a boo-boo. I sent them an editorial I wrote for the Wenatchee World. You'll find it at the end of this discussion of concrete pouring.

The first official pour of concrete for the dam occurred on December 6, 1935, when Governor Clarence D. Martin armed with a vibrator moved the material around in a 50-foot square block. It had been dumped there by means of a four-yard bucket lowered by a hammerhead crane sitting on a trestle above.

The Governor, clad in denim and wearing hip boots, made like a construction stiff as a thousand people looked on and movie and newsreel camera men ground away. They filmed Martin moving the heavy vibrator around amidst regular workmen and their automatic tamping devices. Before going down to the job the Governor pinned on a regulation laborer's badge that he obtained from MWAK. He was actually paid 75 cents for his work. He had been placed on the payroll.

107

A score of speakers emphasized the significance of the event — the actual start of the building of the dam that would ultimately make possible the irrigation of a million acres of land in the Columbia Basin and produce a huge amount of power. Their voices were almost drowned out in the din of jackhammers and other construction machinery.

Among the public figures who spoke were Rufus Woods, The Wenatchee World publisher and member of the Columbia Basin commission; Rep. Knute Hill; Rep. Compton I. White and Banks, the USBR construction engineer.

As laborers for MWAK pressed forward with their work, disregarding the crowd and celebration, Governor Martin spoke fitting his words to his garb. He said "We are not here to make speeches; we are here to build the dam. President Roosevelt is for this project. Secretary of the Interior Ickes is favorable. Dr. Elwood Mead, USBR commissioner, is enthusiastic.

"But there are those in the East who would stop this project right now. We are not going to be daunted by their misunderstanding of the great importance of this project to the nation, as well as to the Northwest." Congressmen, legislators, mayors and other Northwest notables attended the celebration.

Souvenir hunters were active with tin cans. They flocked to the forms and the Governor dipped the cans full of the freshly poured concrete and handed them back.

An early morning snow left the ground white around the project but it ceased falling before the ceremony.

Except for the Governor's hand operation in "tripping" the bucket, the entire operation was mechanical and most of it automatic.

A long belt conveyed sand and gravel across the river to storage bins, near where blended cement and water also were stored. More automatic operations delivered the materials to the "House of Magic", as the concrete mixing plant was called, in response to operators pushing buttons.

The properly proportioned mixture was dumped into a mixing drum. It turned for exactly 2½ minutes and automatically dumped the prepared concrete into a bucket waiting on a flatcar nearby.

A 10-ton diesel locomotive moved it swiftly along a trestle to the form prepared for the first pour. A huge crane picked the bucket from the flatcar, swung it through the air until it was directly over the form and lowered it several feet. Then Governor Martin pulled a steel bar to open it.

All concrete to be poured will flow into 50 by 50 foot forms in layers five feet deep. It will be allowed to "set" 72 hours before another layer would be poured.

The trestles to be used each will carry three railroad tracks of standard gauge and traveling cranes with a reach of 115 feet. They will lower 4-yard, 11-ton buckets from the cars into the forms and return them empty to the cars.

Crane operators and signalmen below will communicate with each other by telephones.

Mixing Plant Noisy

I wrote a story about the mixing plant. I said it was the noisiest place in the state of Washington or the United States or maybe the whole world. On several floors of the structure the terrific ceaseless racket of vibrating screens and rocks tumbling down on top of them with nozzles of water spouting under high pressure was so great that a person cupping his hands over his mouth and shouting as loud as possible could not be heard.

Guides attempting to explain the mechanisms would have to point since to try and talk was utter nonsense and a waste of breath.

No One Buried In The Concrete

Many visitors came to the project firmly convinced that the remains of many employees were embedded in the millions of tons of concrete. Vista-house lecturers were often "peppered" with inquiries about it.

A sample conversation:

"You know what I heard," said one sight-seer. "I heard that..."

"Don't tell me," said an announcer, speaking from experience. "I'll tell you what you've heard. You've heard that workmen are buried in the concrete out there."

"Yes," said the visitor in a surprised manner. "How did you know?"

The government man then went on to relate how impossible the story actually was. For a man to be covered in the concrete would require that he either lay flat on his back or on his stomach directly under a bucket.

The buckets were lowered to within a foot or 18 inches of the previous level and no man could possibly be accidentally buried. With a half-dozen men engaged in the operation, it is hardly likely, the announcer said, that a man might fall flat on his face or back and be covered before someone could see it.

Concrete was poured in four-yard batches, not in a continuous flow through a spout or chute. Workmen themselves not giving any substance to such stories was proof enough that such an accident never happened.

It's Concrete Not Cement

Everytime I saw a publication calling concrete cement (a frequent mistake) I sent it a copy of the following column I had written to its editor.

"A lot of people don't know the difference between a mule and a jackass, or between a ship and a boat. But an even larger percentage know less about the difference between two of the great things that built America.

"Among the misinformed are such prestigious people as those who edit Time Magazine. Also in that category are Sports Illustrated, United Press International, artists who draw daily cartoons, authors of books, and others, such as Emmett Watson of the Seattle Post Intelligencer.

"So as the one writer in the United States who can claim the distinction of having written more about the subject than any other, it is time we wrote this overdue editorial.

"We speak up in the defense of concrete.

"That wonderful, beautiful substance out of which many American buildings are comprised, out of which highways and bridges are made, and which you probably use everyday to get into your house has been repeatedly maligned and downgraded.

"Most everyone except construction workers call it cement.

"As the writer who, for the Wenatchee World, Associated Press, other newspapers, and magazines, wrote the day-by-day, on-the-scene story of the building of the entire Grand Coulee Dam — biggest mass of concrete on earth — we can readily explain the difference.

"Cement is the powdery stuff that is mixed with gravel, sand and water, to make a solid substance.

"That substance is concrete.

"Just as recent as a couple a weeks ago, Time said in its article on the Kansas City hotel disaster that killed more than a hundred people that "some of the victims were pinned for hours under tons of steel, cement and cable" and that rescue crews "struggled to peel away the twisted beams and cement boulders."

"Our clip file shows other examples. Sports Illustrated said Chinese tennis fans sat in "cement bleachers." The same magazine said long distance runner Steve Lacy went by Steve Scott like the latter was wearing "cement boots." It also said the trainer of a prize horse wasn't going to allow it to run on those Southern California "cement tracks."

"United Press International in a story on the collapse of a five-story condominium under construction in Florida said that reports had it a crane had dropped a "huge bucket of wet cement", Runners World magazine in a story on a woman long distance star, Grete Andersen, said her family once lived in a "green cement" building.

"Even the comics go wrong. "Heathcliffe", the cat, is shown threatening to wade through a box of fresh concrete near which was a sign reading "Wet Cement." Several books contain the error, too. Emmett Watson said that "most cooks handle fish as though they've studied to be cement contractors" and Jean Enerson of KING-TV spoke of a construction accident involving "wet cement."

Everytime I read about a "cement" highway there comes to mind a vivid picture of cars stirring up great clouds of cement dust.

Our fettish dates back to the early 1930's, when, as a cub reporter just out of the University of Washington journalism school, I began covering the building of the big dam. When the initial concrete pour was placed I said so many yards of "cement were poured." I was immediately bombarded by engineering friends who noisily pointed out what an ignoramus I was. I never made that boo-boo again.

Later, I used to take the privilege in the newsroom, as managing editor, of hollering at the top of my voice: "What do you mean cement?" whenever some unfortunate writer got cement and concrete mixed up.

No longer having any authority in the newsroom, I take delight in clipping errant items from magazines and books and sending them to the editors. The more prestigious the publication, the happier my response.

I had been finding the common error in so many places that I made a trip to the big dictionary to see if the words cement and concrete were perhaps interchangeable. But no, it indicated they are not.

No Flaws in the Concrete or Bedrock

As I've said many times over, no reporter has seen as much concrete poured as I have.

I've followed the trail of "mud" from the gravel pit to its final resting place in the Grand Coulee Dam.

In explaining the attention paid to the make-up of the concrete, I wrote that it might be alright to get a shovel full of dirt in a little patch of concrete sidewalk because it doesn't matter if a sidewalk is a little weak in spots, but that won't do in such a large structure as a dam.

The "G-Men" of the Bureau of Reclamation were Orin Patch, Chief of Concrete Control, and Bert Hall, Chief Inspector. They ascertained that there were no flaws in any yard of concrete going into the dam structure. They checked the gravel and sand at the pit, at the screening house, at the storage piles, and the concrete at the mixing plant. That concrete was carefully tested for strength and all rules for placing materials in the dam were obeyed.

The inspection of concrete at the dam proper was managed by Hall. His men were given exact measurements by surveyors showing the exact location of each block in the structure. Hall's inspectors then checked the grouting and cooling pipes in each form to see that nothing had broken in the process of the "pour." The mix was vibrated after it was unloaded out of the four-yard buckets in order to move the soft mix into every nook and cranny and to remove all voids from the mixture. Voids are weak points in concrete.

But even before the actual pouring began, a clean-up inspector recorded his approval of the concrete before another five-foot pour was added on top. All foreign particles on the blocks were carefully removed, everything had to be clean. Sand, water, and air-hoses, scrub brushes and plenty of "elbow grease" were used on this extensive cleanup prior to each pour.

Removed from the damsite, the Bureau of Standards did its share of inspection taking samples of the cement at every plant that supplied the project. Cement was tested for chemical composition, strength, fineness and soundness. Here, too, no item was overlooked in the detailed procedure to make concrete in the dam "perfect."

At the silos, another government man was on duty every hour of the day to see that the five grades of cement, sent by five mills in the state, were blended properly. The modified Portland cements varied in make-up slightly. Some needed more water than others and some created lighter colored concrete. The five cements needed to be blended into a uniform mixture to eliminate the possibility of having light or dark streaks showing on the outside of the structure.

After the thorough investigation of every step taken with the concrete in its journey from birth to final resting place, there was little doubt that when Uncle Sam said the dam was "finished" it would not lack strength to hold back the turbulent waters of the powerful Columbia River.

Granite Bedrock Tested

The USBR was mighty finicky too about the quality of bedrock on which the dam was to sit.

Extensive examinations of the granite were made by various means, including the diamond drilling of 31,000 feet of holes, some to depths as great as 800 feet. Many holes, 36 inches in diameter, were drilled to depths of 29 to 68 feet. Such holes permitted the inspection of bedrock in place.

Another activity aimed at accomplishing this test involved slicing up the cores of granite on which the structure was to rest. Cutting through a one-inch core of close-grained granite, as hard as flint, with the seeming ease of a butcher slicing a piece of bologna is interesting enough in itself. But when you take a sturdy piece of granite and grind it down so thin that you can actually see through it, that's worth writing about!

Both of these feats were accomplished in a small room in the concrete testing labs maintained on the east shore of the river near the highway bridge. This research department was manned by Grant Gordon of the USBR and Will Irwin, geologist from Columbia University, New York.

The slicing of a granite core such as brought up by the Lynch Brother's diamond drills, and the subsequent grinding of the slice down to one-thousandth of an inch, permits the geologist to study the composition of the particular granite. Years of study allowed Irwin to tell engineers exactly what the history of the piece was, if it had been crushed millions of years ago, where it came from, if it was squeezed by mammoth forces of nature, and what caused its formation. In fact, Irwin could read the granite like people read a book.

Then, knowing what caused the formation, he was able to estimate what to expect in the future and, if it was faulty, how to correct it. For instance, if the MWAK Co. found a poor grade of granite, Irwin was able to decide if it ran deep and thus be impossible to excavate or if it was shallow and would be easy to remove.

A diamond-saw, which is a revolving disc set with real black diamonds, was used to cut out slices as small as one-eighth of an inch in about 30 seconds time. Then, by holding the granite slice, which had been glued to a slide on a horizontally revolving disc, and applying, in order, four sizes of carborundum powder, it was ground down to 1/1000th to 1/1500th of an inch. About 120 of these slides were made by the two experimentalists.

In future study of the Grand Coulee reservoir, it would be possible to make basalt formations into slides and reveal what leakage, if any, to expect. The slides would reveal the history of basalt, its future, how and when it formed, what it was composed of and many other valuable facts.

The Denver office of the USBR had a similar set-up. Cores of concrete from the dam were made into thin slices. This allowed government men to see if the cement was properly joined to the sand and rock - if there were any voids between grades, what chemical action had taken place, if the concrete was strong enough, etc.

Concrete Testing Exacting Process

As stated earlier, the US Bureau of Reclamation put the concrete of which the structure was composed through exacting tests.

This is the way I wrote up the process:

There is a low humming noise in the Bureau of Reclamation laboratory. The hum increases in intensity, louder and louder.

A small cylinder, six inches in diameter and 12 inches high, composed of concrete taken from a batch as it leaves the mixer, is being put to the strength test. Tons of weight are being pressed onto the cylinder. A needle points higher and higher towards the capacity of the press, 200,000 pounds.

As the hum increases, the needle moves steadily on until suddenly the hum changes. It's quiet in the lab. The cylinder has cracked, the amount of pressure it withstood is marked down and the bureau has again added another bit to its vast store of information concerning tests and elaborate inspections that precede the final placing of concrete in the dam.

No "Hawkshaw the Detective" was ever more observing than is the bureau with its eye on the cement, gravel, sand, and the ultimate concrete. No flaw passes the eyes of Uncle Sam's trained crew in their ceaseless watch.

It's a long process — this inspecting and testing of materials that go to make up the the dam. In explaining it, it is best to split the procedure into three divisions: one, the inspection by the Denver office and at the gravel pit and screening plant; two, the mixing house supervision and concrete block inspection; and three, the laboratory tests.

The Denver office of the bureau handled the original details of the proposed concrete manufacturing when the project was young. Its staff of about 100 men, aided by men in the field, chose the pit to be used and decided what percentage of gravel and sand and water should compose a yard of concrete — so as to use the pit to the best advantage. Distance from the dam, the quality and quantity were also vital factors.

Several carloads of gravel and sand were sent to the Denver office for elaborate studies. In testing the pit, 10 holes were dug, one as deep as 381 feet.

The general make-up of the pit strata was discovered and the percentages of each size of material to be used in the concrete decided.

All these tests, it should be explained, are needed to obtain economy and perfection in concrete production. The fundamental problem is to use the least amount of cement consistent with good results. For instance, without elaborate tests to show the strength of the concrete it would be necessary to use more cement to be sure that the concrete was strong enough. Even then, there might be some doubt.

On a small job, it might be cheaper to use the extra cement and take a chance that the concrete would be good enough. On a large job, such as the dam, no chance can be taken, and the cost of extra cement on the present contract of about 4,500,000 cubic yards of concrete might easily run as high as a million dollars.

However, too much cement would cause too much heat — the more cement, the more chemical action – thus entailing more elaborate and expensive cooling apparatus.

The first step in the exacting inspection system takes place at the excavation of the pit by MWAK. Weeds, roots, and dirt are first stripped off the 70-acre plateau. An inspector watches this work closely, and surveyors measure yardage excavated. The inspector also watches for pollution of the aggregate during excavation, that is he makes certain no weeds or other foreign matter enter the gravel that leaves the pit over the conveyor system.

Stationed in the screening plant were three government men on each shift. Their sole, but important job, was to see that the material, once mined, was cleanly washed and properly graded into four grades of gravel and one sand.

In one of the testing procedures, some of the grades of gravel were at times actually washed by hand. If the material was found not clean the amount of dirt removed by hand-scrubbing was measured and the contractor notified.

One of the principal inspecting jobs was checking the grading. Screens of various sizes were used. The particular grade to be tested was then weighed, shaken on the screens and weighed again. The loss of weight revealed whether the company screening plant was working properly. Sand was even more elaborately graded with more screens and carefully tested, six to eight times per shift.

At the screening plant, inspectors again watched for silt, weeds, or other pollutants before the material was allowed to continue to the storage piles – and then more tests.

Dam Workers Down On Their Knees

The story I wrote about this ran as follows:

"Mrs. Housewife, when you become a little disappointed and discouraged about cleaning your floors, just take a trip down to the damsite and see what a lot of cleaning the poor male has to do to earn his bread and butter.

"For Grand Coulee has the biggest housecleaning department ever heard of. Some say, and they are undoubtedly correct, that it is the biggest cleaning job in the world. Down on his hands and knees, in the midst of a hundred kindred souls, a poor man is scrubbing and washing harder than any housewife ever thought of. (P.S. This is written by a man).

"So clean must the granite bedrock be before concrete can be poured on it, that it is possible, although perhaps not appropriate, to eat one's meal off of the rock without danger of foreign atoms sneaking in. Brushes, sponges, wire brooms, water and air hoses and sand are called into use in this exacting preparation.

"It generally takes a crew of seven men and a foreman three to four hours to clean a block. They pick up loose fragments, scrub the surface with a wire brush, sponge out the moisture between the crevices, and do general cleaning by air and water forced through hoses which spout foreign substances in all directions!

"The cleaning of the bedrock for the initial pour is only a part of the cleaning process. Each concrete block must be thoroughly purified over and over again after each five-foot lift has been placed. This ablution is no small item in the expense of building the dam.

"About five hours after the pour, and before the concrete has become too hard, a crew, armed with compressed air and water hoses, swarm over the block and blow off the top "scum", about one-fourth inch thick.

"If the force by air and water does not dislodge all of the debris a sand blasting process is resorted to. This consists of sand mixed with water and air being forced through the hoses. The result is a sort of emery wheel effect on the concrete. Then comes the hand-and-knees work as the final scrubbing with wire brush is given the surface. An air hose follows the workmen, who might leave a little waste of their own. This hose not only cleans the material but also dries it. The concrete must be comparatively dry before a perfect seal with fresh concrete can be expected.

"According to MWAK officials, about 25 percent of the water provided on the west side is for cleaning concrete. About 600 feet of air and water hoses are used per block.

"All in all, it's a 'million dollar cleanup,' not only in the cost to the government but also in the 'million dollar' results obtained."

World's Record Pour Made

While MWAK was most efficient Consolidated Builders Incorporated (CBI), the contractor building the upper portion at the dam, was even more so.

On May 25, 1939, it set a world record in concrete placement.

It poured 20,685 cubic yards in a 24-hour period.

While CBI, headed by Edgar Kaiser, poured a good many yards of concrete everyday, I suspect it made an extra effort to set a record. It still stands.

Cement Disappears

Talk about a disappearing act! Grand Coulee had one that was in a class by itself.

An early story explained that the USBR, working through the general contractors, made 75,000 sacks of cement disappear into the solid bedrock of the west shore. (Later that would be done elsewhere, too.)

The process used was referred to as "grouting." It involved forcing a mixture of cement and water into the rock. To do so, many holes two inches in diameter and 30 to 300 feet deep were bored into the granite, a pipe connected onto them and a force of air used to push the mixture into the holes. The grout would spread, still under pressure, into all the fissures of the rock.

The purpose of grouting was to make the rock on which the dam rests absolutely solid without any cracks.

Photographers Took Great Pictures

Photography played a major role in the construction of the dam and the irrigation facilities of the Columbia Basin Project.

At the peak of activity, there were 17 photographers at work, five of them at the damsite.

Among the most popular photographs taken, aside from those showing the spillway waterfall and the dam in general, was one taken by Wayne Fuller, that showed a big band of sheep crossing the dam, and one taken by chief photographer Frank Pomeroy called "The Blue Bucket."

Although the photo appears to show the bucket coming down during the late evening actually it was taken in mid-morning.

Pomeroy, who now lives in Bellevue, just printed it dark so as to make it look like it was evening. He then tinted it light blue. This was sometimes done back then, because color film was not yet available.

He arrived at the damsite in 1935 from Seattle as assistant to the chief photographer and assumed that position himself in 1937.

Pomeroy, called "Bill" by his many friends had a couple of real challenges.

One photo job required that he be lowered by crane along the face of the dam riding a "skip." The engineers needed close-up photos of water action over the "eyebrows" above the outlet tubes in the spillway. These caused the sheet of water plunging down the concrete face to jump over the 8-foot openings.

Dangling in the sky in front of the waterfall on a small platform he had never ridden before was very scary.

Another time while standing on a small platform he was lowered by crane cable 40 to 50 feet into a 36-inch-diameter hole drilled into bedrock. Close-ups showing the makeup of the granite on which the dam was built were needed by the engineers to detect faults and examine the efficiency of grout forced into the rock under pressure to make it watertight.

In preparing for the assignment, Pomeroy's 5-by-7 view camera, which was equipped with a wide-angle lens to provide the largest possible image was pre-focused in a replica constructed in the photolab. In the actual deep hole, he was rotated from above according to marks of a compass out there. Scary as that sounds, Pomeroy had no problems with claustrophobia in the confined space.

Pomeroy also was a key figure in taking motion picture shots of the constrution, some of which was used to produce the first documentary "Building a Future." Much of his footage was also used in the bureau-made movie "Columbia Frontier."

Noted Geologist Explains Granite

Man's attempt to place a block of concrete across a river seemed mighty insignificant in contrast to the work done by nature in the creation of the actual damsite through millions upon millions of years, as explained by Dr. Charles Berkey, USBR geologist from New York's Columbia University.

Although he had visited 17 damsites and traveled 30,000 miles, Dr. Berkey, silver-haired and always pleasant, never failed to enjoy telling any interested party the geological wonders of this area. In his room in the

Mason City Hotel he gave me his official version of how the place where men, like ants, were building for the future, was originally formed.

First, how did the granite come to the damsite? Dr. Berkey explained that liquid material millions of years ago oozed up out of the earth. As it came out, it pushed up ancient rocks above it. Then, the fluid crystallized and there was granite, as it is today. Millions of years of erosion scoured away the ancient rock leaving the present granite bare.

Following the creation of granite, great volcanoes erupted and sent layer after layer of molten lava across the granite surface. This lava is the basalt we see today. The geologist said that there was evidence that several volcanoes existed in the area which is now the Grand Coulee. The basalt flow in the area was one of the greatest in the world.

The next step in nature's creative work was done by streams. Water had to find its way out somewhere and through millions of years cut its path through the granite and other rock until we have the rivers and valleys of today. Following their creation came the ice age, the most interesting of all geological occurrences.

Dr. Berkey said the river was dammed near the vicinity of the damsite by two giant ice blockades. The first ice movement occurred to the south in a sheet formation. As it worked its way along it cut deeper and deeper and mud settled on the bottom. All this was before the coulee itself was formed.

For reasons unknown, the ice dam then thawed and the river drained itself, carrying with it silts, such as were found in the excavation area. Then repeating itself, nature sent another ice glacier and this second one created the valley in which the Columbia and actual damsite became located.

As the ice moved it carried material, gathered enroute, along with it. This gravel and sand pushed to the outer edges of the general movement and created the high Brett pit, from which was taken the sand and gravel for the dam's concrete.

At the time of the second ice dam across the river, the Grand Coulee itself was formed. Before this ice stage the region in which the Grand Coulee is located was flat. The big lake created by the ice dam finally cut a big groove into the earth as it thawed, leaving a bed of silt. This occurred about 25,000 years ago.

That the ice once moved in the coulee can be proved by the fact huge pieces of granite, half the size of an ordinary room, are found near Coulee City, where no granite ever existed.

No boulders were found directly over the bedrock at the damsite because the ice probably swept the floor clean as it moved, Dr. Berkey said. It is extremely unusual to find clay settled on bedrock without a layer of gravel or rock.

Colossal Waterfall One of Biggest

June 1, 1942, was a big day in the history of the Grand Coulee Dam.

I told my readers that for the first time water rising behind the dam would spill over the top in a vast silver sheet. A waterfall 1,650 feet wide and 30 stories high would be created. A waterfall that was unparalled.

Eleven huge gates in the crest of the immense dam were lowered to permit the waters of the Columbia River to make their spectacular descent. Simultaneously, engineers closed gates in the outlet tubes that had been carrying the stream through the dam at lower elevations.

No event in the building of this huge dam aroused so much public interest as the plunge of the big river over the spillway. It was of particular interest to the USBR because it signified that additional electrical energy was now available for war industries.

To spill water, a practically full reservoir had to be provided, and a full reservoir meant that the generators would be able to deliver their maximum amount of power. It was the first time that the big machines would be provided with full "head."

Grand Coulee Dam had three of the world's largest hydroelectric generators, each rated at 108,000 kilowatts, in operation, and before the end of the year would have available the output of two others, each of 75,000 kilowatts.

Everywhere in the Pacific Northwest, industries vital to the war and dependent on the Columbia River's low-cost electricity were operating at maximum speed. Out of these plants flowed aluminum for planes, phosphorous for incendiary bombs, carbide and chlorates for explosives, and metal alloys for ships and tanks. Additional production facilities were being provided as fast as possible.

After doing research, I told readers that Grand Coulee Dam's man-made cataract surpassed all but one or two of the world's major waterfalls. Its height was equal to that of Victoria Falls in South Africa and double that of Niagara. At the average peak of the yearly Columbia River run off, the volume that would crash over this precipice would be a third greater than that of Niagara, four times that of Victoria Falls.

Waterfalls, of course, can only be compared on the basis of the horsepower they generate. Some are wider, some carry more water, some plunge a greater distance. I found that only the Aughrabies in South Africa exceeded the horsepower generated by the falls plunging over the spillway at Grand Coulee Dam.

If the flow, moving seven miles per hour as it does below the dam, were confined to a channel the size of the average large city main street, it would fill 30-story buildings to their roofs.

The mighty discharge, a quarter of a mile wide and 320 feet high, hurtled over the spillway in a 15-acre curtain, white as snow. At the bottom it dissolved into a spectacle of boiling foam 50 or more feet high. Large tongues of silvery spray projected skyward, and above these floated ever-changing clouds of mist.

The thin sheets of water that glided over the concrete when the drum gates were first lowered, reached a thickness of several feet within 15 or 20 minutes.

About 10,000,000 horsepower of energy would go to waste at the peak of the year's giant fall. Could this power be harnessed and used to manufacture aluminum for warplanes, it would produce in a single day the amount necessary to make 500 flying fortresses or 2,600 fighters.

The overflow would supply all the residents of Chicago with a gallon of water in two seconds time, all the people of New York with a similar amount in just five seconds. In one and one-half minutes it would provide every person in the United States with a gallon-bucket full.

Construction Stiffs Well Served

The contractors provided many facilities for its workers.

A giant ironing machine, capable of turning out 50,000 pieces per week, and a shirt department, which was able to wash, repair and iron 1,400 shirts per week, were just two of the big pieces of equipment in the Mason City laundry.

Fred Borella, former superintendent of the Covey laundry and the Quality laundry in Seattle, was in charge of the plant, equipped with $20,000 worth of machinery in a building 50-by-100 feet located near the general store.

The plant had a 150-horsepower boiler, which at one time was used to heat the store.

It had a form-a-collar machine to take the rough edges off the shirt collars (which made many a man smile). In another corner, Borella had a triple-head press which ironed the neck and two arms of the shirt simultaneously. Another machine, the bosom press — fool proof so that a worker would not get his hands caught in it — ironed the shirt front and back.

Another big washer could wash 150 sheets in 50 minutes, and, still another smaller one, was capable of 100 sheets. A piece of apparatus known as a "tumbler" dried the towels in such a way as to leave the nap on the towels which was otherwise flattened out if they were ironed.

A curtain stretcher and a mangle were the other two big machines. The boiler evaporated into steam 3,000 gallons of water a day, but because the water was brought back into it from the steaming of laundry, it only used 500 gallons. This method made the hard water soft. When it was steamed, it was also distilled.

But all the above technical details don't mean half as much to the ordinary work man as did the advertisement "The Mason City laundry darns all socks, repairs all shirts (unless they are too badly torn) and sews on buttons."

That service made all bachelors happy.

Free Coffee

The two strangest restaurants in the state of Washington were located at the damsite.

The peculiarity of the eating places was that they only served one commodity — coffee. But there was a good reason behind it all.

Because it was too far for workmen in the west bank excavation and cofferdam areas to walk to the MWAK messhall across the river for coffee, two shops, were set up in the district.

Lunch with piping-hot coffee is a necessary item for hard working laborers. At the two buildings, which had three open sides each, the men were able to obtain their coffee free gratis if on the company boarding list. At noontime, the gathering of the clan at these places was quite a sight.

Sweet Tooth

MWAK also provided a service to the workmen through "Archie the Candy Man."

For three years, A. L. MacLennan, with a cardboard box under his arm, could be seen plying his trade in the excavation zones. Later, he graduated to a glass-covered box, and, still later to MacLennan's pride and joy, a refrigerated box from which he could sell ice cream. He used his truck for storage.

Soon he had a full-fledged candy counter mounted on his truck. The roof of the contrivance was built so that it could be lifted up and Archie could stand erect inside his "store." He carried candy, cigarettes, chewing gum, and, in the summer, ice cream bars, pop, etc.

Like the Toonerville Trolley, which allegedly met all the trains, Mac-Lennan met all the day time shifts. Business was particularly good between 7 and 8:30 a.m., and, in the summer, from 3 to 4:30 p.m.

"The fellows don't care much for the small, fancy, candy bars," he said. "They like the big ones. They want something that will last them until they can have a regular meal."

Archie would extend a little credit when the jobs were going full-blast. "The boys are pretty good about paying," he said.

The candy man was assured that he would be allowed to drive his candy truck into the work areas on the next contract.

Harvey Slocum, when he was general superintendent, told MacLennan, "You're as good as ten men," meaning that his service of making candy and cigarettes readily available kept the guys from spending time "bumming" them from others and thus slowing up the work.

Workmen Had Big Appetites

The MWAK messhall always made good copy for me.

I reported at one time that it took a stack of hotcakes 71 feet high to feed the hungry workmen at breakfast time.

Averaging three hotcakes apiece, the 950 men that were being fed in the modern, spacious mess hall building in Mason City, consumed 3,000 cakes per meal.

Bill Arndt, head chef, was rather reluctant to give out specific figures. Within a few months time, he and his force would be feeding even more men, he said.

In addition to hot cakes, 200 pounds of bacon were eaten at each breakfast.

More than a thousand eggs, three cases full, were prepared each morning. Twenty-five gallons of syrup was spread over the hot cakes and 120 pounds of sugar was used each day. Six sacks of potatoes lasted but one day as did 230 gallons of milk. It took one steer to furnish the beef, 40 loins to furnish the chops and 75 gallons of coffee was made.

It took 12 cooks, 32 waiters and six dishwashers, aided by machines, to take care of the men.

Breakfast usually consisted of fresh or canned fruit, hot cereal (25 gallons), bacon, eggs, sausage, ham, toast and hot cakes. At lunchtime, the following was served: soup, salad, two kinds of meat, three kinds of vegetables, pudding and pie, coffee and milk, and three kinds of breads.

At supper, the men got beef steak, pork chops, fish, cutlets, roast or beef stew, three vegetables and the rest was similar to the lunch.

Arndt, who worked for Guy Atkinson at the Bonneville Dam and who since 1914 had worked on many of the big construction sites in the United States, showed me many interesting features of the great mess hall.

The building contained an ice cream plant with two separate ice machines of approximately 25 tons each. Doughnuts, fish, chicken and all kinds of meat were fried on an electric fryer. A dough mixer of two-barrel size mixed the flour for cakes, biscuits and other pastry. A big trunnion kettle was used for mass cooking. Coffee was made in a 250-gallon urn. Two 20 foot steam tables kept the food warm after it had been prepared.

Two three-bushel capacity pressure cookers, three steam jackets, 40, 60, and 80 gallon size for cooking vegetables, boiled meats and so on were also used in the preparation of food. A total of 25,000 dishes an hour could be washed in a big electrical machine.

The butcher shop contained a gigantic meat grinder, a big slicer, and other abnormally large equipment. Meat was unloaded off the trucks and taken to the refrigeration room on a monorail. Nearby was a refrigerator box for vegetables and fruits, and another for storage of other produce. Boxes had been built to hold smoked meats, fish and dairy products, and there were two, 3-by-10 pantries.

Steam was furnished from a boiler driven by a 10-horse-power motor.

The west side of the big dining hall was used for breakfast and the east side for lunch and dinner.

All in all, the MWAK mess hall was nothing short of a wonder in convenience considering the quantities of food that was served there.

Ten Towns Had to Move

While I never saw much of what was taking place, there was considerable activity in the area upstream from the damsite which was to be inundated in the big reservoir.

Ten towns had to be relocated, numerous Indian graves moved and many roads rerouted.

The first story I wrote about the reservoir clearance was the following which I headed, "Engineers Play Hide and Seek Looking for Old Landmarks."

Trying to find marks on rocks and cuts on trees, which were placed there more than 50 years ago to establish section corners, is the interesting and difficult job of Fred Berry, a party chief of the Bureau of Reclamation. These were needed to determine what land had to be condemned in back of the high dam for the reservoir.

Engaged in what is technically known as "retracement" work, Berry and his parties have progressed up the Columbia river past Hunters, which is about 70 miles from the damsite following the river. They started this survey in April. They will continue up to the Canadian border, probably entailing another year's work.

Berry, well-known in Wenatchee, related interesting phases of the work while at the damsite.

The section corners were established on the Lincoln, Grant and Stevens county side of the river from 1880 to 1890 and on the Okanogan and Ferry side from 1906 to 1907. The corners of the sections were marked so that people could settle there and be officially recorded. There are 40 townships with 36 sections in each.

With these marks having been made 30 to 40 years ago, many of them have been obliterated, and that's where the fun begins. Add to this the fact that the surveys made by various contracting companies, who were in many cases inaccurate, made Berry's job no easy one.

"Some trees, which we knew were marked, had to be cut into as far as six inches to find the old section marks," Berry explained.

Old settlers were interviewed in nearly all cases and their stories as to where the corners were located were then compared. Many times the stories varied and failed to tally correctly.

Berry was especially proud of an old established corner. In this instance, the survey party did not know where the point was located. By calculation and measuring, the group decided where the exact point should be. On digging down to place a marker Berry was rewarded by finding the old stonemarker. He kept it as a souvenir paperweight.

One mark, located about a mile upstream, was set in 1860 before Lincoln's first term in office. This marker was as far north as a party of engineers went at that time. They had worked up from a point in Oregon and ran a line due north so that settlers could designate their property.

This mark, placed on two pine trees, one of which remains standing to this day and still has the figures on it, was the point where the party first reached the Columbia River. In the notes about the "due north" line located two miles west of Almira by a Civil War engineer, were such descriptions as "Indian trails, creeks and mountains." At every section corner this man planted an osage orange seed.

Berry said that there was considerable placer mining for gold on the Columbia. One man using a small shovel at Keller's ferry is reported to have moved 300 yards of placer a day and to have made about 25 cents per yard.

Snow covering the few marks visible, necessitated Berry's return to the dam site, temporarily.

Kettle Falls Lifts Self by Bootstrap

Towns situated in the 151-mile long reservoir had to be moved or abandoned ahead of the rising waters behind Grand Coulee Dam.

They included Kettle Falls and Marcus, the largest towns, and Keller, Plum, Peach, Lincoln, Gerome, Gifford, Inchelium and Daisy.

Kettle Falls solved the situation in the most unusual way. It lifted itself by its own bootstraps, you might say. It was legal for the 400 residents to do what they did. It was the first time in the history of the United States it had been done. Here's the story:

Kettle Falls, 104 miles from the damsite, was to be flooded by 10 feet of water, the falls itself by about a hundred feet. The town had a mayor, city council, city treasurer and pride in its name, given in 1888.

The townspeople had realized for some time that they would have to move. They didn't mind the moving so much, because the government paid them well, but they did want to keep the name of their town intact.

They hired Lon Johnson, a former lieutenant governor of the state, to create what he facetiously called his "Polish Corridor."

It had been agreed that the town should move to Meyers Falls, four miles away, where about 100 people lived. It was first thought that Meyers Falls would be made an addition to Kettle Falls, thereby keeping the Kettle Falls name intact. However, there were legal difficulties. Law books said no town can annex a plot of ground unless it is contiguous, that is, connected to the original townsite. But Johnson found a solution.

People of Kettle Falls voted to annex Meyers Falls and a strip of land 60 feet wide running parallel to the state highway connecting the two communities. The idea carried by an overwhelming vote in Meyers Falls also.

In about six months, the people of Kettle Falls had moved to Meyers Falls, and then they voted to abandon the old townsite and the 60-foot wide strip — the "Polish Corridor" —placing Kettle Falls where Meyers Falls used to be.

As a result of the unusual legal step, the town of Kettle Falls had two postmasters, the only town in the U.S. at that time so blessed and that included New York City, Chicago and Los Angeles.

Although the Meyers Falls office, operated by Postmaster Myron D. Spencer and Mrs. Spencer, still had that name, it was legally "Kettle Falls", and genial J.B. Robertson continued doing business as the latter town's postmaster.

Meyers Falls was a "jerk water" on the Great Northern Railway, with about half a dozen business houses. It soon became the site of considerable real estate trading. It was located on a flat and could adequately hold all the houses to be razed because of the coming flood.

The hectic history of Kettle Falls began way back in 1889 with a spectacular boom which saw a New York land company plan the town as a rival to Spokane. It ran special trains from the east and erected a three-story hotel there. Town lots sold for $1,500. The town was once a "hot spot" of the west.

Last Salmon Jump

The town had moved in 30 days and planned a big celebration — a last salmon jump at the falls in the river, but it found there were no salmon eventhough the reservoir was not yet full when the town completed its move.

Publicity men for the celebration apparently had forgotten, it was pointed out by local USBR men, that all salmon were being trapped at Rock Island Dam and taken to tributaries below the Grand Coulee Dam to use those streams as their spawning grounds.

Thus, the jumping so often seen at Kettle Falls was already history. Residents of the area said that as many as10,000 Indians used to gather there for Indian celebrations about the time of the year that the fish started migrating upstream to deposit their eggs.

Indians To Last Resting Place

A significant phase of clearing the big area that was to become the Grand Coulee Dam reservoir was moving the remains of Indian burials to other areas.

The bones of about 700 people, ranging from tiny babies to Indians more than 100 years old, were carefully excavated and reinterred in cemeteries high above the peak flood limits of the Columbia River lake.

Ball and Dodd of Spokane employed about 15 men at the peak of operations. The government required the contractors to hire Indian laborers to transfer Indian remains. Relatives of deceased were given the privilege of taking the remains to cemeteries other than those stipulated by the government, if they bore the expense. Few did.

Because Indians chose the water's edge for their winter camp sites, many natives were buried within the reservoir boundary. Surprisingly, few artifacts were found. USBR engineers explained that most of the graves were relatively new, having been dug after the practice of burying the personal belongings of the deceased with them had been abandoned.

Most of the dead were found in reclining positions. Early Indian practice was to set the deceased erect in the grave. Some were found buried in hollow logs but by far the majority had the orthodox box.

All the new graves were properly marked, either by existing markers or by metal ones. Curious people were kept away from the digging scenes out of respect for the departed.

Women Have Major Role at the Dam

How women fared when their husbands went to work at the dam was described for Wenatchee World readers by Anne H. T. Donaldson. She was the wife of Francis Donaldson, top engineer on the job for the MWAK.

Her story also described what Mason City and its environs were like, and what happened in transforming the area of sagebrush into a bustling community.

This is what she had to say:

"Less than six months ago the site of the world's first all-electric town, Mason City, Washington, was a desert waste of sagebrush and sand. To a New York tenderfoot, viewing for the first time last August the location of her future hometown (soon to be built by the Mason-Walsh-Atkinson-Kier Co.) the sight was not inspiring. To be sure, after the monotonous hundred mile drive from Spokane across brown and yellow parched plains, the sudden drop into the magnificent gorge of the Columbia River was a thrilling experience. We seemed to have reached without warning the rim of another world. We looked down a thousand feet and several miles across one coulee to the wildest and finest stretches of the glorious "River of the West."

"Dark and towering granite walls form one side of the basin. Through these walls a jagged chasm indicated that there the Columbia once, ages ago the geologists say, cut herself a new course for an unknown period of time, forming that spectacular river bed with its Dry Falls, known as the Grand Coulee. Within our present view the stream, swift and imposing, makes two wide bends, coming out of the east and turning due north, and at the far end of the gorge, disappearing westward. Undisturbed by man through the ages, ranges of high bare hills of every shape and shade surround these grand sweeps of the river, forming a scene of wild beauty.

"But already the site of the future dam was shown by earthworks just below the first bend. The government engineers had been making preliminary excavations, and everywhere could be seen disfiguring but eloquent signs of the arrival of desperate job hunters. Hideous shanties and houses on wheels were grouped into little settlements here and there, where, according to the optimistic real estate notices, all-electric cities would soon develop.

The particular spot pointed out as the future Mason City seemed the most remote and desolate in the whole, wild landscape, a high plateau 250 feet above the river, so perpendicular that the road to the top was cut zigzag along the cliff, and the river itself could only be seen from the edge of the plain. We ferried across in a small but jaunty boat, which was suddenly snatched by the swift current in midstream and whirled around alarmingly, but miraculously managed to edge itself back to the landing. We climbed the bank through sand a foot deep and there surveyed our future home. Not a tree or shrub in sight on the whole extent of the plateau, not a sign of life except one immense jackrabbit that resented my attempt to share with him the doubtful shelter of a sagebrush. As the first woman visitor, I was offered the privilege of turning the first soil of the future city, but the heat of midday, 110 degrees, and the prospect generally did not combine to make me appreciate the honor. I should be proud today to say that I had accepted it.

"As I write, the first of March, we are a full grown town of 2,500 inhabitants. There are more than 280 bungalows, two, three, four and five room houses, all with baths and excellent modern plumbing, with garages and leveled lawnspace. There are 10 blocks of bunk houses for men, comfortably furnished, and an attractive dormitory with dining hall for women. There is a huge mess hall, where 1,000 persons are fed three meals a day, and a good hotel of 40 rooms that cannot begin to take care of the daily visitors. There is a well-equipped hospital of 37 beds, a large general store, where every kind of household necessity, excellent food and clothing, and many luxuries may be purchased at the prevailing prices of the region. There is a post office, a branch of one of the Spokane banks, a model laundry, a fine garage and service station. There is a recreation hall with billiards and poolrooms and a well-managed lunch-room, a theater which seats 450 people and has good moving pictures every afternoon and evening. All this was in addition to the splendid administration building and other offices, the carpenter and paint shops and boilerworks. These composed the elaborate and most up-to-date plant required for the actual construction of the largest dam in the world. All are working now full speed ahead in order to finish the gigantic west cofferdam before high water.

"During the autumn months, the women who were waiting in Spokane to join their husbands at Mason City wondered just what was to be their part in such an absorbingly masculine undertaking in so remote a section of the country. There were predictions of a long, cold winter. How did we expect to keep warm in the 20-below-zero weather that was predicted? All this talk about electric heating! Who knew that it would work? Only Juan Hargrove, the architect responsible for the electric heating, cheered us by his assurance. The houses we saw being built in sections in Spokane and carried out on trucks were to be assembled without chimneys or cellars, without plaster or insulation, stuck up on concrete blocks and banked with earth. No hope of other heating than electricity. Would there ever be enough power available for all the needs of a town in zero weather? My own heart failed when my husband pointed out the three slender wires bringing, from 30 miles away over the mountains and a long span across the river, the wonderful "juice" that was to work the miracle!

"It was the last of November before there was enough electrical current for domestic use, and the first houses ready. The small three-room cottages were in great demand. We drove out through the first blinding blizzard of the winter, the last 20 miles entirely in second gear, unable to see beyond the hood of the car or steer straight on the icy road. Arriving cold and hungry, I found that they had forgotten to "connect up" the just completed house assigned to me, which I had planned to "get in order" as a surprise for my husband who had gone east on a business trip. The three rooms were piled to the ceiling with crated furniture from the second-hand stores in Spokane. It was icy cold and damp; there was no kitchen range, heat or water. In less than an hour all these important details had been supplied by a simple process of hooking up. The house was marvelously warm and dry, dinner was cooking on the excellent electric range — rented from the company at $2.50 a month — and I had become a convert to electricity. We spent December and January in this small cottage, and except for space — there were three of us — we could not have been more comfortable anywhere.

"At the end of January, during the coldest week of the winter, we moved into our five-room bungalow on the exposed hill top overlooking the town, and from our well-heated living room, we incredulously watched the thermometer on the front porch descend to 12 below zero. In these larger houses we are trying out different kinds of insulating materials between the siding and insulating board, and are finding that these greatly reduce the amount of electricity required. The heating units in general use are of different sizes and power according to the size of the rooms. They "plug in" and turn on and off as simply as the lights. They are equipped with fans which keep the heating air circulating and the whole room at an even temperature. They heat the house very rapidly and are now being built with thermostats so that they will operate automatically at a given temperature. They require no special care and have safety devices, making it possible to leave them turned on in a closed or empty house. It is expected that the fan device will keep the house more comfortable during the hot summer months.

"Because of the low rate for current charged us by the MWAK company, we women have become electrically minded, and use freely all the wonderful appliances on the market — water heaters (furnished in all the houses), refrigerators, washing machines, vacuum cleaners, coffee percolators, toasters, and irons. All the more difficult problems of housekeeping are thus solved for us. Camp life in the wilds offers none of the usual hardships. We have time and leisure to appreciate and enjoy our privilege in watching the miracle of the slender wires under man's competent control and management transform, almost between two seasons, a wilderness into a complete and attractive city. We have strength left over from our daily tasks to help with the big achievements. To interest ourselves in the school with its first new building soon to be started, in organizing the several churches to be built shortly, to visit the sick, the recreation hall, the movies, and the library. Yes, we really have time for books and study. Some of us are pouring over garden catalogs and botanies, preparing ourselves for gardening intelligently in unfamiliar soil and climate, and for familiarity with the particularly beautiful wild flowers of the region. Already spring is throwing her veil of tender green over the barehills and canyons, and we are preparing for it.

"If our government will be able, by harnessing these great waterways of our country, to develop electric power to the point of practical everyday use by all the people (as we are using it now), there will be a new era of emancipation, a veritable new deal for women. The machine age will not have deprived us of our jobs, but will have released them from drudgery and set our spirits free for greater and more inspiring accomplishments. We women of Mason City will then be proud indeed to have our small share in the building of Grand Coulee Dam, which is to pioneer electricity."

Women Scarce On The Job

For a while, not many women were to be found among the horde of males on the actual construction site.

An early one was Margaret Dodd, wife of W. S. Dodd, rigger foreman for CBI, the second large contractor on the dam. Her job was to operate a switchboard, together with several men, in the main field office. The building was located in the heart of the construction area, below the concrete mixing plant, above the forms and along the deck of the busy trestle.

The switchboard, which synchronized the phones in the construction areas, was in direct contact with the dam's toughest foreman. The CBI hesitated placing women operators on the board for fear the men would swear at them. No construction job can be finished without swearing, old timers said.

Mrs. Dodd bravely held to her post, despite a little resentment on the part of some of the men. On the other hand, the other women employed on the project, 75 in number, said: "After all, it's a women's job to run phone exchanges, isn't it? Why have men?"

Since the beginning of construction, she was the first of the feminine sex to invade the stronghold of man. Women were not allowed to even visit on the project by company order. "First thing you know, we'll have one bossing us around," one mucker said.

The CBI employed two girls, Miss Katie Kirsch and Miss Helen Peacock, in the warehouse office, which was located on the fringe of the work zone, where the belt conveyor starts its journey upward to the concrete plant storage bins. They performed stenographic, secretarial, filing and other work.

The remainder of the feminine staff was employed away from the actual construction, such as in the laundry, general store, beauty shop, the hotel, the theatre, coffee shop and in the Mason City business district.

The USBR had two capable women employees, Miss Helen Newell, secretary to James Miner, office engineer; and Mrs. Winifred Williams, stenographer.

Miss Newell was practically brought up in the construction game. Her father worked on many projects, and was in charge of the Owyhee project of Ontario, Oregon.

Aside from the women employees, the CBI employed about 4,300 white men, 30 Blacks, and 30 Indians. No Japanese or Chinese were allowed under provisions of the contract with the Federal Government.

Daughter Arrives on the Scene

On my beat was an establishment that gave me a constant supply of news.

It was Mason City Hospital, constructed by MWAK.

We always ran the birth announcements. The most newsworthy one, to me, occurred on April 22, 1939. Julie Blonk was born.

As a birth announcement, I issued one I thought was quite unique. It was a 10-by-7 inch front page headed by the title: THE STORK NEWS.

The major headline read: Bouncing Baby Born to Blonks! The subhead read: Baby Girl Arrived 10:15 P.M. Saturday, 6 Pounds, 10 Ounces.

The story read: An event of super-sensational importance occurred here at 10:15 p.m. Saturday with the arrival of a bouncing girl to Mr. and Mrs. Hubert C. Blonk of Electric City.

The auspicious occurrence took place shortly after Mason City Hospital attendants noted a strange man, whom some said was the father, pacing nervously and endlessly up and down the corridor.

Immediately upon the announcement, this person was seen leaving the hospital, two steps at a time, and, later, frantically passing out cigars everywhere.

A check made with doctors immediately following the arrival of the healthy youngster showed she weighed 6 pounds, 10 ounces at birth, had blue eyes and a bountiful supply of brown hair.

Further statistics reveal the Blonk heiress is the granddaughter of Mr. and Mrs. Carl Haskin of Almira and Mr. and Mrs. Leonard Blonk of Auburn.

Another top of the page story was headed, Youngster Named Julie Ellen Blonk and read:

In an exclusive statement to The STORK NEWS today, Mr. and Mrs. Hubert C. (Pa and Ma) Blonk announced today that their first offspring would be named Julie Ellen.

They made the selection they said, after several months of consultation with one another. It is expected the youngster will be pronouncing her own name in two or three months.

The little newspaper even had a Bulletin!

It reported: In an important bulletin issued a few hours after the Stork left a bundle of joy for the Blonks of Coulee Dam, Dr. R. V. Moore, the stork's technical assistant, declared:

"Both mother and baby are doing fine. The father, one of the worst patients I have ever had, is still a bit delirious, but will recover."

A story under SPORTS FLASH read: Baby Julie Ellen Blonk, late arrival at Mason City Hospital, was heralded here today as the winner of the "baby bawling" contest. Judges said the entrant clearly out-shouted all other youngsters born here to date.

Politics were featured in the little newspaper, too.

A story headed MAKES PREDICTION read: Washington, D.C. U.S. Senator Paul E. Ticks, in a statement to the press here today, predicted that a woman, Julie Ellen Blonk of the State of Washington, would be the first woman president of the United States in 1990.

Senator Ticks said the candidate is already being groomed for the post.

In another story headed Baby No.1 Has Many Wellwishers: all the relatives were listed and in yet another story headed FIRST STATEMENT this is reported:

The scoop of the century was recorded by THE STORK NEWS today when one of its representatives was able to secure the first statement from the young Blonk thus beating all other papers.

When questioned about her health, the youngster said:

"Waah . . . waah . . . waah!"

The paper even had a classified ad. It read:

WANTED — Capable, energetic, untiring washer woman to wash several hundred diapers weekly. Must have iron constitution and be able to work all hours of the day. Apply: Mr. and Mrs. Hu Blonk, Box 1583, Grand Coulee.

Julie grew up to be a daughter to be proud of. Like her mother, she is a kind person whom everyone loves. She won several distinctions, including being "Miss Maritime" in Seattle while serving as secretary to the vice president of the American Mail Lines. As such, she was a Seafair celebration princess, rode on a float in two great parades and joined the mayor of Seattle in placing a commemorative plaque on the waterfront.

Julie has held jobs in Wenatchee with the Washington State Apple Commission and Chelan Public Utility District.

For the latter she served as its hydro-logistics supervisor. Two sons were born to her during her first marriage to James Caldwell. The oldest is Jim, who presently works for an electrical and refrigeration firm in Wenatchee. They have sent him to numerous training schools. The youngest, Jeff, is serving six years in the Navy. He scored high enough to attend electronic schools in Chicago and San Francisco.

Julie has a very happy marriage with Dean Yeager who works for Alcoa and is an officer in the union.

First Prepaid Medicine in the U.S.

While Julie's arrival was big news in the Blonk and Haskin families, there was bigger news associated with the hospital. It was there that the first prepaid, comprehensive, group, medical practice originated. I didn't learn about it until my retirement years.

This occurred in the late 1930's during the construction of the upper part of the Grand Coulee Dam by a syndicate of major contractors known as CBI, for which, the Henry Kaiser Company supervised the job. The lower contractors operated the at-site hospital in what was then called Mason City.

A booklet printed by the Kaiser people describes how the "then radical idea that changed the face of health care delivery throughout the nation" came about at the damsite because of Dr. Sidney Garfield.

Edgar Kaiser, who, as a son of Henry, was in charge of the construction for the combine, discovered he had a problem with medical services. Workers under previous contractors were treated on a prepay basis but they found themselves not treated as well as those who paid a fee. In light of this shaby treatment, their unions wanted to set up their own program.

This was a challenge to Kaiser. He didn't want unions involved in medical care. So he sought help. He got Dr. Garfield, who ran three Mojave Desert hospitals involved with the 100-mile long Los Angeles Aquaduct construction, to come to the damsite.

Kaiser asked Garfield a crucial question: "Could prepaid coverage be provided to dependents as well as to employees?" He didn't want a two-tier system with the employees receiving prepaid care and their dependents having to pay out of pocket.

A friend of Garfield named Dr. Wally Neighbor, who had grown tired of "taking care of the movie colony and the neurotics" in Southern California, was induced to take charge of the hospital. Other physicians were also persuaded to come but not without considerable resistance.

In that period, prepaid medicine was considered an "unethical" way to practice medicine, and its practice could cause a physician to lose his status with medical societies and be barred from them.

The Grand Coulee Dam group plan called for Garfield and his

associates to be paid a percentage of the worker's compensation premium for industrial coverage. A voluntary payroll deduction of 50 cents per week per employee insured coverage for non-industrial injuries or illnesses. Wives and children, however, continued to be treated on a fee-for-service basis.

Dr. Garfield at first objected to further expanding prepaid medicine, because he was unable to devise "a satisfactory computation of prepaid rates for dependent coverage." This resulted in dependents deferring the medical attention they needed which led to more serious complications.

Soon the union leadership began to put pressure on the Kaiser Company and Dr. Garfield to provide coverage for dependents. They even threatened to strike. Thus pressured, Kaiser and Garfield almost arbitrarily settled upon a rate of 50 cents per week per adult and 25 cents per week per child.

The prepaid comprehensive medical plan resulted in a high level of preventive medicine. Doctors saw simple acute appendicitis instead of peritonitis, earaches instead of mastoiditis, upper respiratory infections instead of pneumonia, etc.

For the doctors, the hours were long and the work intense. They worked six days a week with only two or three Sundays off a month. Since three shifts were working on the dam around the clock, up to 50 workers could show up for a midnight sick call.

But the physicians and nurses enjoyed what Dr. Neighbor said was "experimenting in what was in those days unethical or that they later said we were."

Nurses and doctors' wives also contributed to health care at the damsite. They started a "well-baby" clinic in a local community church. They solicited funds for it door to door. These included the houses of ill repute on B Street. One physician's wife said about the latter: "The church provided the space and the 'houses' the money — a very compatable community."

As the end of the construction neared, doctors began speculating about establishing prepaid, group medicine in other communities such as the San Francisco Bay area and Los Angeles. That eventually came about with the Kaiser Permanente Medical Group, a leader in achieving it.

Back of the By-Line

Now and then a reporter from the World would visit the damsite to write a colorful piece or two. One such was Karl Stoffel. He wrote the following article about what my job was like:

"This is going to be different. It's a story about the man behind the by-line and the date-line — a story about Hu Blonk.

"Hu is the chap who writes every day about the things going on at the 'busiest place in the west,' Grand Coulee Dam, for the Daily World. He is also the chap who represents the Associated Press.

"For four years, Hu Blonk has been at Grand Coulee. He went there almost directly out of the University and before there had even been any of the numerous sprawling townsites started at or near the site of the big slab of concrete. He wore high boots in the summer to keep out the dust. He wore them in the winter to keep out the mud and the cold. He wore no hat and his blond hair bleached whiter in the sun. And there was no part or place about the damsite that he didn't go.

"You might have found him most any day riding one of the big shovels, climbing down one of the test holes, or crawling over piles of debris to see what was going on underneath.

"His was a familiar voice to engineers and early contractors, and at the time when the damsite population was still numbered in dozens, he was known to everyone. He still is almost universally known there despite the population increase to an estimated 12,000.

"Whether it is in the administration building of the Reclamation Bureau engineers, in one of the galleries far down in the dam or in a townsite beer parlor, he is still a familiar figure. They hail him from many parts of the job and they call him at night. He knows what's going on.

"If a writer or photographer or distinguished visitor comes to the damsite, more often than not Hu is the guide. He knows as much about the project, what it will be, what everything is for and why this and that, as any non-technical man in the vicinity, and he wants to know more.

"Hu Blonk was born in Holland and still remembers the sea sickness of the Atlantic crossing. He decided to become a newspaperman while attending the University of Washington and began learning that business as University correspondent for a Seattle daily.

"During his four years at Grand Coulee, Hu has written for the Daily World a little more than a column of news a day. A column is about a thousand words. He sends in this budget six days a week, for a total of 120 inches. In 52 weeks of the year, he sends in 6,240 inches, and in four years it amounts to 24,960 column inches.

"That volume of copy is equivalent to 1,250 columns, 156 pages, or thirteen average sized Daily World newspapers.

"If you double that amount of written information, then add about one-fourth as much again you will have the amazing total written about the dam job by one man. In his sparetime, he handles publicity and promotion work for a theatre at the damsite.

"In all those four years and throughout those millions of words, there has not been one proven error chalked up against this aggressive correspondent. And that in spite of rumors that fly as thick as the dust at times, in spite of petty townsite bickerings and in spite of private or special interest groups.

"Hu has been married on the job, bought a car and a house and paid his University bills.

"He was at the damsite when only jackrabbits and sagebrush were to be found, and he was there when the President came. He wants to stay until water is thundering over the giant spillway of the high dam.

"Hu likes his job. He's the man behind the Grand Coulee dateline."

Colorful Characters Abound

If you wanted to know history at the damsite, you always went to see Charley Osborne.

He lived in a cabin in what we called "Engineers Town." I wrote a lot of stories about him but fellow Wenatchee World writer Karl Stoffel said it best.

This is what he wrote under the heading:

Half A Century Of Life In Grand Coulee Packed With Adventure, Hardship, Action. Six Shooter Justice Was Cattlemen's Law.

Charley Osborne Pioneered the Area

Charley Osborne at 70 is one of those men who might step into the pages of an adventure novel and be perfectly at home. He is tall and lean and leathery, with thinning gray hair. His face is deeply lined but not wrinkled and his 51 years of pioneering in Grant County have left the indelible stamp of the out-of-doors.

Osborne lives in the midst of the hub-bub and uproar of the Grand Coulee Dam construction. His present two-room residence is crammed in between two buildings of the model engineers townsite. A road leading from an excavation pit to the dam runs by the door, and, at clock-like intervals throughout the day and night, the house quakes as the trucks rumble past.

One of these days soon his home will have to moved. He'll take his belongings to one of the dormitories. When the job is finished he will be caretaker in the engineers' town.

Half a century ago, on a spring day when the sun and a chinook wind had wiped the snow from greening acres of wild hay and sagebrush, a young lad from Tennessee had his first look at Grant County. He was Charley Osborne, 18 years old and lost.

He knew where he was going but didn't know how to get there. For three days he had been hiking across the country from Spokane, looking for two brothers who had wintered somewhere in the Grand Coulee. With the aid of a cattle owner, Len Armstrong, Osborne found their home and what a home!

Life in the Raw

Oscar and John had built a house out of logs and mud. The logs weren't very big and they had to drag them quite aways with saddle horses. The house didn't have any floor and the roof was made of mud and brush. It was in the lea of Steamboat Rock. They'd lived there all winter and their horses had run away. They were out of grub and had about $20 between them.

"I had a little money and we pooled our resources to buy three horses," Osborne said. We paid $40 for them and found out later they had been stolen from a neighboring cattleman. They were probably the meanest and poorest horses in the country, but we rode all over Eastern Washington on them looking for a place to go into the cattle business.

133

"We went all over the Moses reservation and up in the Okanogan country, but nothing looked any better than the Coulee. By exercising preemption, timber culture and homestead rights, we were able to get 1,320 acres of fine land. It was really fine, too. At that time wild hay grew thick enough in the Coulee to cut with a mower, and a good many times I've put up as many as 800 tons of it for winter feeding. I guess at one time we had either acquired, bought or rented the entire mouth of the Coulee, and we went into the cattle business."

It was in 1883, the same year that the Northern Pacific was brought into Spokane, that Osborne came west. He was born in 1865 in Louden County, Tennessee. His father was a farmer and slave owner.

Lacked Market

There was plenty of range in what was then Douglas County. Cattle fattened easily and rapidly. The trouble was finding a market.

"You couldn't sell a pound of beef in Spokane," Osborne said, "because cattle thieves were supplying that market. They were as thick as fleas in the Inland Empire country at that time."

Osborne went to Ellensburg and there found ready buyers. His first sale was to an old Scotch butcher.

Beef On the Hoof

"That was a funny deal, that first one," he said. "This Scotchman said he'd give me three cents a pound for about 35 head, but they had to be there, in Ellensburg, within eight days. There I was with a good sale but 135 miles from where the cattle were — Well I made it, but I'd hate to have eaten any of the meat off those critters after that drive. It took me a day and a night of hard riding to get back to the Coulee, and I got a bunch of boys together and rounded up the cows and headed back for Ellensburg. I'd get so sleepy at night that I'd turn my horse around so he faced down hill and go to sleep with my head on his rump. As soon as the cattle moved in the morning, the horse would start after 'em and I'd wake up.

"We had to ferry the cows across the Columbia River below Wenatchee on an old, hand ferry. Later they put in a steam ferry there called the Rattler of Portland. It was all two men could do to paddle that barge across with half a dozen steers on it. Well, I drove that bunch of beef into Ellensburg on time, and the Scotchman was some surprised, but he paid all right.

"I took a lot more over the Colockum Pass later but never in such a hurry.

Vigilante Justice

"But about those rustlers and horse thieves — they were thick and slick. We had vigilantes out after some of them most of the time. Once they caught a half breed, who'd stolen some horses, way out in the sagebrush. They had to kill him, you know, but there wasn't a tree for miles around. They argued and discussed it for quite a while and finally decided to shoot him. But after he was tied to a sagebrush most of 'em lost their nerve. After they'd stalled around still longer and it was getting dark one young fella pulled out his .45 and ended it for the half breed. The man that did the shooting lives around here yet.

Bad Bill Mathews

"There was another one too, about the worst of the lot. Bill Mathews was his name. He's serving a life term now in Walla Walla for train robbery. He was caught in Nebraska the last time but was first rounded up by some of our vigilantes near Spokane. He'd been working for H. W. Lang near Coulee breaking horses. I worked with him for a while and advised Lang to let him go. He was a bad one. Big and husky and good looking, but with a smile like a wolf. And he'd have killed his best friend for $5. He'd been stealing cows and horses for years.

"After Lang fired him, Mathews tried to blow up the safe in George McDonald's trading store at Coulee. He and his gang got the safe opened, but the noise woke up the country-side and a posse trailed after them. Mathews was cornered in a cabin over near Ritzville, and, after a gun battle, was shot in the neck and captured. He got six years for that job but was out before his time was up and went to robbing trains.

"They finally caught him again near Lincoln, Nebraska, after a country school teacher had discovered his gang hiding in the attic of the school house. He was in on a dozen different jobs before that."

The railroad was built into Coulee City in 1890, Osborne said. "They were planning to run on through to the coast but ran out of money when they got this far. They even had it graded for 18 miles further. There wasn't much to Coulee City then. I think it had one general store. Sprague was the closest town this side of Spokane. This whole country was all Douglas County then.

Pioneer Entertainment

"There wasn't much to do besides work in those days. We did have some pretty good poker parties though, and, sometimes in the winter, we'd go out roping coyotes. We could run 'em down on horseback when the snow got deep.

"I never married. The first women that came out to this country were either already married or weren't the marrying kind, and, when some good ones did get here, I had gotten out of the notion. My sister came out and kept house for me in later years, after I had built the big house down in the Coulee." That big house of which Osborne speaks is still standing in the Coulee, a monument to the prosperity and productivity of those early days. Osborne later sold all the house furnishings at a public auction. That was after he had poured thousands of dollars of cattle money into wheat farm mortgages and other real estate, he said.

Cattle-Killing Winter

The winter of 1889 was the most severe in Osborne's memory. He had sold 100 tons of hay in the fall, and, when the unusual snow and cold came, he was as unprepared as many other stockmen. He lost 100 head of cattle that winter.

"Snow was belly deep on a horse," he said. It rained all fall up into December. Overnight the rain changed to snow and fell on the unfrozen ground. It was so soft and sticky in the spring it would have mired down a shadow. I lost some cows in the mud.

135

"There was one winter worse than that one, but it was in 1879, before my time. Hardy and Austin, big cattlemen, brought 3,000 head of cattle in from Idaho that fall. In the spring they had 800 left, gaunt as rails and all steers.

"Here's something queer too. A steer in good condition can live three months without a bite to eat. I've seen a herd of them stand in the snow for weeks at a time and never eat a bite. They live off their accumulated fat like a hibernating bear."

Charley Osborne knew Chief Moses when that famed Indian leader was at the height of his prowess. Moses didn't come by his chiefship rightfully, according to Osborne's story, but used his cunning to accomplish the desired end.

"Moses was second brother in the Indian family. He was a medicine man."

Moses Becomes Chief

"His father, Chief Talthscosum, was killed in a raid on a Blackfoot buffalo meat cache. Moses' older brother became chief and after a short time yielded to Moses' persuasion to go on the warpath. He also was killed. This left Moses, next in line as chief, and, although some of his people protested at a medicine man becoming a tribe leader, his dominating influence won out.

Indian Strategy

"Moses was smart. Shortly after he became chief he also went on the war path against the whites. But he didn't fight hard and let himself be captured and then made a deal with the United States Government, whereby he was to get a thousand dollars a year for himself in cash, besides numerous other concessions, in return for keeping his people on the straight and narrow path."

One more story Osborne told:

"There was one old Chinaman, among the many who worked the bars of the Columbia for gold near the mouth of Grand Coulee, who would pack up and go to Walla Walla for the winter every fall.

"A trio of cattle rustlers waylaid him, robbed and killed him and then hid his body in the shale rock, wrapped in canvas. No one missed the old fellow, and it was not until 20 years later, that the murder was discovered.

Murder Will Out

"In hiding the body, the outlaws had inadvertently scooped out a place in the shale rock where an icy current of air came from the ice that never melted beneath it. The Chinaman's body was preserved so remarkably that a partial identification was possible. The men who did the killing, however, were never caught although one of them was later killed as a cattle thief and another was killed in the Nez Perce war."

"The men who found the Chinaman's body thought for a time that it was that of a chap named English who also disappeared mysteriously about the same time. English's death was never cleared up, but a man who had been a neighbor of his turned up sometime later with a deed to his place, and so a lot of stories went the rounds."

136

Six-Gun Justice

Osborne's parting shot was this: "If I had the running of this country for a week or two, I'd clean out this racketeering in a hurry. I'd make it compulsory for every man over 21 years old to carry a six-shooter. I'd offer rewards for bandits, dead or alive. They wouldn't last long.

"I think all politicians are liars. I'm a Democrat but it doesn't make any difference. All legislation now is compromise legislation. Anyway, vote for my bill and I'll vote for yours.

"I've had a lot of money and lost a lot in marginal land farming. I sold my lease on this damsite property for what the government thought it was worth. I've got plenty to keep me busy, and I'm well satisfied with life as it is. Even these trucks and machines that I thought at first were coming right in the window, don't bother me any more. It's all in getting used to things — and that reminds me — did I tell you about that big train robbery at Coulee City in the 1890's. . . . ?"

"Rattlesnake" Smith fond of Reptiles

Another most interesting and quite visible character was W. E. "Dad" or "Rattlesnake" Smith.

This is what I wrote about him under this heading:

Veteran 'Chute Jumper' Turns To Reptiles For Thrill.

"How would you like to catch rattlesnakes for a living? That's the strange profession of 'Rattlesnake' Smith, of Coulee Dam.

"For 36 years this well-known whiskered man of 68, who never tires of talking about his reptiles, has been engaged in taking these dangerous creatures from the sagebrush wastes. More than 800 snakes, big and small, have left their happy homes, never to be seen again, except as belts, or neckties or in Chinese medicinal offices.

"There is no more unique business, certainly none with less competition, than this rattle snake catching profession, but 'Rattlesnake' Smith loves it and as he says, 'I'll do it till my dying day.'

"Dangerous as the reptiles may be, only twice has Smith been bitten. During his first year at the game, if it can be called that, way back in 1898 in Garrett County, he was struck while transferring a snake from a dry goods box to a showcase in a beer parlor museum. Again last April, Smith was bitten. Quick action in both cases saved his life.

"But snakes aren't dangerous,' Smith emphasizes, 'I see thousands of them every year. Visitors to the dam don't have to be afraid of getting bit because the snakes will always rattle before they strike.'

"Rattlesnake has big ambitions. 'I own a little farm along the Coulee City highway,' he says, 'and I'm planning to start a rattlesnake ranch there next fall. I'm going to build a big den with rock piles and so forth and I think it will draw people from all over. I'll have thousands of snakes in there and free camping grounds for the visitors.'

"Smith lives in a little gulch directly in back of the mushroom town of Grand Coulee. No tent covers his belongings, no chairs grace the floor. A cleared away area among the sagebrush is his carpet and when he offers you a seat, it is a gunny sack on the sloping gully side.

"Dad" is happy in his work and his memories. His mind loves to wander back to the days when he was a lad of 25, and he took his first balloon ascension. Then called "Daredevil" Smith, he was once a regular parachute jumper back in 1890, and he made a regular tour of all the fair circuits.

"Born in north central Missouri, as a boy he always wanted to go up in the air. Today, he is the only living parachute jumper who was in that profession in the 1890's. He drifted from place to place after his ballooning experience, married and raised two boys and two girls, proud of them he is too.

"He later came to California and then three years ago to the State of Washington. And he's 'gonna stay here till the dam is built.'

"I catch snakes because I get a kick out of it,' Smith says, smiling through his bushy whiskers. His record catch was set right here in Grand Coulee, 36 snakes in three hour's time. The biggest one he has captured was 4-feet-9 inches long, 2½ inches thick with fourteen rattles. Smith has heard of snakes with 34 rattles, signifying 34 years of age.

"He is surprised at how little people know about snakes. Three common mistakes about the reptiles listed by this strange man are:

1. A snake doesn't have to coil to strike.

2. He bites, not with the two points of his tongue, but with two teeth-like fangs located in the upper jaw.

3. Snakes are not dangerous; they always warn you of their nearness.

"To show the amount of poison a rattler may carry, Smith teased one of them. It struck seven times, depositing half a teaspoon full of poison. The way the venom is taken from them is to hold them by the jaw, make them strike and catch the poison in a whiskey glass. However, snakes replenish their venom in about two weeks.

"In case you're interested, here's how Smith catches snakes: He takes a forked stick with which he pins down the snake. Then he takes a flat stick, such as a lath and works it along the body of the snake to a point back of its head and then lowers it, tail first, into whatever container he has at hand. That's all there is to it. Simple, isn't it?

"And snakes are wonderfully delicious to eat, Smith explains, 'they taste better than venison, and rattlesnake on toast is really something to be sought after.'

"I don't make much money' says Smith, 'but I get a kick out of it. This July and August when the snakes go blind, I'm going to catch a lot of 'em and make neckties out of them and sell them as souvenirs at the dam. After the snake has shed his skin, the new skin is as soft as velvet. They make dandy ties."

Sam Seaton Ran the Ferry

A little guy named Sam Seaton ran the ferry that crossed the Columbia at the damsite.

The government took his land for the dam which made Sam pretty mad. But he got along, starting a townsite called "Seaton's Grove."

His story went like this under the heading:

"Sam Seaton Doing Well, Thank You!"

"The Grand Coulee Dam and hydroelectric project drove Sam Seaton, pioneer farmer and ferry operator at the damsite, from his home. However, Sam took a note from the engineers' book and built a dam and hydroelectric power project of his own.

"And it's netting him a comfortable living.

"Sam once lived on the east shore of the Columbia, a spot now covered by 150 feet of concrete. He operated the old cable ferry, raised chickens and pigs and a few flowers amidst the dust from the road leading to the Colville Indian agency at Nespelem to which his ferry was the main access.

"He now resides at Elmer City (Elmerton) and manages Seaton's Park lake, about two miles downstream from there. The popularity of the place is attested by the 250 people who come there on warm days.

"Sam built a dam of his own at the far end of a small valley situated in the shadow of an 800-foot vertical granite bluff. He diverted the creek, running in another direction, into the valley and made a 3-acre pond.

"He also installed a 6-volt, DC, hydroelectric generating plant and started selling electricity through another party to settlers on his land. Sam now has 53 home owners on his property, 25 of whom use electricity and pay from $1 to $1.40 per month.

"Sam collects ten cents from everyone who swims in his homemade lake. He has a hotdog stand on the edge of the pool, a high and low diving board and a special chute, on which you can ride for 25 cents an hour.

"Pioneer Seaton even had fish in his lake. When asked how they got there, he only smiles. One winter, however, some lowly individual set off dynamite in the pool and killed all the fish.

"Sam still deals in his horses. He's particularly proud of one having a large white swan marking on his side. He said, 'I don't make any money off the horses, but I like to have 'em around. I guess it'd kill me if I didn't have a horse or two.'

"Sam has lost little of his bitterness toward Uncle Sam for taking his home. He joined with other landowners in a court fight to secure more money. Sam finally obtained $8,400, about what the government offered him in the first place. 'When I got through, the lawyers had every bit of it and then some,' Sam said, 'I think it's pretty little of the government the way they treated me.''

Woody Guthrie Wrote Songs at the Dam

One celebrity who came to the Project was a colorful character who I didn't have the opportunity of meeting. He was the late Woodrow Wilson (Woody) Guthrie, well remembered for writing and singing the popular ballad "This Land is Your Land."

While at the dam, he composed the songs for a film about Grand Coulee that was produced by the Bonneville Power Administration.

Hired as a "public relations consultant" for BPA, Guthrie was chauffeured around the Columbia Basin for 30 days to give him a feel for the land and the issues.

In just 26 days, he wrote and recorded 26 songs, among them "Roll On, Columbia" and "Grand Coulee Dam."

The common-man appeal of Woody Guthrie's music took awhile to catch on commercially. It wasn't until he was slowly losing a 15-year battle with Huntington's disease, a hereditary illness that destroys muscle coordination, that one of his most famous songs, "This Land is Your Land," really became popular. At this time, many of his "countrywestern" songs have passed into American folklore.

But in the town of Grand Coulee, Woody Guthrie and his song, "Grand Coulee Dam," are remembered. Before the radio station KFDR ceased broadcasting it used the song both to sign on and off the air.

Guthrie made people feel good about who they were and where they came from with his words and music.

The fruits of his brief stint with the BPA convey a feeling of love and respect for the land. While they are far from Shakespearean, they are unique to the breed of people who pioneered the Northwest, and those who followed to shape the fertile Columbia Basin from a desert of sagebrush and scab rock.

Following is a verse from the immortal "Roll On Columbia."

"And on up the river is Grand Coulee Dam,
The mightiest thing ever built by man,
To run the great factories and water the land, it's
Roll on, Columbia, roll on!
Your darkness is turning our darkness to dawn,
So, roll on, Columbia, roll on."

In 1943, Leonard Lyons, a well known columnist of the Walter Winchell type, had this to say about Guthrie being at the dam.

"The newest darling of New York's literateurs is Woody Guthrie, the hobo ballad-singer whose "Bound for Glory," has attracted so much attention . . . The most money Guthrie ever possessed in his life was $300 — and he spent that in a few days . . . He now has been retained by the Soviet Embassy to adapt Russia's war songs into singable American ballads . . . Guthrie is the only person ever to have been on the Federal payroll as a ballad-singer. He was hired, for $10 a day, during the battle over Grand Coulee Dam, when the citizens in that neighborhood voted on whether they wanted their power to come from public or private enterprise. The private power companies hired Hollywood stars to ballyhoo their program. The government hired Woody Guthrie, who wrote and sang his ballads against private utilities, and the government won."

Harvey Slocum the Big Boss

A key figure on the project was also a most colorful one.

He was Harvey Slocum, the construction boss for MWAK during the building of the lower portion of the dam. If Hollywood were casting for the role of a typical construction stiff, it would have had to change little if it chose Harvey as a model. He was a handsome, hard-drinking guy, stocky in stature, who had quite a vocabulary of cuss words.

I was told that he never went to school past the eigth grade, yet he was the fellow who came up with the low bid for constructing what was called the low dam.

At first Harvey avoided me as a reporter. If I was in the waiting room to

140

see him, he'd disappear out a back door. When I did see him, he'd say as little as possible. But he developed faith in me to the point that when there was an accident he'd get a hold of me even though someone had done something stupid to cause it.

Harvey sometimes would disappear from the job several days at a time. Often as not he'd be on B Street visiting the girls and having drinks with them. In the heat of summer the upstairs joints would get mighty hot, because they were under flat roofs. The girls complained about it, so Harvey sent up a plumbing crew from the damsite and had them put a sprinkling system on the roof of the whore house. I think it was the Swanee Rooms.

The likeable guy vanished once too often, so he was fired. I asked George Atkinson, the son of Guy F. Atkinson, one of the partners in the combine of contractors building the dam, what I should state was the reason for the dismissal. He said "Ill health."

A day or so later, I wandered into the Continental Cafe in Grand Coulee Center. Suddenly, I heard someone shouting my name. I turned and noticed it was Harvey Slocum. He appeared to be angry and to have been imbibing.

I walked up to Harvey, who was seated at a counter with another man, and said "What's the matter, Harvey?"

He replied "You put in that goddamn paper of yours that I was canned because of 'ill health.' Now you know damn well I got canned because I was drunk."

Harvey was extremely popular with his men. They refused to let him quit. The dam site was soon "flooded" with petitions asking MWAK to retain him for the remainder of the contract, I wrote "Thousands signed the petitions Sunday."

The petition read:

"We, the undersigned, feeling that in the final analysis, construction of the Grand Coulee Dam is in our hands and with an intense feeling of loyalty to the company and the job, and also feeling that Mr. Slocum is in absolute earnest in that his actions during the balance of this contract will only be in the best interest of the job and in consideration of the work he has done to date, particularly in saving the job during the cofferdam break.

"Do hereby respectively petition that Mr. Slocum be reinstated as general superintendent, above our feeling of loyalty for Mr. Slocum as our leader, we feel that this will be in the best interest of the job."

The company did not change its mind, however.

But the workmen did one more thing for their beloved boss. They presented him with a large new automobile as a token of their "great regard and fondness" for him.

I wrote: "The car was purchased by the laborers, from the lowest 'mucker' to the highest 'uppity-up' superintendent."

The presentation was entirely a surprise to Slocum and his wife. "The 'supe' beamed all over," witnesses said, when they turned the car over to him. I was told that Harvey wiped away a few tears.

I later learned that Harvey sobered up after he left the job. He must have, because he wound up building one of the great structures of the world — the Bakhra Dam in India.

But he remained the same Harvey I knew at Grand Coulee Dam. I know this for he was written up in "True," a highly popular men's magazine. It reported that when Khrushev visited the project, he told the Russian leader "I could probably do your job, but you'd play hell doing mine."

Buck Buchanan Damsite Poet

Bryan Buchanan, nicknamed "Buck," used to hang around the Grand Coulee News office a lot being a good friend of publisher Sid Jackson. Buck was a big, soft-spoken fellow who got around among the B Street crowd and fellow workers at the river below.

Memory fails me as to what job he had. It wasn't a high-paying one, I do recall. Buck's claim to fame was that he was a poet. You might call him "The Poet Laureate of the Grand Coulee Dam" because he wrote a lot of poetry on various phases of the construction, always stressing the construction stiff's view of things.

His stuff appeared in the weekly paper, and, later, he published some of his best in a small booklet, which unfortunately I no longer have access to. In the Grand Coulee News his writings were carried under the column heading: "Bunkhouse Baloney." A sample was one which he headed: "Every construction camp has seen the old-timer who drifts in, tells about the good old days, spears a few drinks, and goes on his way." Here he is:

The Old-Timer

I went into the beer saloons
And recreation halls,
And there was many a husky lad,
All dressed in overalls.
Oh, there was many a miner there
And riggers by the score,
But never a one of the good old gang
That I shall see no more.

Chorus:

It's early in the morning,
In the winter time.
Out upon the skidroad
Stemming for a dime.
When you're young and husky
It's fun to blow your pay,
But life is not so easy
When you're gettin old and gray.

There was Waterliner Murphy
And Hard Rock Dan McGee,
Big Oscar Olson, Horse Malone
And Frisco Slim and me.
A bunch of young construction stiffs
All set to blow our stake,
To do some serious drinking
And to give the girls a break.

But Frisco Slim was killed in France,
And so was Dan McGee,
While Horse Malone was put away
In the penitentiary,
Big Oscar died at Boulder Dam
And Murphy in Peru.
We'll have a drink to them, my lads,
Of course, it is on you.

I cannot work at Coulee Dam,
Though I came here to try.
The company won't put me on
Because I've lost an eye.
So thank you lads, for all the drinks
You've given me today.
I guess I'll take my old balloon
And I'll be on my way.

Mike Gilmore Rode a Horse

I didn't know Mike Gilmore, superintendent for Goodfellow Brothers of Wenatchee, very well, but he was an unusual character in that he rode a horse among the construction machinery as he supervised early excavation on the project.

He was a big, rawboned individual, probably of Norwegian descent. The sight of a horse at work at the dam certainly warranted attention, so I wrote it up.

One of the Goodfellows told me the horse had been the proud possession of the firm for three years and had been used on every road job the company had contracted. Because long stretches of ground had to be covered on those jobs, "Mack" was purchased and he faithfullly fullfilled his duty whenever called on.

The use of a horse on construction projects dates back to the era when railroad foremen were called "riding bosses."

Mike Carr is Damsite Shoemaker

It took all kinds of people to build the dam . . . one such was Mike Carr. This is his story under the heading:

"Damsite Mike Friend to All."

"Let me live in a house by the side of the road and be a friend to man."

Although he may never have heard that poem, it seemed to be the life axiom of middle-aged Mike Carr, the damsite's best-known shoemaker.

Living along the dusty highway leading into Grand Coulee in a ramshackle place which looked very much like a woodshed, "Damsite Mike" as many workmen called him, was one of the area's most interesting people.

Mike was one of the new pioneers here, and one of the first to start a business at the original business site, near Sam Seaton's old ferry. He bought an old house belonging to Julius Johnson, Almira banker, and moved in his needle and last, plus a couple pair of heels and soles. For a long time, he was the only shoe repairman around.

His "office" was most interesting. The front portion was his workshop, the back was his sleeping quarters. Part of the building was painted a worn-out green, the rest consisted of rough boards. On one area, old 1907 Saturday Evening Posts were tacked up to keep out the winter blasts. One of them had a picture of Grover Cleveland.

No job was too big or too small for Mike. He wasn't interested in making money, he'd refuse money for small jobs. His main love in life was to help others.

His quarters were located on a high bank between the Center and Grand Coulee. People would pass his place over a small path used as a short cut. During winter when the path would get snowy and icey, Mike would keep it shoveled so no one would slip and fall.

Many of the children would stop and see him on their way to and from school. They liked to see the picture posters of old movies that lined the walls of his cabin.

With an "Old Mike — Damsite Shoeshop" sign on the building, dozens of people stopped on the weekends to take pictures of his place.

A well-known cigarette company offered Mike a dollar a month to put a big sign on the shabby building, but the old shack was home to him and he was proud of it. "Nothing doing" was his answer.

You had to know Mike to appreciate him.

Hermit First Man in Coulee

It was an old, old story that Mike Leahy told. So old in fact, that few people had ever heard it.

Leahy, who with three of his brothers founded the town of Leahy, 18 miles northeast of Mansfield, came across a gulch, now known as the Grand Coulee, on their way from Canada to Foster Creek.

Leahy provided me with the story about Rufus Hardy, whom he called the first inhabitant of land around the present damsite. Hardy was a hermit who raised cattle in the Grand Coulee. He lived around Steamboat Rock in a house built of cottonwood logs at a time when the Indians also used the land there for grazing.

"Hardy wasn't the talking kind," Leahy said, "no one knew when he came to the Coulee, but it must have been in the 1860's. He had about 4,000 head of cattle, which he drove to the nearest railroad point heading for the big stockyards in Chicago. Spokane was only in the process of becoming a city at that time. There wasn't a brick building in the town. Davenport was then known as Cottonwood and Walla Walla was the nearest place to buy supplies."

During the years around 1882, Leahy and his three brothers settled in what is now Leahy. About the same time Oscar and Charley Osborne settled on a ranch where the town of Osborne was later located.

"Sometimes we didn't see another white man for months at a time," Leahy remarked.

Cattle Stealing and Socials Spiced Early History

A lot of frustrated homesteaders lived in the area from Grand Coulee to Steamboat Rock in the early days. Sometimes they were visited by thieves escaping from lawmen who would not venture into the upper Coulee.

I was told this by Jess Canady, who resided on his father's homestead in what is now called the Delano area. He expressed disgust at stories being told that very few people lived in that area in the early days.

He recalled the days of cattle stealing, socials at the schoolhouse or in private homes, moonshining "all over the country," homes built from logs pulled from the Columbia River, community rodeos at someone's corral, cattle crossing on the frozen-over river, and big wheat threshing crews.

There were a lot of families here, Canady said, talking about the 1905 to 1919 period. Drought finally drove nearly all of them out. When construction on the dam began in 1933, there were only six families left — the Nobles, Partees, Charlie Osborne, Oscar Osborne, Dan Lael and Jess Evans.

Canady's father homesteaded in the area in 1905, coming from Kansas via the Palouse. He remained with his wife and children — Les, Naomi, and Jess — until about 1919, when he moved to Nespelem and later to Almira. The family, working with Stringfellow and Halloran, real estate men from the coast, subdivided the property when the dam construction began. The town was named Delano which was President Franklin D. Roosevelt's middle name.

The Partees lived in the Canady root cellar until they could build a home of their own. They, like other home-steaders, attempted to raise cattle. A big apple orchard, run by Frank Davis, was located where Crescent Bay is now. Canady hauled lots of fruit over plain dirt roads.

It would take all day to get to Coulee City, he said. Usually folks just stayed overnight and came back the next day.

He also recalled the first road built around 1910 from the coulee to the river below. His father and Sherm Scott did the work, using an old steamshovel and a jackhammer. The road was used to haul wood and stuff from the river.

There was no town in those days, no store. A key structure for the scattered farmers was the schoolhouse that sat where the North Dam is now situated.

Thirty-one kids went to school there. It served also as a dance hall, and a place for pie and ice cream socials and other gatherings, such as taffy pulls. There was another school near Steamboat Rock, and one near Coulee City. The closest high schools were at Almira and Coulee City.

Recreation consisted of celebrations at someone's corral where men would try to ride bucking horses and wrestle steers. Swimming and ice skating in Buckley Lake was another seasonal activity.

A lot of gunfighting occurred across the coulee, but there never were any shoot-outs of the "O.K.-Corral" type. Participants were men of questionable honesty who rode through the coulee on the way to hide out at Wallace Canyon, along the present rode to Bridgeport.

Lawmen chasing the culprits from Almira to Wilbur would never come beyond the coulee wall. The thieves, some of them bank robbers, were plenty tough and dangerous.

"You didn't want to stick your head out or they'd hit you, they were good shots," Canady said. He recalled Bectel Wallace being killed while taking "slick-eared" (rustled) cattle to Spokane. He lived in the robbers roost up in the canyon named after him.

Another man was killed in one of the three saloons in Govan (near Almira), after he had boasted that he could lay his hands on the man who had killed a couple in the area. The killer escaped to the upper Grand Coulee, knowing that it was unusual for the law enforcement to come that far.

The area's religious services consisted of revival meetings in the local schoolhouse.

Canady's memory was keen and he remembered the location of all the homesteads. He listed the owners as follows: Canady, Partee, Earl Thompson, Oscar and Charles Osborne, Hans Lange, Frank Davis, Mark Noble, Herb Buelen, Sherm Scott, Emmett "Turkey" Martin, Ernest Martin, Jess Evans, Buckley, Ed Goodman, Cy Buckley, Lincoln Stock Farm, a man named Scheibner, Carl McKinley, Cliff Stearman, Alfred Feese, and Carp Dyer.

These and others purchased their groceries once a year, either at Almira or Coulee City. Their load consisted of barrels of flour, several sacks of sugar, salt, pepper, and coffee. The rest of their larder was raised on the family homesteads.

Rattlesnake Canyon Home for Indians

One of the most prominent land features at the damsite, in addition to the Grand Coulee itself, was "Rattlesnake Canyon."

It is now a lake into which for many years sewage from the town of Grand Coulee was dumped. This prompted local citizens to name it "Lake Urine." Now freed of pollution, it may one day border a major resort development.

I wrote the history of the canyon on which Daily World editors put a heading that current newsmen wouldn't think of putting at the top of an article. It read: "Those Palefaces! It Seems Redskins Cannot Have Even a Place for Winter Camping." Following is the story:

An Indian, stoically erect as his forefathers in years gone by, and his squaw, stood on the edge of Rattlesnake Canyon overlooking the landscape in front of them.

He saw the canyon filled with the biggest earth pile he had ever seen. A belt was dumping even more into the 400-foot deep canyon which already held 13 million cubic yards of earth that had been excavated in building the dam.

Workmen said the Indian and squaw stood there for a long time, finally leaving. Although it is not definitely known, the history of Rattlesnake gulch probably caused them to gaze so intently at the earth mass.

According to Charles Osborne, a pioneer who came here in 1882 with his brother, Oscar, the bottom of Rattlesnake canyon was once a favorite winter camping grounds for Indians. Every year they'd come in great numbers to spend the colder months here. They caught fish on the shallow bars of the Columbia located just out of the mouth of the canyon, he said.

During extreme cold weather, when the tribe ran out of food, they lost a number of the older people and buried them there. Osborne said a large number of Indian graves are probably located deep under the excavated material from the dam.

Osborne said, incidentally, that he believed cold winters sometimes made cannibals out of the Indians. His brother digging in the Grand Coulee one year found buried, about six feet under the ground, a campfire with human bones split open and human teeth marks on them. The campfire was undoubledly buried in a gradual movement of earth from the coulee wall.

The history of Rattlesnake Canyon had an added interest named "Texas Jack." Osborne called him a cattle-rustler and horse thief whom the ranchers at one time thought about hanging. He was the first resident of the deep coulee. He squatted there in 1887 and lived there until he was chased out of the country.

Then came Sam Dillman, who homesteaded the property in 1888 and built a fine orchard which proved a paying investment. Bill Zimmerman and a man named Pitt then purchased the orchard and continued to make it pay. Then it was sold to A. L. Davis and in turn, in 1914, to the Noble family.

The only person ever to live on the canyon floor at the place where the overburden was actually dumped, was Herb Bulen who came in 1906 for the sole purpose of catching timber and lumber in the bend of the river near the present damsite. The material he gathered he sold to ranchers in the area. In 1913, however, his bare existence caused him to give up his small ranch house located at a spot deep in the heart of the company dumping ground and it was vacant until project construction started.

Spider Fights, Other Tidbits Paid Off

I was paid so much a column-inch for my writing, so I submitted a lot of copy that might be labeled "Trivia."

Here are a few sample items:

A Spider Fight

A new fad has taken Mason City and the damsite by storm. Replacing the old rooster fights held in old deserted barns with spectators keeping one eye out for the cops, the newest in mortal combat is black-widow spider fights.

The poisonous creatures are so bountiful here that they are easy to find and the hunt for the biggest of the species is constantly on. Owners or finders of these spiders then match each other's proteges within the battleground, a large glass jar.

Yesterday's crucial battles were all won by "King" owned by Andy Seresun and Duncan McPherson. The giant spider killed ten adversaries.

The first round of the battle consists of lowering the two enemies into a common jar. Round two sees them eyeing one another (if spiders have eyes. do they?). In the third round the spiders stick their feet or arms or fangs or whatever you may call them, into their mouth and fill the ends with poison.

Round four is generally the last canto. The two spiders crawl toward one another with spinning mechanisms ready for instant action. As the two meet they both attempt to spin a thread around one another. Within a few seconds one or the other always wins, tying the other fast. Cannibalism then takes place.

"King" is to be matched, after a few more preliminary bouts, with another great fighter owned by Earl Schreiber of the Coulee Trading company. Both managers report their charges in great shape, (if you like a spider's shape).

More and more men are hunting spiders and entering the fray. It's quite a thing in Mason City.

Stick of Gum Brings Letter From Governor

A little fellow living in Grand Coulee by the name of Blaine Madden (he's seven years old) is going to be the proudest boy at the damsite soon.

A letter sent by Governor Martin to Major Fred M. Weil of the new Continental Hotel, explains it all.

"During the dinner Saturday evening," the governor wrote, "a little boy came and gave me a piece of gum. Later, his mother talked to me and I gave him my card. I seem to have forgotter the young man's name although as I recall it his first two names were Blaine Martin, but I fail to recall the proper name. I thought I would like to drop him a little line but without this information I am unable to do so."

This Is Dam Lingo

When in Rome, do as Romans do. When at Grand Coulee speak as the Grand Couleeites (or Grand Couleeians) do.

The damsite has a lingo of its own.

Here are a few of the terms used by laborers and even the common citizenry at the damsite:

Muck — Excavated earth.

Spoilbanks — Dirt and rock removed from the excavation area.

Catskinner — One who operates a tractor, either diesel or gasoline.

Kiddie Kar — Auto-cars belonging to E. Paul Ford, contractor boss, these haul 5½ yards per trip.

Up the Hill — The private townsites.

Down Below — The damsite proper.

Powder Monkey — One who loads holes with dynamite or black powder.

Le Tourneaus — Big 15-ton, 12-yard automatic scrapers used in the grading and leveling of the town and on the lower end of the joint highway and railway entrance.

The Pit — The site where operations are being carried on.

Coyote Hole — A big hole drilled in rock in which dynamite and black powder will be deposited for blasting.

Dumps — The spoilbanks or piles of earth removed.

Jackhammer men — Laborers who operate jackhammers, an instrument equipped with a steel chisel or hammer which is operated by means of air compression and makes a staccato-like noise as it hits rock.

Grease monkeys — Men who grease trucks and other machinery.

P and H's — A type of excavation shovel.

Shovel runner — One who operates a shovel.

A card — Meaning a registration card from the national re-employment office, needed by laborers in order to be permitted to work.

Cut — A large gap necessary for the railroad line.

Fill — A crevice that must be filled up for the railroad and highway line.

Maniac — Term used jokingly in referring to a mechanic.

City Without A Chimney Has Snake Fence

It seems that the damsite is a veritable gold mine for strange facts that can be used in the famous Robert Ripley "Believe It Or Not" cartoons.

Three major items have been submitted on request by Mrs. Marie Telford of the MWAK company, all of them accepted.

The first, already printed, brought attention to the fact that Mason City, a community of 3,000, is without a chimney. Since the cartoon was published, the MWAK has been literally flooded with requests for information on electric heating from all parts of the United States, including letters from mayors of many cities.

The second oddity is that "Electric City" in the Grand Coulee has no electricity. This was true a few weeks ago; now the little community has both phone and light service.

The third strange thing is the snake fence built by George Atkinson around his home. About a foot high, it was designed to keep dangerous rattlers from the Atkinson yard.

Another item to be submitted is that the damsite possesses the world's largest rubber band, that being the longest section of rubber belt on the conveyor system.

Exclusive Taxicab Has Clientele At Dam

What is perhaps the state's most exclusive taxi service is run by the state patrol and the police force of Mason City.

Because women are not allowed to walk through the single men's dormitory section by company rule and as this section lies between the girls' dormitory and the headquarters building, it is necessary for the patrol or camp police to take the "telephone" girls to and from work.

The "hello" girls are said to be elated about the condition.

At Last! A Place For Razor Blades

The age-old, bothersome problem of what to do with old, used razor blades will be no problem at all for engineers who will shortly move into the spacious and beautiful $40,000 dormitories in Administration City.

Instead of wrapping them up in paper, placing them in an awkward box,

149

or otherwise disposing of them — and how men hate to bother with these dangerous blades — a small groove had been made in the cabinet above the sinks in each of the rooms.

It is plainly marked "Razor Blades." Engineers simply insert the used blade into the slot, and presto, the job is done. They are lost within the walls of the building.

Husband In Distress

An ad appeared in the Grand Coulee News and its editor, Sidney Jackson, swears that it's genuine.

"FOUND — Lady's purse left in my car while parked. Contains papers, $5 in change, etc. Owner can have same by describing property and paying for this ad. If owner can explain satisfactorily to my wife how purse got into my car, I will pay for this ad myself. R. C."

Is Climate Too Healthy?

Ladies, if you want to keep that sylph-like figure, don't come to Grand Coulee dam to live!

That, in toto, is the warning to be taken at its worth from a check-up by the Daily World correspondent this week to learn the reason for the apparent consistent increase in poundage among the damsite's citizens.

An unofficial survey shows that the majority of Grand Coulee Dam people have gained weight since coming to this area to live, some gaining only a few pounds but most of them from 10 to 20 or even as high as 30 pounds.

Warren Hockaday, secretary to M. Harvey Slocum, reports gaining 20 pounds (he blames it on "middle age"). Jack Murray, MWAK employment manager, added 10 pounds to his waistline, Clint Heid of the company machine shop, a similar amount.

Sidney Jackson, newspaper editor and publisher, reports a boost in poundage of about 10 pounds. Bill Rosholt of the Electric City "Trading Post" grocery had added about 20 pounds. And so on down through the list of people.

What is the cause for this mysterious appearance of bay-window protrusions?

Dr. A. S. Baker, head of the district state health office in Grand Coulee says, "It's the climate."

"This is simply a healthy climate," he said. "There is plenty of sun and dry, stimulating air. The dust seems to affect some people, particularly in the spring. We seem to have the most pneumonia cases during that time of the year. However, after that, the sun comes out and sterilizes the dust."

As for the ladies they, too, report difficulty in keeping that girlish figure. It was impossible to learn, for publication at least, how much some of them had gained since coming to live at the damsite. It was admitted, however, that dieting is a much-practiced, but unpopular, indoor and outdoor sport.

Walking Bombs Have Damsite In Jitters

One hears a lot of wild stories at the damsite, but the wildest of these (although they say it's true) was printed in the Grand Coulee News yesterday.

In a small community in the Coulee the folks have the jitters, the story goes. Whenever a hog says, "oink, oink", they start to run. A squeal is the signal for a hundred-yard dash for a cellar, and even the sight of a razorback honing himself on a fence post gives them the heeby-jeebies.

It all came about when two pigs tried to make hogs of themselves.

The pigs were said to have discovered a dynamite cache along the government railroad that was being built. Being hogs, they devoured as many sticks of dynamite as they could.

The owner was in a quandry. Should he butcher the hogs and take a chance of them blowing up in his face or should he take them down to the contractor and say, "Here they are?" Or should he drop them off the top of Steamboat Rock and pick up the baloney?

Dynamite is indigestible and remains ready for business in the hogs stomach, it should be explained. To make matters worse, the two hogs joined their fellow hogs, about 18 in number. Imagine the chagrin of the owner to find the two dynamite eating hogs mixed in with a herd of 20.

And now, so the yarn goes, the conscientious engineer is careful to toot his whistle when his engine passes that particular spot. He cups his hand behind an ear to hear the "oink, oink", of a wandering porker. Far be it for him to run into a hog and have the cowcatcher blown over the moon.

Yes, folks have the jitters down the Coulee. And pigs is pigs and treated with a great deal of respect.

Dog Dies, Refund Asked

Tragedy stalked into the Grand Coulee police station one day recently.

A wee lad, six or seven years old, walked in with an old dog collar held behind his back, shyly but solemnly. The officers paid no attention to him at first; "just another kid hanging around," they thought.

But the youngster, sad-eyed, wasn't long to be denied.

Screwing up his courage, he said, "Kin I get my money back?"

"What money, sonny?" policemen asked, puzzled.

"Well, I got my dog a license," the child softly said, his eyes turned to the floor. "My dog got killed, and now I don't need no license no more."

Another youngster recently came to the station to get a license for his dog. However, he didn't have the $2. He told the policemen, "I'd like to pay you 25 cents a week until I get it all paid for."

Reading Tastes Differ

By the magazines they read, ye shall know them! These are the approximate words of J.J. Murphy of Tacoma, who has charge of the cigar, candy and magazine stand for the MWAK in the Coulee Trading company store building.

Murphy, by the way of explanation, has been engaged in this particular type of work for years and years. In fact, his present job is the sixth time that he has been engaged in building a dam. Murphy has worked on the Fort Peck Dam, the Guernsey Dam in Wyoming, the Alexander Dam in Idaho, the Monticello Dam in Indiana and the Safe Harbor Dam in Pennsylvania. So he should know whereof he speaks.

Murphy, who studies all types of characters from behind his counter, judges that the men employed on Grand Coulee Dam are of higher type than he has ever seen on any project since he has been in the business. And why — because the men read better types of magazines.

Although there is a great demand for Western magazines, Murphy reports that he has frequent calls for such as Cosmopolitan, Collier's, Saturday Evening Post, Liberty, Redbook, Readers Digest and Time.

He has on his shelves such publications found supposedly only in the best of families; Esquire, Review of Reviews, Harpers, Current History, Forbes, Barron's Weekly, Today, etc. As a good businessman, he wouldn't have them unless there were calls for them, and there are many, Murphy explains.

"The men do not read the trash you find in most construction camps," Murphy declares. "You'd never find these higher type magazines in any other camp. Here we have men on the job who formerly had money, ex-bankers etc."

Of the 600 magazines per week, Murphy reports little call for movie magazines, joke magazines and sex stories. The family man, of whom there are many here, prefers deeper reading, he says.

"And love stories don't sell at all," he concluded. "In other camps, you'd sell lots of those but here most of the men are married, and I guess they are past that stage."

Poison Ivy And Snakes

Among the complications arising from the construction of Grand Coulee Dam was the curse of poison ivy.

Engineers working in the Colville area in the upper reservoir region are having trouble with a skin ailment.

In an effort to check the recurrence of the malady, the U. S. Public Health Service has sent several dozen jars of a poison ivy protective ointment.

The men will not only protect themselves but will report the success of the lotion to the health service which is anxious to learn the powers of the medicine.

Nearly all engineering parties sent out by the USBR are equipped with snake bite remedies as protection against the reptiles striking them as they work in the sagebrush. During this season of the year, the snakes are particularly dangerous. They are shedding their skins and during that period they are partially blind.

Workmen To Use Vanishing Cream

On the surface of things, one could easily preclude that hardened and tough workmen engaged on the dam construction have gone "soft."

Can you imagine any group of workmen using 100 pounds of vanishing cream? Heretofore, the usage of such was confined mainly to members of the female sex to make themselves more becoming.

However, 'tis true that the workmen will soon be using some of the same type preparation. Of course, there's a story behind it all. The cream, similar in content to the vanishing cream with the perfume removed, is a protective lotion to be used on the hands of the workmen engaged in handling bulk cement.

The chemical formation of cement is such that it will cause irritation on all soft tissues. The effect on one's hands is similar to a lime burn. In order to prevent this, the pores of exposed areas are saturated with the cream.

Barking Man

When a dog bites a man it's news; when a man barks at a dog, that's news again.

A Grand Coulee citizen was released this week after serving a short jail term. He had been found sitting in the mud on a Grand Coulee street, holding a bulldog by the neck and barking in its face.

No Ringa' Da Bell

Workmen engaged in digging a ditch as part of the gravel carrying system in back of Mason City are telling a story on an Italian workman.

It seems the men were busy digging the ditch when a rattlenake, still somewhat sluggish at that time of the year, peered over the edge of the gully.

The Italian fellow, with presence of mind, suddenly grabbed the snake in back of the head and shouted, quite loudly:

"You son-a-gun, why you no ringa' da bell?" Obviously meaning that the snake should have "rattled."

Strange Machine Displayed in Store

A unique machine, never before seen at Grand Coulee Dam, was on display in the Coulee Trading Company general store the other day.

The apparatus, which in the memory of one of the oldest inhabitants, has never been used here before, seemed so out of place that it aroused considerable interest.

It may not arouse attention any other place, but the very idea of having grass to cut here is no small novelty. Yards in Mason City will soon demand the attention of this unique piece of equipment, a lawnmower!

Writing On Wall Shows Genius

Judging from "the writing on the wall," the jail in Mason City has housed a group of poets, philosophers, artists, engineers and essayists.

An inspection of the writings on the boards, ceiling and bunks, reveals a myriad of literary genius. Consider this one for instance:

"Take the Rocky Mountains, put them in the Atlantic and raise it to the level of the Pacific and thereby do away with the Panama canal, a PWA job of the future." USBR and MWAK take heed.

Another prisoner was evidently a "knock-knock" fan. He scribbled with a dull pencil, "knock! knock! Who's there? Ammonia. Ammonia who? Ammonia a bird in a guilded cage."

Still another recent inmate learned his lesson. He scrawled "I may as well put mine (his message) here too. I always wondered about jails. My curiosity is entirely satisfied. I think I'll be hard to find in one when I get out of here."

Here's another poetic delivery:

"The saddest words of tongue or pen are these few words 'In jail again'." Another person complained about being "soaked" $250 for selling what he called "pop." Patrolmen found it to be mighty intoxicating "pop."

Criticism of the patrol bastile was voiced by many inmates. Some called the local justices "numbskulls" and quite a few insisted they had been "framed."

Workers Start Own Security System

Lay offs were tough for some workmen because they were off the payroll.

A social security program of their own was adapted by five Mason City bachelors to take care of their expenses during the winter lay off of work at the damsite.

A back-to-nature movement was combined with it. The idea, which met with success, was explained to me by Bill Pearson, retail clerk in the big Coulee Trading Company store at Mason City.

The plan used by the men was simple. During the working months of the busy summer the five men each "chipped in" $5 per week to raise a grubstake. When the lay off came they left for the back woods country near Priest Lake, Idaho, where they established themselves in a cabin with the secure feeling that they could last six months.

"We struck upon the idea one night when we were chewing the fat in one of our cabins," Pearson explained. "We discussed what we would do during the lay off and what we could do to keep ourselves alive without the usual reliance on government aid.

"We decided to build up a grubstake, and the next day I put up the first $5 to start the pot. When the boys were off work because the shutdown at the dam, the fund had built up to $200. Chef Bill Arndt of the mess hall said that due to quantitive buying the money would last the five of us at least six months.

"The prime object of the plan was to build up our health. At the same time, we could live cheaply yet pleasantly away from the humdrum of civilization."

The men taking part in the private social security program were: Pearson, about 45; Ned Klein, about 30, a camp office worker; Les Mumson, about 25, time-keeper; John Burton, about 28, welder; and Don Wells, about 30, cat-shop worker.

The men lived in a cabin owned by Klein. They spent their idle moments clearing land and planned to build more cabins. About 300 books from Pearson's library were taken up into the wilds, and these furnished evening enjoyment. All the men were of a philosophical nature and single.

Pearson estimated that $200 lasted one man about 5 months only at the damsite. For future posterity, the men also kept a diary of their experiences and someday may write a book.

A Sleeping Giant Goes to Work

Publisher Rufus Woods used a lot of large black type and flowery words on the front page that reported the first power would be produced by the Grand Coulee Dam on March 23, 1941.

One read: "CONTACT." It ran above smaller heads reading: "Grand Coulee Turns on First Electricity Saturday," "Sleeping Giant will Awaken" and "Biggest Thing Coming to Life."

My story read:

"A sleeping giant goes to work tomorrow. Seven years and seven months from the day the first worker started his labor, the Grand Coulee Dam — a monument to the ingenuity of man — will start to harness the surging waters of the Columbia River to convert that energy into man's most precious commodity — electricity.

"Two 10,000-kilowatt generators will begin to turn and electricity adequate for a city of 60,000 persons will flow into the Bonneville lines to be distributed to awaiting industries and homes in the Northwest and to answer the cry from national defense.

"And the general public — always before told that the construction area around the "biggest thing on earth" was no-man's land — will be welcomed with open arms to see the monster go into action. Estimates of the anticipated crowds, who will take advantage of what probably will be the only opportunity for a long time to enter the sanctity of the powerhouse, run as high as 8,000.

"A two-and-a-half-hour program has been planned by the reclamation bureau, starting with talks by dignitaries, including Governor Arthur B. Langlie, carrying on with a half-hour ceremony in the powerhouse, a program from Bonneville Dam with music, and ending with a tour of the big station, two city blocks long and rising to the height of a 21-story building.

"Powerhouse ceremonies will start with sounds from the spillway waterfall being picked up by suspended microphones and broadcast to the thousands gathered at the west vista house.

"They will then be permitted to hear the actual starting of the machinery. James Miner, assistant supervising engineer, will twirl the knob that will turn the turbine blades into the 200-foot deep body of water stored in the reservoir.

"When the turbine revolves, James Wallace, master mechanic, will regulate the speed of the generator seated overhead, while C. P. Christensen, chief electric inspector, will stand ready at the voltage control. When the needles give the signal, A. F. Darland, construction engineer, will throw the switch that will send Grand Coulee Dam's first electrical energy surging into the Bonneville circuit."

What is described was the preliminary to the "official" start of production which was headlined the following day as follows:

The story, by the United Press, read:

"Chief Jim James of the Nez Perce Indians pushed a button in the powerhouse of giant Grand Coulee Dam today, sending the first electricity surging from two 10,000-kilowatt generators.

155

"Then he stepped to a microphone and spoke briefly in his native tongue on a nation-wide broadcast. 'Pride and humility mingle in our hearts today,' the chief said. 'We Red Americans are glad to join the White Americans to celebrate the beginning of a generation of power at the largest plant in the world.'"

"Thus in a strange linking of the past and present, descendants of northeastern Washington's first inhabitants gave their approval of a $167,000,000 project that will carry light and power to homes and farms, Indian reservations, and metropolitan cities, small businesses and big national defense industrial plants, and irrigate a million acres of fertile land.

"President Roosevelt, in a letter to Dr. Frank Banks, supervising engineer, called the project 'a fine job, well done.'

" 'I want to congratulate the Bureau of Reclamation upon putting the great Grand Coulee Dam to work two years ahead of schedule,' the president wrote.

" 'It is thrilling to contemplate the prospects that this dam opens. A tremendous stream of energy will flow continuously from the dam to turn factory wheels and make the lives of men and women more fruitful. It will light homes and stores in towns and cities. It will ease the drudgery around the farmyards and farmhouses of the Pacific Northwest. In short, it will bring to millions the benefits of plentiful, low-cost public power. Water will flow through the canals of the dam to lands now dry and barren but which one day will be made fertile by irrigation. This water will serve thus to create houses for thousands of families on farms and in new towns and villages.

" 'Floods will be controlled and navigation will be improved so that much of the commerce of this new empore may cheaply be water-borne.' "

An NBC radio announcer, later to become famous, covered the historic event in a national broadcast. His name was Chet Huntley.

The appearance of Chief James and other aged Indian leaders was arranged by me, then a reporter, at the request of the information officer Sol Hutton who knew I was acquainted with them. I remember asking Hutton if it was alright to pose some of the Indians on top of the generators for the photographers surely would want to put them there. He said it was "okay" and the Indians were posed there.

The first big generator of the 18 ultimately installed in the project's initial two powerhouses began production on October 4, 1941. The units were originally rated at 108,000 kilowatts but currently are capable of producing 125,000 kilowatts or more each, having been rewound.

The generators went on the line just in time for their kilowatts to contribute to the World War II effort.

They made possible the manufacture of the great block of power needed to produce the aluminum with which to build war planes and to provide through Hanford the plutonium required to make the atomic bomb.

Who Should Get Credit for the Dam?

One bit of history about the Grand Coulee Dam needs to be told here to set the record straight. It involves U. S. Senator C. C. Dill, of Spokane, who was referred to as "the father of Grand Coulee Dam."

The senator didn't call himself that, but he kept saying "some papers call me the father of the dam" for the same self-serving purpose.

I now quote from a letter dated October 28, 1942, written by the head of the "National Grange" to clear the record and thereby give the credit to the people who earned it: Rufus Woods, James O'Sullivan and U. S. Representative Sam B. Hill.

"Dear Rufus:

"Through your courtesy, I presume, I am receiving copies of the Daily World for which I thank you. In one of the copies I noticed a statement by former Senator Dill telling how he had secured the appropriation for the Coulee Dam. In my present position as Master of the National Grange, I cannot take any part in the election controversy, but, personally, it burns me up to hear him claim credit when I know how hard it was to get him to do a thing when I came back here as the representative of the Columbia Basin commission to try to get something underway.

"The man who deserves the credit for the appropriation for the Coulee Dam is Judge Samuel B. Hill. Senator Dill was doing his best to prevent prompt action and it was not until Judge Hill offered to go with me to the White House that Senator Dill acted.

"You will recall the situation because you were on the Commission at the same time and I reported in detail. Also in October 1940, I spoke at Wenatchee, and you asked me about the situation. I think you reported the case quite fully in the Wenatchee World, and, if you have not done so, it occurs to me that you might like to review what was said.

"I know nothing about the many reports for the various reasons why Senator Dill was not pushing the Coulee Dam in the Spring of 1933, but I do know that he was not only not pushing it but he was doing his best to discourage it when I came to Washington. He told me there was absolutely no use of taking it up at this time and that we ought to wait until the press of immediate work was over. I talked with Judge Hill about it on several occasions, and, each time, I found that he was meeting opposition in the Senate, but was continually working in the interest of the Dam. I do not know whether or not Judge Hill would be willing to say anything, but it occurs to me that if you want confirmation of my statement you might call him up. If he is willing to talk, he will tell you that what I say is absolutely true.

"As a matter of fact, Dill never got a single appropriation for the Dam. Judge Hill got them all. It is also a fact that Dill was working for a low dam while Judge Hill was working for a high dam. Before leaving Congress, Judge Levy put in the record a statement of how helpful Dill had been to him in securing the appropriations for the high dam. This is nothing but Dill propaganda because all the work for the high dam was completed before Judge Levy came to Congress and Judge Hill and Senator

157

Schwellenbach worked them through together. I think that some of you Washingtonians should dig up these facts and make them known. If you will call Judge Samuel B. Hill, Emerson 5004, Washington, D.C. and ask him a few questions, I am very confident that you will get information which you can use to good advantage because Dill is up to his old tricks of mis-representing this situation.

"Senator Dill claims great influence in Washington. As near as I can find his influence is practically nil. I do not know what Judge Hill would say to a question on that point, but if he is willing to talk I am sure he would tell you the same as I have told you, because the Judge always tells the truth."

Yours sincerely,

A. S. Goss
Master, The National Grange

How Wrong Some Critics Were!

There were many people who scoffed at the idea of building the Grand Coulee Dam.

When the dam produced its first power in 1941 and the occasion was celebrated I wrote the following about the sceptics who opposed it years earlier.

"I recall a photographer for LIFE Magazine taking a thousand photos when the first power was produced at Grand Coulee Dam."

"What finally appeared in LIFE was a single photo. It was displayed prominently on the page entitled 'Picture of the Week.' "

"Did it show the big generators, the big dam or the ceremonies? No. The full-page photo featured a Nespelem Indian woman at an old washing machine on a dilapidated back porch."

"It was the national magazine's way of saying: "There's no market for the power; the only potential customers are a scattered bunch of Indians."

"Grand Coulee Dam was used to abuse such as this by the time the switch was thrown that turned on the first of the generators which subsequently made the project the biggest producer of power in the world."

"Those who fought for the project were for many years subjected to ridicule, antagonism and the might of money as they went about with the frustrating promotion job of selling the Northwest and the Congress on the worth of the Grand Coulee Dam project."

"Renowned national magazines and newspapers found it fun to laugh, editorially, at the nincompoops and dreamers who figured there was need for a Grand Coulee Dam and for the power and subsequently the crops it would produce."

"Said the Public Service Magazine "Only a Dr. Gulliver is competent to write about the enormity of the potential power production of Grand Coulee on the one hand and THE MICROSCOPIC VISIBLE AND ECONOMIC MARKET for this mobilization of kilowatts on the other."

"The Washington Post criticized the project too, saying that now

Governor Roosevelt "adds the immensely costly Columbia River project to the list of squanderings to be made if he should become President of the United States."

Said the Farm Journal: "No private power company would risk a cent in plants to manufacture power for a non-existent market . . . Of all the outrages on agriculture, we are beginning to think the Columbia Basin Project takes the cake. Who wants it? Nobody!"

"In the Congressional Record, an Eastern member of the House of Representatives — Rep. Francis Culkin — called Grand Coulee Dam "the greatest fraud ever perpetrated on the people of the United States."

"Business Week added its caustic comment "Grand Coulee Dam is typical of those things that won't have anymore usefulness than the pyramids of Egypt."

"Colliers spoke in a similar vein: "What are they going to do with it? (the power) . . . The largest possible markets would be Seattle and Tacoma. But these cities are 300 miles away. To drag Coulee power over the Cascades to Seattle and Tacoma might easily make the consumer's meter rate prohibitive."

"Closer to home, the Spokesman-Review, under the heading The Columbia River Damsite Fiasco," said "There was never justification for the demand for borings for a possible damsite. Now that these borings have proved the utter futility of the search for bedrock, the state and federal authorities ought to give no further consideration to the clamor of Hugh Cooper (a nationally known engineer) and the little group of land speculators in Grant County who noisily demanded the wasting of the state's appropriation." Later the Spokesman-Review became a staunch supporter. It helped expedite irrigation of a half million acres of land and today offers editorial backing toward the completion of the project.

"The Bellingham Herald joined the chorus: "Washington has started into an enterprise that is almost certain to be disastrous. It should stop it NOW!"

"The Business Chronicle of Seattle said "Why not take the proposed $200,000,000 which the completed Grand Coulee project is supposed to cost and spend it right away (to provide work during the depression); and then turn around and squander an equal amount (to be provided by taxes and bonds or printing press money) to tear the thing down as soon as it's completed."

"The Bremerton Searchlight added "Nothing more visionary or impractical or ruthless with waste of public funds has come in amongst the mass of schemes to use taxpayers' money than is the Grand Coulee project."

"Today — you see how wrong, how utterly wrong editors can be."

"The 'useless' Grand Coulee Dam has produced, in three decades, power having a dollar value of approximately $5 billion."

The abundance of power that was produced at a strategic time made it a weapon of peace for it allowed the production of the atomic bomb, which shortened World War II.

Some of the Grand Coulee energy was used to pump water to meet irrigation needs in the Columbia Basin where a half million acres of desert land have been turned into fertile farms, with bustling communities providing, along with the farms, thousands of jobs in service industries.

The big "slab of concrete across the Columbia" also has created benefits in flood control, and it has helped keep power rates for homes and industry down to the lowest possible figure.

And as to the much-worried-over waste of taxpayers' money: Grand Coulee is way ahead of schedule in repayment of the federal investment.

We at the Wenatchee World are proud to recall the vision and energy of its original publisher and one of the project's staunchest supporters — the late Rufus Woods. He made it possible for us to boast today that for many, many years the Wenatchee World was the only daily newspaper in the State of Washington to stand up and fight for the Grand Coulee Dam.

PHOTO SECTION CREDIT

The next section of the book contains 40 pages carrying 71 pictures.

Most of those of scenes at the damsite were taken by Bureau of Reclamation photographers. None were shot by the author for the Wenatchee Daily World did not furnish him a camera and those he took for the Spokane Chronicle were not saved.

Photos of Bureau of Reclamation activities originating out of regional office in Boise were taken by that agency.

World features written in the author's days as managing editor and later as a special writer were illustrated with pictures he himself took.

The Blonk family in Holland

Grade school graduate

A skinny runner, left, at the U.W.

A cow milker

P-1

This is the house in Holland in which the author was born. Posed with it are his father, right, and his dad's parents

The author worked with his parents on a dairy farm and later a chicken ranch

Daughter Julie Yeager

Hubert C. and Martha Blonk

Grandson Jim Caldwell

Grandson Jeff Caldwell

This is what the famous B St. looked like in 1938. It sprung up in 1933. Earlier photos were destroyed in a fire

The first residents of the B St. area got their water from a big tank on a truck

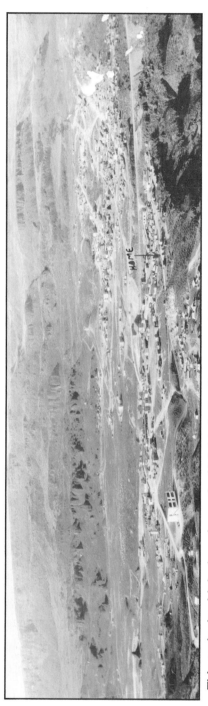

This early day high view shows the Heights in the foreground, the Center above it, and the B St. area beyond

The Continental Hotel, mid-photo, and the Roosevelt Theatre, left, dominated Grand Coulee Center

It was in a barren area they built the Grand Coulee Dam. At first the only activity here was a cable ferry

Friday was payday at the damsite. That day a lot of construction stiffs headed for B St.

B Street suffered three major fires. In one a woman was killed. In another the files of the Grand Coulee News, including early-day pictures, were destroyed

Diesel-electric trains ran over low and high trestles hauling concrete

Being a sandhog was a scary experience. It required going below the river surface under pressure during the building of a bridge

When President Roosevelt visited the dam in 1937 the author, second from left, was assigned to report what he asked project head Frank A. Banks seated alongside him

Construction took place behind cofferdams. As it proceeded, Mason City, at left, and Coulee Dam, the engineer's town, came into being

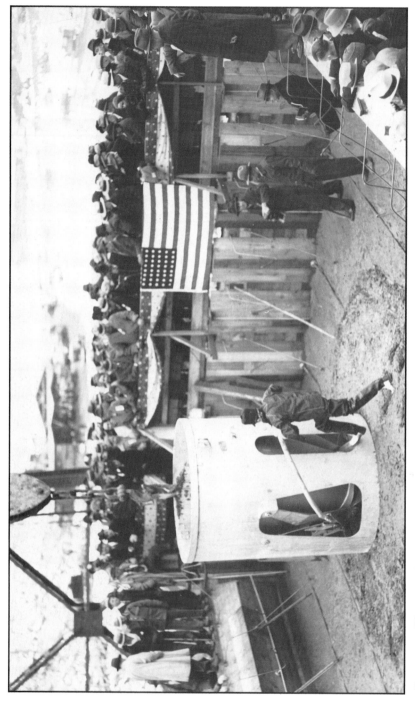

Governor Clarence Martin made the first official pour of concrete at the damsite on Dec. 8, 1935. He opened a four-yard bucket

A plant near an abutment called the the "House of Magic" provided the concrete

A hillside was frozen so that mud would not ooze onto an area where concrete was to be poured

As the Grand Coulee Dam-to-be grew, water was diverted by means of low gaps in the concrete poured earlier

Frank A. Banks
Project head

Harvey Slocum
Construction boss

Charlie Osborne
Area pioneer

Sid Jackson
The first editor

Ida Fleischmann
Early promotor

Robert Hunter
Early-day lawyer

Joseph Wicks
A key attorney

Francis McGinn
The law

Jackhammering was a noisy activity required to build the Grand Coulee Dam. The chattering machines made holes in rock preceding blasting

Ten towns had to be moved and a vast area cleared in the reservoir

One of the longest conveyors anywhere brought the concrete aggregate from a pit to the dam

Indians featured the start-up of power production in 1941. They were:
Chief Jim James, left, who spoke, and Harry Owhi

President Truman spoke to 8,000 in Mason City in dedicating the dam and reservoir. He was quite jovial, as he was found to be earlier at Hungry Horse Dam

This striking aerial view shows the scope of the magnificent power and irrigation development that was created

Homesteads were awarded to war veterans at a drawing on the Yakima Project. Supt. Ole Lindgren, near mike, looks on

A Congressional party was escorted to Western projects and the Grand Canyon. Rep. George Schwabe of Oklahoma is shown at right

The Bureau of Reclamation bowling league in Boise was nationally publicized for having fun. Don Price awarded five silver dollars in "cold cash" — frozen in a cake of ice — to Carl Hopt

As a celebration publicity stunt governors were asked to send water from a local stream to be dumped into the first irrigation water pumped. Posed with the jugs is Lily Jo Hammans

Commissioner of Reclamation Michael Strauss helped deliver the first irrigation water to the Columbia Basin. A working farm was created in a single day as part of an 11-day celebration

The "biggest button in the world" started up the third powerhouse. Senator Henry Jackson was the principal speaker

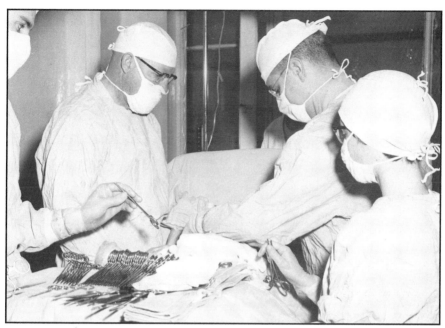

Armed with a bulky Speed-Graphic the author covered a major surgery

TV star Telly Savalas posed at a golf match

The coldest the author ever got was taking a picture showing water whipped out of Blue Lake becoming frozen

When a national ski jump record was set at Leavenworth, this layout was used to show how far the skier jumped

"Fishermen are so enthusiastic" was the caption for this specially-arranged photograph

A photo of a dog nursing a fawn drew lots of attention

As a gag, the World ran a reverse of the usual early-day deer picture. It showed the hunter instead of the deer laying on the fender

Jogging in strange places was fun. Here a typhoon shelter in Hong Kong is in the background

Being a "ham" actor brightened life in Wenatchee. With the author, wearing derby, are June Taylor, Jerry Barash, and an unidentified person

Daughter Julie rode a Seafair float in Seattle as "Miss Maritime." She also helped the mayor unveil a plaque on the waterfront

Governor Dan Evans used wooden scissors to cut a ribbon that officially opened the North Cascades Highway. He was aided by long-time road booster Les Hollaway

Another master of ceremonies job involved dedication of Rocky Reach Dam

The World was allowed to be present at the spring feast and funerals by the Wanapum Indians

The author had a pencil in his mouth all his newspapering days. He was given chocolate-covered ones on his retirement

LIFE magazine purchased this photo and published it half-page size under the title "Doe On a Floe"

Yes, It's A Different Page 1; Its Date: The First Christmas

The first Christmas!

Surely no news story in the history of mankind can begin to compare with the occurence of that day.

But how would it have been had there been a daily newspaper coverage of the news of that day 2,000 years ago today?

For your reading on this eve of Christmas, the Daily World herewith presents an unusual page: The Page 1 that might have carried the news of that first Christmas morning.

So, as you read this page, consider that TODAY is the original Christmas.

You find that the total Christmas story is not unfolded in the news articles. Only a handful of persons on that morning knew of the significance of what had happened. Even they could not envision that centuries of man in the future would be altered by the birth of Jesus Christ that day.

A touch of imagination was necessary to present the events of the first Christmas in modern news form. But extensive research went into the stories on this page. Thus, despite the touch of imagination, the essentials of the articles are accurate.

Every member of the Daily World news staff has worked in the preparation of this page. Each writer found it stimulating to research in more depth the story of that first Christmas.

We hope you find it a page as interesting to read as it was to prepare.

Merry Christmas . . . . .

King Herod In Trouble?

Ruler Of Judea May Face Loss Of Throne

ROME — Is the reign of King Herod of Judea nearing its end?

That is the question raised by many political observers throughout the Empire nowadays.

There are rumors that Emperor Augustus might depose King Herod, the emperor's one-time favorite.

Sources close to the emperor indicate that the emperor feels Herod is losing his grip on Judea. Jewish unrest has been growing in recent years. Although nominally a Jew himself, Herod has subverted his allegiance to his God to his allegiance to the emperor.

King Herod shows obvious symptoms of uneasiness.

Recently he slew three of his sons whom he felt might offer a challenge to his throne. That act prompted the emperor to comment at the time: "It is safer to be Herod's pig than Herod's son."

KING HEROD
Political observers wonder if his days are numbered.

Should Herod be deposed, two of his surviving sons, Archelaus and Antipas, would be considered contenders for the throne. Archelaus advocates harsh treatment of the Jews.

Time has apparently worn the emperor's fondness of Herod. That fondness began when Herod stood with Augustus in the battle of Actium, against Mark Anthony and Herod's former wife, Cleopatra.

Many rumors have circulated about Herod's jealousy of this throne.

One observer today remarked that Herod could become concerned about the so-called Messiah babe born last night might be a threat to his throne. If that should happen, the king would probably seek to have the infant eliminated.

THE WENATCHEE DAILY WORLD

THE FIRST CHRISTMAS

Emperor Urges Cooperation In Census; Towns Crowded

Transients Clog Roads; Housing Short

ROME—Emperor Caesar Augustus today ordered total cooperation in the census being taken to plug tax loopholes.

An imperial rescript recently ordered all subjects to return to the cities of their ancestors so that a census can be made.

The result has been a heavy flow of subjects on roads and some serious crowding in the towns. Many report acute housing shortages.

Transients themselves say their forced migration is working an economic hardship on them.

Imperial sources say the census is necessary to effectively carryout the imperial tax program.

One spokesman said: "Corruption among petty officials, who presumably are taking bribes to keep merchants off the tax lists, have made the census Rome's only alternative."

"The amount of taxes being collected is simply not in line with the number of subjects. A proper tax program is impossible until Rome has an accurate idea of the population in the provinces."

The imperial order, urging cooperation in the census declared: "Citizens and other residents of the empire should recognize their obligation to the state."

It was pointed out that hardships are being endured everywhere in the empire. There have been reports of congestion and difficulties in the migration in Judea. The same is true in Egypt, along the Rhine and elsewhere in the far-flung empire which now almost completely rings the Mediterranean Sea.

NEW MOTHER—A woman named Mary during the night gave birth to a child in Bethlehem. The birth, surrounded by unusual circumstances, occurred in a stable beneath the inn at Bethlehem. Mary and husband Joseph had just arrived in Bethlehem after a long trip from Nazareth.

BRIGHT STAR SEEN IN AREA

JERUSALEM — A bright star was seen over the area last night and astrologists today have been unable to explain it or identify it.

Many reported seeing the bright star.

Most agreed it seemed to hover over the town of Bethlehem.

Astrologists are pondering the fact that a bright star had been reported seen earlier in the direction of Persia.

Reports indicate that three Persian scholars, named Gaspar, Melchior and Balthasar, have been following the course of the star.

Because they have been traveling, the three men could not be reached for comment.

But, in the absence of any scientific information, a Persian merchant here indicated the star has a special meaning. The man, Ishmael, suggested a connection between the star and the religion of his countrymen: a creed opposed to the worship of graven idols, and professing belief that there is but one God for all men.

Emperor Augustus Unconcerned

ROME—There is no fear in the royal palace of Emperor Augustus that the babe in Bethlehem might be a "Messiah" come to rule the earth.

EMPEROR AUGUSTUS
He indicates no concern over report that a savior has been born.

Messengers bearing news of the rumored birth of a "Jewish king" were brushed aside by palace aids.

The emperor and his council were feasting in celebration of the success of Gaius, son of Agrippa, in Armenia where he established order.

Serving as spokesman for Augustus, a senator told the messengers it is no concern of the world if the Jews, a minority group of strange teachings believed that a new leader had been sent to them from heaven.

"What have we to fear of the wailings of an infant?" asked the senator. "Augustus has the world well under control with no help from the God worshiped by the Jews.

"His name will be recorded in history as greater even than that of his uncle, Julius Caesar. He has settled troubles all over the world. The state coffers are overflowing.

"There is evidence of much prosperity throughout Rome. Many merchants, risen in a few years from obscurity, have palaces rivaling kings. They live in luxury never known before, with many slaves, handmaidens and dancing girls. Their stables are filled with the fleetest of steeds, their chariots are gilded and encrusted with jewels.

"There is much feasting on spiced foods fetched from far lands. Their vessels are filled with rich wines from vast vineyards.

"Let a Messiah come to the Jews. He cannot shake the power of Augustus."

Strange Birth Reported

BETHLEHEM — Strange circumstances surround the birth of an infant here during the night.

There are rumors that the mother is a virgin and that the infant is the promised Messiah.

Other phenomena are linked with the birth.

Excitement has been swelling among many believers who cite ancient Jewish prophecies which foretold:

A king of Israel will be born here;

A "virgin will be pregnant and give birth to a son, who will be called Emmanuel, which means 'God with us'";

The Messiah would be called "Wonderful, Councellor, The Mighty God, The Everlasting Father, The Prince of Peace."

All of those meanings, believers say, are embraced in the infant's reported name, Jesus, which means "God is Savior" and "God Saves."

Details of the birth are scarce at this hour and no authoritative comment has yet been offered. The infant was born, oddly enough, in a cave beneath an inn — a cave in which the inn's small domestical animals were kept.

One lower priest in Solomon's temple doubted reports of the Messiah's birth. He offered the opinion that the promised messiah would probably not arrive on earth in such humble surroundings as a stable, but would instead descend in triumph on a cloud.

The infant Jesus was born in Bethlehem shortly after the arrival there of the mother, Mary, and her husband, Joseph of the House of David.

They had migrated with many others to Bethlehem on the order of the emperor, for the census count. It was explained that they could find no room at the inn and thus took quarters in the stable.

The father, a carpenter, had walked the 90 miles from Nazareth. Mary, although great with child, had ridden a donkey.

Reports indicate that Mary is the niece of Elizabeth of Hebron with whom a miraculous birth was associated only a few weeks ago.

A son was born there to Zacharias and Elizabeth, who were considered too old to have children. Zacharias had said that birth was foretold when he was visited by an angel of the Lord who told Zacharias that his son, John, would be born and the boy "shall go before the face of the Lord to prepare his ways."

Later Elizabeth met Mary and was reported to have told her:

"Fear not, Mary: For thou hast found favor with God. And, behold, thou shall conceive in thy womb and bring forth a son, and shall call his name Jesus.

"He shall be great and shall be called the Son of the Highest: and the Lord God shall give unto Him the throne of His father David: and He shall reign over the House of Jacob forever; and of His kingdom there shall be no end."

Messiah? High Priest Says 'No Sign Here'

JERUSALEM — If the long-prophecied "Messiah" has come to the Jews, the religious leader in Solomon's Temple has received no sign this morning.

The high priest retired to his inner room for daily rites as usual.

An attache of his office, a priest of lower order, told the multitude that thronged the gates to go home.

"We have received no sign here," he told the clamoring crowd. "Would not we, who keep the law of Moses and the scrolls in the Temple, be the first to know? The time for fulfillment is not yet. There is peace in the land. Jews are no longer in bondage. Return to your homes and forget this fanciful story told by the shepherds."

The excitement stemmed from rumors that certain shepherds had seen "angels", and had followed a "bright star" to find a newborn babe in a manger. The mother, Mary, is claimed to have been a virgin.

A scribe from the temple said it is written in the Holy Scrolls by a long-dead prophet of the Jews: "Therefore the Lord Himself shall give you a sign. Behold, a virgin shall conceive and bear a son and shall call his name Immanuel."

The number of the writing is Isaiah 7:14, the scribe said.

He added that there are many writings of prophets to indicate that the child is to be of the house of King David. These writings are cherished in the hearts of the people, he said.

Joseph, the husband of Mary, the mother of the babe born in the stable near the inn last night, claims to be of this line. Mary also is said to be of David's house.

A very old priest at the Temple, Simeon, lamented that he was unable to make the journey to Bethlehem himself to see the child. He claims to have had a vision in which the Lord told him he would see the Messiah before he died.

"When they bring the child to the temple for circumcision in seven days, I shall see him and know," he said.

In the women's quarters at the Temple, a priestess of great years, Anna, also expressed a desire to see the child.

The younger priests scoffed, saying: "They are old and of wandering minds. Pay them no heed."

Sea Of Galilee Marks Explained

GALILEE — The strange markings in the sand along the Sea of Galilee are no longer a mystery.

They are pictures of fish.

Fishermen reported seeing symbols of what might be a new cult imprinted in the sand.

One morning two small boys, sons of a fisherman, were seen prodding the shore with sticks as they played.

"We're making pictures of fish," they said.

Their names were Simon, called Peter, and John.

'OTHERS SAW IT'

Young Shepherd Tells Of Angels' Appearance

BETHLEHEM—Angels appeared over a group of shepherds near here during the night, a young shepherd reported today.

He said they spoke of the birth of "a Savior, which is Christ the Lord."

LEVI
Young shepherd says he and others saw angels in sky.

The shepherd is Levi, son of Ezra. He lives outside Bethlehem and he reported that the angels appeared there to tell of a child being born there in the City of David.

The youth said a multitude of angels appeared in the sky over him and other shepherds who were tending their flocks. He told of the angels singing.

The apparition disappeared after one angel told of the birth of a Savior.

The 17-year-old shepherd said the angels spoke of the birth occurring in a manger. (That might be considered a reference to the birth of the child Jesus in the cave beneath the inn in Bethlehem. That birth occurred in a stable where the inn's small animals are kept.)

Levi said the other shepherds departed at once to seek the Savior of whom the angel had spoken.

Levi, who was left to tend the flocks, said early today he had not received word of their search.

There were no reports from any Bethlehem townspeople of the appearance of an angel.

Obviously excited over the event, Levi said he was convinced that "the child (of which the angel spoke) is truly the Messiah."

He added there was also no doubt in the minds of any of the other shepherds who saw the appearance of the angels.

Rich Cargo Lost In Sea Disaster

ROME — A cargo of silks, spices and brass work from India was reported lost today by Julia Marciana Metelli, widow of Senator Agrippina Lucus Metelli.

Mrs. Metelli said word has just reached her from Alexandria that the Ship Fortuna was lost in heavy seas on the eastern shores of the Cape of Good Hope.

Antonia Brutus Livie, captain of the Fortuna's sister ship Legend, said all hands were lost and the ship broke up on rocks in a heavy gale in June.

Disappointment was expressed by Mrs. Metelli over the loss of what she described as "the most elegant silks ever seen here."

"Two years ago," she said, "I had ordered several hundred bolts of exquisite fabrics. They would have made perfectly beautiful togas for my friends.

"Some had gold and silver threads interwoven with the silk. They'd be so much more pleasant in the summer than our usual woolen togas."

Also lost along with the fabrics were several boxes of ivory, silver and gold hair pins. Most were mounted with precious stones.

LINK WITH 'MESSIAH'?

Temple Priest Tells Of Pair Of 'Miracles'

JUDA — An elderly priest here claims two "miracles" came to him during the past year.

Struck mute for several months, he is now able to speak fluently, with no recurrence of the affliction.

The return of his speech was simultaneous with the birth of his son, John, also regarded as a miracle.

A strong, healthy child, the boy was born long after Zacharias and his middle-aged wife, Elizabeth, had given up hope of having a baby.

"For many years we prayed for a son," Zacharias said. "I served in the Temple and both my wife and I kept close to the Lord. Yet for some reason our prayers went unanswered."

When Zacharias learned that at last he was to have a child, he was literally struck dumb.

"I was burning incense in the Temple, according to the law," he said. "When the angel appeared and told me I was to have a son, John, who would lead many to turn to the Lord, their God.

"I thought the years were fogging my brain, increased by the smoke from the incense.

"I scoffed, I'm afraid.

"It's hard to believe, but from that moment I could utter not a sound until the birth of my son.

"When he was born my speech returned and my rejoicing was heard to the heavens."

Zacharias admitted knowing Mary, the mother of the babe born in the stable at Bethlehem last night.

"She is a cousin of my wife," he said. "She came to our house for a visit when she learned Elizabeth was to have a son. Although only betrothed to Joseph at the time, Mary was already with child. She came to Elizabeth for comfort.

"It's a strange thing, very strange," mused Zacharias. "I would swear at the altar of the Lord that Mary is a virgin.

"It may be that I really heard the words of the angel that day as I burned the incense.

"Perhaps my son, John, indeed is the herald of the Messiah."

At one Christmas the front page was made to look like it had been published the day Christ was born. A regular front page followed. Reporter Dick Larsen wrote the stories and did the art work

THE HOME EDITION

Tammie Bakker says Watkins was financial adviser
— *See story on page 54*

Blustery
(Watkins' windiness)
Highs: Every night
Lows: Every Morning

THE WENATCHEE WORLD

Published in the Apple Capital of the World and the Buckle of the Power Belt of the Great Northwest
Wenatchee, WA 98801

Saturday
Sept. 19, 1987
83rd year, No. 68

35¢

Watkins loss minor, happy publisher says

The Wenatchee business community was saddened today, well, not the whole day, maybe just an hour or so or probably just a few minutes, to learn that Jack Watkins had retired at The Wenatchee World as general manager.

He was a sucker to deal with, merchants reported.

Mildewed records show that Watkins worked an occupied a desk at the newspaper for 36 years. He was controller until things got out of control, Publisher Wilfred Woods reported.

After that Woods put him in a vacant room not used for anything else and gave him the harmless title of general manager. That job required very little skill, had little authority, and was most apt to keep him out of trouble.

Asked to analyze Watkins' departure, Woods said:

"The loss will be minimal. I expect profits to rise sharply, almost immediately."

The publisher made it clear that the remodeling of the World building was not done to fumigate the place after Watkins leaves or to find out where he has hidden part of his loot from the World profit sharing fund.

Wotkins' biography shows that he was graduated from Weatherwax High School in Aberdeen in 1940. There he was a thespian always seeking roles that required a lot of smooching. He was known as "Hotlips" Watkins in those days.

He was a member of the high school golf team which is best remembered for having to stop league play in mid-season because it ran out of funds to replace golf balls Watkins lost in the rough.

Upon graduation Wutkins entered the U.S. Air Force causing World

War to be extended several months because he couldn't make it to his departing plane on time or was playing poker at strategic times when he should have been on the front line. Earlier he had tried to enter the Navy but he got seasick in the recruiting office.

Watkin graduated from Pitiful State with a degree in hog-calling. He subsequently won a Northwest competition with a decibel reading of 150. Associates of Watkins report he exceeded that high peak quite often in dealing with fellow employees. In 1948 he managed to graduate from the U. of W. and get his CPA rating but not without having bribed the license examiner.

In adult life he participated in numerous activities. He was a leader in the Boy Scout movement until parents forced him out because he made their children carry him up

steep portions of trails.

He belonged to the Applarians, which was appropriate because their uniforms of Pepto Bismol pink matched Watkin's complexion after a long night out. But he suffered some trying to keep up with floats at apple blossom festival time. For him it became the "grunt parade."

The departing employee was finance chairman of many organizations — Mission Ridge, the economic development association, the Kiwanis Club, various political campaigns and many civic groups. With the commissions he earned he is paying for his country club retirement bash.

Whatkins is a quiet-spoken individual who seldom raises his voice. He has a reserved, almost bashful manner in expressing himself. This personality trait has prompted Republicans to urge Whitkins not to

enter politics under their party label. So Watkins will become campaign manager for Gary Hart for he feels that the press has been hard on Hart.

The honored guest at a retirement party held at the Thunderbird Hotel and Wenatchee Golf and Country Club joined the business end of newspapering only after being frustrated joining the editorial side, a search of his records reveals.

He made an application to become photographer for the Wall Street Journal and medical writer for the Christian Science Monitor.

The last act Watkins performed for the newspaper was to officially order that no paper be published Monday, Sept. 21, in order that people will have two days to recuperate from extending him the great honor that is due him at the country club.

READY FOR HIS PARTY

Talking It Over
with Wilfred R. Woods

When I hired Jack Watkins in 1951 to help Warren Woods look after the World's books, I expected him to be a permanent member of the staff.

But here it is, only 1987, and he's decided to leave already.

I think he came to the conclusion that he'd never get those books straight anyway. So he might as well call it quits.

—FREE AT LAST!—

Watkins perfect hubby

Jack Watkins' wife, Marianne, was asked to express her opinion of

---

For the retirement of department heads and a publisher's anniversary phony front pages were issued to staff members.

Kathy survives quarter century with Wilf Woods

The highlight of the Eastern Washington social season is to take place tonight at the Fontanelle Club House.

Thirty couples are to pay tribute to the former Kathleen Kingman on the occasion of having survived 25 years as a wife to journalist Mr. Wilfred Woods.

In attendance will be the three irascible children, Rufus, Kara Sue and Gretchen, who are normal in every way except they take after father.

It could not be confirmed but it is reported that Mr. Woods has rearranged his busy schedule to attend the affair. He was due on the same date in Washington, D.C., Ocean Shores, New York, Malaga, San Francisco, Israel, Fairbanks and Mozambique.

A check of the Wenatchee Daily World files revealed that the Woods actually were married, contrary to present-day custom.

A clipping from a 1951 issue of the Wenatchee World reads, in part:

"Miss Kathleen Kingman, daughter of Mr. and Mrs. L. H. Kingman of Chelan, and Wilfred Woods, son of Mrs. Rufus Woods and the late Mr. Woods, exchanged marriage vows last Saturday afternoon in the Chelan Methodist Church.

"The lovely bride wore black, with sorrow about the loss of her freedom.

Several years after this photo was taken, this sweet, innocent child became the bride of Wilfred Woods, the only man available at the time. A long search by Miss Kingman failed to reveal any

Here's a graphic picture of the financial condition of the bridegroom immediately after the marriage. It was caused by him being paid what he was worth. The impoverished condition forc-

to be out playing hopscotch with the boys. Her frock was a miniature copy of the bride's dress, this giving Miss Kingman, a crafty shopper, a bargain in a two-for-the-price-of-one arrangement. She carried an old-fashioned bouquet of slightly wilted flowers, another bargain the bride was able to arrange, and a white tiara.

"Robert W. Woods of Wenatchee skipped duck hunting and attending a Husky football game to be his cousin's best man, and Richard G. Haley of Tacoma and Walter F. Hiltner of Mercer Island, ushered, they giving the best seats to those who tipped profusely.

"The Kingman house at Lakeside was decorated in a white and green motif for the wedding reception, the first time the place had been cleaned up in months.

"Mrs. Kingman received in a silvery taffeta gown with which she wore a rosebud corsage. Mrs. Woods was attired in blue lace with pink accessories and a rosebud corsage.

"Presiding were four sisters-in-law, Mesdames Howard Kingman, Elwyn Kingman, Richard Haley and Walter Hiltner. (The latter two had been smart enough to marry a prosperous candy manufacturer and a well-known scientist, instead of a journalist of

To show what the effect a war bomb striking Grand Coulee Dam might have in Wenatchee reporter Dick Larsen drew this sketch

An illustrated story was written about what it was like to be a blind man on a city street.

Japanese erected a huge sign to welcome Wenatchee Sister City friends

Governor John Spellman speaking and fireworks set off on top of the dam featured celebrating the 50th anniversary of the start of construction

A recreation highlight was flying high up attached to a parachute behind a boat on Lake Chelan

A chromium-plated crowbar intended for use in keeping public doors open was an Allied Dailies gift

Cameras in the courtroom came about in most states
after Washington put on a demonstration

"What's
this I hear
about you
retiring,
Hu?"

A photo of President Nixon telling editors at Disney
World he was not a crook became the cover of the
author's retirement program

Present publisher Wilfred Woods stands at the mike with the author at the celebration marking the 50th anniversary of the start of construction of the dam

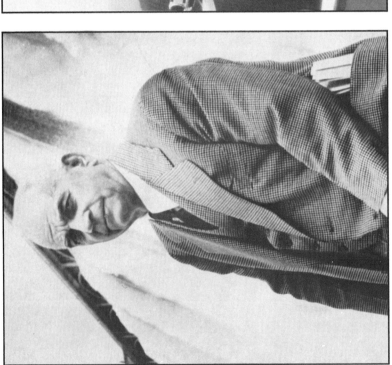

Rufus Woods, early-day Wenatchee World publisher, was a key figure in bringing about the Grand Coulee Dam

Milestones in Building the Project

The Bureau of Reclamation provided the following about important milestones in development of the Columbia Basin Project of which the Grand Coulee Dam was the principal feature.

1918 — **July 18:** The Wenatchee Daily World published the first newspaper story ever written about Grand Coulee Dam. Rufus Woods, publisher, reported on the idea for the project put forth by Ephrata lawyer Billy Clapp. For 18 years the paper was the only daily in the state to promote the dam.

1925 — Congress approved the Rivers and Harbors Act, authorizing the Corps of Engineers to submit a report on the Columbia River.

1932 — **January 11:** Bills were introduced into congress by Congressman Samuel B. Hill and Senators C. C. Dill and Wesley R. Jones for the construction, operation and maintenance of the Columbia Basin Project.

1933 — **April 26:** President Roosevelt advised that a low dam could be constructed for $60 million.

July 11: A contract was executed between the United States and State of Washington to utilize $377,000 appropriated by the State of Washington to begin construction of Grand Coulee Dam.

July 16: Governor Clarence T. Martin and Senator C. C. Dill marked the beginning of construcion of Grand Coulee Dam by driving the first stake and turning the first shovelful of dirt.

July 27: $63 million was allocated by the Federal Administration of Public Works for construction of the dam.

August 1: Frank A. Banks was appointed Construction Engineer of Grand Coulee Dam.

1934 — **June 18:** Bids were opened in Spokane for the construction of Grand Coulee Dam and its two powerplants. Two bids were submitted: MWAK, $29,339,301.50 and Six Companies, $34,555,582.

August 4: President Roosevelt visited Grand Coulee Dam.

December 13: First actual construction work on the dam began.

1935 — **June 5:** Secretary of Interior Harold Ickes signed Change Order No. 1 providing for the construction of a base for the ultimate high dam in lieu of original low dam.

August 30: Bill passed Congress authorizing the Grand Coulee Dam Project.

December 6: Washington's Governor Martin made the first official pour of concrete at Grand Coulee Dam.

1937 — **May 31:** Employment at the construction site reached 7,053.

July 28: About 1,000 landowners attended a Columbia Basin irrigation meeting.

October 2: President Roosevelt again visited the dam and addressed approximately 10,000 people.

December 10: Bids were opened for the completion of Grand Coulee Dam, the left powerhouse, and the foundation for the pumping plant. Interior Construction Company, consisting of M.W.A.K. Company and 7 other firms, was low with a bid of $34,442,240.

1938 — **February 7:** Consolidated Builders, Incorporated was awarded the contract for the completion of Grand Coulee Dam (Note: This is the same company referred to on December 10, 1937).
December 20: WPA participants began clearing for Lake Roosevelt.

1939 — **February 18:** Quincy Irrigation District was formed.
December 9: East Columbia Basin & South Columbia Basin Irrigations Districts were formed.

1941 — **March 22:** The first two generators at Grand Coulee Dam (two 10,000-kw service units) were placed in service.
December 31: The main structure of Grand Coulee Dam was completed.

1942 — **January 1:** Work was started on the right power house.
January 14: CBI completed their contract.
June 1: First water was spilled over the completed spillway at Grand Coulee Dam.

1943 — **March 31:** The Columbia Basin Commission was created by the Washington State Legislature.
May 8: Excavation was started on the Main Canal, marking the beginning of the construction phase of the irrigation portion of the project.
August 28: Construction work was begun on the Equalizing Reservoir's South Dam near Coulee City.
December 18: An agreement was signed with the National Park Service to establish and administer the Coulee Dam National Recreation Area on Lake Roosevelt.

1945 — **July 21:** 98% of the irrigation district voters accepted the proposed repayment contracts.
August 31: All three irrigation districts signed their payment contracts.

1946 — **March 20:** Morrison-Knudsen Construction Company was low bidder for the construction of the main canal.

1948 — **May 15:** First Project irrigation water (obtained by pumping from the Columbia River near Pasco) was delivered to Block 1.
June 12: The greatest flood level since 1894 reached its peak of 633,000 cfs at Grand Coulee Dam.
November 15: First drawing for Government-owned settlement units was held at Pasco to determine order of selection of applicants wishing to buy 15 available farm units in Block 1.

1949 — **May 20:** The first generating unit in Right Power house, R-1, was placed in service.

1950 — **May 11:** President Truman named and dedicated the reservoir behind Grand Coulee Dam, designating it Franklin D. Roosevelt Lake.

1951 — **June 14:** First irrigation pump in Coulee Dam Pumping Plant was started, lifting water 280 feet out of the Columbia River canyon for testing the irrigation system prior to the start of irrigation in 1952.

1952 — **March 18:** First water was released into the Main Canal from the Long Lake Reservoir and subsequently to the East Low and West Canals. This began the 1952 testing year and brought irrigation water from the main irrigation system to more than 65,000 irrigable acres.

May 29: Symbolic delivery of first irrigation water to the "Farm-in-a-Day" northeast of Moses Lake, was a feature of the Columbia Basin Water Festival.

July 10: An agreement was signed with the State of Washington for the administration for recreation purposes of the lands in the Potholes Reservoir area. Other reservoirs and waterways were covered by supplemental agreements made at later dates.

1955 — **September 6:** Land was transferred to the United States Bureau of Sports Fisheries and Wildlife for use as The Columbia National Wildlife Refuge.

1957 — **September 2:** The Columbia Basin Project Act was amended to allow a member of an immediate family to own a total of 320 acres instead of the previous limit of one farm unit or 160 acres.

1964 — **September 16:** The Canadian-U. S. Columbia River Treaty was ratified. The treaty calls for Canada to build three storage dams which will help to reduce fluctuation in the flow of the river throughout the year, thus reducing floods, and will enable 11 main Columbia River dams in the United States to produce an additional 2.8 million kilowatts of power. This treaty, therefore, increases the feasibility of a third powerhouse at Grand Coulee Dam.

1965 — **October 27:** The Columbia Basin Job Corps Conservation Center was opened at Larson Air Force Base.

1966 — **June 14:** President Lyndon B. Johnson signed Senate Bill S. 1761 authorizing construction of the Third Powerhouse and a supplemental authorization for $3,000,000 to begin the work. Although original plans called for a powerhouse with twelve 300-megawatt generators for a total cost of $390 million, manufacturers stated that generators twice this size would be economically feasible. Hence, on January 13, 1967, Secretary of the Interior Stewart Udall announced plans for six 600-megawatt generators in a powerhouse that would eventually hold 12 units.

1967 — **March:** Construction of facilities for the irrigation of Project lands reached the halfway mark. Of 1,029,000 acres authorized for development, a total of 502,091 irrigated acres had service available for agricultural production.

1975 — **October:** The Third Powerplant became operational with the first generator (Unit 19) on the line.

1983 — **July 15-17:** The 50th anniversary of the start of construction of Grand Coulee Dam was celebrated.

BOOK THREE
BUSY BUREAUCRAT

Goodbye You Construction Stiffs

In 1940, the construction of the Grand Coulee Dam was nearing completion. More and more of the news coverage was becoming routine. While I was still earning sufficient money, space-rate wise, I felt I was beginning to coast. The thrill was disappearing.

That year the University of Washington School of Journalism contacted me to ask if I'd be interested in joining the Fairbanks (Alaska) News-Miner as its senior reporter and replacement for a writer going into the Army. I was also to be interior Alaska correspondent for Life, Time and Fortune magazines.

Replying that I might be interested, I was induced to come to Seattle to be interviewed at the Washington Hotel by "Cap" Lathrop. He was known as "Mr. Alaska" for he owned coal mines up there along with the newspaper, a bowling alley, KFAR radio station, and a theatre.

While I was not definitely promised the job, Lathrop started sending me the paper so that I could become acquainted with it. It turned out that I was to receive it for eight years. This annoyed my wife, Martha, who saw that I made little use of the publication.

The journalism school had recommended me for the position.

The fact that I was leaving the damsite for Alaska became known around the project. This prompted the USBR to suggest that I go to work for it. I remember telling someone I was not interested, because "after two years in the government you're not worth a damn!"

The USBR countered with the suggestion that I take the civil service examination. I did on the basis that a job might open at some distant date, say the next depression . . . when I might need work. A mere two or three weeks later, I was told that I had passed, and that the job with the Bureau was mine. Not having heard anything definite from Fairbanks, I decided I'd join the government.

The date was April 21, 1941. The job title was Assistant Information Specialist, the Grade 11, and the pay $2,600 per annum.

I was well acquainted with the job to be done, having worked with Major Sol Hutton, the information officer, as a reporter.

I became acquainted with William E. Warne, the bureau's information officer in Washington, D.C. He was to play a major role in my life for the next 12 years.

My job consisted of writing news releases, issuing photo releases, and handling visitors of prominence. I enjoyed the work as much as I did the earlier reporting, and I worked just as hard, particularly after the Japanese bombed Pearl Harbor on December 7, 1941. This caused stringent restrictions to be put on visitations.

A Japanese Attack Feared at the Dam

When the Japanese bombed Pearl Harbor USBR higher-ups immediately figured that the Grand Coulee Dam would be a prime target for the enemy.

So at once they started planning protective measures to prevent sabotage, theft or military attack.

One of the first things done was to stop access to the dam and the powerhouse by visitors who came to the dam by the thousands each year.

Such access was limited to guests accompanied by a couple of top USBR officials, the chief guide, and the two-man public relations staff. Such restriction put a tremendous load on the latter's men — Major Hutton, and myself.

I spent many of my days off and weekends taking groups over the dam. I did so as late as 7 p.m. feeling it was good public relations for the Bureau. To escape the frequent requests to tour the project, I had to get out of town.

Other security measures taken included increasing the Federal Guard staff from 16 to up to 65 and having the Department of Justice deputize five of them as deputy United States marshals.

In addition, a 10-foot high metal fence was constructed around each end of the dam to prevent access to it and the powerhouse and a similar fence was installed around the two switchyards.

A heavy log boom was placed across the reservoir some 1,500 feet above the dam to prevent access by boat.

A U. S. Coast Guard base with up to 40 men and four boats was placed on the reservoir to enforce motorboat and navigation regulations and to assist in the protection of the dam and other government property.

Fifteen guard stations with glass windows on all sides were placed at appropriate locations, at designated gate entrances and other strategic points.

Floodlights were installed to aid the guards inspecting the areas and fencelines. Gooseneck flood lights were placed the full length of the upper side of the dam roadway.

The area behind the pumping plant was partially flooded to discourage entrance to the dam via pump discharge tunnels and to protect pump inlet pipes.

Concrete bulkheads were placed in the galleries (tunnelways) inside the dam at critical points to prevent flooding of the powerhouses. Metal and wooden doors equipped with strong locks were installed at all points of entry.

An alarm system was added that would immediately warn of any attempt to open doors of either structure.

An air-raid siren with a minimum sound capacity of two miles was placed in operation at the east end of the dam. More radio equipment and more guns were provided.

No employees were permitted to pass the guarded entrances to the dam, powerhouses and switchyards without new badges that carried a 1 by ½ inch photograph of themselves and their payroll number.

After the Japanese lost the war, the size of the guard staff was greatly reduced. It currently consists of 18 firefighters who double as security staff. But the men are provided with all sort of electronic surveillance instruments, such as cameras, motion detectors, and electronic door access devices.

All during the war, I felt an obligation to contribute to the war effort, so I got the USBR, on September 17, 1942, to give me permission to get a commission in the Navy. Frank Buell, later a good friend and president of the Farmers State Bank in Winthrop, sought to recruit me. However, the effort was not a success, because I had not been a U.S. citizen long enough — I was naturalized in Superior Court in Ephrata in 1937.

Buell and I then sought to have the commander of an aircraft carrier at sea to specifically ask for me as an intelligence officer. That failed because he had to go through the regular recruiting process. Subsequently, I wound up as a member of the Washington State Guard and the Virginia State Guard while stationed in Washington, D.C. One night we had a skirmish on the ground where the Battle of Bull Run had been fought.

My first official efficiency rating brought me a "Very Good." Six months later, in December 1942, I received a startling letter from Washington, D. C., marked "personal and confidential." It was signed by Goodrich W. Lineweaver, USBR Information Officer. He offered me a job with him as Chief of Publications at $3,200, which with overtime would amount to $3,900.

I received the letter at noon, and after talking the matter over with my wife, I accepted the appointment a couple of hours later. When Frank Banks, still the man in charge of the project, heard about my plan to leave, he felt that I was making a terrible mistake. Washington was a lousy place to work, he said. In contrast to later years, no one was leaving the field to go there.

On January 7, 1943, Banks telegraphed: "Consent to Blonk's transfer, but regret our loss."

The job amounted to being assistant to the chief of the information division with supervision over publication activities reduced by the war. I was to edit publications, write news articles, speeches, radio and motion picture continuity and general informational matter. I was also to handle administrative functions and do other public relations work.

We had just recently moved from Electric City to Coulee Dam, the engineers town, where we lived in a house closest to the dam which was air-conditioned all day via the cool air off the spillway waterfall. It had been a pleasant place to live with the temperature 11 degrees cooler in the yard than the yards of homes farther away from the water.

Martha took the move in stride as she also did two later moves which would occur in a short period of time. When we went to Washington, D. C., Julie was four years old.

We found a second-story apartment in Arlington, Virginia. Having no car we were dependent on bus transport. With humidity as high as it always is in Washington, D. C., these were uncomfortable rides. Sweat would come through my suit coat. When it rained on hot days, steam would rise from the sidewalks.

Lineweaver was a tremendous worker for whom hours meant nothing. I fit in well with his pattern. I have never worked as hard in my life as I did during my stay in the bureau's head office. Often we would eat in the cafeteria, late at night, with the custodial help.

I would leave early in the morning, before Julie was up, and return late at night, when she had gone to bed. I now regret not having spent more time with her and Martha while we were in D. C.

It turned out that we were to be back East only a little more than a year. Washington, D. C., was not happy with Major Hutton, who pretty much operated on his own, so it was decided I should be transferred back to Coulee to take charge effective January 1, 1944. Major Hutton was promoted to another position but nevertheless my taking charge of Information at Grand Coulee Dam made for an awkward situation. The pay was $4,000, the rating CAF11.

Martha, Julie, and I moved into a house on Ickes Street, situated in what earlier had been called Mason City, the contractors town.

The Cat in the Act

Shortly after returning to Coulee Dam from Washington, D. C., I learned that about a week before a cat had been used in correcting a fault in a 500-foot long drain pipe. No publicity had gone out on it. Feeling that my newsreel camera friends would be interested in a re-staging of the incident with resultant nation wide publicity, I contacted them. Charlie Perryman of MGM News was quite enthusiastic and got his New York office's O.K. to come over to Coulee Dam.

Because the original cat, a brownish one, had an evil temper, a more amiable one (also much better looking) was found. Deep inside one of the galleries of the dam, all sorts of lights were set up. The job of the cat was to pull a string through the tube. Then a rope would be tied to the string and after that a cable to the rope. By means of a sled attached to that cable workmen could quickly be hauled along the pipe so that a block of concrete that was partially obstructing that area could be jackhammered out.

With all the fuss and the bright lighting, the cat was reluctant to enter. A blast of compressed air was set off, and it quickly disappeared into the pipe. A friend named Charlie Zack had been stationed inside to stop the cat from going too far because we were going to be at the other end of the tube to show the cat coming out pulling the string behind it.

Zack was again moved inside the pipe, with the cat in front of him toward the exit. However, because of the lighting and noise, the cat refused to come out. I kept shouting "Charlie, bark like a dog" but he didn't. After five minutes of delay, Zack did bark and sure enough, the cat came out pulling the string behind it.

When I returned to my room in the dormitories, I received a phone call from Ray Paulsen of Paramount News. He said that his New York office had just decided that it wanted to film the scene. After all the trouble the first time, I was not anxious to repeat the procedure, but I did the following day.

167

Still pictures were sent out showing the pretty white cat looking into the camera from the opening in the pipe. Many papers, including the Washington Post, used the picture.

Working the Steno Pool a Whole Weekend

We were barely settled, when Washington called Banks to request that I be assigned on detail back there to write the war history of the USBR for Secretary of the Interior Harold Ickes, the famed curmudgeon. It turned out to be a mammoth undertaking that would separate me from my family for three months. I worked days and nights and weekends.

Most memorable was the weekend before a Monday afternoon deadline. Acting Reclamation Commissioner Warne asked me on a Friday if I would meet the deadline. I told him I was done, but couldn't possibly get the tremendous amount of material typed up. "Why not?" he asked. I told him it would take the whole bureau stenographic pool to do it. Thus, I became the only person ever to work the pool over a weekend. It was hot in the building and the girls walked about in their stocking feet. The document was delivered to the Secretary's office five minutes before the 5 p.m. deadline, August 1, 1944.

Acting Secretary of the Interior Michael Straus awarded me an "especially meritorious" promotion entailing a pay increase from $3,800 per annum to $4,000 per annum. My Washington, D. C., efficiency rating was "Excellent."

Straus wrote in praise "The assignment required a study of voluminous records of the USBR and its accomplishments under the war program, citing legal authorities, reviewing construction programs, priority procedures, agreements with cooperating agencies, etc., which in view of the extensive activities of the bureau, constituted an enormous undertaking."

I was glad the job was over. Staying at the YMCA for that long a period of time had been taxing, particularly nights when the radio announcer would say "The temperature is 90 degrees and the humidity is 90."

Enroute to Washington for this assignment I had been asked to meet Bill Warne in Boise, Idaho. The bureau was setting up a regional headquarters for the Pacific Northwest there. Warne suggested he and I take a walk one evening. He said he wanted me to become regional information officer. I objected, not wanting to move once again and to a town that I said "Probably doesn't even have an AP bureau."

But I gave in, telling Warne that he had been so good to me that I would do what he wanted. The job was to pay two grades more than the Coulee job, so moneywise, it was enticing. I had earlier objected to moving from Washington back to Coulee Dam even though it entailed a one grade payraise. The Boise job was rated CAF12, paying $4,600.

I assumed the position of Chief Branch of Information and Public Relations in Boise, on December 6, 1944. I had returned to Coulee Dam from Washington, D. C., early in March and had been granted deferment from military service, because it was felt that my role in government work was more important.

Aiding Truman With His Trip

While in Boise, I was once assigned to the White House.

It occurred when President Truman was about to make a train trip through the West in the fall of 1952. He would be making short speeches in whatever towns he stopped.

To make him sound knowledgeable about each community, his staff wanted a notebook prepared containing a paragraph or so of facts about each town so he could refer to it before stepping out into public view. I was assigned to prepare the portion involving the Pacific Northwest.

For instance, in coming into Boise past a lot of sagebrush I had him say how delightfull it was to come into this empire of green that reclamation brought about after so many miles through the dreary desert area.

While this was done for the White House, I was never actually in the place. I worked in a building adjacent to it.

Helping the People Celebrate

One of the most interesting and challenging of the duties that I performed for the Bureau of Reclamation was the planning of celebrations recognizing major achievements.

The two most satisfying celebrations were the start of irrigation pumping at the Grand Coulee Dam and the initial delivery of water to the Columbia Basin Project. Later while employed by the Wenatchee World I was involved with four more celebrations.

Bringing the Columbia Basin Water

The start-up of the world's largest irrigation pumps involved water being lifted 280 feet out of Lake Roosevelt into the feeder canal. It lead to the Grand Coulee, which was to be the project's equalizing reservoir. How to publicize this historic event nationally was the problem that confronted information men. Some sort of gimmick had to be dreamed up, of course.

This is what was done. The Columbia Basin Commission, a state group devoted to promotion of the project, at my suggestion, sent a letter to the governor of every state requesting that he send a gallon jug filled with water taken from some stream in his area. He was told that his state would benefit from the great irrigation development through the market for goods and supplies that the new irrigated empire and its environs would create. For instance, new farmers and new people in the towns that would spring up would buy cars from Michigan, clothing from New York made out of the cotton from southern states, insurance from Connecticut, etc.

Nearly every governor participated. The one from Delaware sent his jug accompanied by a note saying he had taken his water from the stream over which George Washington threw a dollar. The governor of Arizona, who was embroiled in a dispute with California over who had the water rights to the Colorado River, sent only half a jug. He said California had stolen the rest.

On celebration day, June 14, 1951, all the girls from the royal court of the Washington State Apple Blossom Festival were present at the head of the feeder canal where the program was to take place. Each had a jug of water at her side.

I was master of ceremonies of the program. It consisted of band music and speeches, including one by Commissioner of Reclamation Michael Straus. The climax of the affair was the broadcast of remarks by Secretary of the Interior Oscar Chapman in Washington, D. C., and his order to Grand Coulee Dam officials to "turn on the water."

Soon, a huge surge of water came up the 14-foot diameter pipes into view of the audience. At the same time, the colorfully clad young ladies emptied their jugs of water over the railing above the initial irrigation supply. The sight of almost 50 tiny streams of water falling 20 or more feet was spectacular. A LIFE magazine photographer was among the many shooting the event, and a radio broadcast carried the message to distant listeners.

Commemorative Stamp Issued

Between the first pumping and actual use of the water to Columbia Basin lands about a year later, there was a smaller celebration. It occured on May 15, 1952.

I had maneuvered the Post Office Department into issuing a commemorative stamp showing the Grand Coulee Dam. It was intended to commemorate the initial delivery of water to the Columbia Basin Project and the golden year of Federal Reclamation.

With so many requests for special stamps it took a powerful figure to get this done. U. S. Senator Warren G. Magnuson was the man I got to help. I made a trip to Washington, D. C., in connection with designing the stamp.

When the postal department released the stamps they were sold at all government post offices and also from little stands erected at Grand Coulee. They were sold individually and in blocks, also on envelopes with the Grand Coulee cancellation stamp on them.

There was a "First Day of Issue of the Commemorative Stamp" ceremony staged at the west vista point at the dam. An official program was printed with the stamp in black and white on it.

The Honorable E. W. Schwellenbach, chief justice of the State Supreme Court, presided. There was music by Grand Coulee and Coulee Dam High School bands and the Ephrata High School Glee Club and a solo. The address was given by Osborn E. Pearson, assistant postmaster general, who also presented albums to dignitaries.

The Washington office of the bureau was mighty pleased with what our crew of information men had accomplished.

Farm in a Day a Spectacle

The most pretentious and significant celebration of all those I arranged for the Bureau of Reclamation during my years in Boise occurred near Moses Lake. It commemorated the initial delivery of water provided by the Grand Coulee Dam to the Columbia Basin Project.

Nation-wide attention was focused on the USBR program through a sensational stunt which saw a 60-acre piece of sagebrush transformed into a completed farm, including a home, in a single day.

It took place on May 29, 1952.

The affair was the highlight of a series of community celebrations all over the Columbia Basin. As on other projects we of the bureau stayed in the background, but it was our crew of bureau information specialists including Eugene Nicolai and Barnery Molohon aided by Hubert H. Walter, head of the Columbia Basin Commission, which constituted the sparkplug that made it all come about. We formed a group called "Columbia Basin Celebration Inc." It was headed by Walter as president and myself as vice president.

A crowd of 50,000 was present at the "Farm-In-A-Day" site to witness the symbolic, long-awaited delivery of water to the first of a million acres of arid land. 100 to 125 cameras — more than had ever been seen at one time at a major news event by old-time hands among the news media — focussed on the land being cleared of sagebrush, leveled for irrigation by 18 huge, earth moving machines, corrugated to carry the water, crops being planted, a modern house being erected, the furniture being moved in, and Commissioner of Reclamation Michael Straus yielding a gold-plated shovel to turn the water into the farm ditch.

The history-making event, started at midnight with bombs bursting in the air, occurred on the eighth day of an 11-day "Columbia Basin Water Festival." Some 500 volunteers participated.

To attain utmost national attention, I dreamed up the idea of awarding the farm to the "nation's most worthy veteran" and having him selected by the Veterans of Foreign Wars. This allowed us to have press releases issued by every VFW post in the United States and for me to appear to "Welcome Travelers," a popular radio show originating in Chicago.

Walter and I made a trip to Hollywood and got the water festival queen on Queen For A Day, another hit radio show of the era. We also were involved with such national shows as "The Breakfast Club," "People are Funny," and "The National Farm and Home Hour."

The water festival was regarded an outstanding success. The Columbia Basin Commission spoke in glowing terms about what had been accomplished. In an official report on the celebration, it said:

"The event from the publicity standpoint has been one of the most successful in the history of the Pacific Northwest. The millions of dollars in national and world wide publicity which the event received will live for decades to come."

The fortunate veteran getting the farm was a 30-year old GI formerly from Marion, Kansas, by the name of Donald Dunn.

Deschutes Project Gets Water

The first community celebration heralding a significant USBR event that I had to arrange was the one that marked the initial delivery of water to the 50,000-acre Deschutes Project in Central Oregon. It took place on May 18, 1946.

I planted the seed for this gala event, as for others, with a local committee. Local participation is vital to the success of any community

171

event, but the publicity attendant to the affair here and elsewhere was always handled by the USBR.

To make the celebration of interest to more than just local people and attain maximum publicity for the federal reclamation project, it is necessary to tie it in closely with the national picture. Obviously, opening of a 50,000-acre project is not in itself of great significance nationally. However, creating 100,000 new farming opportunities in the West for war veterans and others was newsworthy.

The Deschutes celebration found all businesses in the area closed on the day of the event. It was declared a legal holiday for Central Oregon and high ranking officials, including the governor, were present. A morning pageant was staged to tell the story of how the project came about, followed in the afternoon by the highlight of the occasion — water being turned on and being diverted onto a farm by old-timers.

The ceremonies were covered by two newsreel cameramen and broadcast over a 22-station Mutual Radio Network, and the development was saluted on the National Farm and Home Hour of the National Broadcasting Co. Numerous local radio stations in Oregon also covered the event.

Tieton Project Pays Off

A less pretentious celebration that required some imagination, occurred in Yakima in 1947. We called the affair the "Tieton Pay-off Party." The excuse for it was that the Tieton Division of the Yakima Project had become the first irrigation district to pay off its construction cost obligation under the Federal Reclamation program.

The goal was to draw national attention to this important aspect of the USBR activities.

Through the organization of a local committee the presence of the Secretary of the Interior, Julius Krug, was arranged. He arrived mid-morning and was taken to the Wapato Long House, where the Yakima tribe made him an honorary chief called: "Chief Bring the Water." They wanted to call him "Chief Always Up in the Air," because he traveled by airplane so much. I talked them out of that title, fearing columnists in Washington, D. C., would use the occasion to make fun of him.

For the celebration, Yakima was decorated with flags and window displays on Federal Reclamation and workers were given time off to see Mr. Krug go by, in a convertible, with Governor Walgren by his side. After a luncheon, the Secretary was given a two-hour tour of the project during which time schoolchildren stood along the roadside and greeted him with banners. That was followed by a big banquet and a mass meeting in the towns' largest theatre. Widespread publicity through newspapers and radio resulted from the celebration.

State attention had been drawn to the affair by the governor declaring "Reclamation Week." National publicity was gained in two ways. U. S. Senators Harry Cain and Warren G. Magnuson presented President Harry Truman with a box of Tieton Delicious apples and the Washington delegation put on the desk of every congressman a Tieton apple around which was a special wrapper explaining the benefits of Federal Reclama-

172

tion. Pictures of the presentation to President Truman were used nationally.

Hungry Horse Project Celebrates Twice

Twice celebrations involved the Hungry Horse Dam in Northwest Montana.

The first one, on July 10, 1948, heralded the start of construction of the big power dam situated on a tributary to the Columbia River. Working with local people, Jack Criswell, project information officer, and I arranged for a dynamite blast to go off. An ordinary explosion would not do because it would simply lift up the rock. So black powder was spread over the rocky hillside. When the powder was ignited, by Montana Governor Sam C. Ford pulling a switch, a huge yellow flame shot skywards. It made a beautiful picture for the photographers.

Present for the occasion were the Commissioner of Reclamation Straus; Chief Information Officer Warne, Blackfoot Indians, and many others.

In the fall of 1952, the project was ready to produce its first power. That brought out President Truman and his daughter, Margaret, to dedicate the dam. They came by train. That mode of transportation allowed the popular Truman to make rear platform speeches for the Democratic candidate for the presidency, Adlai Stevenson, as he traveled throughout the country. The train's end had the sign, "Vote for Stevenson and Sparkman" prominently displayed.

What happened on presidential visits is that about 10 days before the celebration, two Secret Service men came out to check arrangements. I learned that you cannot have the President speak in a cul-de-sac, from which his car could not readily get out. Nor can you put him below an overhang, such as a cliff, from which he could possibly be shot at.

Much detail is involved in these visitations. For instance, you have to have a nail on the front of the speakers' stand on which the Presidential seal can be displayed. Any luncheon in the plan must be checked as to where the food is to be prepared.

On the actual day of the festivities you are joined by many more Secret Service men. You never really know how many. They are particularly anxious about any "crackpots" being present.

In connection with the Hungry Horse celebration, a parade was to be held in Kalispell. In such, the car that carries the President has to be preceded by a car of Secret Service personnel. These men insisted that someone acquainted with the town and the festivities should ride in the car with them so I wound up preceding President Harry Truman down the main street of Kalispell.

As a publicity stunt, we arranged for two hard hats to be prepared for the honored guests. One read "Harry," and the other "Margaret." Each had a sketch of a hungry horse on it. The President put on the hat immediately, but his daughter hesitated, apparently not wanting to mess up her hairdo. When Truman said "Margaret, you put that on!" she quickly did.

When Criswell and I were brought up to Truman's car, he thanked us both. Photographs of this incident are very precious to me.

173

The President was popular with the working press who had accompanied him. I found this out first hand on riding to Spokane on the train. The President wandered through the cars to talk to reporters and almost joined one group at a game of poker.

Truman Dedicates Grand Coulee Dam

One of the major jobs while I was stationed in Boise was to organize the program for the dedication of Grand Coulee Dam and Lake Roosevelt in 1950. President Truman was to be the honored guest. While President Roosevelt had preceded Truman to the project on two other occasions, those visits were not dedications.

In planning for major events, it has always been my practice to put assignments to others in writing. This prevented anyone from saying that they hadn't been told what to do. I would up with an eight-page, single-spaced list of jobs that were to be done.

It included having Construction Engineer Banks check the lapel of the suit coat that he planned to wear to see if it had a hole in it. I did not want President Truman to have any problem in pinning on Banks the Distinguished Service Award that was to be presented to him.

As usual, I was joined by two Secret Service men 10 days before the dedication date. They only became excited once. That was when a sub-contractor working at Coulee City telegraphed the President to ask him to have breakfast with him. As I said earlier, the agents were always concerned with people showing unusual behavior.

The ceremony was to be held in Mead Circle of Mason City, now called Coulee Dam. A grandstand to hold 150 people had to be built, for a large number of distinguished guests were to be honored by being allowed to sit with the President. A luncheon was to be served in a gymnasium at the Circle. I remember that Mrs. Banks was in charge of it and she kept asking me if I felt that the menu was alright. I kept telling her she was better qualified to make that decision than I was. Health Department clearance had to be gotten because having meals served by other than commercial places was frowned upon. Ham or desserts (among other foods) that were left out in the open could be contaminated.

About 8,000 people were there for the ceremony. The grandstand had been roped off. Only invited guests were permitted to pass through the ropes, which had been ordered by the Secret Service.

The program was to be a two-part affair with the dignitaries being introduced to the crowd before the President was to appear. In order to make the introductions as meaningful as possible, as co-master of ceremonies, I had prepared a card for each person on which was listed something of interest about him or her. As an individual came through the entryway to the grandstand his name would be checked and a Boy Scout would bring to the public address system the card describing him or her. The guest would then get something more than "Mr. Tom Jones of the So and So Company."

A Seattle man, who thought he was important, tried to force his way through the ropes. A Secret Service man glanced over at me, and, when I shook my head to denote that he was not an invited guest, they hustled him out, promptly.

When President Truman arrived by motorcade with his party of VIP's, I turned the program over to Secretary of the Interior Oscar Chapman, who served as master of ceremonies from then on.

A luncheon followed in the high school gym which was located behind the grandstand. There Mr. Truman presented Mr. Banks with his award.

I did not get to shake hands with the President as I had done earlier at Hungry Horse.

The affair had gone off without a hitch despite the many things that had to be planned. I was again recommended for a superior accomplishment award. I turned it down on the basis that many other people had also contributed to the success of the event.

Truman a Handy Man at the Dam

Two years earlier President Harry Truman had also made his presence felt at the damsite, by telephone.

He was a key figure in reducing the devastating impact of the monstrous flood of the Columbia River.

Involved in the incident was Al Kelso, the first mayor of Elmer City, a settlement of 200 people situated about a mile downstream from the face of the dam. The time was June, 1948. The Columbia River, due to fast melting of snows and rain, has reached the second highest crest in its history exceeded only one in 1893.

Kelso saw his little town partly covered by the flood. Three houses were floating away and another five were threatened. Kelso tried to get equipment from the Bureau of Reclamation and the Bureau of Indian Affairs but was told these federal agencies had no authority to loan him items.

So Kelso called the White House where he told an aide to Truman that there was a "terrible flood" hitting his town. No sooner had he gotten the words out of his mouth when he heard: "This is the President." Kelso told Truman that he could not obtain the 20,000 to 30,000 sandbags and equipment that he needed from the two federal agencies in his area because they said they did not have the authority to loan them.

The President cussed and told Kelso he'd get the authority, just stick by the phone because he'd call him back. Kelso later reported that he told Truman that he might have trouble getting him back, that he was on a 10-party line and part of it consisted of a barbed wire fence as a circuit. "Let me worry about that," the President replied. In "no longer than 20 minutes," he called back to report he'd contacted the Department of the Interior and the Air Force and they would send the bags and equipment. They did.

Five houses were tied down, lots of bags placed, and much earth moved around to keep the river under control. A headrigger on the project named "Harry" Nelson was in charge of the effort.

The water of the river came up to the porchlight of one house. It is now an apartment located at a higher portion of the shore.

Kelso was "dumbfounded' during the President's visit two years later to find he remembered his name when seated nearby him at the banquet.

Kelso was mayor of Elmer City for five years. The first year of that public service still sticks in his memory.

He said "When you incorporate you have no money. People donated their services, such as the city clerk, and they paid their own expenses, for such items as stamps and envelopes. We had a city marshal and he didn't get paid except from fines. And there were not many of those as people didn't drive very fast because the roads were poor."

On Stage with Eisenhower

Besides Truman and F.D.R. I also came in contact with Nixon and Kennedy and I saw General Dwight Eisenhower when I was on detail in Washington, D. C. I was coming out of the Department of Interior building when I noticed a large crowd across the street at Constitution Hall.

I asked someone what was taking place. I was told it was a charity program featuring Helen Hayes and that General Eisenhower would be in the audience.

I mingled in the crowd at the entrance and was asked for a ticket. I put on an act of great surprise that one needed a ticket! I hung around and soon the ticket-taker let me in.

During intermission it was announced that Miss Hayes and the President would be backstage to meet guests. I, crustily, joined the group to see the famous individuals there.

I didn't loiter long; I saw Eisenhower close-up and that was all I intended to do.

A Day of Near Disaster

While information officer in Boise I got involved in a minor way with a near disaster at Grand Coulee Dam. I had to bring pressure on skittish project officials who were not fully cooperating with Murray Morgan, a prominent writer, who wanted to write a book about the sensational incident.

On March 14, 1952, an accident in the spillway section of the dam resulted in a huge volume of water flooding the lower parts of both powerhouses.

For a time major industries in the Northwest using Coulee power were partially shut down as one after another of the 108,000-kilowatt generators had to be taken off the line because the water threatened to intermingle with the oil in the bearings of the turbine.

At the peak of the trouble, as more and more of the water engulfed the powerhouses, nearly half of the 18 generators were shut down to prevent their being damaged at a cost of millions of dollars.

What happened is that three men employed in the left powerhouse were sent into the dam to close gates in outlet tubes, each 8½ feet in diameter. Each tube had an upstream gate and a downstream gate. The men were to close the upstream gate in connection with painting the insides of the tubes.

At one of the tubes the upstream gate had been opened by error

176

allowing water to flow into the upper part of the tube above the downstream gate. It was under high pressure because of the great body of water in Lake Roosevelt above it. What wasn't known to the men was that a manhole in the tube had been accidentally left open.

Thus, the minute the water entered the tube it gushed out of the manhole and soon reached to the top of the gallery, or tunnelway, where the gates were operated.

This was shortly after 10:30.

The escaping icy water rose up the legs of the startled trio as they sought to meet the crisis. They finally had to give up and they made their way out of the dam itself, after having alerted the powerplant people that there was trouble in the dam, the exact cause of which they did not know.

A small, swift-flowing river formed in the tunnel, headed toward both the left and right powerhouses.

The water cascaded down spiral steel staircases and elevator shafts, down a couple hundred feet or so to the bedrock gallery. There it began a steady rise.

A number of key men rushed out of the powerplant into the dam to see what was happening. Several frustrating incidents occurred because gates installed inside the dam as safety precautions against possible saboteurs were locked and keys not readily available. This delayed reaching the trouble spot.

The USBR men faced a torrent of water as they sought their way up the concrete tunnelway to the gates. The nearer they came to the gate the higher and swifter the water became. They were waist-deep in the "water," chilled to the bone and out of breath.

They tried to open the control box for one of the gates which they figured was spewing out the deluge, but the key didn't work and there was no crowbar handy to break it open. In despair the men returned to the left powerhouse.

Meanwhile water began pouring into the powerhouse. Ultimately it reached the turbine pits, where it was feared the water would mix with the hundreds gallons of oil lubricating the bearings.

Key powerhouse people faced the decision as to whether to shut down the powerplant, with devastating effect on power use throughout the Northwest, or to let the turbine-generators run until instruments definitely showed the bearings were heating up. The latter plan was resorted to.

Some of the powerhouse crews began to build improvised dikes in strategic places. They threw plywood clothes lockers into certain places and erected a plywood barrier in a tunnelway. It subsequently collapsed under the pressure of the growing volume of water and then a real flood reached the powerhouse.

On the other side of the river the water also was cascading into that powerhouse.

In the right powerhouse, operator John Picken had been among the first to hear a sound of water and cool air coming into his area.

He advised operator Jack Denny and checked further to discover water about an inch deep coming towards him. The two men, who later operated at Chief Joseph Dam, were to find themselves in 15 to 16 inches of water.

The two and other operators were watching their control boards to keep track of what was happening to the various generators. They knew that if all the power units had to be shut off there wouldn't be any power to close the gate in the tube from which the water was cascading.

As extreme danger neared at the power units other men entered the dam. They made their way up the tunnelways. At times they were forced against the wall by the torrent, hardly able to move forward. Again they couldn't reach the gate they wanted.

Others joined in the rescue effort. Among them was the late Norm Holmdahl. Deep inside the dam he learned from a painter that a manhole cover had been left open in one tube. That pin-pointed the source of the trouble.

The water was flowing faster than ever as Holmdahl and Dan McGregor sought to reach the control box that would close the gate. As they neared it they were almost swept away by the strength of the rushing water. The men smashed the cover off the box and Holmdahl pushed the right button.

Very quickly the flood began slackening. The gate was closing.

When the water was finally shut off the lake water had been pouring through the manhole for more then two hours.

But the threat in the powerhouse continued for the water kept draining into the buildings. About half of the 18 turbines were running under water and the bearings were overheating.

About noon — before the water had been shut off — the first of the generators in the left powerhouse was about to be pulled off the line. Shortly afterwards the turn-off switch was thrown for the first of the nine in the right powerhouse.

To replace the Grand Coulee output that might all be lost Northwest, steam plants were started up. Bonneville Power Administration officials ordered cuts to industries, a sudden danger particularly to aluminum-producing ones where a power shutdown can cause great damage.

Through the Northwest there was consternation among power distributors and major users.

Radio stations asked people to cut power use to a minimum.

Commercial and industrial plants were requested to cut their loads to the fullest extent possible without damaging equipment permanently.

A lot or all power was cut off for industrial plants in Spokane, including the Kaiser Aluminum Co.'s rolling and milling plant. Kaiser's Aluminum reduction plant was also cut off.

Approximately four hours after the flood began the water was under control and enough steam plants were in production so that the BPA could let the industries start up again. By early evening all the Grand Coulee units were back in production.

During the night hours, when power demands are down, it was possible to take the generators off the line one at a time and inspect them for possible damage. No serious damage had been done.

The AP reported no estimate was officially made of water that entered the dam. But it was about 75 feet deep in the bottom of the left powerhouse.

In the aftermath one man was transferred to another project because of the error he reportedly made, and nine persons were given medals.

They were: Norm Holmdahl, Don McGregor, Milton Berg, John Bates, Harold Parmenter, Jim Slaughter, Perry Crandall, James Green and Roy Peterman.

Author Morgan was allowed to get all the facts and subsequently told about the near disaster in his book "The Dam."

He commented on the opinion of some powerhouse workers as to who should have been regarded as heroes in the near disaster and on the punishment meted out to Vick Chrishman, the man blamed for the accident:

"A few felt the blame had not been passed out evenly. Chrishman's friends feel he was treated too harshly. 'So he made a mistake,' one man said.

" 'So what? These other guys never make any mistakes? Who designed the dam so water would drain into powerhouses, huh? Who figured out it was smart to have all the doors locked against saboteurs so we couldn't get around when there's an honest accident? Who set up the procedures and forgot to have a check on the manholes. Who?'

" 'After all,' said one of the World War II veterans 'there was a glorious snafu and somebody had to catch hell. That's the way it is with an organization. You got to have one or two fellows absorb the blame so the organization itself does not look bad. That's how things worked. Carter gets bounced and everybody else gets a medal.'

"The distribution of medals by the Bureau of Reclamation to the heroes of the flood stirred as much feelings at Coulee Dam as the flood itself.

"No one objected to the decoration of the heroes. But who were the heroes? "Holmdahl obviously, and Berg and McGregor — they had turned the water off? But what of those tried and failed? And what of the ones who had fought the flood with brooms in the turbine pits. What of Ray Seely who had put up the barricade around the control panel and governors?"

Getting Landowners to Sign Contract

Before the government could build the facilities needed to irrigate Columbia Basin lands, the landowners had to agree to sign a contract saying they would return that part of the investment that was within their ability to repay. The rest could come from power revenues. That was the Federal law.

The state Columbia Basin Commission undertook the big task of getting what was called "recordable contracts" signed in 1937. The USBR did not wish to be in the role of promoting the project.

The commission chose an excellent man to get the job done. He was Charles Cone, superintendent of Chelan County schools and the father of a son of the same name who became a Chelan County Superior Court Judge. I was assigned to join Mr. Cone at his Spokane office at times.

Cone got out significant material about the contract and arranged for numerous meetings in the basin and elsewhere in the state where absent landowners lived. One meeting drew a thousand people.

While at Boise, I announced the winners of homesteads on the Minidoka and Yakima projects at public gatherings.

On the Stage in Las Vegas, etc.

Probably the most exciting and unusual experience of my days as Regional Information Officer at Boise, was escorting three members of the House Subcommittee on Interior Appropriations throughout the West. The year was 1948.

It started with a phone call from the Commissioner's office in Washington, D. C., to Regional Director Robert Newell in Boise. Two bureau men had started the trip by driving the party to Spokane, but the Congressmen — Ben Jensen of Iowa, Dr. Ivor Fenton of Pennsylvania, and George Schwabe of Oklahoma — had taken a dislike to the driver from Washington, D. C. It was later reported that he drove the car wearing white gloves, refused to stay at the same hotel as the Congressmen, and had feminine ways.

Newell was asked if I could be spared to replace the driver. The answer was yes, so I joined the party at the Davenport Hotel in Spokane. I was to drive one of the big Buicks and Ralph Williams, a regional officer from Denver, was to drive the other.

It proved to be a strenuous trip that took us through Washington, Oregon, California, and other Pacific Southwest areas. Enroute, the Congressmen were entertained at breakfasts, luncheons and dinners in various towns as local interests made the pitch for their project appropriations. We were well fed, thick steaks being served quite often.

The Congressmen were an amiable, hard-working lot, who made no great demands. Because of the earlier experience with the other driver, I made it a point to be a good fellow. It was important that no baggage was left behind, so Williams and I always loaded the bags in the trunks in the same spots, so it would be readily apparent if one were missing.

Exchange of humor was frequent. For instance, on entering California from Oregon it was apparent that we were to undergo an agricultural inspection. I mumbled something about Californians being so high and mighty when the truth was that Washington crops were probably cleaner, insect-wise, than those in their state.

As I stopped the car, an inspector asked me to open the trunk. He then pointed to a bag that he wanted opened. It was my own. He had me take a lot out of it and he then proceeded to further "mess up" my personal belongings.

When we got back into the car, I further cussed the Californians. That brought a shout of laughter. It turned out that one of the Congressmen had told the inspector to "give him the works."

I attempted to get even by trying to get Rep. Jensen to eat a green olive off the trees. I said that they were delicious. He didn't take the bite. Untreated olives taste like quinine.

When we reached Los Angeles — after many luscious meals — I asked the Congressmen what they would like to eat the night we were on our own for a change. One said "What I'd like is a hamburger and a malted milkshake." Another added "Me, too."

Then I sought to determine what they'd like to do for entertainment during the evening. "What is there to do?" one asked. I suggested they might like to see the stage show "The Drunkard,"which had been playing in Los Angeles for 26 years. I advised everyone that you drank beer, ate peanuts, and hissed the villian.

It was agreed that we'd go there, if I could get tickets. I called the theatre and told the people there of the very distinctive group that wanted to see the show. When advised that this would be possible, I was asked to give the names of the party. I listed Congressman Jensen, Congressman Schwabe, Congressman Fenton, Williams, Blonk, and Bill DeErmand, (Jensen's secretary).

During the play we booed the villian, ate peanuts, drank some beer, and had a general good time.

After the fun, the M. C. conducted an "oleo" — an "after the show" festivity - during which he introduced people in the audience. He was uncanny in knowing where everyone was seated. After a few introductions, he said "We have seated over there — (pointing) — a most distinguished group from Washington, D. C. We have Congressman Jensen from Iowa, (Ben took a bow), Congressman Schwabe from Oklahoma, (another bow), Congressman Fenton from Pennsylvania, (another bow), and Congressman Blonk from Idaho!" I heard Rep. Fenton say "Oh, my God!" I sort of ducked down. Later on the M. C. mentioned several people from Caldwell, Idaho. They were seated in the balcony. When they stood up, he asked them if they knew Congressman Blonk? I could see them shaking their heads "no."

There were other stops of more than casual interest. We visited Yosemite National Park and Alcatraz. While at the prison, we got more than the usual visitors tour because Rep. Fenton was on the House Prisons Committee. Hardened criminals were pointed out to us, something that is not done for the usual visitor.

From Los Angeles, the two Buicks headed east toward Las Vegas. There in the "Flamingo Club," which was owned by the mobster, Bugsy Siegel, who incidentally was later murdered, the Congressmen became acquainted with a prominent contractor. He invited the party to be his guest at the nightly show. It was headed by singer Barry Wood.

The club was packed with several thousand people. After the dinner, Barry Wood began singing, a rendition called "When the Idle Poor Become the Idle Rich." This song greatly aroused Representative Jensen, who saw a Communist behind every bush.

The star's appearance had been preceded by a never-to-be-forgotten incident in which I participated. A member of a troupe of acrobats came to our table to ask the Boulder Dam information officer to join their group. When he wouldn't they asked me if I would. I did so as part of my role of being a "good fellow" for the Congressmen.

When I got on the stage with the acrobats, I was asked to lay flat on my back with my legs up in the air. It must have been a laughable sight. As I tried to straighten out my wrinkled down socks, I was told "Keep your knees bent." Then suddenly from across the stage a scantily-clad gal came somersaulting at me. I caught her with my feet. Soon another gal came whirling through the air, then another, and another, etc. All the while I was being told to keep my legs bent (I remember being concerned that I might get kicked in a sensitive area). The crowd roared with laughter. When I returned to our table, three gleeful Congressmen welcomed me.

This was not the last time my Las Vegas stage appearance would be mentioned.

When Rep. Jensen's committee had its formal appropriation hearings in Washington, D. C., he recited what had happened after first telling the committee secretary "This is off the record."

He ended with the statement "Mr. Commissioner, I want you to know that Mr. Blonk had not been drinking."

A report of the hearings of Jensen's Subcommittee on the Appropriations Bill for 1949 included laudatory comments about Williams and myself.

Representative Jensen said "I would like to say, on the record, that if Hubert Blonk and Ralph Williams are a sample of your information officers you have good men because they certainly gave the committee that traveled with them last fall a lot of information. It was all good information. They were well informed and right on the job every minute."

Mr. Strauss (Commissioner) "They are samples and I think they may be outstanding."

Mr. Jensen "I am inclined to think that you do not have all men that can come up to the qualifications of these two men."

Mr. Schwabe "I think that that is the unanimous opinion of the committee."

The trip was exciting but it was also strenuous. I ended up with nervous exhaustion. On getting back to Boise, I took a month off.

The assignment had another good side, too. I was presented a superior accomplishment award by the Commissioner. It cited "the extraordinary manner" in which I was said to have performed my duties as official escort on the trip, and it also cited contributions at the Hungry Horse celebration and the Tieton Pay-off Party.

Making a Film Was One Of The Final Tasks

One of the major tasks done in Boise was to produce a 30-minute motion picture entitled, "Columbia Frontier."

Ray Schrick of the Coulee Dam information staff wrote the script. Stan Rasmussen of the Boise office took the footage that we needed in conjunction with what had ben filmed earlier by construction progress for the engineers.

Rasmussen worked from my shooting script.

The filmmaking job took me to Washington, D. C., where the federal government's motion picture laboratory was situated.

There, motion picture experts showed the formation of the ice dam which blocked the Columbia River during the Ice Age. They drew an ice dam, and then, with the camera directly above the drawing, they continually scraped more and more of it away until there was none left. Each step was filmed showing the ice dam getting smaller and smaller.

Then by running the film in reverse, the dam was shown growing into full size.

We had no funds to make a musical score for the film, so we had to use leftover music fron other films. Surprisingly, this feature of the film is one of it's most outstanding ones.

The production was one the Columbia Broadcasting system used in its "Golden films" series. TV networks were hard up for films to fill its early TV programs. The film also won an award overseas.

"Columbia Frontier" can still be seen at the North Central Washington Museum in Wenatchee.

A "Screwball" Made Bowling Fun

Bureau of Reclamation days in Boise were not without recreation. The most popular was bowling.

A league made up of Department of Interior teams was formed in the late 1940's. I was named as its president. I immediately made "fun" the prime goal of play, not just winning the games. Our activities were described in the July, 1950 issue of "Bowling Magazine" in an article titled "Screwball." It read "Most bowlers use a hook ball, back-up ball, or a straight ball. In Boise, Idaho, one league makes good use of a screwball. He is Hu Blonk."

"Blonks' mission in life, he'll tell you, is to prevent bowlers from taking themselves too seriously. He'll go to any end to keep things on a high plane of tomfoolery.

"Blonk is president of the Bureau of Reclamation Bowling League, made up of 14 teams of the Department of the Interior. The circuit hasn't set the world on fire with bowling skill but, Blonk's boys have more fun than anybody.

"Through a plea for gags, published in Bowling Magazine, Blonk received a lot of ideas, all of which he used to needle his league bowlers. In return, other league officials throughout the country flooded him with requests for his own favorite horseplay ideas.

"Blonk is a 40-year-old former newspaperman now regional information officer for the Bureau of Reclamation, a federal agency which builds dams for irrigation and power production. He has headed his unusual bowling league since its start five years ago.

"Life in Blonk's league is never dull. One week a high-scoring bowler found his ball having a fondness for the gutter. He wound up with the low series. The league awards a weekly cash prize for this achievement. The next week, instead of simply being given the dough, this bowler found a large weather balloon floating above his alley. It was appropriately worded.

"Blonk likes to hear noise when the league is in action, and he has helped his men achieve the distinction of being the loudest bunch of bowlers in Boise by awarding a season's prize for the 'most enthusiastic bowler.' One year the prize was a hand-embroidered megaphone complete with pin-up girls.

"Weekly prizes were paid off in dozens of ways. One bowler won $8 from some 20 bowlers, and each man threw 40 pennies at his feet. Another found $5 stuffed inside a dozen boxes, the largest box was 3 by 4 feet in size.

"One winner got the weekly dollar bill for the high individual series. It was fastened securely with rubber cement to a board the same size of the dollar bill. He could not get the greenback off, but it made a good souvenir.

"Mysterious and insulting signs appear over teams battling one another in a particularly crucial series.

"One bowler received a gift of a pair of dark glasses on which a pattern of bowling balls had been painted...to help him see the maples on the alleys.

"Why all the monkey business? Blonk put it this way: 'When fellows in an organization begin to think that winning is the prime reason for bowling, instead of the good fellowship that it affords, the whole value of the sport is lost. In our league we try to keep everything good natured. I like to think we have succeeded. Our bowling league has helped provide for our government agency a closely knit group with a high morale and friendship toward one another. That's mighty important in any organization."

The photographs accompanying the article showed "Low-Point Pete" (a bowling pin decorated to look like a human figure) which was awarded to the captain of the team with the lowest score of the week. A bowler who had scored the seasons' highest average was given a $5 award. It was five silver dollars frozen in a 50-pound cake of ice.

A magazine called "All Stars Sports" also featured a story on the unusual stunts perpetrated. Entitled "Bowling for Fun," it mentions, in addition to several humorous incidents, the fact that Blonk conducts an airmail bowling tournament among Reclamation bowlers in offices throughout the West. The scores were all sent to him to evaluate. One year 115 teams competed for prizes totaling $300, the money provided by entry fees.

In the mid-80s, the tournament had been going for about 40 years.

Interest in the league was kept alive by a weekly mimeographed publication that I put out entitled "Pin Points." It contained all sorts of tidbits, announcements, scoring and other what nots. One time a bowling test was included. Bowlers had to pass it before being allowed to start the fall season. It contained such difficult questions as: A ball has how many holes? two, three, none, twelve, or one for each finger? The ball should be thrown: In dropkick fashion? with both hands? with fingers in the holes? overhand like in baseball?

Hells Canyon Dam Got Me Fired

My USBR career in Boise was dominated in the latter stages by what might be called "The Battle of Hells Canyon Dam."

It changed my life around completely.

I "bumped my head up against an anvil" again, to use the expression voiced by that professor at the outset of the battle of the Thursday Noon Club on the U. W. campus. The bumping consisted of losing a high paying job because I felt that the people were entitled to know the government's Hells Canyon Dam plans.

184

My adversary was the Idaho Power Company and the Idaho interests that it dominated; such as the Idaho Chamber of Commerce and the Boise Statesman and Congressman Hamer Budge.

The issue was whether to build two small, private power dams in the Hells Canyon stretch of the Snake River which formed the border between Idaho and Oregon, or whether to build a large, government storage dam.

Of course, the latter would produce much more power than two run-of-the-river plants because it would store excess summer flows for use in turning the generators during the winter.

But Idaho Power didn't want that fact explained to the people. So as information officer I became the focal point of attack because I consistently accepted invitations to speak. I felt that the people had the right to know what their government was planning so they could decide what course of action they preferred. The Regional Director was reluctant to take on such an adversary.

But to me the issue was fundamental — whether to be a coward and keep quiet, or to speak up for what I thought was right.

Over the course of several years, it was never possible to give the Idaho people the benefit of a debate in the controversy. Idaho Power spokesmen wouldn't agree to appear on the same platform with me. The company always insisted that I speak at one meeting and that they appear at a subsequent meeting. This protected them from the embarrassment of being questioned about the truth of any statements that they might make.

A graphic demonstration of this occurred when a Boise radio station asked that I debate the governor and the Attorney General. Aha! I thought, here is a chance to corner them about the many falsehoods that Idaho Power was uttering.

However, the confrontation was not to be. The station questioned me for 15 minutes, and, later, questioned the Governor and the Attorney General. Then, they put the pieces together for the program. They sought to outfox me in another way. The interviewer asked innocuous questions of me, not getting down to fundamentals. That made me suspicious about a put-up job being done on me, so I answered the harmless questions in a sentence or two, then drew in the basic facts that the listeners were entitled to know. That way I told the Hells Canyon story rather fully, but it was a frustrating experience.

The Idaho Power Company, as explained earlier, had control of the Boise Statesman. Therefore, its editorials were vitriolic. One time, they called me a "parasite," another time "un-American." However, I continued to speak up whenever an audience requested a USBR speaker.

My sin was explaining that Hells Canyon Dam was the necessary tool for fully developing that stretch of the Snake River. My facts were wholly based on engineering studies made by the the finest dam building organizations — the Bureau of Reclamation and the Corps of Engineers.

But for the vast curtain of silence that the Eastern-controlled Idaho Power Company dropped on Idaho, the people of that state would have been strongly in favor of this great multi-purpose development. So The Hells Canyon Dam would have been authorized. Now, two small dams sit in the river, meaning a tremendous amount of energy has been lost forever for the power-hungry Pacific Northwest.

The company sought to shut up anyone opposing its questionable proposal. When the Idaho Hells Canyon Association, which boosted the project, spoke in a weekly series over the radio station KDSH, the Idaho Power Company forced the association off the air.

Another example of the "Keep Idaho People Green" campaign fostered by the power company occurred when the Armed Forces asked the USBR of Reclamation to put up an exhibit showing the relation of resource development to defense of the Nation. A display was made to show the overall, region-wide, resource development aspect of the project. It stressed hydroelectric power for building planes, for the production of food from newly irrigated areas, and many other contributions. No mention was made of Hells Canyon Dam or public power.

Within an hour after the exhibit was placed in the Dufresne Motor Co. store window, the owner called up to demand that it be removed immediately. It seems that the firm sold trucks to the Idaho Power Company. It had objected to the display and threatened to cancel future orders.

The IPC exerted similar pressure on the bureau's regional Office, so that the engineers feared to answer requests for information from the public. My effort to get out an unbiased statement was opposed for fear of antagonizing the power company.

I was not speaking of promotional material or of an attack on the company, I was talking about statements as to the engineering and economic feasibility of Hells Canyon Dam without reference to any other plan. I was unalterably opposed to government informational specialists engaging in promotion of a governmental agencies or projects. I was just as strongly in favor of the government explaining to the people what it was planning to do when asked for such an explanation. For a government official to do otherwise is cowardly, shameful and definitely harmful to the American way of life, and I wanted no part of it.

But it cost me my job!

In 1953, the regional director received an order that the job I held was to be abolished — the standard governmental way of getting rid of someone. In December of the same year — after five months delay in putting the order into effect, because I was being considered for a foreign aid job in Iran — I left the Bureau of Reclamation. But not until I was offered a report-writing job in the planning division, a job I refused to accept, because I am a newspaper man at heart. I would have felt like a leech.

During the five-month period of uncertainty, I was asked to submit my record to a Salt Lake City advertising agency handling the account of the nation's sugar beet industry, consisting of 11 refineries. It was seeking a man to replace one who had failed at the public relations job. He had been paid $25,000 a year, a sizable salary in the 1950's. The total budget for the beet industry was a whopping $1,000,000 a year!

Immediately upon receipt of my career summary, the advertising agency contacted me to request that I come at once to Salt Lake City to meet with its people and the officials of the U and I Sugar Co., which had been assigned the task of finding a suitable public relations man.

After two days there, the people involved notified me that they were doing something unusual. They were not going to interview anyone else.

They wished to employ me subject to the approval of the industry's board of directors.

Subsequently, I was interviewed by the board in Denver, Colorado, and upon walking out of the session with the key figure in the Salt Lake City advertising agency, he said to me "You made a good appearance; you're in!" I had freely discussed Hells Canyon Dam on questioning.

Shortly afterward, the IPC started a vicious campaign to stop me from getting the job, claiming that Blonk was against private enterprise. The action was an example of the lengths to which the firm was going to punish those who dared to say that there are two sides to every story.

Not only did it get me fired from a federal position, working through a stooge congressman named Hamer Budge, but when I was about to land an important job in the sugar beet industry, it turned its wolves loose to prevent it. It followed me out of the government, so to speak.

In drumming up support on my behalf, the advertising people wrote to every member of the Boise Rotary Club (I put out its weekly bulletin) and questioned them about my attitude on private enterprise. All but three members supported me. The three who did not were the president of the IPC, its chief engineer, and the representative of the Idaho Chamber of Commerce — which annually received a big contribution of company money on which to operate.

While this was taking place, the U and I Sugar Co. asked me to handle arrangements for opening its new refinery at Moses Lake. The company said it was not a test to determine how well I'd do handling the bigger job.

It turned out that the affair, which I handled while on annual leave from the government, was highly successful in regard to the publicity and attendance it generated.

Newspapers, such as the Portland Oregonian and Spokesman-Review, devoted full pages of pictures and ran many stories about the affair. Others gave it wide publicity also. Likewise, radio and TV devoted much coverage to the event.

On the first day of the grand opening, a Saturday, a huge crowd was present. It heard music from three sources, a Western orchestra, a school band, and an organist. The head of the Mormon Church was present. He and 400 other dignitaries were fed a scrumptious meal in the bag room which had been prepared by the Davenport Hotel of Spokane.

Moses Lake people, whom I'd trained as guides, handed out brochures I had written and explained features of the refinery to people on the tours. Everyone was served a glazed doughnut and apple cider.

The U and I people were greatly impressed with the first-day response to their open house invitation. However, officials warned me not to go overboard in ordering doughnuts and cider for the following day which was a Sunday. I remember saying: "You haven't seen anything yet!"

Sure enough, we were overwhelmed the next day. Cars were backed up for three miles trying to get to the plant and luckily I had ordered 500 more gallons of cider from Wenatchee. I was able to keep up with the demand for doughnuts, because they were being made on order by an Ephrata bakery. Serving glazed ones instead of cake ones meant that they had to be fresh.

To handle the crowd expeditiously, it was necessary to abandon the guided tour arrangement. I placed the guides at specific spots to which the guests could walk without the delay that guided tours would have caused.

We put 13,000 people through the refinery in the two days it was open to the public and disposed of a whopping 16,000 doughnuts. I forget how much cider was consumed.

A rather humorous incident sticks in my mind in regard to the function. The sales department of the sugar company wanted to serve cocktails to its commercial customers. However, the Mormon Church being against liquor consumption raised a problem. It could not show on the record the purchase of a large quantity of booze, so I bought $115 of the refreshments and listed it on my personal expense account.

However, despite the Moses Lake expericence — which was lauded in a letter to me by the sugar beet people — the Idaho Power Co. was successful in stopping my employment by all industries involved with beet sugar. Ten of the 11 companies continued to favor my employment, but the eleventh wouldn't. Of course, one could not operate successfully unless his hiring was unanimously approved.

I was never one to carry a grudge. But I surely did in regard to Homer Budge the Idaho Congressman who got me fired.

After he lost the election I wired him and said: "That's the best thing that happened to Idaho since Lewis and Clark."

But from the long-range point of view, the rejection was a fortunate one, because it allowed me to become employed (three months after being fired by the bureau) as managing editor of a fearless, high-principled newspaper.

It was during 20 years at the helm of this publication under Wilfred Woods, the son of the original publisher, the great Rufus Woods, that I was able to make a real contribution to the "people's right to know" . . . not only on the homefront . . . but throughout the state and nation.

For that, I received a number of awards, which I'll mention elsewhere.

BOOK FOUR
"WORLD" WONDERFUL

Wenatchee Newspapering

It was an exasperating experience in Boise to be out of work. I had never been before. I had sent out a lot of job applications to companies and agencies but they of course do not act at once. Some never reply.

I wrote Wilfred Woods, publisher of the Wenatchee Daily World, asking him if he had some kind of job I could do while waiting for permanent employment. I told him I was going crazy not doing anything and would do any kind of work, no matter what the pay. I would even "sweep out the joint." I had to find something.

I got a letter right back telling me to come over. I started out writing stories. Got three or four features the first day covering Chelan. Within a week, Wilf offered me a job but I told him I had better stick to public relations, newspapering didn't pay enough.

Maybe it will, Wilf said. I replied that I'd decide the minimum I would take and he'd decide the maximum he could pay, and if they didn't match, we'd still be friends. They matched and I accepted the job of managing editor.

Wilf immediately wired news of the appointment to the Associated Press. It happened that friends of my wife in Boise started calling her about reading it in the paper before I had a chance to tell her myself. She was not pleased.

I was later offered a job as public relations director for Tacoma City Light which would require me to leave the Daily World. Of course, I didn't do so having just accepted the job there.

In 1954, there were about a dozen people employed on the newsroom staff — Ralph Wood, Bob Woods, John Richardson, Genevieve Strand, Jim Lieb, Lona Courtney, Beulah Davenport, Dick Pieper, Dick Larsen, Herb Jenkins, Millie Barnett and myself. The sports department consisted of just one man. Pieper and Bob Woods on occasion single-handedly edited all the local and wire copy, wrote all the heads, and dummied all the pages. After a while, I gradually took over some of that work with a wire editor handling the Associated Press wire.

The reporters used bulky, Underwood typewriters. All of them took their own pictures using Speed-Graphics. You had to be alert with these as they had two shutters. One worked in conjunction with a Compur-Rapid lens in the front of the camera, the other consisted of a plate that moved up and down in the back. It was used for fast action. If one left that shutter down, as most everyone did at one time or another, it would shut off the image coming through the front lens and there would be no picture.

189

The film was developed and prints made by a darkroom employee working about two-thirds of a day. Today, we have three photographers and a part-time one, plus a full-time darkroom assistant.

After 20 years as managing editor, I retired in 1974 but have spent 18 or more years as a special writer working whenever I wanted.

Few men have had such an enjoyable career. The work was always exciting, and Wilfred Woods was a most considerate publisher who gave me much latitude in editing and writing and also in performing extra-curricular activities.

The latter involved two major fields:

1. Bench-Bar Press relations as they pertained to fair trial and free press, and

2. Freedom of Information as it pertained to public agencies. Both of these were conducted on the national, state and local levels. I will discuss these in detail later.

I was considered a tough editor, one who demanded the utmost from his employees. My Dutch temperament showed at times. However, editors of other newspapers were not reluctant to hire someone who had worked on the World, because they knew they had been Blonk-trained. Some of these later became managing editors of dailies and held other responsible positions such as serving as investigative reporters, photo editors, etc.

While managing editor, I did some reporting, because I enjoyed that more than running a newspaper. I did not send another reporter up in the Methow, because I liked the area and its colorful people. The Grand Coulee dam area also was covered by me, for it was "old home" to me.

Because of my experience as reporter at Grand Coulee Dam, I covered the construction of all the dams in North Central Washington. These included Chief Joseph, Wells, Rocky Reach, Wanapum, Priest Rapids, and of the new powerhouse at Rock Island.

I never considered myself a great writer, although I have won some state awards including a first place one and two second places in the feature category.

In editing our copy we used a heavy black pencil. Sometimes the story would look pretty messy with all the scratch-outs. Another early-day messiness resulted from using paste to join pieces of paper together to an article. To do that, we used a small brush attached to the top of a paste pot. When the "slopover" dried it was an ugly sight.

In the "back shop", the page was made up in hot metal. I still miss that nostalgic, wonderful smell of the composing room. The paper later adopted an new printing process called "offset." It eliminated hot lead.

We redesigned the paper taking off an "ear" situated alongside the logo. It had read "Greatest Daily In The World For Cities Under 16,500" (or whatever the circulation was). We also took out the "Daily" from the original "Wenatchee Daily World." We left the subtitle "Published in the Apple Capital of the World and Buckle of the Power Belt of the Great Northwest."

One of the fortunate things I seemed to have, was a "nose for news." I was always proud to come up with four or five good features on every two-day trip out of town. And that production continued well into the 1990's.

While in charge of the newsroom, I acted more like a city editor than a managing one. I edited copy, wrote heads, dummied the pages and made assignments. I never felt a great need to spend full time on administration.

One of the most unpleasant things in putting out the paper was turning down people who had been arrested and wanted to keep their names out of the newspaper. You had to handle that gently, which at first I did not do. A prominent businessman who had been arrested for drunken driving said he'd beg me on his hands and knees to keep his name out of the "News of Record." I refused, and he subsequently pulled out $5,000 in advertising.

People thought it easy for me to do what they asked, but it wasn't. I would never have had a clear conscience, if I had submitted to a big advertiser's request and then turned down a wife and mother whose husband had been arrested for a misdemeanor, which publicity she felt would hurt her children.

Wilfred never once interferred with a decision — much to his credit. When two members of the World staff were charged with drunken driving their names appeared along with the others.

He also had integrity in relation to politics. Never once was I asked to slant a story in favor of a candidate that he might personally be supporting. In that regard, I always felt I had been objective when both Democrats and Republicans were mad at me at the end of a campaign.

I've been lucky not to have been sued for libel.

However, a number of years ago, the advertising department was hauled to court. An older woman advertised in the classified for work at her home. The wording was perfect but the ad was placed in the wrong column under "breeding stock." This resulted in her getting many strange phone calls.

After a lot of fuss, her lawyer agreed to settle for $200 but publisher ' Woods refused and the case was dismissed.

A couple of times members of the composing room staff caused us trouble.

I was called into the General Manager Jack Watkins' office with the publisher and Editorial Editor Bob Woods present. I was told someone had told Watkins a person had succeeded in keeping news of his arrest for drunken driving out of the paper.

I was instantly mad and hollered "That's a damn lie!" When the alleged facts about the particular news incident was revealed, I called in George Richardson (later managing editor) who would have written the story. He, startled, vigorously denied keeping it out.

As both he and I and the whole newsroom staff were under suspicion of having done so, I suggested we give everyone a lie detector test. When news of how serious we felt the charge was spread through the plant, a couple of composing room employees admitted having thrown the story away as the man involved was a friend. They barely escaped getting fired!

The second annoyance was not that serious. It started when "Jeep" Miller, who owned a major car company and was a good advertiser, came into the plant to say a news item about his son being punched in the nose by some man while involved in a car accident was not true.

I called in Richardson, who wrote the small item, and he said he had not written the "punch in the nose" portion of the story.

It turned out a close friend of Miller's son who worked in the composing room had put it in as a joke and forgot to pull it out before the press run.

I enjoyed working with new people, especially the summer help. I always told them at the start of the employment that I was not interested in winning a popularity contest with them. I just wanted to make the best newspaper man or newspaper woman out of them that I could in three months time.

Quite a few aspiring journalists were error prone I found. I used a couple of unusual tactics to cure them. I told a girl named Penny, after repeated other efforts failed, that if she continued to make the same mistakes I was going to dock her pay $5. She never made them again. At the end of her stint with us, I asked her about it, and she replied, "Mr. Blonk it wasn't the $5."

One young man just out of the U. W. was really careless with the spelling of proper names and other important facts. I did everything I could think of to straighten him out without success. I praised him, cussed him, I tried this; I tried that with no luck. Finally, in desperation, I told him he'd have to put a red dot under every proper name. I was told that TIME Magazine assured accuracy that way. It worked! Later this very aggressive reporter assumed the difficult task of becoming an investigative reporter for a leading Midwest daily and later a managing editor in the East.

I Loved Photography

I took many pictures myself and won some state awards.

The most unusual photograph I ever took required no skill at all but the subject made it one in a million. The humane officer called me from Fifth Street and told me what was happening. I grabbed the camera and sped down to the pumping plant on the Columbia River. As I knew what I was about to shoot I pulled out the back slide and focused the camera as I ran to the shore so I would be ready the instant I got there.

There it was! A deer floating down the Columbia on a cake of ice, very alert with its ears erect. It had probably floated on the ice chunk all the way out of the Wenatchee River. It was a sensational sight. I shot quickly for I feared the animal would jump into the water with all the people gathering near the river. It finally did jump a few hundred yards downstream.

LIFE magazine borrowed the negative from me for $75, which was quite a lot in those days. It ran the picture two-thirds of a page in size and gave it the clever head "Doe on a Floe." In the transaction the negative disappeared but I still retain a good print.

On one full-page spread, I ran photos of dead trees under the title "Death in the Mountains" and used as captions the phrases of great literary writers.

The biggest picture, about a third of a page in size, which showed a picturesque dead tree, had the caption "The day without a cloud hath passed — and thou were lovely to the last." —Byron.

Another shot was a section of a fallen, dead tree which had an interesting pattern of knotholes, and I used as the caption, "All that lives must die. Passing through nature to eternity." —Shakespeare.

I also liked to take the color photo of Indians dressed in native garb, dancing at Nespelem. It showed a close-up shot of a small Indian boy blowing bubble gum. I felt it was a contrast between the old and the new.

I loved to use close-up lenses and color film to focus on tiny things, for instance, a toad stool in the lawn or a butterfly on a flower. I also used this technique to do a spread under a heading saying, "farm crops are beautiful." Extreme close-ups of frost on road gravel, pebbles, tumble weeds, and wheat stubble also made unusual pictures.

A color photo of tall aspen trees in the snow with the caption "Winter's Picture Postcard Country" won me a first prize in the Washington State Press contest.

One photo I figured was going to be great proved to be somewhat of a dud. It was of a beautiful, red-haired girl nibbling on a Red Delicious apple. It ran full page. The problem was it was too closeup and greatly exaggerated the skin texture of the girl.

The Most Satisfying Stories

One of the most satisfying stories I ever wrote really took some doing. A hermit-like mountain man named Gordon Stuart lived year round at Domke Lake above Lucerne on Lake Chelan. He rented out a few cabins to hunters and fishermen during the spring, summer, and fall. In winter, he trapped, as far away as the Entiat Valley, using snowshoes to get about.

Of course, he was newsworthy, but he steadfastly refused to grant an interview. Not even the National Geographic could get his story during the time it had two men there to interview him. One time, I offered to let him read the story before it was printed. He scoffed at that. I then offered to let him read it but not publish it until he died so that he would not lose his beloved privacy. He scoffed at that, too. He mumbled something about my coming back in 10 years.

Several years later, when he was suffering with emphysema, high blood pressure and other things, he decided, to the surprise of friends, to build a large cabin. He had been living in a small, cluttered-up shack. Pre-fit logs were to be dropped in by helicopter. Learning of this, I flew into Domke Lake with Ernie Gibson, the veteran seaplane pilot.

I was fully prepared when I reached the cabin. I had my camera pre-set so I could instantly take a picture of Gordon if I wanted to, and I had decided not to ask him if I could interview him. As I entered, I greeted him and immediately got out my note pad and started asking questions. He had a hairlip, and this, plus his deteriorating physical condition,made it nearly impossible for me to understand him. An employee of his, Sandy Norris, sort of interpreted his answers for me.

I did not stay as long as I wanted, because I feared he would cut me off at anytime. But I got the long-sought-after story and took two pictures of him using light coming through a small window as illumination. I just shot. I did not ask him first as I did not want a turn-down to keep me from getting the photos.

Sandy said Gordon wanted to see the story before it ran, and I agreed to that. It was three weeks after I sent it to him, before he replied. I had already surmised that he had decided not to let me run the story, but I was in for a great surprise. Sandy wrote that Gordon liked the story and for me to go ahead and run it.

We ran the article about a week later. Surprisingly it was on the day he died.

Later I asked Gordon's good friend, Stan Norris, why Gordon had let me run the story. He said because he had told me, in rejecting me earlier, to come back in 10 years, and I had. Truth is, I never realized it had been exactly 10 years since I had tried to interview him.

I also much like the one headed "The Gandy-Dancers Are One-Day Millionaires. . . ."

Probably there are two reasons for this: One it won a first place award in the annual state writing contest, and, secondly, I think it was headed by the best lead I ever wrote. The first few paragraphs went like this . . .

"The life of the gandy dancer is no waltz!

"There's no doubt in your mind about that after you've spent a few hours talking to the workmen on the 'extra gang' laying spur track on the Great Northern a few miles above Rock Island Dam. 'Gandy Dancer' is their nickname, and it's not generally held in very high esteem.

"One of them summed it up quickly and straight-forward: 'Nine-tenths of us are alcoholics.'

"While there are some regulars in the crew who don't drink and who save their money, most of the tracklayers have their failings, and they know it. They don't feel sorry for themselves, nor do they brag about it. Facts are facts.

"When one talks to you, he generally speaks in the third person about the group at large not being able to handle its liquor, but he doesn't hide the fact that he is one of them. 'If they can get by payday, they're O.K.,' said the tall guy in the baggy, wrinkled pants. 'Maybe they can go 6 to 8 months before going back to town.' "

"They call them 10-day gandys, they work ten days and then head for town. The first liquor store, and they're gone. They're one-day millionaires with all the money in the world while it lasts. They treat everybody. One or two days, and it's all gone. Then they come back and start all over again.

"The name gandy dancer comes from the fact that in the early days of railroading the track workers stomped the gravel around the ties with their feet, thus appearing to be doing a dance."

Other happenings you don't forget:

The Day Kennedy Died

A most exciting and tense day in the newsroom occurred when President John F. Kennedy was killed in Dallas, Texas, on November 22, 1963.

We got word of it from the Associated Press. Its teletype was usually noisy as it clicked out the news articles. On this historic day, it stopped and rang a bell to summon editors. Then we were advised that the President had been shot. The item was only a paragraph long. Then silence, for the AP wanted the wire clear for subsequent reports.

In about 10 minutes, came the report that Kennedy had been severely wounded and was in intensive care in a Dallas hospital. After this report, the news started coming in faster and faster, in an endless stream of copy. Then came the bulletin that the President was dead.

When we got the initial report of his being shot, we had already made up page one so we immediately tore it apart for a makeover and the big headline story.

I held the paper about an hour and a half past deadline in order to give our readers the very latest details. I knew the front page would be a historic one saved by many, so I wanted it to be spectacular. Two lines, two inches high read: "President Kennedy Killed by Assassin" and below that "Fatally Wounded in Texas Parade; Johnson Becomes New President." The headlines were in bright red color and occupied close to half of the front page.

Covering a Murder

I covered a murder for the paper. It was a tragic affair that involved a personal acquaintance, a beloved businessman of the Methow Valley. He was Otto Wagner, who operated a big mill at Twisp and had just recently contributed a swimming pool to the town. I had served as master of ceremonies for that dedication.

The following fall he was murdered and found in a closet of his home. It was a week before his body was discovered. It subsequently developed that the killer was his nephew, James Hayden, for whom he had financed a cattle spread in Montana. They had argued over money matters. Wagner was a prominent, kind, quiet man, so the crime was sensational in the valley.

It was quite awhile before they located Hayden in Scottsdale, Arizona. He was found guilty in Okanogan County Superior Court.

He had been in Walla Walla State Prison only about three years when Mrs. Wagner learned that he was to come up for parole. That greatly disturbed her, Sheriff Fred Horner and myself. We felt the term was way too short.

After learning about the possible parole, the sheriff had someone tip him off whenever the murderer was to appear again before the parole board. He would then let me know and I would call the board for news about it. They must not have wanted the publicity, and, so, reconsidered turning him loose so soon.

It was important that he be kept locked up, because Mrs. Wagner was afraid for her own life. She kept a gun in her purse and in her home. She would not travel alone to Hawaii, for instance, where she previously often went. She had an elaborate security system installed around her big ranch. It allowed her to summon aid from her helpers no matter how far from the ranch home they were. She also had a state patrolman living nearby.

After Hayden got out, he embezzled money in Idaho, then ran his pickup into a river to make it seem like he had drowned. Later he was arrested in California.

195

Over the Arctic Circle

During the course of my life, I encountered some unusual experiences. I once typed out a story while over the Arctic Circle. I was aboard one of the Pacific Western planes which the Wenatchee World chartered.

Chester C. Kimm, associate editor of the Wenatchee World, was trip coordinator. The excursion was called "Survey '68." It was a flying seminar to provide organizational, business, and governmental leaders — both in Canada and the United States — an opportunity to see the natural resources, observe economic development, and to become acquainted with other business and political leaders of the Greater Pacific Northwest. Of the 6,000 miles flown, about 2,400 were over the United States and 3,600 over Canada.

There were 80 people aboard.

This was about the time that California had eyes on the Columbia River because of the threat of water shortage in its area.

Our plane stopped in several places, including Prince George, White-horse, Fairbanks, Prudhoe Bay, which had no airport at that time so we had to descend by stepladder, Yellowknife and Edmonton. Near Inuvik, an Eskimo village, the plane suddenly vibrated and the pilot came on to say, "Sorry ladies and gentlemen, we just crossed the Arctic Circle hence the bumpiness." Everyone had a good laugh, and champagne was brought out to celebrate passing over the landmark. We were all handed commerative certificates.

I had a portable typewriter on my lap; I was writing up the trip for the paper and wanted to get everything down quickly rather than wait until we got back to Washington state.

My most memorable aspect of the trip was seeing Eskimos pushing shopping carts down the aisle of a supermarket.

Movie Stars Interviewed

I've interviewed a lot of movie stars on the practice green at Pebble Beach during the Crosby and AT&T Golf tournaments.

I went to the celebrity tournament as a result of my knowing Ted Durein, a close friend of Bing Crosby. Ted was in charge of the press and put me up with Dave Schutz, retired editor of the Redwood City Tribune. We got our lodging free and, for a number of years, also our meals.

Each of the 11 times I went to the tournament, I would do tid-bit interviews with the stars, who played as amateurs in the pro-am classic. A combination of these stories was featured in the Wenatchee World's Kiosk, the entertainment section of the paper.

A few of the celebrities I talked to over the years were Lawrence Welk, Telly Savalas, Tommy Smothers, Jack Lemmon, Phil Harris, Burt Lancaster, Robert Wagner, the Gatlin Brothers, Charlie Pride, Hank Ketcham (Dennis the Menace creator) and Charles Schulz (Peanuts cartoon).

The luminaries were always quick with a quip. I asked Chi Chi Rodriguez how he'd played that day. He said: "Like Doug Sanders this morning (he was a top golfer always flashily dressed) and this afternoon like Colonel Sanders (of fried chicken fame.)"

The VIP's told funny stories (a few dirty ones amongst themselves). Phil

Harris, who M.C.'d the "Clambake Bake" — as Crosby called the banquet for some 900 or so volunteers — with a glass of Jack Daniels always in his hand, told singer Charlie Pride not to feel offended with the joke he was about to tell. Pride, seated in the audience, grinned as he shouted back, "Go ahead." Harris then told the story about a nurse coming up to an old man and asking him if he was the husband of the young lady who just had twins. The guy proudly said "yes." She then asked him how old he was. The man said "94." She expressed surprise, and he responded with "Well, you know there may be snow on the roof but there's still fire in the furnace." She replied: "Well you better check your flues, these twins are both black."

Editor Made To Get Some Staffers Drunk

No doubt the most unusual assignment given me by Wilfred was the one in which I was told to get three members of the staff and the son of another drunk!

He, who never accepted liquor advertisements, wanted to find out how much beer or liquor one had to consume before he would exceed what the state law defined as legally drunk. Drivers arrested by the State Patrol for drunken driving repeatedly kept saying they had had only a couple of drinks, yet were shown by the breathalizer test to have exceeded the state standards.

Wilf was particularly interested in finding this out because of the paper's long-standing policy not to accept any liquor advertising despite the fact that there was considerable money to be made from it.

I gathered the people who were to be subjected to the test in the lunchroom, which in the early days was located upstairs, together with two members of the State Patrol. The latter were to keep record of how much beer the beer drinkers consumed and how much hard liquor the others drank over a certain period of time. They were continually tested as the drinking proceeded.

I don't recall what the consumption amounted to over the period of about an hour, but for sure at least two people present got drunk. The noisiest was "Skip" Mussen, who later became general manager.

Next noisiest was Richard Snodgrass, son of Roy Snodgrass, long time press cameraman. Mussen was tested with hard liquor, Snodgrass with beer. The other two participants were members of the World advertising staff, Gene Robards and Ernie McCart.

I remember "Skip" looking up in drunken fashion to the much taller Snodgrass, and shouting "You can't drink worth a damn can you?"

After the test was finished, I took the entire group to the Chieftain restaurant for dinner so they would not be driving under the influence.

When we got through eating, "Skip" was still tight. I remember a state patrolman asking him if they could drive him home. To which invitation, Mussen replied "I ain't going home with Smokey the Bear!" Someone else drove him home. The experiment proved a motorist had to consume a lot of alcohol in order to be guilty of drunken driving. One fellow had drank 9 or 10 beers in the hour-long test.

197

Other Unusual Subjects Made Good Stories

I loved writing stories on unusual subjects such as the above. Two others follow:

When the Kingdome was under construction in Seattle, I rode a rickety elevator to the top when only three of the approximately 40 concrete roof sections were in place.

Later under the heading "Roll Up the Carpet", in a full-page spread with many photos, I described how the Kingdome floor was converted from a football field to a basketball configuration.

Once I traveled from the Canadian border to the Oregon border along Lake Roosevelt, Banks Lake, the canal system and McNary Pool for a story saying that Washington State was the only one in the United States that can be crossed entirely by man-made or man-shaped waterways.

Colorful Experiences Galore

The fun of reporting is the variety of experiences that it offers the reporter. I had lots of them.

Up In The Air

Parasailing was one. It came about as the result of having two good friends at Manson on Lake Chelan — John and Cora Picken, orchardists. Each year for many years they offered me a two or three-week stay in a cabin that partially hung over the lake. They refused to let me pay for it and when I offered gifts, such as a dinner out, they would turn about and do the same thing for me.

In preparing for the ride into the sky, I was strapped into a harness fastened to a balloon held open by several fellows. It was fastened by a 300-foot long rope to John's boat.

As he hollered, "Go," he raced the boat forward. It made the rope between the boat and me taut. I ran forward on the lawn to the edge of the lake and then was swung in a big arch over the water. As the boat raced along I went higher and higher until I was about 250 feet in the air.

John could control the height I attained. When he slowed the boat down, I would drop down. When he put on speed, I'd go up. It was a great feeling.

At ride's end, I was dropped in the water near a dock where John stopped the boat.

Julie, who is scared of heights, took a ride, too. She and John put on quite a spectacle as the "Lady of the Lake," a tour boat, passed by. John dropped her to about 30 feet above the water closely alongside the boat. That was repeated several times. It caused a flurry of picture-taking by the passengers.

Another Airy Experience

Jim Goodfellow of Goodfellow Brothers, a Wenatchee contracting firm with whom I was acquainted because they had worked at Grand Coulee

Dam, asked me if I wanted to view all their projects in the Northwest in a single day. We'd do it by means of the company airplane, they said. We started at Bellingham, then flew to Biggs, Oregon.

Enroute, company superintendent, Tom Reilly, the pilot, asked me if I wanted to fly over the top of Mount Rainier. Of course, I said yes. So Tom had me put on an oxygen mask because of the 14,000-foot elevation over the top. When we reached the top of the mountain, we flew over the big crater. What a sight! I have never forgotten it.

Later, we flew to Whitebird Hill in Idaho and a job in Montana.

A Couple of Helicopter Rides

I accompanied a veteran Manson pilot to the top of Nason Ridge in the Lake Wenatchee area to bring down a couple of mountain goats that were to be transferred to Idaho. The creatures had already been trapped in a wire cage.

They were strapped onto boards fastened alongside the fuselage. In coming down we flew at the outset a couple of feet above the rocky ridge and then headed out thousands of feet above the road where the animals were to be taken. It was a scary feeling. I felt as though my stomach was coming up into my throat.

The Bonneville Power Administration also took me for a ride in a helicopter to show how it was used in the inspection of the high-voltage lines in the area. I got into the rig as it sat on the east side of the river in the Ribboncliff area. The door had been taken off on my side of the 'copter, so that I would not have to take my pictures through glass.

We flew up to a tower across the Columbia on which men were working and passed over it and the accompanying high-voltage lines several times. I didn't think it particularly scary for some reason. However, when I later talked to one of the men on the tower I asked him how high we had been above him. "About seven feet," he said. Wow!

Spectator In Surgery

I found myself on a reporting assignment during surgery one time. A woman patient was undergoing an operation to correct her stomach, which had passed up through the diaphragm and fastened to her lung. It would involve for the first time a local anesthesiologist. My wife suggested I not do the story because I might faint. While I was a bit apprehensive, I ventured forth regardless.

I wore a surgeon's mask and cleaned my hands so everything would be sterile. I was using a Speed-Graphic camera, a bit bulky for the job, but that was all I had. I stood on a chair so that I could see what was going on.

The operation lasted one and a half hours. I was surprised that the incision made by Dr. Albert Stojowski at the beginning of the surgery created so little bleeding.

At one point, I got down from the chair. That prompted Dr. Stojowski to say "What's the matter, Hu, you feeling faint?" I replied "Oh, no, this camera is getting heavy."

I devoted a full page to the story using several photographs. I had received advance permission from the woman to do the story.

199

Stake-out For A Murder

The most unusual investigation which resulted in no story at all began when The Seattle Times's top reporter Don Duncan walked into my office and offered to share with us a possible story that he had started working on in Seattle. I'm sure he felt his prowling around in the Wenatchee police station would have alerted me, and that he might lose the story which centered on the then mayor of Seattle.

Duncan said that an aide to the mayor had quit because he did not like the way the mayor operated. A woman named Hazel learned of this and approached the aide with a shocking story. He told Duncan about it, and Duncan met with the woman in a Bellevue restaurant.

She said she had been in a room at the Cascadian Hotel in Wenatchee doing some typing for the mayor at a Young Democrats convention when a girl named Joy accused him of two-timing her. An argument ensued, and the mayor gave the girl a shove. Her head hit the corner of a desk, killing her.

Hazel screamed. That prompted the mayor to yell "Shut up. You're part of this, too."

According to Hazel, she and the mayor carried the dead woman to her car. He had told her that if anyone approached them they should say the woman was drunk.

Hazel said she had a shovel in her car, and they buried the woman in a shallow grave in one of Wenatchee's canyons.

Neither Duncan nor Ray Schrick, my reporter, could find anyone named Joy missing. Ray went through a lot of registration cards at the Cascadian without success.

Duncan met with Hazel in Seattle several times to try to develop more facts without success. A strange thing happened then. Hazel claimed that she was clobbered in the back of her yard one night when she heard a noise and was taken to a hospital. But the doctor could find no bruises, although Hazel appeared to be hysterical.

Later, I got a phone call from Duncan who said he had gotten the woman to agree to return to Wenatchee to see if she could find the grave. He gave me the license number of her car.

Not knowing what highway she might use to get to Wenatchee, I arranged for a stakeout. I put George Richardson along the Blewett Pass highway posing as a fisherman. I suggested he go unshaven, so he'd look the part.

I put Schrick in a car on the Stevens Pass Highway to watch for her there. Both fellows were near the junction of the two roads. I drove around between the two to keep them advised. I also, had my car ready to follow Hazel.

She never showed.

Duncan was later approached in Seattle by a Sergeant Remington of the Wenatchee Police Department who had become interested in the case. The department had been unable to determine if such a killing had ever taken place.

Strangely, that officer was killed about six months later.

Animals Make News

Animal stories make for great reading. I was able to come up with several.

I did a full page on a pet deer near Twisp. I took it downtown and posed it in a barbershop, cafe and other places. As hunters used to place the game they bagged on the front fender of their car, I did just the reverse. I put a man on the fender and had the deer coming out of the front seat.

At the start of fishing season, I had a bit of fun with fishermen. Under the caption "Fisherman Are So Enthusiastic", I showed a picture of the surface of the Columbia River with a man's arm sticking out of the water hanging onto a pole the line of which was bent as though he had a whopper of a fish on it. His hat was shown floating on the water. The photo, which showed nothing else of the fisherman, is still one of my favorites. (The man under the water wore a wetsuit.)

The deer floating on a piece of ice I've described earlier.

A photo showing a dog nursing a fawn aroused great interest among readers, as did a picture of two fawns trying to hide in the grass. The latter occurred when I was along with a game biologist tagging fawns. He determined if any fawns were present by blowing on a self-made whistle when he saw a doe. If the doe moved toward him it meant she had fawns nearby. The two little deer in the grass had been chased there by a dog the game man had in his pickup. Whenever the dog caught one or more fawns, he'd gently place his front feet over them. It was a thrill to see the two little creatures and hold one of them while the game man was weighing the other.

I once went along with a game biologist to count pheasants in the Columbia Basin. This is done at dawn. At specific points on the route, he listened for roosters to crow and jotted down the number of crows he heard. Using a certain formula he could tell how many hens there were in the area. Of course, I asked him how he knew it wasn't the same rooster crowing. He said roosters only crow once every two minutes and he kept track of the time.

I was fond of a story about the horse called "Badger Mountain," a legend among bucking horses. He had the reputation of throwing even the greatest of riders and was described as "hell on hoofs," the "buckingest bronc," (Time magazine) and by a top-ranking cowboy as "the most spectacular bucking horse I ever saw."

The great horse, who, away from the rodeo arena was so gentle kids could ride him, died at age 29. He was buried near the brow of a hill in Sinlahekin Valley a few miles toward Palmer Lake from Loomis. He was retired there. He used to stand and look down on the meadows of that valley. His owner, rodeo stock contractor Tim Bernard, had seen to it that his close friend "Badger Mountain" did not wind up as cat or dog food as do some horses which no longer serve a purpose.

I have long felt a marker should be put up along the highway pointing to the grave of the great, bald-faced, bay horse.

Two more creatures drew my interest. Up a draw above the Wenatchee-Chelan Highway beyond Rocky Reach Dam, ladybugs by the thousands spend the winter under the sagebrush. I found they sting like the devil should they get on your hands.

Then there was the boa constrictor that a merchant kept in a pen in his factory office on Sunnyslope. I allowed it to wrap its six-foot length around my neck. Surprisingly to me, it was not a fearful experience.

Two talented dogs were worth writing about. One, a dog called "Mitzi," was crazy about television. Her favorite performers were dogs and cats. She walked up to the TV, put her paws on the set and barked and barked and watched television endlessly.

A dog named "Curley" not only made The Wenatchee World but, on the basis of my article also the "National Inquirer." It walked around its Cashmere yard on its hind legs but was never trained to do that, just did it on its own. It took no command of any kind to get it to perform. One would see her stand up erect for half an hour at a time!

Sorrow And Joy Of The Indians Is Shared

Always having been for the underdog, I covered several Indian activities. I knew many on the Colville Reservation and three of the four survivors of what I called "The Vanishing Tribe of the Wanapums."

I shared the latter's joys and griefs at Priest Rapids Dam. Their pleasure was the annual "Washat" dance held each spring, their sorrow the loss of a prominent figure.

The religious dance, held for endless years along the barren shores of the Columbia, is the ceremonial welcome to spring. It features, as it did under the founder of the Dreamer Religion, Smowhala, a sacred wooden bird that has brass tacks for eyes and a sprig of feathers for a tail and sat on a pole outside the longhouse where the ceremony was held.

I was allowed to attend one. Seven drums were pounded, with ear-splitting noise, just as was done when the great prophet was at the peak of his Northwest-wide influence. The affair also featured feasts, much singing, and other traditional activity.

I wrote a full-page story on the funeral for Rex Buck Sr., who along with his brother, Frank, and Bobby Tomanawash, were the only full-blooded Wanapums left of the original 2,000 who were at Priest Rapids earlier. The article was headed "Drums of Sorrow Beat At Feast."

I started the story this way:

"The small handbell had quit ringing and the chanting had ended when the Indians, seated on the floor along two rows of mats or at a center table, drank a quarter cup of water and ate a piece of salmon, the size of a cherry, off their otherwise empty plates.

"It was the saying of grace by 150 people from widely scattered areas at a memorial feast in honor of the man who was leader of the Wanapums here — Rex Buck — who now lies buried along with other members of the proud, but vanishing tribe who refused to give in to the White Man."

During the ceremony, there were the beating of the drums, a prominent feature in the Dreamer Religion, the chanting and wailing of the women, the Indian way of expressing sorrow.

Of course, there was a feast and something strange to the White Man — letting friends of the deceased take home any of his personal possessions, including household items.

202

"Cancer Cure" Story Almost Made "60 Minutes"

A story about a Texas dentist in Winthrop who claimed he was able to cure cancer through diet drew the interest of "Sixty Minutes," the popular CBS Sunday night program.

Paul Loewenwarter, a producer for the show, called me to ask if I could provide him with the number of patients who went to Dr. William D. Kelley. I had written that he drew people from all over the world. By contacting all of the notary publics in Winthrop, where Dr. Kelley had had patients clear him of any blame or failure, I could report to Loewenwarter that the doctor saw three or four persons a day.

The dentist operated up the Methow as a nutritional consultant. He came there from Grapevine, Texas. His practice there resulted in the state's Supreme Court barring him from practicing medicine and distributing his booklet,"One Answer To Cancer."

He asked patients a thousand questions, the answers to which were fed through a box he said was a computer that I saw in his office. The printout of several pages called for some people to take, among other things, a daily dose of as many as 250 non-medicinal pills, wafers or liquids.

He also advocated a coffee enema, "which is very stimulating to the liver" every morning for a month and twice a month for eight more weeks to rid the body of waste products. An enema of yogurt, sour milk or buttermilk was urged in the evenings for the first two weeks of treatment.

Of course, the American Cancer Society, which contacted me from Chicago, and the American Medical Society scoffed at his "cure."

I received several long-distance calls from disturbed relatives of people seeing the doctor asking me if I felt he was a quack. I refused to answer, because I did not know, although I had definite suspicions. I didn't want to be sued for slander.

Kelley, who built quite a complex of buildings to process crops he was growing, left the area after divorcing his wife. I last heard of him when he treated movie star Steve McQueen who also sought treatment in Mexico; in both instances without success. The incident was written up in Newsweek in 1980.

CBS never followed up with its idea of featuring Dr. Kelley on "Sixty Minutes."

Was I a Water Witch?

I have been a skeptic about many things. One of these is that people can find water with a forked willow branch. But I wasn't so sure after visiting Hayo Buse, of Waterville. I wrote as follows:

"Of all the pooh-poohers in the world, we've got as hearty a 'pooh-pooh' as anyone.

"We had a real lusty one already to go when Hayo Buse, a 58-year-old Waterville farmer, took us into the backyard of his home to show his mysterious skill as a water witch. He's one of those fellows who insists, he can find an underground source of water with the fork of a willow.

"He demonstrated by showing that the willow switch, in his hands, moved downward over where he said there was water.

"Oh, nuts!' I said under my breath, fully convinced he manipulated the willow with his wrists. 'Let me try it,' I insisted.

"He handed over the willow, and I started walking over the garden below which there was water, he had said. My sneer of disbelief was well camouflaged.

"But when we reached the spot with the water below, and despite the resistance of all the strength I had in my hands, the end of the willow fork moved down . . . it really did.

"Still not fully convinced, but admittedly somewhat confused by the twisting of the wrists caused by the willow, I tried again. Same result.

"Well, I'll be dawgoned,' I said humbly and put my best 'pooh-pooh' away for use some other time."

Job Was Dangerous Once

Because The Wenatchee World did not operate in a big city where riots and other disturbances prevailed, we on the news staff did not encounter many real dangers, unless we got caught in a forest fire. I did not generally cover these.

But one time, I faced possible drowning.

It occurred when I was writing up the start of commercial river rafting on the Methow River above Winthrop. I boarded a rubber raft at Weeman Bridge along with three or four other rafters. I had my Hasselblad camera with me and was clothed in a sweatshirt and other gear to ward off the cold.

We had rafted less than half a mile when we headed over low rapids toward brushy overgrowth on the shoreline. I thought we were in for a little trouble, because limbs hung over and into the water. Sure enough, we struck the brush and the raft started to tip over. I was dumped into the stream, first placing my camera on the floor of the raft hoping it might not be damaged.

I toppled into the river and went under. Immediately, I felt something above me. It struck fear into me, because I thought I was under a limb and would be snagged by it and be unable to surface. But I felt movement and determined it was another raft rider above me. It took a while to surface, which happened some distance from the shoreline.

I had difficulty swimming in the ice cold water, but I finally made it to shore. A later search revealed my camera had been dumped out of the raft into the water.

However, a year or two later it was found in the river, rusted and useless.

A Flight with Ted Kennedy

I had two experiences with the Kennedy family, one as a spectator.

I saw President Kennedy as he spoke in the Tri Cities and also at a banquet in Seattle, where I left my seat and walked past where he was eating so I could add him to the list of presidents I had seen up close.

I was aboard a Northwest Airlines plane to Washington, D. C., on one of the several details that took me back there when Ted Kennedy, enroute back home from Alaska, came aboard. The flight had been delayed awaiting his boarding.

His group was together in the front of the plane and engaged in much chatter. On arrival at Washington, D. C., his associates got off while Kennedy lingered behind. He and I finally were the only passengers left to leave the plane. I had remained behind because I wanted to see what kind of welcome at the airport he would get.

Kennedy finally left the plane and was met at a door by a mob of reporters who wanted to interview him about an occurrence in Alaska. I was right behind him.

The Weather Makes News

Three occasions when the weather made news remain vivid in my memory.

The Beverly area below Vantage on the Columbia River is known for its violent winds. It drew me one day. I found that the wind had bent over steel highway signs and torn pumice blocks out of a motel building. Standing near it with a group of men I actually found myself lifted to tip toes by the blasts. It was a bit scary at times.

I tried to photograph a strange sight. The hard hats worn by the workmen were whipped to a position over their heads that made them appear to be floating. They did not touch their heads, straps keeping them from being blown away. It made for a sensational picture. Unfortunately, I did not get one because the wind was so strong I could not keep my camera still.

Winthrop still holds the state record for having had the coldest temperature in the state. The thermometer at the fish hatchery read minus 45 one night.

I went up there so I could tell readers what it was like to live in such extreme cold. I found that the oil brought into stoves from barrels outside through copper tubing became so thick it would not run. Burials could not be held. Groceries in enclosed trucks would freeze. For instance, many products in glass jars would freeze and break.

A wintertime storm in the lower Grand Coulee created sensational pictures. At Blue Lake, the wind hurled water onto the main highway. It would then freeze. At one spot, the accumulation of ice on a stretch of guard rail looked like the rib cage of a huge prehistoric monster.

Taking pictures was an ordeal. It was easily the coldest job I ever did for the paper, because the wind was blowing fiercely lowering the chill factor to goodness knows what. The blasts were so strong that I could hardly stay put on the ice-covered highway. They slid me along a number of times but let up momentarily so I could take pictures.

Long Distance News Reporting

Covering the news for the Wenatchee World sometimes took us far afield.

I wrote up a couple of Sister City visitations to northern Japan in as much as I was associated with the group in an official capacity. (More about that later.) I wrote about items of interest while on personal vacations to various countries such as Morroco, Spain, Portugal, Yucatan and other Mexican areas, Holland and other European countries, Taiwan, Hong Kong, etc.

But the longest distance traveled for a specific overseas assignment was to Puerto Rico. I went there in March of 1960 to cover the biggest peacetime airlift ever conducted by U. S. Armed Forces. It was to drop 25,000 men plus equipment.

Accompanied by the editors of the Oroville Gazette — the Doehres — I boarded a plane commonly referred to as the "Flying Boxcar" at Moses Lake. It was a bulky-looking plane in which the military carried all kinds of equipment. Ours had a large truck and other machinery inside. There was no seating provided so we sat and tried to sleep most anyplace there was a flat space.

It took us 28 hours to get to Puerto Rico. Thus it was not particularly a restful flight. However, we had no plane trouble such as another "Flying Boxcar" had. It encountered an airshear in which there is a sudden violent drop of the plane. Unfortunately, a soldier aboard that one was caught between equipment and was killed.

Not all of our time was devoted to covering the airlift. We had at our disposal a frequent shuttle plane that would take us from the airbase to San Juan, the big city on the island, and back.

Two experiences remain vividly in my mind. We had gotten a for-hire car and started to explore the city when we heard a lot of noise — of a crowd cheering. We stopped and found it was a rooster fight, which is legal in Puerto Rico. We entered the place, which turned out to be a 25-foot diameter arena. It had bleacher seats around a pit where the roosters were to fight.

There were a couple ready to fight when we got there. The yelling among the 50 spectators indicated they were betting. Wanting to get pictures of the rooster fight with the Oroville men in the background, I got into the ring. I kept waiting for an order to remove myself but as long as everyone was smiling I stayed put. Then I was told to get out, but I had gotten my pictures.

Not only do the Puerto Ricans bet on which rooster will win but if one is knocked down they will bet on whether it will get up or not.

There may be as many as 20 fights on Saturdays, we learned. The referee puts the birds in cloth bags, with their heads sticking out, and then weighs them. Difference in weights up to one ounce is permissible. When released, the roosters start to fight immediately and may keep at it as long as 15 minutes. One match we saw lasted 30 minutes.

They even have "workouts" at special camps for the birds. There they do roadwork, engage in sparring practice, are fed special diets, and before a fight receive a "beauty parlor treatment."

Birds do not often die in the ring, we learned. Competent doctors attend them, and, in a week or so, a wounded warrior is back, once again "sparring magnificently," as a native writer put it. Particularly valiant birds are "retired" at the peak of their careers and are used for breeding.

To me it is a cruel sport, because the birds had small knives tied to their spurs.

The second incident that I remember is driving the car through the narrow streets of the city. It is hard to find your way about in a strange town where every one seemed to be honking whether it was necessary or not.

I remember being so proud that I finally had found a street, the name of which I recognized, but I soon found out from all the honking of other drivers that I was going up a one-way street the wrong way!

Kicked Out Of The Ballpark

I was once kicked out of a professional baseball park. Sitting in the grandstand during a Wenatchee Chiefs game, I noticed that a cub reporter I was training, who was standing near third base, was using his Speed-Graphic wrong. Between innings, I walked up to him and showed him how to get the best results.

Suddenly, an umpire came rushing up to us from second base and asked me, loud and nasty-like "What are you doing here?" I replied "I'm a photographer." He shouted "Where is your camera?" I then explained that actually I was instructing my photographer. He then hollered "Get Out!" and continued being nasty.

It made me angry so I hollered back at him "Don't make a horse's ass of yourself two nights in a row," tapping him on the chest with my finger. He had made a lousy ruling the night before that brought the wrath of the crowd down on him. This prompted him to shout back "You can't strike an umpire." I said "The hell I can't."

Then the homeplate ump walked up and escorted me off the field as I explained to him that I was wrong in being out there (the inning was ready to start which I hadn't known), but that the umpire certainly did not have to get obnoxious.

The whole confrontation was being broadcast by KPQ Radio. As a result, I could never again walk up to the grandstand without someone hollering "How you getting along with the ump, Blonk."

Sports editor Dick Pieper protested the episode to the president of the league. His reply follows:

"Dear Dick,

"I am sure that Umpire Stone would not have ordered Mr. Blonk from the field had he known the reason Mr. Blonk was on the field. It is unfortunate that he did not introduce himself to Umpire Stone.

"Normal procedure would have been for the umpire to request the attending police officer to escort any unauthorized person from the field but probably the police officer was not in attendance that particular evening so the umpire took it upon himself to eject the invader.

"You can readily understand that if any and all fans were permitted to go on the field a ball game could not be conducted. There is question in my mind as to whether or not Mr. Blonk should be fined.

"Yours Truly,

J.M. Fleishman, President Northwest League

The World Helps Legalize Rural TV

Scrappy people in North Central Washington led by those in Bridgeport brought the powerful Federal Communications Commission to its knees in their fight to get television for their rural areas.

The federal agency had ordered the reflectors that local folks had erected to be taken down or their VHF transmission changed to the more costly UHF.

Boosters for the reflectors recognized there was a provision in the law under which the FCC operated that stated that any mechanism that transmitted in such a way as to cause interference with other forms of communication was illegal.

But, they said, no one ever proved that the TV arrangement would cause any interference.

The Forest Service was opposed to the reflectors claiming the signals would interfere with their communication system. The FCC claimed the units on top of mountains or hills would interfere with the national defense system protecting the U. S. from enemy attack.

In the struggle during the 1950's and 60's local interests were aided greatly by the extensive coverage and editorial support of the Wenatchee World. Feeling it was greatly unjust to keep rural people from enjoying the television that those in more accessible towns and cities enjoyed, I saw to it personally that we ran a great volume of stories, many of which I wrote myself.

The FCC became a subscriber to the paper to keep itself informed as to what was happening.

The fuss began when the FCC ordered the reflector serving Bridgeport off the air saying it was illegal. This made other towns planning such units, including Wenatchee, greatly concerned.

The conflict spurred on the organization of the Washington State Television Association headed by James Livingston, of Bridgeport. Members protested to their congressmen, fought the FCC in U. S. Court of Appeals, got three bills introduced into Congress to legalize the reflectors, testified at FCC hearings, and in other ways aroused a storm of protest which generated tremendous publicity, which federal agencies never like.

The feisty organization even threatened to go to the U. S. Supreme Court to have the TV transmitters judged legal. The group was joined in its efforts by TV viewers in Colorado.

The Wenatchee World carried a head over one story that reporter Stan Pennington wrote that indicated what a furor the FCC had created. It read "It'll Be Like A Civil War If The FCC Won't Allow Reflectors."

The rural folks finally won out, paving the way for the many reflector towers that today bring television to small towns and many rural areas all over the country.

Goldmark Case was Sensational

The Wenatchee World story that drew the most national attention during my regime as managing editor involved the Goldmark case.

It resulted in having our reporter, Dick Larsen, call the Associated Press day and night over a period of 11 weeks with news of what happened in the libel case, because interest was so great nationally.

John Goldmark, a three-time member of the State House of Representatives and a rancher, was the key figure in the case. In his lawsuit, he alleged he was libeled during the 1962 legislative election campaign by being labeled a Communist by Ashley Holden, publisher of the Tonasket Tribune, Loris Gillespie and his Okanogan Independent, and by Al Canwell, who ran an "intelligence service" in Spokane.

Holden had printed in his weekly newspaper that Goldmark "was running on a platform which advocated the repeal of the McCarran Act, a law requiring the registration of all Communist Party members," that his son Charles was a sophomore at Reed College, "the only school in the Northwest where Gus Hall, secretary of the Communist Party, was invited to speak," and that he was a member of the American Civil Liberties Union, "an organization closely affiliated with the Communist movement in the United States."

Holden also made it known that Goldmark's wife, Sally, had been a member of the Communist Party in Washington, D. C., and claimed that the party would not have allowed her to marry anyone who was not sympathetic to the cause.

The trial occurred in 1963 and featured among the witnesses a prominent movie star, Sterling Hayden, several nationally publicized ex-Communists, and an FBI counterspy on whose life a network TV series was based.

Judge Theodore Turner of King County Superior Court presided.

Attorneys for the defendants were E. Glenn Harmon, Ned Kimball, and Joseph Wicks, a retired Okanogan County Superior Court Judge of "great local renown."

Attorneys for the plaintiff were William Dwyer and R. E. Mansfield.

In his opening statement, Dwyer told the jury that the Goldmarks were greatly damaged, because many people believed they were disloyal to their country as a result of what the defendants did.

On the other hand, Harmon stated that everything the defendants said during the campaign was true. He told the jury "We believe you will be compelled to conclude from the evidence presented in this courtroom that John and Sally Goldmark are in fact under Communist Party discipline."

Then followed a long parade of witnesses for both sides in the trial.

Time magazine was to say "The cast of characters reads like the lineup for a movie."

The plaintiff's attorney put into the record Goldmark's naval career, which included disarming bombs and naval intelligence clearance even after he revealed his wife had been a Communist.

When Sally took the stand, she testified she joined the party during the unrest of the Depression and later left it, because she had "changed her mind completely" and had cooperated fully with the FBI.

During Goldmark's lengthy testimony, it was revealed that he remained a commander in the Naval Reserve.

The defense centered its questioning on Barbara Hartle "one of the country's best known ex-Communists." She had been a star government witness for years. She explained how the Communist Party functioned and claimed that a member "does not get married without the approval of the party."

One of the most newsworthy personages that the defense brought to the stand was Herbert Philbrick, on whose book "I Led Three Lives," a then current popular TV series was based. He talked about party discipline in regard to past members, by means of which testimony the defense tried to label Goldmark a Red. Dwyer got Philbrick to admit that a great majority of past members "have settled down and are leading normal lives."

Closing arguments by attorneys concluded the trial. One of them was particularly eloquent. It was delivered by Wicks. He even brought in the Scriptures. Wicks' argument caused Sally to burst into tears and run from the courtroom.

On January 17, 1964, the case went to the jury. On the fifth day of deliberation, it found for the plaintiffs and awarded them $40,000.

The drama did not end with the jury's verdict, however. A few months later the U. S. Supreme Court altered the constitutional rules relating to libel. It held in the New York Times-Sullivan case that false statements about public officials, such as Goldmark was, are protected free speech under the First Amendment unless uttered with "actual malice."

As a result, Judge Turner set aside the verdict and entered judgment for the defendants. He said there was nothing in the record that proved the defendants knew the statements they made were false or not.

William L. Dwyer, in his book "The Goldmark Case — An American Libel Trial" is quoted as saying "The Goldmarks returned to their ranch. The long trial and the jury's verdict had cleared their good name; life could go on with honor."

The Associated Press Managing Editors Association gave The Wenatchee World, an afternoon paper, citation for its coverage, because it meant we had scooped ourselves on a lot of the story in serving morning papers through the AP.

The credit for the recognition should go wholly to Dick Larsen who covered the entire trial except for two days, when I did. I never saw a more masterful job of difficult reporting done or one more impartial.

Larsen rose to become a top editor on The Seattle Times and served as Representative Tom Foley's top aide. He authored a best-selling book about multi-murderer Ted Bundy, and wrote on Senator Henry Jackson. Dick remains a good friend.

There occurred a sad addition to the Goldmark story some 21 years after the trial. A mentally disturbed man who believed the Goldmarks were Communists, murdered their son, Charles, his wife and two children on Christmas Eve, 1985, in their family home in Seattle.

Heart and Eye Surgery in the News

A couple of my personal ailments while working at the Wenatchee World made good copy, which was widely read.

I wrote up operations, because I felt that the stories would encourage others who had possibly been postponing them, to undergo the surgeries.

I had a heart operation in 1980 and cataract surgery with an intraocular implant in 1989.

Test Brings Quadruple Bypass

Below is the feature on the heart as it appeared in the paper.

The subhead read:

"One From the Heart" —
Reporter Tells Story of Own Bypass Surgery.

"You're very apprehensive about someone putting a tube up the arteries of your arm or your leg all the way to the heart.

"You ask yourself, what it he pushes it too far and jabs a hole in the heart? Then what?

"But, if you're going to know how badly your arteries are blocked and where those blockages are, you have to undergo the procedure. It's variously called coronary angiogram, coronary catherization or coronary arteriography.

"The prospect of such a procedure is ominous to most people. Painful it is not.

"I know. I underwent it in Wenatchee, so that a Seattle surgeon would know where to bypass partially obstructed sections in four arteries and bring a full supply of blood to my heart again. Treadmill tests, which involve walking or running on a motor-driven platform while blood pressure is being taken and other circulatory tests showed the heart was not getting enough blood.

"If you're like me, you'll be apprehensive as you enter Central Washington Hospital the afternoon of the day before the examination. In general, you've been told what will happen in the 1½ to 2 hours you're being examined.

"One or more long, narrow plastic tubes will be passed through a blood vessel in your right arm or leg, and into the chamber of the heart. When the tube, called a catheter, is in place, a dye will be injected through it. As the dye courses through the blood vessels, your doctor will follow it by X-ray fluoroscope.

"For the examination by Dr. Dennis Larsen I was wheeled out of my room into the "cath lab," a place with a lot of equipment in it. Previously I had been given a pill to calm me down, should I be anxious. I pretended I wasn't.

"I was then placed on a padded table, my right arm extended at my side. At the outset, cardiologist Larsen anesthetized a small area inside my elbow. Then he made a small nick in the skin and inserted the tube. Sometimes he uses the leg (groin) area.

"Dr. Larsen guided the tube into position in my heart with the aid of a large television monitor. It was hooked up to X-ray equipment situated above and below the table where I lay.

"He then injected the dye. It mixes with the blood and makes the entire coronary arterial system visible on the X-ray camera. He made several injections of the dye through tubes of differing diameter. At various times he had me move about on the table so he could look from another angle. I was strapped to the table so I couldn't fall off when the surface was slanted in this part of the exam.

"I got kind of tired lying there but, if I wished, I could see what the doctor was seeing on the TV screen, which was the movement of my blood and the location, shape and extent of any blockage, plus the movement of my heart. I also conversed with the hospital aides.

"Before the final injection of dye, Dr. Larsen advised me I was going to feel real warm all over because he was going to inject a larger amount of dye. I found what he said to be most accurate. I felt heated up from my head to toes. It was an odd and slightly unpleasant sensation. But, as quickly as the warmth came, it vanished.

"During my confinement under the big camera, I was connected to a monitor that showed my blood pressure and an electrocardiogram (EKG) machine that gave the doctor other facts he needed to know.

"At no time did I feel the tubes moving in my blood vessels nor did I encounter the slightest pain, even though later the areas involved looked bruised. If the doctor had not been talking about what he was doing, I wouldn't have known the tube was there.

"Still, I was relieved when the doctor said, in effect 'That's it.'

"I was returned to my room, where I was required to stay for several hours to make sure nothing had happened to my circulatory system following my stay in the 'cath lab.'

"The risk involved in having someone probe around in your heart is minimal, although my doctor stressed there is some risk. However, the risk is only zero to 0.18 percent, according to the American Heart Association.

"A prominent heart specialist calls the procedure 'the greatest advance of the century in heart diagnostic technology.' The kind of information obtained through this procedure cannot be obtained from any other tests currently in use.

"A few days after this, I was headed for Seattle with a 2-foot-long envelope containing motion pictures, X-rays, and the other medical facts about what had happened during my stay on that padded table. Once there, I handed it to a young surgeon who would make good use of it when he performed my bypass surgery.

An Account of the Bypass

My story of the actual heart operation went like this:

"My heart had stopped beating! It would not beat again on its own for another 33 minutes.

"But I was very much alive. A space-age looking device was circulating blood through my body and doing my breathing for me while I was undergoing quadruple bypass surgery at Swedish Hospital in downtown Seattle.

"I was heavily sedated and remember nothing of what took place during the 4½ hours in that sterile room. But what was to happen to me as I lay on the operating table with my chest and legs exposed through plastic sheeting and green surgical fabric had been explained earlier by Dr. Douglas D. Johnson, my cardiac surgeon, and his staff of specialists. Details were added later by these same people who held my life in their hands.

"I walked into the big building the morning of the day before. I was somewhat nervous, to put it mildly. It seemed like an awful long time to prepare, but the day was pretty well taken up with more X-rays, conducting blood tests and other preparatory tests and swallowing a pill or two, one of which was intended to lessen the anxiety of this 73-year-old guy from Wenatchee. It did.

"I was wheeled into the operating room on schedule at 9:30 the next morning. There a nurse gave me a pill and jabbed me with a needle to make me feel drowsy. I barely recall what the anesthesiologist, Dr. Larry Dobbs, said would be the last thing I'd remember in the operating room. It was the insertion of a little catheter into the jugular vein of my neck. It would allow him to measure pressure and blood gases in my heart. I recall thinking that I'd just as soon he'd do that after I went to sleep. But it was only a pin prick.

"With me passed out, the anesthesiologist slipped a tube past my vocal chords into my windpipe so I could breath as the heart-lung machine took over. It would also circulate the blood, oxygenate it and cleanse it of carbon dioxide. The device would continue to aid my system until 5 a.m. the next day.

"There were seven people in the room which was once described as "a scene out of Star Wars." One of them painted me all over with a rusty colored antiseptic to lessen bacteria.

"Then Dr. Johnson, a personable young man in his 40's who's done more than 3,000 open heart surgeries, and his surgical assistant, Dr. John L. Goodman, went to work.

"As they operated, all sorts of things were monitored, blood pressure was measured, samples of blood were analyzed every few minutes in a nearby laboratory and called in to Dr. Johnson. Urine output was measured often to check metabolism and keep track of hydration. An oxygen line was in my nose to aid breathing and an intravenous needle in my arm near the wrist to monitor blood pressure.

"Next came the big hook-up. The heart-lung machine took over my breathing and blood circulation. To reduce the body's demand for oxygen as I lay there, my blood was cooled down from the normal 37 ½ degrees centigrade (about 87 degrees Fahrenheit) to 32 degrees centigrade. There were other procedures too complicated to explain.

"With these preparations completed, it was incision time. Strips of vein were removed from both legs — leaving a 16-inch scar on one leg and a 6-inch scar on the other. These vein strips were to replace partially clogged sections in four arteries on the surface of the heart that had been reducing blood flow, a potentially dangerous condition.

"The veins, the ones removed when a person had varicose veins, were kept in a salt solution until Dr. Johnsom exposed my heart. The legs don't miss the veins. There are alternate routes for the blood to flow in that part of the body.

"The surgeon sawed my breastbone apart with a power saw, leaving an incision that I later measured at 11 inches. Next, my ribs were spread apart, and there lay my heart — pinkish in color and about the size of a fist.

"Dr. Johnson gently placed it in a support so it would be kept perfectly still while he and Dr. Goodman did the bypass. (I later read that the support is jokingly called the 'cardiac jockstrap' by some physicians).

"The bypass involved sewing one end of the previously cut segment of vein from my leg to a small opening cut in one of the arteries just below the obstruction. They vary in size from the lead of a pencil to the size of a drinking straw.

"The other end of the segment was attached to a small hole Dr. Johnson had punched in my aorta. That's the big vessel about the size of a garden hose which takes blood from the heart and distributes it through the body at the rate of four to five quarts per minute when the body is at rest, more when one is exercising.

"The procedure was repeated four times, one for each potential troublespot.

"Now it was time to put me back together again.

"First thing, the temperature of my cooled-down blood was restored to normal by heating water in the heart-lung machine. Then four wires were run through my chest wall to my heart and fastened to an external pacemaker. It was intended to go to work in case of an emergency drop in my heart rate. I didn't need it.

"My heart now was ready to go back to work. The heart-lung machine was slowly brought to a halt. Simultaneously, the anesthesiologist ventilated my lungs. This caused my heart to swell to full size and resume its normal pumping operation. After further checks, the machine was disconnected and other detailed maneuvers performed.

"It seemed like there were tubes and wires coming out of me everywhere. One tube was put in last. It drained away the blood and fluids that always accompany major surgery.

"Next, I was about to be sewn up again. My breastbone was pulled back together and held in place by stainless-steel wires. I will have them inside me forever.

"After the long hours on the operating table, I was wheeled into a brightly lit intensive care unit. There I remained 24 hours with specially trained nurses constantly at my bedside. Quite a number of instruments recording vital signs would warn them of any trouble. I was still asleep, and they had told me before the surgery that I would remain that way for another six hours. But I required a blood transfusion, so I was kept 'under' until next morning, nearly an entire day in all.

"I can't remember being in the place after I awoke, but they had warned me I'd forget many things that had happened because of the amnesia-producing medication given patients. They tell me the tubes remained in my nose and throat for 18 hours before I was allowed to breathe on my own. Then nurses repeatedly urged me to inhale deeply and forced me to cough to remove fluid from my lungs.

"The coughing was a bit painful even when I held a pillow tightly across my chest. I didn't look forward to having to cough, and made sure I knew where the pillow was at all times.

"Surprisingly, the morning after the operation, I was helped from bed and seated in a nearby chair to eat my breakfast.

"Next stop in the hospital was a semi-private room. I was allowed to leave my bed to go to the bathroom with the support of a nurse, and, the second day I walked down the hospital corridor. My chest wasn't particularly painful, but one spot in the 18-inch incision in my left leg ached. It was to remain so for a couple of weeks after I ended my six-day stay at the hospital.

"Dr. Johnson, who is associated with Dr. Donald M. Miller at Northwest Cardiac Surgery Associates, likes his patients to remain nearby for a week after their discharge, so I stayed in Seattle with my sister-in-law, Ollene Patterson, from whose house I ventured every morning for walks up to a quarter-mile. Dr. Johnson told me he'd have me jogging again in three weeks.

"I had decided to have the $20,000 to $25,000 operation (all but $1,000 paid for by Blue Cross and Medicare) even though I'd never had a heart attack, only a minor disturbance several years before. I had not even had the pain that generally precedes an attack. However, treadmill tests at six-month intervals over the last two years had shown that when my heartbeat reached a certain peak my blood pressure would drop. This meant that not enough blood was getting to the heart due to clogged arteries. I decided on the surgery now rather than after my heart had been damaged.

"The whole experience was not at all the terrifying one I thought it would be. Credit for that is due to the policy of Dr. Johnson and his associates for having anyone involved in the surgery visit the patient to explain their role and to answer questions.

"The most comforting visitor was John Binford who said he'd be running the heart-lung machine. I told him I was not fearful of dying on the table but I was concerned about the pain. Someone had told me that no painkillers could be used in this type operation. I had been too chicken to verify that with my cardiologist.

"That's not so," Binford replied, repeating the phrase three times for emphasis.

"Boy, am I happy to hear that," I replied. A load had been lifted off my chest, figuratively speaking.

"The result of the operation was this: No evidence in a post-operation checkup of an inadequate blood supply to the heart during exercise.

"One uncertainty remains, will I set off alarm systems while boarding airplanes because of the steel wires in my chest?"

An Inside Look At Cataract Surgery

"The road back to good vision was traveled in just 45 minutes.

"That's the time it took to remove a cataract from my right eye at the Eye and Ear Clinic.

"I went there, because I had found it increasingly difficult to read, particularly in subdued light. Also, my vision of distant objects was getting blurry.

"I reported to the clinic at 6 a.m., where a nurse spent the first hour and a half dilating my eye. This opens the pupil so the lens will be fully exposed to the surgeon.

"At 8:30 a.m. I was wheeled into the operating room where Dr. Terry Sorom would do the surgery. There sterile drapes were placed over my head and face and an anesthesiologist inserted a needle into my right arm to provide sedation that would make me relax during the procedure.

"A pad was attached to my left arm to measure blood pressure. A bit later, I was given a local anesthetic to relax the muscles around the eye and prevent movement in the critical area.

"I could hear the doctor and the staff of three confer repeatedly during the 45 minutes I was prone. But, much to my surprise, I never felt a thing, not the prick of a needle that provided the local anesthesia, not the doctor working on the eye, not a thing!

"Dr. Sorom said I might have actually been "out" for a few minutes due to the intravenous sedation. But I don't think I was.

"Dr. Sorom later explained the operation to me. He said the lens of the eye is naturally clear. A cataract is not a film over it, but the lens itself becomes clouded as the result of different things, the aging process being one of them — much like the graying of your hair. The clouding causes dim or blurred vision because light needed for good vision cannot pass through to the back of the eye.

"To do the surgery, Dr. Sorom used a high-powered operating microscope. He first made a very small incision — one eighth of an inch — in my cornea, the clear window in the front of the eye. Through it he inserted a hollow probe that looks like a rod and vibrates at a very high speed.

"The ultrasonic vibration, 40,000 cycles a second, actually broke up my lens into tiny fragments and removed some of it. Through another probe, the remainder of the lens was sucked out. But the "capsule sack" in which the lens was located was left intact.

"Next, the surgeon extended the tiny incision so he could insert into the sack the new plastic lens I was to see through. A quarter of an inch in size, it is equipped with two loops which hold it in place by tension.

"The operation complete, Dr. Sorom then sewed up the incision. Only three stitches were needed. Small incisions allow for more rapid recovery.

"I felt none of the incision-making, nor the vibration of the probe or the stitching. Before I was wheeled back to my room, a patch was put over the operated eye, which I wore home and left on until my examination by the doctor the next morning.

"Dr. Sorom put no restrictions on what I might do except not to "chop wood or ride horses." Three hours after being discharged, my daughter, Julie, and her husband, Dean, drove me to Seattle where I attended a University of Washington reunion in the evening.

"I had been told I could take Tylenol if I developed post-surgery pain, but I never found the need to use it because the discomfort was so minor.

"For three weeks after surgery, I wore a metal patch over the eye at night so I wouldn't scratch or disturb it while sleeping. For five weeks, I used special eye drops at various frequencies.

"The first drop contained antibiotics, the other an anti-inflammatory substance.

"I did not see clearly at once. But in a couple of days I noticed that I could read the fine print that had formerly eluded me. I also found the TV clearer.

"Dr. Sorom found I had 20-20 vision in the treated eye. I could read the whole test chart instead of the three or four lines of days past.

"The doctor said there is a popular misconception that lasers are used in the operation to remove cataracts. But lasers are utilized only in the correction of some other eye problems.

"My operation cost $3,418, which covered the fees of the surgeon, anesthesiologist, and the use of the Wenatchee Surgical Center. Blue Cross and Medicare will pay all but $100. Thus my out-of-pocket expense was minimal.

"Like every cataract surgery patient, I required new glasses because the eye with the intraocular implant now had a different, clearer, refraction.

Dam and Mountain Celebrations

As managing editor of the Wenatchee World, I served as master of ceremonies at several public functions.

Major ones included the dedication of Rocky Reach Dam and the start up of the third powerhouse at Grand Coulee Dam.

The Rocky Reach event occurred on July 20, 1963, outside the powerhouse.

Rocky Reach Dam is Dedicated

I started the Chelan County PUD affair in a most unusual way. I told the audience that I could not understand why I was picked to be the master of ceremonies. I said I presumed it was because I was always full of enthusiasm just as were the PUD board members in bringing the great project about. I went on to say I had just finished a Dale Carnegie course where the teacher tries to get class members to show a lot of enthusiasm about their subject. I'll illustrate how the Carnegie teacher did it, I told the crowd. He asked that you roll up a newspaper and when speaking wave it about in making a point. Like this, I said, waving the roll of newspaper over my head. An inexperienced speaker does not show enough animation, which makes an audience think he or she is dull. I illustrated this by saying, This is a great project brought about by men of vision speaking in a monotone and barely moving the paper about.

But the speech students were told to wave the rolled paper about vigorously in order to show more emotion. Finally, they catch on and do it the way Carnegie wanted them to do. I showed this to the audience by raising my voice and shouting "This is a great project brought about my men of vision!" while hitting the podium resounding whacks which when picked up by the microphone sent out loud bangs.

This was so effective the audience of about 2,000 gave me a loud ovation. It was the first time I ever got such a reaction in relation to making introductory remarks.

Among the dignitaries attending the affair were U. S. Senator Henry "Scoop" Jackson. He said, "Rocky Reach is an example that public and private power have learned to live together." He added that occasional differences of opinion needed to be resolved and continous cooperation attained.

He went on:

"Having said this, let me say also that those in the public sector of river development need to rekindle the spirit that brought us Grand Coulee and the lowest power rates in America. There have always been, even in our own region, doubters as to the role of the federal government and the publicly-owned agencies in river development. And there is a whole new generation of Northwesterners who do not fully realize the Herculean effort of public-spirited citizens that was necessary to obtain an abundant supply of low-cost power, to build dams we tend to take for granted."

The senator recalled "the men of vision" from this area's colorful past — Jim O'Sullivan, Billy Clapp, Rufus Woods and others who set us on this great course of comprehensive river development. He said President John F. Kennedy "joins me in congratulating you who have made this project possible."

Dignitaries from all over the United States and Canada were on hand for the colorful ceremony which christened the $263,000,000 project.

Bright sun shown on the ceremonies and the surface of Lake Entiat sparkled. The 43-mile long reservoir formed by the dam is one of the major recreational by-products.

More salutes to the project came from other people on the program: Ivan Compton, president of the Chelan PUD Board of Commissioners; James K. Carr, Under Secretary of the Interior; Congressman Walt Horan; Major General R. G. MacDonnell of the U. S. Army Corps of Engineers, and Earl Coe, Secretary of State, representing Governor Albert Rosellini. Senator Warren G. Magnuson missed the dedication because he was stricken by illness.

Earlier during the construction, I was on a committee with Kirby Billingsly to check into providing tourist facilities, particularly those needed to view fish going up a ladder in getting past the dam.

I suggested we have a slogan to encourage visitors. I first came up with "A Submarine View of the Fish", but the final suggestion I made was the one used . . . "Look a Salmon in the Eye."

The Priest Rapid guys made fun of my slogan and came up with their own — "Look a Bass in the . . ."

Putting a Highway Across the Mountains

The Wenatchee World has always been dedicated to the betterment and development of the area that it serves, so it was a strong supporter of the building of a North Cross State Highway between the upper Methow Valley and the Diablo Dam area on the west side.

From the time I joined the paper in 1954 until the road was completed, I

218

was a member of the board of directors of the North Cascades Highway Association. I was president of the group in 1966-67.

I attended all the board meetings, and, because no other paper covered the road promotion, I wrote nearly all the stories about the planning and later about its construction.

I made two promotional treks over the route, the first done on horseback during the yellow-jacket season. Some of the horses got stung and I and Ed Chalcraft of the Seattle P. I. were slightly "shook up" plus I lost my glasses. The second was in a four-wheel drive driven by Al Gracey of the highway department. I continued to write up yearly celebrations as the construction of the road advanced.

When the highway was dedicated on September 2, 1972, I was the master of ceremonies at the Winthrop celebration. It was followed by an official opening ceremony at Newhalem on the west side. Governor Dan Evans was the principal speaker on this side of the mountains and U. S. Senator "Scoop" Jackson on the other.

I was quite flowery in my opening remarks. They were:

"This is the day on which a dream of a hundred years comes true.

"This is the day the concentrated efforts of a group of persistent men over almost two decades bears fruit.

"This is the day the majestic, spectacular beauty of the North Cascades is opened for all of our people to see, young and old, feeble and strong.

"This is the day a new avenue of transportation brings closer together the people and economy of the west side and the east side for the benefit of both.

"This is the historic day you participate in making history in the state of Washington.

"This is the day we open the North Cascades Highway!

"The significance of the occasion is attested to by the presence today of the governor of our state, distinguished representatives of key federal agencies, a congressman, the wife of a congressman and others associated with the tremendous task of creating one of America's most scenic highways and developing recreational facilities along its forest corridor."

Many speakers followed and the affair reached its climax when the governor and Lester Holloway of Twisp, who spent years promoting the road and never gave up even when others were discouraged, cut a ribbon across the road.

Two plaques were presented at the affair. They are now located at the Washington Pass viewpoint at the summit of the highway. One cites State Senator George Zahn, of Methow, for his great contribution in promotion of the road and for his many other highway projects, part of the time as a member of the State Highway Commission. The second plaque was dedicated to eight men who served as the most influential members of the North Cross-State Highway Association. Their names are: Sig Berglund, G.

W. Gannon, Sig Hjaltlin, S. S. McIntyre, Jack Abrams, Morris Bolinger, Lester Holloway and Leonard Therriault.

Following is a list of all the men who served as presidents of the association until the road was opened:

1953-54	Sig Berglund	Sedro Wooley
1954-55	Sig Berglund	Sedro Wooley
1955-56	Jess Sapp	Sedro Wooley
1956-57	Les Holloway	Twisp
1957-58	Sig Hjaltlin	Bellingham
1958-59	George Zahn	Methow
1959-60	Chuck Dwelle	Concrete
1960-61	Jack Wilson	Mazama
1961-62	G. W. Gannon	Bellingham
1962-63	Jack Abrams	Twisp
1963-64	Lowell Peterson	Concrete
1964-65	Chuck Hulsey	Oroville
1965-66	Arnell Johnson	Anacortes
1966-67	Hu Blonk	Wenatchee
1967-68	Ken King	Bellingham
1968-69	Clair Penz	Omak
1969-70	Sid McIntyre Jr.	Sedro Wooley
1970-71	Ernie Johnson	Ferndale
1971-72	Leonard Therriault	Brewster

During the Winthrop ceremony, I paid tribute to Mrs. Otto Wagner for it was she and her husband who contributed financially to the transformation of Winthrop into a village of the 1890's era. The old western town is complete with wooden sidewalks, false-fronted buildings and antique looking signs such as the one advertising "Bull Durham" tobacco.

There was a strange follow-up to the celebration. A former aide to Governor Dan Evans claimed that he was the first person to officially cross the new highway, driving the governor in a small van.

I had Dick Larsen, who formerly worked for me and was associate editor of the Seattle Times, check with the governor. Evans pooh-poohed the claim.

The former aide was the notorious Ted Bundy, who was later found guilty of murdering several women and eventually was executed.

Big Button Starts Up Third Powerhouse

When the Bureau of Reclamation asked me to be the chairman of a major celebration at Grand Coulee, I always wanted to stage something out of the ordinary that would draw major public attention — a publicity gimmick.

At the start-up of the third powerhouse on October 12, 1975, we wound up having "the world's largest button" to start the first of six huge generators.

I thought I had a most unusual way to mark the start of the power generation, but we had to give up the idea because of the expense.

This AP story explained it:

"Organizers of the dedication for a new powerhouse at Grand Coulee Dam have abandoned plans to have red, white and blue water pour over the spillway.

"But lest the moment go unnoticed, an eight-foot tall bicentennial emblem will glow with tri-colored neon lights as the first huge generator is turned on.

"Speaking at the dedication will be Senator Henry Jackson, Democrat-Washington.

"Hu Blonk, chairman of the preparation committee, said plans to use red, white and blue water were abandoned because of financial reasons.

"Blonk said it would have required 300 pounds of dye for each color. That would have cost $2,000 for a two-minute display of water pouring down the 300-foot spillway.

"The committee had obtained clearance from the state Department of Ecology to use the dye, providing it was non-toxic.

"The company that was consulted, American Cyanamide, provides the dye that is used to make the Chicago River green each Christmas."

The colored water idea not being feasible financially, we concentrated on the "big button." It was about 2½ feet square and was placed at the top of the speakers platform.

At the actual ceremony I was asked to introduce the Bureau's regional director after having made my opening remarks. This, in short, is what I said:

"This is a momentous day. On occasions like this when you honor the accomplishments of engineers, labor and contractors, one frequently is able to say that this is the day a dream comes true.

"But this can't be said here today. Several years back no one even dreamed of a third powerhouse at Grand Coulee Dam in which a staggering four million kilowatts of hydroelectric power would be produced. No one, not even the farsighted Rufus Woods, or the tenacious Jim O'Sullivan, or the fluent W. Gale Matthews, or Billy Clapp, the man who had the original idea of a dam at the mouth of the Coulee. This quartet of people, now deceased, was mainly instrumental in bringing about this massive structure, minus the third powerplant, that is.

"We are here today not merely to start another generator on the Columbia River. We are commemorating, to use another man's words, 'the spirit of achievement that is the spirit of America.' For this is achievement at its greatest."

U. S. Senator "Scoop" Jackson was the principal speaker at the hour-long ceremony and there were many other dignitaries present who spoke. These included: Representative Thomas S. Foley; Representative Mike McCormack; Secretary of the State Bruce Chapman; Administrator of the Bonneville Power Administration, Donald P. Hodel; and Commissioner of the Bureau of Reclamation, Gilbert G. Stamm.

Jackson said, among other things "Today's ceremony marks the latest in a long series of events leading toward the full development of the tremendous resources of the Columbia River.

"I am particularly gratified to have had a part in bringing about construction of the Third Powerhouse, because it is the kind of resource development which is clearly in the interest of the local people, the State, the Pacific Northwest and the nation.

"Our growth and prosperity and the quality of life we and our children will enjoy in the future depend in large measure upon how wisely this resource is managed and protected.

"As we strive to meet the basic material needs of our expanding population, we discover that new public aspirations have been created. Today these aspirations are directed towards recreation, open spaces, clean air and water, freedom from noise, natural beauty, pleasing design and other amenities which together constitute the 'quality life.'

"The Third Powerhouse symbolizes what can be done with intelligent foresight, careful planning and a balanced policy."

It takes lots of energetic work to put on a celebration of this kind. I was fortunate to have a great committee in staging it. They were: Bob Evans, project manager; Jack Hilson, Grand Coulee Chamber of Commerce; Esther Rice, Coulee Dam Chamber of Commerce; Don Bowsher, president of the Washington State Reclamation Association; John Ulrich, Public Affairs officer for the Bonneville Power Administration, Portland; and Steve Wade, Public Affairs, USBR, Boise.

Dam's 50th Anniversary Celebration Joyous Affair

It was one of the state's most spectacular celebrations that hundreds of volunteers and USBR people staged in 1983 to commemorate the 50th anniversary of the start of construction of the Grand Coulee Dam.

It took a committee of eleven a year's time to plan and direct it.

On the committee in charge of the joyous affair were: Chairman, Hu Blonk, retired managing editor of the Wenatchee World; Vice Chairman, Stephen G. Wade, USBR Regional Public Affairs Officer; State Department of Ecology, Donald Moos; Bonneville Power Administration, Wenatchee District Manager, Ronald K. Rodewald; Director East Columbia Basin District, Earl Terwillegar; Grand Coulee Chamber of Commerce Jack Hilson; Spokane Chamber of Commerce, R. R. "Dick" Ahrens; Columbia Basin Development League President, Wistar Burgess; Colville Confederated Tribes, Legislative Chairman, Ernie Clark; Columbia Basin Project Office, USBR, Carol Prochaska; and Grand Coulee Dam Project Information Officer, USBR, Craig Sprankle.

Twenty-five thousand people attended the three-day affair beginning on July 16, 1983. There were a lot of activities for them to enjoy.

The speaking program was staged at the third powerhouse and featured Secretary of the Interior James Watt as the key speaker. He was loud in his praise of the vision and courage of the men and women who fought for construction of the dam and spoke in spectacular fashion about the project.

"Listen," Watt urged the crowd of about 5,000 people.

They cocked their ears to hear the roar of millions of gallons of water cascading down the dam's face.

"Listen to the sound of power," added Watt.

222

"It is the power to improve the quality of life . . . to make our nation great."

He went on "There are those who say we built too many dams, that we produce too much power, that we are in an era when Americans must accept limitations on our future.

"There are those who say we have an excess capacity to produce food today, that we have no further need for reclamation projects.

"But" the secretary went on, "we won't let this happen because we are in the presence of greatness . . . for here we can feel the spirit of those who launched the building of the Grand Coulee Dam . . . and their spirit is America."

During the speech the secretary promised that the Reagan Administration would support the completion of the Columbia Basin Project, then half-done with irrigation achieved on 500,000 acres.

"This Administration is going to work with the people of this area and the State of Washington to finish the job," Watt said. (In later years, no such support was evident).

Watt went on to say that originally the dam was called "impressive in the magnitude of its folly" and projects on the Columbia River were called "dams of doubt."

"On the contrary, the Columbia Basin Project has been successful beyond the wildest dreams of its early proponents, he said.

"It is because of such men and women of vision and action that today's Americans have a high standard of living, abundant food and power, and, indeed, our very freedom."

With Wilfred Woods, publisher of the Wenatchee World, as master of ceremonies, the program also featured colorful dancing by Indians from the Colville Reservation; a presentation to Elliott Roosevelt, son of President Franklin D. Roosevelt; speeches by Representatives Tom Foley and Sid Morrison; music by two military bands; the Mullen Brothers singing "The Grand Coulee Dam," written by Woody Guthrie; and a welcome speech by Governor John Spellman.

During the ceremony, five bombs burst in the air to signify the first 50 years of the Columbia Basin Project. To illustrate the impact it had on agriculture, small tractors pulling carts filled with produce rolled by in front of the crowd.

Two events later in the day were particularly attractive to those in attendance.

Every person who had worked on the dam was given a 12-by-9-inch certificate featuring a large color photo of the dam with space alongside for the recipient to fill in his name.

A great fireworks display in the evening drew many "Oh's" and "Ah's." The setting for it was perfect — the top of the dam illuminated by the usual colored lights.

As state or federal funds could not be used to put on the pyrotechnics, we had to get funding elsewhere. I wrote the heads of the major companies that had built the dam. The chairman of the board of the Kaiser Company, Steve Girard, who had been a young engineer on the project and a personal friend of mine, sent us $5,000.

There were at least 40 other activities on the schedule including a free barbeque catered by a Spokane restaurant, a carnival, a beer tent, the Wenatchee Youth Circus, a street dance, photo displays, an arts and crafts show, catamaran races, a fun run, a champagne brunch, a dam builders reunion picnic, a celebration of worship, etc.

The Wenatchee World's 64-page tabloid on the 50th Anniversary celebration contributed greatly to the significance of the celebration.

The only annoyances during the program were a few protestors carrying signs criticizing the secretary's environmental policies. One sign stated, "Dam Watts, Not Rivers." There were also some labor unions marching as an exhibition of solidarity against the Reagan labor policies. I feel it was the threat of the latter that kept President Reagan from being at the festivities.

On occasions like this, or, whenever a reporter serving radio, television and a newspaper focussed on a bit of history about the project, Stan Pachosa, a retired bureau man and former construction stiff, and myself were often interviewed. We were portrayed as "old-timers" who were there when it all took place.

The Strange Bank Robbery

Covering a bank robbery in the Methow Valley landed me in the federal court in Spokane.

The case involved a former, Navy petty officer named Anton V. Evalt. He held up the Commercial Bank of Twisp in an odd way.

I wrote that in the Methow Valley, with its rugged individualists and assortment of odd characters, things were done differently.

I said, take yesterday's $4,400 bank holdup, for instance.

"1. The robber is dressed as conspicuously as can be. He wears a sailor hat pulled down over his ears like a northwester, an Air Force rain jacket, red gloves and a loose-fitting shroud, made of a women's scarf or something else sheer.

"2. A Wenatchee businessman who follows the thief into the Commercial Bank of Twisp doesn't realize for a while that a holdup is taking place. He thinks some farmer has come in and failed to take off his beekeeper's veil.

"3. An auto mechanic, on his way to the bank, stops on a corner across the street, sees the thief, with mask and gun, go into the bank but thinks it's all a big gag (even when the robber drives off).

"4. The robber is seen speeding away in an old car with one hand on the steering wheel, holding a fistful of money. He obviously came into the bank without anything to carry away the loot.

"5. The robber burned the get-away car on a new concrete bridge over a clear, blue stream called "Buttermilk Creek.'

"6. A few hours after the hold-up, the town mayor starts a pool, with the pay-off going to the person guessing closest to the time the robber will be caught."

Evalt (the suspect) made his way across the Cascades to Stehekin where he was caught. He was just wearing tennis shoes and had a hunk of cheese and some dates with him.

After he was taken to the Chelan County jail, I got permission to interview him. Sheriff Dick Nickell advised him he did not have to talk to me, and, I myself, told him the same thing, but I did state that if he told his story perhaps it might stop some other person from making the same mistake.

I put no pressure on Evalt.

At the end of the interview, Evalt asked me if I would do him a favor. I said I would if I could. He then said: "Would you tell my wife?" I said I would and did so, his wife breaking down, even though I tried to be as gentle as I could.

George Richardson, a reporter at that time, and myself were subpoenaed by the prosecution to testify at his trial in Spokane. The defense attorney tried to get me to say Evalt appeared crazy which I refused to do, saying I couldn't tell a crazy man from a normal one. I could say that honestly, because a few months before a member of our advertising staff came to me and sought to get his story and a picture of his feet in the paper because he thought he was Jesus Christ. The next day he spread-eagled himself on Wenatchee Avenue. He was sent to Medical Lake. Evalt was convicted.

Evalt's attorney appealed to the United States Court of Appeals in San Francisco which set aside his conviction and critized the publication of his confession to me, because it created the possibility "that the defendant will be unable to get a fair trial."

In the decision, the judges took a crack at me saying too many reporters "seem to regard it as their right and duty to get the story regardless of whose rights they invade or how they may invade them." The judges said we should not have been allowed to testify.

I struck back at the court saying in an AP story that it was "another case of nitpicking in which the higher courts have lately been engaged to the detriment of society."

We testified again in a retrial of the case and Evalt was convicted.

Articles Not Always Wholly Truthful

Except one day a year you could pretty much believe everything you read in the Wenatchee World.

That "one day" was when I described the annual "Ardenvoir Swallow Festival" by exaggerating what took place and adding humorous observations.

A typical story was one "The Bird Watchers Digest" of July 1977, picked up.

It went like this:

"You wouldn't exactly say Ardenvoir, Washington, spared no expense in staging its first annual festival to herald the yearly return of its swallows on March 12. But it did have five "floats." Well, sort of. The parade featured an ancient land cruiser and four pick-ups that definitely showed their age, each bedecked with half a dozen strips of colorful loggers — flag tape strung from cab to tailgate.

"There was no music — only the honking of horns — and a hundred or more spectators, none of whom was seen to applaud or was heard to say what a remarkable spectacle it all was. But there was a swallow queen, 41-year-old Gayla Wellendorf, who was hard put to keep her balance standing up in one of the oldest of the vintage trucks.

"True to tradition, she wore a crown, a sparse creation of a few chicken feathers, which she struggled to keep on her head during the breezy ride. She held a bouquet of large flowers made of crepe paper, because the roses hadn't bloomed yet.

"It was all over in five minutes, but it was good enough, the half dozen townspeople who staged the festival agreed. It properly paid tribute to the 150 or so birds who come up from Central America each spring to mate and nest and raise their young and frolic inside the buildings of the mill that supports this upper Entiat Valley community of 150 people, more or less.

"The parade was lead by Ivan Sloan who was designated "grand marshal," for reasons he didn't know. Maybe it was because he drove an odd-looking, elongated, newly motorized tricycle he'd made out of a Volkswagon motor and a Harley-Davidson front end.

"The mile-long run not only honored the graceful, swift-flying swallows but also the gal who'd correctly estimated their arrival date — Ms. Wellendorf. She works in downtown Ardenvoir's business district, which consists solely of Chuck Cooper's Store, his combination tavern-cafe, and his gas pump. Explaining her accuracy reasonably enough, she said that she just picked her birthdate.

"The correct estimate made her "queen of the parade" — although no one called her that — and, as such, she entertained the loyal citizenry at a reception held at the City Center, otherwise known as Cooper's Store. She personally served beer, Coca Cola, or whatever anyone ordered as long as the $52 she'd won ($2 from each person guessing a date) lasted.

"Her name is now inscribed on the wall of the cafe-tavern along with the last years' winner, Mae Ellis. Near the white cardboard plaque, hangs the arrival times of the swallows, dating back to 1968. The statistics are kept by Tom Raspet, a millworker here for 28 years. He drove a 1950 Chev in the parade, with the sign "Official Record Keeper" on it. His data shows that the dates vary from March 4 in 1976 to April 14 in 1968.

"The making of the festival begins each year when mill workers and others put their money into a pot and start looking for the first swallow to arrive. When someone spots one or more, he or she shouts excidely — in manner of Paul Revere — "The swallows are here! The swallows are here!" The shout is echoed and re-echoed all through the valley.

"It isn't just any old swallow that's honored here. The watchers-for-the-birds will have nothing to do with the common barn swallow. The species heralded in Ardenvoir is the violet-green swallow. Glossy green and purple above, pure white below, it has two white flank patches. Violet-greens, a.k.a "Tachyineta Thalassina," prefer Western fields and canyons, so naturally they like Ardenvoir.

"The birds have to be smart enough not to come too early, because they are sensitive to weather and have been known to be "decimated by cold spells," as the ornithologists say, which is every bit as bad as being wiped out by a blizzard.

"This writer, who rode in the newest of the old pickups with Harvey Seat which carried a sign which proclaimed "Hu Blonk, Swallow Festival's Official Reporter," feels he must preserve what's left of his integrity by admitting, although he is sorry to have to do so, that he never has seen a single swallow. He asked the Official Record Keeper, Tom Raspet, "Why?"

"Putting down his bottle of beer at the queen's reception in Cooper's Store, Raspet deliberated only momentarily. "There's too much wind," he said. "They don't like wind."

"To which, between gulps, parade-arranger Jim Smothers added "They're so light, you know."

"Because the men have honest-looking faces, I am inclined to believe them."

Spectacular Pages Brighten Paper

News events of significance warranted spectacular front pages. It was always fun to dream up unusual make-ups.

When man first landed on the moon, we published a particularly colorful one. Red, yellow and blue predominated, and there were only three stories on the front page, all relating to that subject.

The headline was in red. In letters three inches high it read "Man on Moon." Below it was a photo of the landing printed in blue that took up four of the five columns of the page and ran 12 inches deep. Along side the picture was a three-deck subhead of large letters that read "July 20, 1969, 7:56 PM."

Below the photo was a block of yellow, four columns wide which carried the head "This Is Way It Was on Earth." The block of copy started out "To Readers of the Daily World In the 21st Century" and was followed by short sentences citing individual situations. Here are a few:

"A quart of milk cost 30 cents, a loaf of bread, 37 cents . . . Nixon was President . . . Wenatchee had a population of 19,000, East Wenatchee, 11,000 . . . the North Cascades Highway is due to be completed soon . . . A box of Red Delicious brought growers $8 at the end of the season . . . the state record low temperature was at Winthrop at 48 degrees below zero . . . the second Wenatchee River bridge is being designed . . . No cure for cancer has been discovered yet . . . Juvenile delinquency is a major problem . . . etc."

I ran this thinking that the historic issue would be read many years later and therefore readers would be interested in such a summary.

On December 24, 1962, we made Page 1 look like it had been published on "The First Christmas . . ."

To make it look old we gave it a yellowed look. Dick Larsen did the whole page for me, including the sketches. Dick was quite an artist.

The top head read "King Herod In Trouble?" Another large one read "Emperor Urges Cooperation in Census; Towns Crowded." Another sizable head read "A Strange Birth Reported." Others read "Temple Priest Tells of Pair of Miracles." "Bright Star Seen in Area." etc.

On a Leap Year one February, we ran a full page of mug shots of eligible bachelors under the head "Calling All Girls: It's Leap Year." We said we were doing this "as a public service for girls."

Under each photo, we gave the man's occupation, his height and weight, and the color of his eyes and hair. We stated that, "we have not provided phone numbers, figuring you should be allowed to exert some initiative."

About a month later, we had a dandy follow up. A handsome farmer shown on the page got married to his bankteller after she started kidding him about the story. So, we had a second good story.

Under the letters heading of the story "Campaigning In the Rain," I drew in raindrops an inch or two long that looked like they were about to strike a tent showing youngsters inside.

I printed a 3-column punch card over a story about a study to be made on the effect of pesticides on humans. It read "Are You Still Alive? If Not, What Happened?"

An unusual display was on the story "Physician Tests Heart by Phone." This dealt with taking a cardiograph of a heart by long distance telephone. On the right side of Page 1, I showed the wires being attached to the patient in Soap Lake, Washington, and, at the left, Dr. D. J. Hoxey reading the electrocardiograph in Wenatchee. Through the four columns of type between the two pictures I ran what looked like a telephone line connecting the two scenes.

Alongside a story called "William Greime, 40 Movie Years," we carried what looked like a strip of 35 millimeter film including rachet marks and four pictures of Greime's head, one above the other, just as faces are shown on a real strip of film at a theatre.

Looking Ahead to the Year 2000

The most spectacular section printed was published on June 28, 1965, the sixtieth anniversary of the paper. It consisted of six pages headed "Headlines of Tomorrow" and it was profusely illustrated with sketches and photos depicting what advancements in technology would exist in the year 2000 or earlier.

Nearly all the articles were provided by various agencies. For instance, the U. S. Atomic Energy Commission predicted a visit on Mars and electronic libraries. The Inland Empire Waterways Assn. forecast a "NCW Waterway to Alaska." General Motors said that cars would follow an electric beam in a highway and relieve the driver of the necessity of steering. They would also have built-in shopping carts.

The Pacific Northwest Newspaper Assn. predicted that future readers of the Wenatchee World would get their news and advertising off TV screens in their homes. "Medical Discoveries Amaze the World" the American Medical Assn. told the paper. "Pocket Phones" were forecast by General Telephone.

"Tree Overcoats" that will literally turn North Central Washington into a vast series of plastic greenhouses as protection against insects and disease were foreseen by a Washington State University official. A fourth powerhouse at Grand Coulee Dam was predicted by the Bureau of Reclamation. A French scientist announced a hormone that will eliminate the need for men to shave their faces and women their legs.

Russians claimed they would be the first to reach the center of the earth just as they did in outer space in the 20th Century. Boeing told us planes would carry 1,000 passengers on the World's 100th anniversary. Surgeons are considering the possibility of replacing entire natural organs with artificial counter parts (that has come about).

Ohio Turnpike officials announce wheelless transportation was forthcoming using a self-generated cushion of air that would save millions in the upkeep of highways.

The Washington Apple Commission manager, Joe Brownlow, said nuclear-powered trains will bring about faster service into Eastern and Southern markets.

The Radio Corporation of American predicted TV sets that would fit into a lady's handbag, wall-size TV screens and changing of channels on the screen by means of the viewer's voice.

The Department of the Interior saw a huge water supply network to move converted ocean water to key areas all over the U. S. The State Highway Department forecast a nuclear-powered machine that would go through virgin ground and spew out in its wake a completed paved road and signals that "speak"to the driver.

Other predictions included long malls downtown and many new industries along the Columbia River. J. C. Penney foresaw clothing made of stretch paper and "Forecast" magazine thought that "Spaceliners" of the future would fly to the moon where there would be hotels with underground golf courses and a 150-pound man would only weigh 24¾ pounds.

Lots To Do Besides Newspapering

Wenatchee World Press Run

For seven or eight years, one of my favorite tasks was to stage foot races in town. We called it the "World Press Run" a name suggested by press boss Bud Preston. It was a 10-kilometer and a 5-kilometer competition for about 300 runners pounding down Wenatchee streets.

Our awards were "the most unusual in American Road Racing," I claimed. They were aluminum press plates on which front pages were printed. These carried the names of winners in individual headlines such as "Mary Jones First in Press Run." The rest of the page contained photos of runners and a list of the winners.

Those finishing highest got the plates mounted on hard wood, others were framed and still others were presented unframed.

Each entrant had a colorful T-shirt and a certificate saying he or she had competed.

The races were very popular but were abandoned to give publicity to the more civic "Ridge to River Race."

I Talked A Lot

In addition to my newspaper duties, I took on other things that were of interest to me.

I gave many speeches, about 250, possibly more. Many were on the "people's right to know." Others involved appearances before newspaper groups and civic clubs on various topics.

The course on public speaking at Auburn High School and the University of Washington plus a Dale Carnegie course in Wenatchee stood me in good stead.

In my boyhood days in Holland, I had inclinations toward speaking in public. My mother once told me that as a child I would get on a chair and pretend that I was giving a speech. One time, I thought it would be nice to be an orator, not thinking that one could hardly make a living doing that.

"God's High Table" Brought an M.C. Job

A most memorable M.C. job occurred in Twisp.

Leland Cooley, the brother of Lew Cooley, Twisp banker and real estate man, wrote a book called "God's High Table," the setting of which was the Methow Valley. He was the producer of the Perry Como Show on television, and his wife, Lee, was choreographer for it.

The author, who became a good friend of mine, used local people as characters in the novel, such as Putt Darling, who ran the Wagner mill. The cafe now called the "Branding Iron", became a cafe and rooming house in which the heroine lived, Washington Pass the location where a religious sect settled. Twisp was called "Mill City."

To drum up publicity for the book, people in town decided to honor Cooley. They hung a big banner across the main street reading "Mill City" and staged a banquet. They asked me to M.C. the affair.

I remember my remarks in introducing Cooley. I said something like this:

"Ladies and gentlemen, I find it difficult to introduce our honored guest. I can't call him Mr. Leland Cooley, for no one in the Methow Valley is introduced so formally. I can't call him Lee Cooley, for his wife's name is Lee.

"So I figured another way of introducing the author, Ladies and gentlemen, here he is, 'the Grand Cooley.' "

Cooley hoped to have the novel made into a movie but never succeeded. He figured Clint Walker would be the ideal actor to play the role of Jeremy Godbolt, son of the patriarch of a religious sect, who fell in love with Clara Logan, an attractive widow who owned the leading bar and restaurant in Mill City called "the sinful Sodom."

Cooley later wrote a number of books, autographed copies of which he sent me. These included a prestigious one named, "California."

Ham Actor at Large

About six months after arriving in Wenatchee, I became involved in "Little Theatre." While I had very little talent, I earlier had been on the stage in minor roles and had written some skits in Boise.

230

My initial appearance was in "Two Blind Mice" presented by the Wenatchee Theatre Group. It was a three-act comedy directed by Beryl Briggs. I played the minor part of Major John Groh, USA.

The play was presented in the former Columbia Hotel as a theatre-in-the-round production. That involved the audience completely surrounding you. For a beginner it was a scary experience.

In the cast were Alma Trub, Tessa Bish, Bob Satterwhite, Kay Wagner, Harold Gribnau, Keith Sexson (a new arrival in town who went on via Wenatchee Valley College to direct and participate in many plays), Don Burns, Wayne Noyd, Donna Garrett, Ken Allen, Bob Firman, Bob Soth, Louis Crollard, Harold Walz, Neil Gellatly, Elmer Jacks, Dr. Ernest Movius, H. E. Miller, and myself.

The Junior Wenatchee Hospital Guild used to stage "Follies" periodically. These involved local actors and actresses and a professional New York producer.

In the "Follies of '55", I was in a skit entitled "Believe Or Not" with Joy Arch, Aileen Ramsey and Pete Painter. My role was of a Hollywood press agent, a gruff character.

In the "Follies of '58," I played a tough gangster in a sketch entitled "14th Street Speakeasy." Also in it were Chuck Wallach, Donna Garrett, Glen Siler, Dale Woods, Cal Paxman, Eric Erickson, Barry Fry, Ed Engst, Dick Riley, Lois Evans, Olive Schrengohst, Walla Evans, Nick Travers and Jim Schrengohst.

This performance is still vivid in my memory for something very unusual happened. I was to shoot somebody but for safety reasons the noise of the actual firing was to take place off stage.

For some reason, I thought about what I ought to do in case the noise of the gun firing did not take place. And sure enough it didn't.

So I looked into the barrel of the gun. Then the noise of the gun going off occurred off stage. The audience really roared. Someone whispered in my ear "Milk it Blonk . . . milk it!" So I looked in the barrel of the gun some more and said loudly (as I had planned), "Must be that cheap Talbott an Conway ammunition." That was the name of the leading sporting goods store in town.

At the beginning of the mishap I could see, out of the corner of my eye, that the producer was on the floor laughing his head off.

I did not continue long in Little Theatre, because I was always fearful I was going to muff my lines.

Radio Fascinated Me

I was a short wave radio listener, not a ham who talks by punching Morse Code or speaks via a mike.

I had a powerful Hammarlund HQ-140-XA, with numerous frequencies that I bought from my friend, Bill McGaughey of the Wenatchee World composing room staff.

With it I picked up news being broadcast in English by countries all over the world.

By telling these different countries what I'd heard and giving them a "SINPO" rating (Strength, Interference, Noise, Propagation and Overall reception), they'd send me a distinctive postcard from their country. I wound up with over 50.

Short-wave intrigues me as it seems a miracle that you can pick up someone talking as far away as South Africa and many other distant places.

Could Mr. Blonk be a Trifle Pink?

Newspapermen never escape criticism from readers. Sometimes it comes in a considerable quantity. I was the subject of two such. One came early in my editorship, when I described the area around Priest Rapids Dam as "desolate and God-forsaken." Our letters to the editor column called "Safety Valve" got some strong worded letters that said the area was beautiful and suggested Mr. Blonk be confined to coverage of Wenatchee Avenue or PTA goings-on. I never made that mistake again.

But the real deluge of letters came when I wrote a story under the heading "Writer Spends a Night with Birch Society."

I was in Seattle one night and noticed a large crowd mulling about at the Eagles Auditorium. I found it to be people waiting to hear Robert Welch, founder of the Birch Society. I wrote that a "mannish-looking" woman of middle age had a fistfull of tickets near the door. She was arguing with a couple of U. W. students who were trying to get in. She felt they were there to agitate but she finally let them in. I quoted an onlooker after asking him what the gathering was all about as saying that this was a "new racket in America."

I further wrote "Several times a wiry, pale-faced individual came up to the ticket taker to converse." He looked familiar.

Finally it dawned on me. This was Don Caron, the Conconully forest ranger, who said he quit his job when the Forest Service said he'd have to stop stirring up controversy with his writings on Communism, because it adversely affected good public relations.

I stated that he had called Dick Larsen, one of my reporters, "tricky Dick" after a recent interview. Thinking Caron, state coordinator for the Birchers, was going to be the speaker, and, thus give me a local angle, I flashed my press card and went in despite some effort to stop me. But it was Welch who was to speak. I described him as the man who had once called President Eisenhower "a dedicated, conscious agent of the Communist conspiracy."

I quoted him as saying that Senator Joseph McCarthy was unjustly attacked, that several thousands of Protestant clergymen were Reds, that President Roosevelt purposely enticed Japan to attack at Pearl Harbor to get us into war as part of a Communist conspiracy, and that the U. S. built air bases and powerful shortwave radio stations in some countries knowing the Reds would take them over.

I went on to write that he said there were Communists in government with Harvard accents, that to think Russia would never attack us was "sheer nonsense", because it would only be a mop-up operation after the country had been weakened by infiltration, that the Russians would take over American newspapers "which won't be much of a change," that

Communism never starts from the bottom. In Russia, it was forced on the people from higher stratas of society, Birch said.

I ended my story this way:

"In this country beware of Reds among the rich," said Welch in much fancier words.

Communism among the rich?

At this point we left."

Some letter writers took exception to my description of Caron as being "pale-faced" and the ticket-giver as looking "mannish."

One woman said she was cancelling her subscription. "My reason? I have yet to experience more disgust than I felt when I read Hu Blonk's account of Robert Welch's recent talk in Seattle . . . His description of Mr. Caron was as far from the truth as anything I've ever encountered." She added that my work should be "confined to writing fictional dime novels."

Another woman wrote "The main thing I got from Mr. Blonk's article was that we can't all be as good looking as he thinks he is."

A man wrote "I must regard his article as a masterpiece of sarcastic innuendo in complete ignorance of the truth."

Another writer said I must be a "frustrated juvenile."

Some indicated they suspected I had Communist leanings. One wrote "I would be interested in knowing exactly what Mr. Blonk's views on Communism are."

And another started her letter with the question "Could Mr. Blonk be a trifle pink himself?"

Nasty Letter Puts Writer in His Place

The severest rebuke I ever got came from Stella Stevens, the movie star, who had a ranch up Libby Creek in the Methow Valley.

I had interviewed her several times, and we got along fine, although she was moody and I never knew in what mood she was going to be.

A story about her opening a children's art gallery in Twisp got me in trouble. In the story, I made what I thought was a minor mistake. However, she wrote a nasty letter to Publisher Woods. I got to read the letter after he hollered for me to come into his office. I found him in hysterics over it. I laughed as hard as he did on reading it.

In the first paragraph of her letter she complained about the error I had made and in the second paragraph she said "Don't ever send that senile old fart up here again."

I quickly wrote Stella a letter saying I was sorry about the error and that it hurt, especially since I was trying to do her a favor in publicizing her gallery.

"But," I wrote, "I am coming up to see you again despite what you said, for I want to write up what it's like to have a part as an extra in the movie you said you were going to make up there. Surely there must be a role for a senile old fart in it."

Stella wrote back immediately to commend me for having such a good sense of humor. "I wouldn't think about doing a movie without you," she said. Later, she got annoyed about something else.

Treated Like Royalty in Japan

In 1970, I began an association that was to land me in Japan twice. I became the vice president and later the president of the Sister City movement in Wenatchee.

In 1970, Mayor Walter Young was contacted by the people of Kuroishi seeking a Sister City relationship. That community is situated in Aomori Prefecture in northern Japan, the same one in which Misawa, the city we later became aligned with, is located.

In 1971, Kuroishi sent over its deputy mayor to push for a tie-up with that community.

The town, located 50 miles or so from Misawa, is in an apple growing area and had an experiment station as Wenatchee did, so there was a natural alliance between it and Wenatchee. The two towns also shared an interest in the 1931 Pangborn-Herndon non-stop flight across the Pacific Ocean. Both had erected monuments honoring the intrepid flyers.

The mayor turned the problem over to a committee. On it were Ralph Nakata, Gene Snyder, Beulah Davenport, Doris Kirkpatrick, and myself. By April of 1972, a Sister City organization was formed headed by Paul Larsen, who was in charge of the experiment station here. The name given it was "International Cooperation Committee of Wenatchee." I was the vice president and the late Gregg Bitter its secretary-treasurer.

The group adopted by-laws and filed for articles of incorporation in Olympia, and we joined the Town Affiliation Association of the U. S. State Department.

Mayor Young died in November of 1972, after which Jack Grover served in that capacity and continued Young's involvement in international affairs.

In 1973, fifteen Japanese from Kuroishi visited here. They were greeted by 500 junior and senior high school students at the airport and otherwise given royal treatment.

In October of 1974 a Wenatchee delegation visited Kuroishi. In the party were Mr. and Mrs. Grover, Mr. and Mrs. Larsen, Mr. and Mrs. Marvin White, Mr. and Mrs. John Windhusen, Mr. and Mrs. Jim Kane, Mr. and Mrs. Harold Bidwell, Jean Miller, Barbara Hein, Mrs. Ivan Scates, Mr. and Mrs. Ron Reimer, and my wife, Martha and I.

A most unusual thing happened at a banquet in Kuroishi. We found large live fish on a number of the serving platters. They had been filleted but continued to move. One flopped off the platter. Mayor Grover said one winked at him. Japanese said this presentation of the fish constituted the greatest display of hospitality they can render visitors.

After the 1931 flight, the then-mayor Jack Rogers had sent apple saplings to Kuroishi. One tree, somewhat out of shape, was still growing when we visited.

There was only one exchange of visits between Wenatchee and Kuroishi.

In the early 1980's I became head of the Sister City committee, Mr. Larsen having moved to Utah. Mayor Grover and I sent individual letters to the mayor of Kuroishi, but got no response so it was felt that the association had ended.

In 1980, we helped bring about the issuance of a stamp honoring Clyde Pangborn and Hugh Herndon. The Hon. Osborne E. Pearson, assistant postmaster general, came here for the ceremony.

The alignment with Kuroishi brought about the Japanese Room you see in the North Central Washington museum. Ralph Nakata contributed considerable financial help toward making it a reality. Mayor Grover's $1,500 kimono, given to him in Kuroishi, is displayed there.

In 1981, Misawa came into the picture.

A delegation from that city came to the Washington State Apple Blossom Festival in Wenatchee. I remember being surprised because I had not been contacted by the group. Nevertheless, we made the Japanese feel welcome.

After the parade, a luncheon was served to them at my home in East Wenatchee. The food was Kentucky Fried Chicken along with beer and Coke. During the lunch, the Japanese took me aside to discuss a Sister City arrangement. I told the mayor of Misawa, through an interpreter, that Wenatchee already had a Sister City in Japan, and I did not know if it was permissible to have another.

The matter came to a head when the interpreter, a woman from Seattle whose husband, Bob Burnett, had worked for me, sort of whispered we would be given one million yen to help cover expenses when we visited Misawa. That would total about $5,000.

Subsequently, before our visit to Misawa in 1984, our group received half a million yen. While in Misawa, a small package was put at my table with the whisper not to open it then. It contained the other half million yen. That money aided our group for many years.

After the visitors departed, I asked the Town Affiliation office if it was O.K. for us to have two Sister Cities in the same country. It said it did not recommend such an arrangement. However, our group decided to go ahead without official affiliation with the national body. We now had two Japanese cities under our wing. Later, all interest in Kuroishi died.

Taking part in the initial visit to Misawa were: Mr. and Mrs. Ron Reimer, Mr. and Mrs. William Stewart, Helen Hathaway, Louis Bovee, Mr. and Mrs. Al Kane, Jean and Mark Miller, George Battermann, Marlind Nelson, Bob Curtis, Mildred Naughten, Margaret Mussen, my daughter Julie and myself, Martha having passed away.

During the visit, a formal ceremony featuring the official signing of the Wenatchee-Misawa Sister City agreement was held in the town convention center. Television and still cameramen filmed the event. Memorable moments of the affair were seeing and hearing several hundred school children sing American songs and a Japanese military band play "The Battle Hymn of the Republic."

While we were trying to decide what to take to Misawa as the offficial gift, Al Kane, rather sheepishly, had asked me if it would be proper to present a light off the wing of the plane in which Pangborn and Herndon had crash-landed at Fancher Field. I said "Yes." Wenatchee had the bent propeller.

In presenting it to the Japanese, I told the audience that Kane had saved the memento all these years so today it could be given to Misawa. By their laughter, they indicated they understood.

The Sister City alliance remains strong here because of the energetic leadership of several people and a loyal membership.

Of all the gifts presented to the Japanese visitors while in Wenatchee, I am most fond of the one I gave to a Japanese chicken farmer. I presented a live chicken to him at the headtable "so he would not be lonely for his flock." In the transaction, the excited bird left a messy deposit on my notes. This fact drew a roar of laughter.

During a half dozen visits I sang a song I had written to the tune of "I've Been Working on the Railroad." We had been told that the Japanese liked to sing at banquets. Much to our surprise, when Mayor Grover and I sang it in Kuroishi, the crowd hummed along with us. It seems the tune is a well known one in Japan.

In 1991, both cities celebrated the 60th anniversary of the Pangborn-Herndon flight and the 10th anniversary of the signing of the Sister City agreement.

Jogging Around The World

I guess I've only had three hobbies in my life — newspaper writing, photography and running.

I've pursued the latter since my days in Auburn, when I ran through Dad's cow pasture to the highway to get in shape for intramural cross country at the University of Washington.

When I went to work in Wenatchee, I took up jogging, competing in Saturday races in different towns. I won first place quite often in my age category or as the oldest jogger.

Whenever I took trips I ran in the mornings. That resulted in an article in the "The Jogger," published by the National Jogging Association. The magazine devoted two full pages and seven photographs that my wife had taken of me. The article was entitled "Traveler Jogging the World" and went like this:

"The moment we stepped outside the Kyoto, Japan, hotel for our morning jog, we could hear what sounded like the pounding of distant drums. It was barely dawn and the sun had not yet risen above the low roofs of the small houses in Japan's ancient capital. It was not yet light.

"For a few blocks, our footsteps were not diverted from our anticipated route by the mystifying noise we heard. Then our news instinct took over, and we wound our way through the narrow streets toward the rhythm, in one place passing large decorative signs leaning against a house denoting that someone had died.

"It did not take a long series of footsteps on the concrete to reveal the reason for the odd-hour commotion. A highly colorful scene came into view. All around a small track were to be seen large, highly colorful signs, none understandable to an American. But from all the shouting and excitement it was readily apparent that a track meet was taking place, with people of all ages, from children to bow-legged older men, participating.

"There were cute, teenage, yell leaders waving pompoms and leading songs, one surprisingly to the tune of "I've Been Working on the Railroad," which was popular in Japan.

"Questioning of some friendly Japanese who knew a little English disclosed that this was Sports Day in Japan. That's when all the government office buildings and stores close, and the nation has a full-fledged holiday to emphasize the importance of exercise. The competition here involved not schools but company trade unions.

"Running into sights such as this in a strange land is one of the extras in the world of jogging that many runners may be missing. To jog international is to make jogging educational, and it keeps you in tune with the schedule one maintains at home.

"Take Hong Kong, for example. There one can brighten up and make the daily run seem much shorter by galloping along a typhoon shelter. This is where junks and sampans are tied up to one another behind a breakwater in the busy harbor.

"As our feet moved forward, a constantly changing scene came into view and it aroused enough curiousity for us to later learn that in one place, 35,000 people spend their lives on these small craft, some reportedly never leaving the scene of poverty with its floating, smelly debris. One vessel had a TV set on it, we noted.

"In Taipei, Taiwan, near the Grand Union Hotel, one of the most ornate in the world, this lone American jogger was greeted by friendly family groups heading into the jungle-like hillside. We cut short our run to join them, going up a narrow gravel and dirt path leading into the dense forest."

"There a most un-American sight was revealed. At various levels of the sloping ground, one could see badminton nets spread across flat, dirt surfaces, near which adults were either doing their Chinese exercises or were gathered under tiny open-air shelters drinking tea or just chatting.

"Breaking out in a broad smile and moving our hands up and down alongside our head to denote exercising, we were invited over by a group grinning at our gestures. We joined them in their physical fitness activities which differ greatly from the American version.

"The Chinese have long studied the activities of animals indigenous to their land — the quickness of the tiger, the gentleness of the deer, the clumsiness of the bear, the nimbleness of the monkey and the gracefulness of the bird.

"The Chinese have attempted to adapt these movements into their martial arts, dance and sports, but they also have made them a part of their exercising. It's called "Wu chin hsin" (the frolics of five animals).

"If one's traveling on a luxury liner in the Caribbean or off Mexico, he will find the morning run a great experience. Dawn is a thing of beauty on the ocean. One can look directly into the sun as it comes into view on the horizon, it having a subdued but bright orange color.

"Dawn is also a great time to jog along the rim of the Grand Canyon. It offers one of the most spectacular jogging sights one will ever see, the sun gradually illuminating more and more of the rugged walls of the deep gorge as though a curtain of light was dropping to reveal the various geologic ages.

"The great tourist attraction is situated at an elevation of 5,000 feet so a jogger finds his breath coming a little bit harder than when he runs at sea level, such as at Waikiki, Acapulco or the scenic Oregon coast.

"For those who do their visiting at a nine to ten minute-per-mile pace, there are numerous other attractions — the park near Buckingham Palace, the monorail at Disney World in Florida near which the plants are in the shapes of animals are intriguing, the huge golf ball on a tee that rises 25 feet above the golf course at Taxco, Mexico, and serves as a huge water tank, Central Park in busy New York, the nations capitol, where guards holler "good morning" as you pass by and Cannery Row at Monterey, California where you hear seals barking from an island beyond the breakers.

"For those who insist on running on the level, the 'Forum' in Los Angeles and the New Orleans Superdome are excellent spots. The latter offers an obstruction-free run at the entrance level, which we found to be a half mile around. Level, too, is the four-fifths of a mile straight-a-way offered by the roadway that tops the Grand Coulee Dam.

"There, if one knows the right person, one can take the most unusual run of all, jogging a half-mile round trip in one of the galleries inside the 10½ million-cubic yard structure. There are 8½ miles of such tunnels in the dam.

"One of the worst places to jog is Bourbon Street in New Orleans, which one only does to say he did it. Sidewalks have purposely been left broken and twisted to retain the old French Quarter effect, and a turned ankle could be your reward if you do not keep your eye on the pavement ahead.

"Late afternoon is a total loss there for runners, because the narrow thoroughfare is jammed with people trying for a peek at the nearly naked girls who cavort on tiny stages in the semi-darkness of a number of places.

"If during your travels, you're confined to your hotel by the vagaries of weather you may have to jog inside your room, preferably in front of your TV set, to make the boring time go faster.

"But we must warn any jogger from doing what one super-enthusiast is supposed to have done. He ran in place in the confined lavatory space of the airplane he was on.

"That sent a concerned stewardess scurrying to the front of the plane to alert the pilot about a strange pounding in the rear of the aircraft that should be investigated right now!

Olympic Trials and Marathons

I paid my own way to the Olympic track & field trials in Eugene, Oregon, and Los Angeles, California and to a NCCA National Championships. Each of these lasted about a week. Armed with press credentials, I could get into the press tent where the top athletes were. I was a hero worshipper and enjoyed that tremendously.

In the Los Angeles Coliseum, my seat mate in the press box was Wilt Chamberlain, the tall professional basketball star.

One of the favorite running events that I covered at my expense was the Honolulu Marathon. I first attended because I had won an expense-paid trip by having the winning ticket in a drawing held for press guys who had run from Northgate in Seattle to the Kingdome.

During one of the Honolulu races, I stood near the starting line where the VIP entrants were lined up. One runner motioned to me on noticing the word "Press" on my official T-shirt. He asked me if I was going to be at the finish line and I said, "Yes." Then he asked me to carry his old sweatshirt and to give it to him at the end of the race. So I proudly carried the shirt belonging to Frank Shorter, the Olympic Marathon winner, a running legend.

The Honolulu race is a fun one. I saw five guys dressed in Santa Claus suits running the course. They were tied together with a rope. At the finish line I asked one "Why the ropes?" and the leader who was the head of the Honolulu Bar Association, said "Because we're Santapedes." Corny, huh?

Jogging With the Governor

Except for the difference in elevation and climate, a sore toe, a shoe lace untied, and the wife saying, "Don't you dare beat the governor, he's supposed to win," this jogger, age 66 at that time, would have beaten Governor Dan Evans in an early-morning, two-mile run.

That's not to belittle Evans for he was trim and in fine shape. He set a brisk pace for the six times around an old school field in Olympia, beating most of the 40 who joined him for the 11th annual invitational "Governor's Own Track Team Race" although it wasn't exactly a race.

Not as much can be said for some of his department heads.

Fishery department boss, Don Moos, lagged way behind, claiming afterwards "I'm too valuable, I can't kill myself."

Attorney General Slade Gorton was seen stepped off the running path trying to catch his breath.

Among the runners were three Evans-appointed Superior Court judges wearing sweat clothes that read "Caution. This Body is Protected By Contempt of Court."

Also represented was the Washington State Women's Council. Their sweatshhirts read "Women's Council Track and Hopscotch Team."

The start of the race, begun in semi-darkness, was given a Longacres touch. Ann MacRae, a former Tenino High School "tooter" played the "Parade to Post." MacRae was secretary to James Dolliver, who was an aide to Evans and later became a Supreme Court judge.

On the victory lap, the Governor told this writer that he got to jog about two times a week, if it didn't rain.

239

Big Crew Needed to Produce The World

In 1992 when this book was published, some members of the current staff had been serving as long as 50 years. Those who had served 15 or more years were:

50 YEARS or MORE
    LeRoy Snodgrass — Press-Camera
    Robert Woods — Associate Publisher
    Wilfred Woods — Publisher

45 YEARS or MORE
    Hu Blonk — Managing Editor and Special Writer

40 YEARS or MORE
    Dave Graybill — Packaging
    Bill McGaughey — Composing

35 YEARS or MORE
    Pat Green — Press
    Gary Montague — Classified Manager
    George Richardson — Managing and Executive Editor

30 YEARS or MORE
    Ralph Mitchell — Composing
    Skip Mussen — General Manager
    Gene Robards — Display Advertising

25 YEARS or MORE
    Nancy Dahlen — Credit, Purchasing
    Karen Kell — Ad Services
    Dave Kraft — KIOSK
    Gary Phippen — Display Manager
    Jean Smith — Classified

20 YEARS or MORE
    Marv Barham — Regional Editor
    Jim Beam — Controller
    Larry Chapman — Composing
    Irma Ficke — Accounting
    Betty Harris — Composing
    Jim Maxey — Display Advertising
    Mary Jo Milne — Editorial
    Ted Weaver — Composing

15 YEARS or MORE
    Nick Babcock — Sports Editor
    John Barta — Photo Lab
    Linda Barta — Library, TV World
    Sheila Graves — Editorial
    Marj Kearny — Composing
    Bob Koenig — Press Foreman
    Steve Lachowicz — Asst. Managing Editor
    Ernie McCart — Display Advertising

Christy Mirabelli — Circulation
John Moffat — Wire Editor
Kelly Murphy — Composing
Mike Reister — Composing
Dee Riggs — Editorial
Lory Rowe — Advertising
Toni Stubbe — Advertising
Tracy Warner — Copy Desk
Linda Worley — Art Supervisor

Current department heads who joined the staff 10 or more years ago were:

Linda Murphy — Circulation Director
Jay White — Advertising Director

Besides top newsroom personnel the following who are no longer on the paper were key figures in its production for many years during my term as managing editor.

Harlan Honeysett, who headed the composing room
Charles "Bud" Preston, who was the press foreman
Jack Watkins, General Manager
Eva Anderson, History Writer

While I was covering the damsite, Kirby Billingsley was in charge of the newsroom. He hired me.

When this book was published the following served in the editorial department (some have been mentioned earlier).

Kay Andreini — Copy Editor
Nick Babcock — Sports Editor
Marv Barham — Regional Editor
Hu Blonk — Special Writer
Kimberlee Craig — News
Debbie Duke — Newsroom Asst.
Susan Gillin — News Editor
Kathleen Gilstrap — Newsroom Asst.
Sheila Graves — People
Laurel Helton — Food
Mike Irwin — News
Dave Kraft — KIOSK
Steve Lachowicz — Asst. Managing Editor
Barbara MacLean — (People Editor until her retirement in late 1991.)
Steve Maher — Business
Jeannette Marantos — News
Doug Mattson — Copy Desk
Michael McCluskey — Sports
Mary Jo Milne — Fantasy Farm
Bruce Mitchell — Historian
John Moffat — Wire Editor
Michelle Partridge — Schools
Marla Pugh — Reporter
Lew Pumphrey — Crime

George Richardson — Executive Editor
Dee Riggs — People Editor, Religion
Dave Riggs — Sports
Robert Siler — Ephrata
Rick Steigmeyer — News
Tracy Warner — Copy Desk
Dan Wheat — News
Evan Wood — Sports
Rufus Woods — Managing Editor
Patricia Wren — Okanogan

Working in photo department were:
Don Seabrook
John Barta
Mike Bonnicksen
Kelly Gillin
Tom Williams

Historian Bruce Mitchell was extremely valuable to me in my "special writer" days and the following, among others, also aided me in various significant ways:

Cheri Rayburn	Phil Rayburn	Charlie Karl
George Ulin	Tim Patrick	Lory Rowe
Ray Viall	Lorna Lorti	Rolf Wagner

Those who served as reporters or worked in photography during my years as managing editor and are no longer there include:

Bob Burnett	Cliff Cameron	Dorothy Cameron
Jane Cartwright	Mike Cassidy	Dorothy Coryell
Lona Courtney	Beulah Davenport	Jeanne Doering
Neil Felgenhauer	Virginia Fish	Judy Gardner
Ray Halleran	John B. Harrison	Mary Hart
Keith Haugen	Herb Jenkins	Charles Kerr
Phil Kipper	Richard Larsen	Jim Lieb
Vern Matthews	Chris Meller	Mike Nickel
Dave Offer	Les Parr	Dick Pelto
Stan Pennington	Helen Peterson	Dick Pieper
Dave Rea	Larry Rader	John Richardson
Ray Schrick	Betty Skelton	Roger Simpson
Wey Simpson	Ronda Sisson	Genevieve Strand
Grace Weber	Jane Weber	Erika White
Bill White	Robert Woehler	Ralph Wood
Cliff Latimer		

In listing the many people I associated with in my 38 years on the paper, I particularly want to pay tribute to the great role Dick Pieper played as sports editor over nearly four decades. He died of a lingering illness in 1991. No employee was ever more loyal or hardworking.

This Hiring Was The Most Satisfying

Of all the employing I did the most satisfying was the one that added

Vern Matthews to the payroll. I contacted him in Ephrata after I had asked my friend, Dave Johnson, who published the Grant County Journal, if he knew of any good reporters available for I had an opening on the staff.

He had replied: "Yeh, if you can keep him sober — Vern Matthews. He's working for me."

I knew of Vern's ability because I saw his work when he published the "Post-Register" in Quincy. So I hired him, saying to myself that I'd have to let him go the first time he slopped over. Actually I knew I'd give him a second chance.

Vern never took another drink!

Not only that but he would go to Soap Lake weekly to help fellow alcoholics at "Alcoholics Anonomous" meetings and spend the night with those in Wenatchee who needed help.

I recall that Vern, who sometimes was assigned to come to work early in the morning in an editor's capacity, saying to me: "If someone had told me a year ago that I would be trusted to come to work by myself in the morning I'd have told them they were crazy."

His early death was a great loss.

So was that of my long-time friend Ray Schrick, who died of a heart attack at an early age. Joining us from the Wall Street Journal, he was the greatest investigative reporter we ever had.

Practical Jokes Brighten Life

In my high school annual under my senior class picture are the words:

"If someone couldn't laugh and be jolly, this world wouldn't be what it is by golly."

That was the first indication that I might become a practical jokester in later life. I can't remember the things I did to warrant the annual editor to say what he or she did, but I surely played a lot of practical jokes thereafter.

Fun In Boise

The joke involving the Boise Rotary Club and its aftermath is one of my favorites.

I was editor of the "Boisetarian", the club's weekly bulletin, during my days with the Bureau of Reclamation. I made it a fun publication. For instance, I pretended to be feuding with the club president, once publishing the bulletin on wrapping paper and then crumbling it up before mailing it because, I said, the president had been too tight to buy more stationery.

I had a friend, Barney Molohon, who published, for the fun of it, a publication entitled "The Burp Hollow Bugle" in "Burp Hollow, Maryland." That became my tool for a real practical joke.

I announced in the bulletin the club bulletin had been entered in a national contest to determine the best service club publication in the United States and said nothing more for about three months. Then the fun started!

243

I announced that the Boise weekly had been judged the best in the U. S. by the "Burp Hollow Bugle" in conjunction with the University of Maryland. I attached an issue of the "Bugle" that told of the award to the weekly issue of the "Boisetarian."

The "Bugle" said our publication had won the judges' praise because it had conducted a program to prevent Rotary Club International from becoming a club for be-mustached men only, the Club's past president, the present president and the past Rotary International president being so adorned.

The publication went on to say that the "Bugle" had found in two of three such cases that persons with unnatural growth had been removed from office and the existing president could not last much longer.

As a result of the achievement, I was to get an expense-paid trip to Washington, D. C., and tour the Pentagon (which was so big and elaborate that people were getting lost in the structure). Editor Blonk would also be interviewed over Radio Station "BURP" on time donated by a beer concern. And he would "visit the gas chambers of the House and Senate."

Each issue of the "Boisetarian" was mailed to the two daily newspapers in Boise. Much to my surprise and consternation, the afternoon paper took all this seriously and printed an eight-inch article headed "Rotarians' Weekly Publication Here Wins Nation-Wide Honors."

I had just finished reading it when the morning paper called me and in effect asked "What about this, Blonk?" I told the editor "It's all a hoax!", and he came out with a short article headed "Rotary Club Publication Award Is Termed Hoax."

That was followed by the evening paper's editor calling me up and shouting "Damn you, Blonk, you made us look like a horse's ass!" and me replying "Ernie, don't ever believe anything you ever read in the Boisetarian." The paper followed up with a story headed "Editor Says Story In Rotary Paper Was Merely Gag."

Then to make matters worse a morning paper columnist took a crack at the afternoon paper with this item: "The reddest face in Idaho: The Evening Statesman editor who fell for Hu Blonk's story hook, line and sinker. It was printed Thursday and it was one that will be remembered for a long time."

How any editor could take seriously such a silly article as I had written was beyond me.

The Seance

I was not always on the giving end of a practical joke. On two occasions, I was on the receiving end. The best one started with my receiving a phone call in the Wenatchee World lunchroom from someone who said "Mr. Blonk I understand you are interested in spiritualism?" I replied, "Maybe so." Then the caller went on to invite me to a spiritualistic sceance featuring "Madam Sobochowski" of Detroit.

I asked where it was to be held, and the man said the Burke Hotel. I told the newsroom people what had happened, and then added that I thought the Burke was a whorehouse and I wasn't about to go there. The next afternoon the same person phoned to say the seance had been moved to a house on Cherry St., so I said I'd be there.

On the day the seance was to take place, I had been up a side road off Entiat Valley to interview a rancher. I had difficulty getting back because a heavy snowfall occurred. After getting home, I got a phone call asking me if I was coming to the seance. I said no, I was worn out from the trip down the mountain road, and, besides my wife had the car. However, the caller said, the house is only a short walk from your place, and the seance would sure make a good story. The word "story" has always spurred me into action so, of course, I went to the affair. The house was an old one with a full-length front porch and a narrow, vertical slot in the front door. When I knocked someone opened the slot and I saw an eye but little else. Like Cyclops, I thought.

Once inside it was weird! Across the darkened room sat a large woman with a deeply lined face looking into a large fishbowl. I thought it must be some kind of a cult, because she didn't use a crystal ball. In the corner of the room sat a guy looking into the corner. He just sat there; didn't move. All the while the "Song of India" a melancholy tune, was being played in the background. It was spooky.

In a couple of minutes, I moved to a small table across from "Madam Sobochowski" and started asking questions and taking notes. She said I was full of spirits and would travel soon. I replied I had just gotten back from Hawaii. After a while the lights went out.

My reaction was "What kind of nuts am I involved with?" and "No one knows I'm here," because I had not told Martha. I was just a little apprehensive as to what I had gotten into. Suspiciously, I also checked on my wallet in my back pocket.

I was continuing to ask questions, when I heard a rustling noise to the left of me and felt something going through my hair. Later something went through my hair again in the opposite direction.

All of a sudden THE LIGHTS CAME ON! Who was there? The whole newsroom! Some gag, eh? I just loved it and have repeated the story dozens of times.

The Big Sign

Our engraver and later press cameraman, jolly Roy Snodgrass, a big fellow, had a lot of fun with people around the plant. He is best remembered for giving just about everyone on the paper a humorous gift at Christmas, most of them risque. So I got the idea of repaying him for his kindness by placing a large billboard in the front room of his house while he and his wife, Vi, were at work. She was a nurse. It read "A Big Thanks to Big Roy From His Big Bunch of Friends." City Editor George Richardson helped me put the sign up. It was so large that it split the room diagonally in half.

We learned later that Mrs. Snodgrass on seeing what had been done peered at the ceiling to see if we had done any damage, because it had just been given a new finish.

There was a sequel to this practical joke. Read on.

The Mailman

About three weeks after this episode, I started getting a lot of mail. In succeeding days, I got more and more, so much so, that the mailman had to put it on the front porch one time because the mailbox would not hold it.

The letters in the deluge tried to sell me a course so I could get my high school diploma, told me how to become a physical specimen like Charles Atlas, or how to go into nurses training, and it brought little gifts, like tiny flower pots, all sorts of things.

I soon figured out that Mr. Snodgrass had put me on numerous mailing lists. So much mail came, that Martha, an even-tempered person, actually became angry. It took me months to get off these lists, follow-ups continuing to come all the while. Roy later told he had given my name to 115 companies. I thought it was funny, Martha didn't.

Front Pages

Each time a department head retired, I put out a special front page in his honor. These contained humorous headlines, photos, and stories. I must have put out a dozen of these.

The headline over the one for Roy Snodgrass read "Odd Character Finally Disposed Of." The page on Jack Watkins, company general manager, said in one story "What can you say about Jack Watkins that hasn't already been said about hemorrhoids?"

Special front pages also came out on other occasions. When Publisher Wilfred Woods and his wife celebrated their 25th wedding anniversary, a story page said "The reception will be held in Chelan at the home of the bride's mother. It will be the first time the place has been cleaned up in months."

On the occasion of my speaking to the Wenatchee Kiwanis Club, I issued a silly front page with Kiwanis-oriented articles and a photo showing me speaking alongside two Kiwanians. I had newsboys hawk the paper at the luncheon. What surprised members was seeing this picture, which they had seen taken only a few minutes before, printed that quickly. Of course, I had had it taken earlier with us posed exactly as shown in the picture.

Besides the humorous front pages I produced, there was one that really topped them and "I" was the victim!

I had had a gallbladder operation and had returned home. I was sitting in the front room on Tyler Street when I noticed the newsboy plunk a paper on the doorstep. Martha went and got it.

I opened up the July 9, 1959, issue and was startled to see a black, five-column headline reading, "Medical Mystery Solved; Lost Gallbladder Found." For an instant I thought "How stupid to put out a headline on that," then I caught on. It was a humorous front page poking fun at me. It turned out that reporter Dick Larsen had put it together.

I could only read a little at a time, because with my new incision, it rather hurt when I laughed.

The story under the main head read:

"As a screaming, cheering throng jammed sidewalks and streets along the route from the Deaconess Hospital to a modest white house on Tyler St., Hu Blonk returned home.

"Washington State Patrol officials estimated the screaming, cheering, throng at nearly four persons, including a three-year-old boy who had wandered into the neighborhood by mistake.

"Blonk, sometimes gardener and house painter, was home again after surgery. Physicians ordered the operation last week after Blonk reported the disappearance of his gallbladder.

"Discounting the theory of Wenatchee World staffers that their managing editor needed no gallbladder, because he vented all his gall on them anyhow, Dr. Alfred Stojowski and Dr. George Krakowka decided to take a peek.

"Word trickling out of the somber, brick clinic where Blonk was taken indicated the hardest part of the preliminary diagnosis was in getting him to pose for X-rays. Blonk, star of many community theatrical productions, insisted on putting what he termed his "best profile" towards the machine.

"Technicians distracted Blonk momentarily by marching a parade of gorgeous nurses past the X-ray machine and were finally able to snap a series of pictures.

"The pictures, however, all turned out to be of the gorgeous nurses, but the physicians decided, after determining that Blonk carried medical insurance, to open him up.

"Blonk entered the hospital Thursday. During the days preceding the event, Blonk showed little sign of being nervous, although co-workers found a drawer full of sawdust, apparently from pencils he had chewed up when no one was looking, and a hole worn in the new flooring under his desk.

"Circumstantial evidence," Blonk muttered as he was informed of that discovery. "I'm not at all concerned about this."

"While he spoke, a staff of some 30 physicians, plumbers chiropractors, and spiritualists hired by Blonk to see him through the ordeal, conferred outside his door.

"The consultation broke up when a doctor, who declined to be identified, threw down his cards and stalked out the door.

"Blonk was under the lights for nearly two hours, before his wife persuaded him to come down and get on the table for his operation.

"He was wheeled back to his room several minutes later, given a pre-digested diet of pencils and told not to laugh until the incision healed. The contents of what appeared to be a gallbladder was turned over to Dr. Robert Bonifaci and Chelan County Sanitarian Lloyd Ajax for further investigation.

"Blonk seemed his usual self when he was about to return home. While carefully scanning the report of his operation, he screamed, "Say, doc, you sure you spelled gallbladder right?"

A caption under a photo of a Leavenworth twirling group of young girls read:

"Learning that Hu Blonk would be hospitalized there, Deaconess Hospital took some precautionary steps. It immediately ruled that all third floor nurses would have judo training and calisthenic conditioning. "We hear Blonk's a frisky one with the girls," explained head of the nursing staff, Mary Murphy.

Another article on the phony front page read:

"The Wenatchee World, a local newspaper, may be putting out another edition again one of these days.

"That's if we get around to it," explained acting managing editor, Beulah Davenport. She added "Yahoo! Pass the cheese dip!"

"The paper suddenly halted production in early June, when members of the news staff decided it would be more fun to have a party than write news stories.

"A vacant desk in the center of the news room was converted into a bandstand for a jazz group, and the dancing crowd can be seen whirling around it most days and nights. Chinese lanterns brightly decorate the newsroom.

"Occasionally the voice of Bill White rises above the din shouting, "Hey, Beulah, it's my turn to be managing editor!"

Angry Angler

When on a hiking trip with three Okanogan County commissioners, I wrote a story on the mountain experience. But at the urging of two of the commissioners, Jack Abrams and Ed Winslow, I said that John Carlson, the other commissioner, had caught a fish using a spoon. Being a member of the Okanogan Fly Fishermen Club, he was met with all sorts of scurrilous remarks on returning to Okanogan from acquaintances who had read the article.

In about three days, I was served with a legal paper suing me for a $1 million dollars for defamation of character. Carlson had put a fellow fly fisherman, a lawyer named Reese Mansfield, up to it.

Fun With a Debate

While with the bureau in Boise, I was asked to debate Assistant Regional Director Lyle Cunningham on the subject of "Should I Induce My Son to Enter the Government Service?"

I took the negative side, never having been a rock-solid bureaucrat. Lyle, on the hand, having come to Boise from Washington, D. C., had all the attributes.

I made my presentation humorous. I stressed the deplorable plight USBR employees lived under, showing a picture of a housewife cooking on an old wood stove. I also drew up an organization chart which showed a lot of boxes, denoting positions on the staff but, of the 30 or 40, only one was a production unit.

I presented a lot of statistics none of which were the truth. I quoted the "Western Governmental Research Association." There was no such association, so I made up any set of facts that I wanted to use.

Trail Side Humor

The Forest Service took official groups into the back country. On one trip there were some county commissioners and also Heather, the wife of Congressman Tom Foley. She was always a good sport. Once the hired

248

help threw her into the lake with her clothes on, after she had been kidding them.

Everybody on these trips rode horses. I never felt at ease with them so this trip I decided to walk out the last 17 miles. It was mostly downhill.

I started early and enroute got the idea to write short, fictitious press releases and place them on rocks along the trip route.

One of the five I wrote read "Washington, D. C. — Congressman Tom Foley announced today that he is filing for divorce. He said that his wife had deserted him for a horse."

More Trail Jokes

On one of the many mountain trips the World sponsored annually, I took along a little bag of horse manure.

Attached to it was the following:

Pasayten Fragrance
Manufactured by Claud Miller and Associates
Boyd Walter, Distributor
Guaranteed Produced by Native Inhabitants
Have Memories of Your Trail Hike All Year Long

INSTRUCTIONS FOR USING: Allow contents to age in sunshine on the back porch, then put into the freezer compartment of your refrigerator.

When used, take 8 ounces of contents and allow it to thaw by placing it in front of the hot-air outlet of your furnace.

Do not use to excess as this genuine Cascade mountain product is the most odiferous obtainable anywhere.

Surprise your friends at Christmas time. Use "Pasayten Fragrance" in place of the smell of pine cones . . . Or at Thanksgiving instead of the odor of musty pumpkin.

GUARANTEED: If not satisfied return unused portion to Boyd Walter, Route 1, Box 560, Manson WA 09931.

Fun at Open House

The paper had periodic open house parties, generally on the occasion of some anniversary. As people toured the plant, those of us whose byline was well known were asked to be present because sometimes people wanted to meet the person behind the name.

During a late stage of my retirement, in a prominent spot on my desk where we kept our name plates, I had put the sign "Oldest Geezer Here."

Most people laughed as they saw it, but a couple of older ladies felt I ought to feel offended. One said to me, "Why I think that's awful, I'd make them take it down!"

Mountain Top Humor

Once I carried humor to great heights — to the top of Mt. Hood in Oregon.

Don Pugnetti, managing editor of the Tri-City Herald, and I were induced by Erwin Rieger, M.E. of the Vancouver Columbian, to climb the mountain with him.

We had never attempted climbing to any appreciable heights. Erwin had been doing so for many years.

We started at 2 a.m. and reached the top at 2 p.m. I had carried in my pocket a sizable banner which Don and I unfurled at the crest of the peak. On it, I made fun of the Bellingham Herald M.E., Ben Sefrit, who was head of the Allied Dailies of Washington and happened to be vacationing in Hawaii at the time.

The sign read "Where in Hell is Ben Sefrit?"

Of course, we took photos to present to Ben when he returned to Bellingham. I was told he got as big laugh out of it.

The "Absentminded" Professor

One time, I was involved with something humorous but not by choice.

It was the result of my life-long absentmindedness which early in life caused my mother to describe me in Dutch as "the absent-minded professor."

The incident occurred at a car wash.

Rolling down the car window and carefully reading the instructions, I put six quarters in the coin box and drove into the car wash.

As I neared the rotary brushes, the water came in. I was immediately drenched. I had forgotten to roll up the car window!

And because I had power-driven windows it took a little time before I could find the right button, mainly because I couldn't see in the spray of water. The brushes were nearly inside before I found the button to close the window.

The People's Right to Know Defended

It was in Phoenix, Arizona, in 1954 that my 25 years of fighting for the people's right to know through the Freedom of Information Committee of the Associated Press Managing Editors Association (APME) began.

I had been sent there by the publisher to accept a citation the organization was to give us for the utmost cooperation we had extended the Associated Press in the coverage of the sensational Goldmark case in Okanogan County.

During one program of the convention, it was announced that the Freedom of Information (FOI) Committee would meet in such and such a cabin. I decided to follow a group headed in that direction but held back because I was a stranger in the organization. At one point, I almost decided not to proceed further. Later, when I was welcomed enthusiastically, I decided to join.

As I have done all my life, I pitched in zealously to do what I had been assigned. The major effort was towards assuring freedom of the press in relation to court procedure.

After little more than a year on the committee, I received a phone call from the APME president, Charles Roe, Fredericksburg, Virginia, asking if I would assume the chairmanship of the committee because the chairman, an editor from Perth Amboy, N. J., had labor trouble and could not continue to carry on. I said, "Why don't you make the vice chairman the chairman?" He said he preferred me because I had been so active.

I retained the chairmanship for three years, then served as vice-chairman four years. As a result of my work I was selected to the APME Board of Directors in 1966, just two years after I had joined the organization. Later, I was re-elected for another three-year term.

In my first official report in the Red Book, (the annual report of the APME activities) I said "In the halls of Congress you score what a headwriter not too finicky about cliches would call a smashing victory. In the courtroom, you take a poke in the nose, and you're told to go out and sin no more."

For in the Congress, we and other news organizations had been successfull in getting the Freedom of Information Act passed after a long struggle by a 307 to 0 vote. But in regard to keeping courtrooms from being closed by the bench and the bar to assure fair trials we were about to take a beating

Fair Trial — Free Press

In regard to the court problem, I reported that the U. S. Supreme Court had ruled that Dr. Samuel H. Sheppard did not receive a fair trial on the charge that he murdered his wife, and it criticized the presiding judge for not keeping the trial under control so that Sheppard could get a fair trial. He also lambasted the press for permitting gross abuses in news coverage and courtroom behavior.

While the court placed no restrictions on the press, the wording of the edict was such that Freedom of Information was apt to suffer through the interpretation that judges, lawyers and police officers would put on the court's opinion.

The criticism accentuated what the Warren Commission on the assassination of President Kennedy had concluded earlier "The experience in Dallas is a dramatic affirmation of the need for steps to bring about a proper balance between the right of the public to be informed and the right of the individual to a fair and public trial."

That prompted the American Bar Association (ABA) to name an advisory committee on the fair trial-free press issue, later known as the Reardon Committee, Paul C. Reardon, a Massachusetts Supreme Court judge, heading it. It subsequently issued a report that sought to curtail news coverage of the police and the courts.

The ABA aimed to have the legal profession of each state adopt standards to control what lawyers might tell reporters about pending cases. It also urged law enforcement officials to establish strict internal codes governing the release of crime news during the pre-trial hearings at the request of the defendant.

Further, the Reardon Report also called for contempt of court citations against anyone who published an "extra-judicial statement willfully designed to affect the outcome of a trial" or that "seriously threatens to have that effect."

APME and other press groups attacked. I and others met with the Reardon Committee in New York and in Hawaii to voice our strong objection to the proposal. My role was to advocate achieving the fair trial goal through codes of voluntary restraint such as we had in the state of Washington. We, of the press, knew that the Reardon standards would result in most hearings being closed.

After much turmoil over a long period we won out. Today nearly every state has a code of voluntary restraint, many containing some of the words we had put in our Washington State code.

Freedom of Information Act Passed

The passage of the Freedom Of Information Act in Congress in 1966 which the President appropriately signed on the Fourth of July, opened records of the government to the people for the first time.

Glowing language was used by some congressmen to praise the result. Rep. John Moss, of California, who was the sparkplug who got the bill through the Congress, said the legislation would for "the first time in our nation's history guarantee the people's right to know the facts of government."

Rep. David S. King of Utah said: "This guarantee of the people's right to know will surely stand as one of the milestones of mankind's long and troublesome quest for greater liberty."

Later Rep. Moss named the key editors who helped him get the legislation enacted in the Congressional Record, the official publication of the Congress. I was most pleased to find my name listed.

I sought to strike a further blow for open government during the 1968 election. I asked the two candidates — Richard Nixon and Hubert Humphrey — to advise me what "their pilosophy and intent in regard to freedom of information as it pertains to the federal government in all its aspects" would be.

I had found in less significant elections, that candidates are apt to make statements that later I could use against them if they deviated from the statement while in office.

Humphrey conceded that a communication gap does indeed exist between the government and the citizens it serves and declared he would take this attitude "Either there is a valid reason for withholding — and the government has the burden of proving this — or the information will be available."

Nixon said "I believe a President must, whenever he can, make the decision for more knowledge rather than less. I do not believe in the right to lie."

In light of Watergate, one might say Nixon did not always stick to the truth.

Openness Sought in Other Ways

Down several other Avenues I tried to help newspeople prevent infringements on the people's right to know.

In that regard a notable event occurred early in my FOI chairmanship. I had just returned to Wenatchee from climbing Mt. Hood in Oregon when I received a phone call from a Eugene, Ore., attorney who was representing Annette Buchanan, a 20-year-old editor of the University of Oregon

252

campus newspaper. She was charged with contempt of court for refusing to give a grand jury the names of students she interviewed in writing a story about the use of marijuana on the campus.

The attorney said he was having difficulty getting Oregon newspapermen to testify in her behalf. I accepted immediately, and, in a matter of hours, was on my way to Eugene.

I was the first person to testify in the crowded courtroom. My pitch was that protecting one's news sources was as much a part of journalism as the typewriter.

While I realized that the case had drawn national attention, and my title as AMPE FOI chairman was of some significance, I was still surprised on leaving the courtroom to find television cameras from ABC, NBC, and CBS pointed at me. I subsequently found my picture on the front page of the Portland Oregonian and in the Seattle Post-Intelligencer.

The editor was convicted and fined $300 which the publisher of the Oakland Tribune promptly paid. The ruling brought about considerable talk about getting a national shield law enacted that would protect writers from being cited in cases of this kind, but nothing ever happened.

A lot of my time was devoted to trying to get law schools to teach the importance of free press and journalism schools to teach the importance of fair trial.

I succeeded in arranging a day-long meeting in Chicago of several deans of law and journalism schools to discuss bringing this about. It took place during the Christmas-New Year holidays of all times. I was never successfull in this venture because law schools refused to pay much attention to newsmen.

I helped fight the ABA in yet another way. It had persistently objected to having cameras in the courtroom. Our state accomplished it early by putting on a demonstration of how little disturbance they caused. While I was not a member of the committee in charge I kept close track of the test because I thought it would be very helpful to other states seeking to get their photographers in the courtroom. I issued an APME report entitled "Cameras in the Courtroom — How to Get Them There." Now, most state courts have removed the restriction, and even the federal courts are considering doing the same.

I also had printed another court-related report. It was entitled "Courtroom Design — Preferences of the Press." It included suggestions from editors as to how courtrooms might better serve the press and justice if they were arranged differently. I made the study in connection with one undertaken by the American Bar Association and American Institute of Architects.

I quoted a prominent architect as saying "There has been no new thinking in courtroom design in the past 150 years."

Back Room Was a Busy Place

I spent a lot of weekends working in my back-room den on other Freedom of Information topics.

Here summarized are a few:

— Inspired a study to be made as to whether there were any threats to Freedom of Information in guidelines that some officials urged to be drawn up in connection with coverage of riots. The report summarized that there was "no real threat at the moment to Freedom of Information" but in view of the trend of times a serious warning "to keep the guard up."

— Supervised the making of a survey among the general public to determine attitudes on the right of a man to have a fair trial in relation to the right of the people to know. It revealed that the people do not want less news about judicial processes and law enforcement.

— Initiated an unsuccessful campaign to bring about a National Freedom of Information Day to focus attention for a single day on the importance of the First Amendment. The proposal was supported by Editor and Publisher, a major news media magazine, and several other publications.

— Sparkplugged the conduct of a study to determine what barristers do in the courtroom prejudice-wise. Fifty experienced court reporters were contacted. The consensus felt that a small, but nevertheless significant, number of lawyers use prejudicial tactics that can be construed to be more prejudiced and damaging than any newspaper article. The study summary stated a better job of court reporting would definitely be in the public interest.

— Initiated a study to determine press restrictions on court news coverage in eight countries behind the Iron Curtain, and how they compared with U. S. procedures. The study was made for us by the Library of Congress at the request of a congressman. Its report featured 44 pages dealing with news coverage and 22 pages with photography in the courtroom. It disclosed that restrictions ranged from prohibitions on the use of a typewriter in Rumania to giving certain trials in Bulgaria and Czechoslovakia greatest nation-wide attention to prevent the spread of crime. No direct comparison between news of American and Communist justice was possible because of conflicting philosophies in government.

— Made innumerable speeches in many parts of the country advocating the protection of freedom of information in all forms, but particularly on bench-bar-press relations, such appearances having been made among other places, in Chicago, San Diego, Oklahoma City, Hawaii, Berkeley and Portland, Oregon.

— Wrote the section on Bench-Bar-Press relations for the Associated Press Managing Editors Association manual for managing editors of some 400 daily newspapers in this country. It stressed precaution against encroachment on freedom of the press but urged restraint in news coverage of the courthouse and police station so that a fair trial would be assured.

— For three years personally complimented, by letter, many reporters, photographers, and editors who refused to "knuckle under" when threatened by public agencies or officers. This was done in the thought that unless skirmishes are fought on the home front, the battle for the people's right to know would be lost nation-wide.

— Had a study made to determine the dangers of news stories being attributed only to "sources, reliable sources, or a 'high government official'." Some responsible editors felt that under non-attribution, the news media itself was violating the concept of freedom of information and also violating the right of the people to know all the facts.

— Fought the attempt of the Defense Department to combine the New York Bureau of "Stars and Stripes" with the Armed Forces News Bureau in Washington, D. C., a move seemingly aimed at news management. Alerted key congressmen with the result that the Pentagon dropped the merger plan, thereby escaping a Congressional investigation that seemed certain as a result of the complaint.

— Dispatched, hurriedly, 33 individual letters to key Congressmen to prevent the Subcommittee on Foreign Operations and Government Information from being abolished through lack of funds resulting from a political maneuver. This prompted Rep. Moss, on May 15, 1968, to say "Many thanks for your timely and effective support in the battle to retain Subcommittee on Foreign Operations and Government Information I shall forever be grateful to you and the others who helped in so many ways . . . the Subcommittee will vigorously pursue its role as watchdog over government information policies and practices."

— Stimulated the FOI committee to make certain that the American people were being told the truth about the Vietnam War through a survey of editors and war correspondents.

— Responded by mail to dozens and dozens of requests for help from editors throughout the country who faced specific threats to the people's right to know. The correspondence totaled 278 letters in one year.

Prepared a list of 150 speakers from the journalism profession who could emphasize the press role in schools of law, where future lawyers, prosecutors and judges are educated.

— Had the courts covered extensively for the Wenatchee World for which effort it was awarded a certificate of merit under the American Bar Association's program "for an outstanding system of law and justice."

Court Relations Argued in State

My long participation in the controversy over fair trial and free press started at the state level in early 1964, because of my having been invited by Superior Court Judge Lawrence Leahy, of Chelan County, to speak to a group of judges on the subject of news treatment of juveniles in trouble.

This was followed by another speech on juveniles at a state meeting of Washington's Superior Court judges in Spokane.

Thus, when the chief justice of the State Supreme Court Richard Ott decided to establish a bench-bar-press committee to assure amiable relations between the three interests I was one of the editors named to it. The committee sought to draft guidelines to assure fair trial and free press in the state. The judge appointed the committee of 22 at the request of the Washington Judicial Conference, because the legal profession had become concerned that excessive publicity given sensational cases prevented a defendant from getting a fair trial. It pointed to the abuses of the press in coverage of the trial of Dr. Samuel Shepherd on charges that he killed his wife.

The portion of the guidelines that would cover coverage of juveniles in the arrest and trial stages were drafted largely by Judge Charles Stafford, of Skagit County, and myself. I was appointed to that phase of the guidelines because of my earlier speeches on that subject.

Once the document was approved, the committee held annual meetings to discuss specific problems in news coverage as they arose, for instance, a judge closing a courtroom, which was annoying to the press, and newspapers publishing confessions, which was annoying to judges. The committee also held regional meetings throughout the state to educate all who were concerned with fair trial and free press about the guidelines.

To make the bench-bar-press committee more effective, the committee in the early 1970s established a liason committee, later referred to as "the fire brigade." In case of any complaint, either by a judge or a newspaper, about some phase of a trial such as a request by lawyers to close the courtroom, the committee would spring into action. It would call the judge and meet with him in person.

The "fire brigade" consisted of a representative of the broadcasters, a Superior Court judge, an attorney, the excutive director of the Allied Dailies of Washington, and a member of the press, namely me. Surprisingly, the committee had utmost success though it actually had no powers nor brought great pressure on the jurist involved. Just a discussion of the troublesome situation did the job.

One memorable situation involved a Snohomish County judge. He was presiding over a sensational murder trial involving a man who had killed his wife, a neighbor and a baby. The defense asked that the courtroom be closed during certain phases of the trial.

The judge asked for the aid of the committee in preparing to make his decision, so we met with him in Everett for breakfast. In the afternoon lawyers formally presented arguments for and against the closure. The judge ruled in favor of the press position and, in doing so, stated that he had met with the "fire brigade" earlier. Afterwards the attorney representing the news media said that no doubt the committee had brought about the favorable opinion, rather than his presentation in open court.

We, of the "fire brigade", got involved with another sensational case. The Ellensburg judge presiding over a trial of 17 Seattle police officers on conspiracy charges asked for the committee to draft a special set of guidelines. He sought to prevent publication of testimony and arguments that occurred during the many days of preliminary hearings. We drafted these with the result that after the trial, the judge praised the committee for having helped assure a fair trial while protecting the people's right to know.

Through the many years on the state committee, I was called upon by various newspapers, TV and radio staions to offer help in specific problems they were facing. The longest journey I took in being of assistance landed me in Anchorage, Alaska.

Bob Atwood of the Anchorage Times called one afternoon to ask if I could be in Anchorage the next day because the judges were having the Alaska press in for a luncheon and there was to be a panel discussion. He said he feared the judiciary was trying to put "something over on us."

I said I would come up but how would I get there so quickly. He said take such and such a plane in Seattle. I did and found myself arriving at the meeting place at noon. The judges were very friendly and even suggested I get on the panel with them. I did. All that happened was just talk. The judges said nothing about putting restrictions on the press.

After the meeting, I called on Atwood to tell him he had nothing to worry about. The problem was that the Alaska press and judiciary had not been talking to one another. I strongly suggested dialogue. That's what made the Washington bench-bar-press relationship successful.

My presence cost Atwood $300 in airfare and lodging.

Awards presented

It was most pleasing through my many years of newspapering to receive recognition for having aided the profession in a number of ways. Some of the awards are below.

FOI AWARD — The Western Washington chapter of Sigma Delta Chi award for "distinguished service to journalism" was given in 1966. It heralded activities in the field of freedom of information.

BOSCH AWARD — This one, a plaque, was presented for "serving humanity through journalism." It was accompanied by a $500 check. The award was established in honor of Susan Hutchison Bosch, a Seattle P. I. reporter who died at the age of 25. The presenter mentioned protecting the people's right to know in bench-bar-press relations in the state and in the U. S.

HALL OF JOURNALISTIC ACHIEVEMENT — The Washington State University's school of journalism presented this award in 1979. A large framed photo of the annual winners, hangs in the journalism building of the university.

JOHN PETER ZENGER FREEDOM OF THE PRESS AWARD — This beautiful large plaque was issued annually by the Fraternal Order of Eagles to the editor of a newspaper or the radio or TV station having done the most to protect freedom of the press in this country. It was presented in 1970. The winner the previous year was the Kansas City Star.

CHROMIUM-PLATED CROWBAR — It was presented by the Allied Dailies of Washington so it could be used to continue to pry open doors behind which business was being conducted secretly.

SDX AWARD — This plaque was presented by the Inland Empire chapter of Sigma Delta Chi in 1965 for "distinguished service to journalism."

BUREAU OF RECLAMATION AWARD — Called the "Citizen Award," it was presented for "unusually well informed coverage of land and water resources programs in the Pacific Northwest."

257

SUPREME COURT CERTIFICATE — This large framed scroll signed by all members of the State Supreme Court was presented in 1974 during the retirement banquet at the Elks Lodge. It cites contributions toward improving bench-bar-press relations through formation of guidelines and mentions other court-related activities in the state and nation.

WRITING AND PHOTOGRAPHY AWARDS — These focused on various categories of writing and picture-taking over many years.

WEEKLY PUBLISHERS AWARD — This framed certificate dated October, 1964, was awarded by the Washington Newspaper Publishers Association, an organization of weekly papers, "in recognition of meritorious and valuable services rendered the association and the press of the state as a whole."

APME MERITORIOUS SERVICE AWARD — 1991 was the first year this coveted plaque was issued. It cited 25 years of service through membership in the Freedom of Information Committee.

FREEDOM FOUNDATION AT VALLEY FORGE AWARD — In 1972, this foundation represented the "George Washington Honor Medal Award" for "Freedom of the Press/Fair Trial Activities." The organization is dedicated to preserving the American heritage for future generations. The selection was made by an independent national award jury consisting of 13 state supreme court judges and 29 national representatives of civic, educational, patriotic, veterans and service organizations.

CIRCULATION MANAGERS ASSN. AWARD — The International Circulation Managers Assn. in 1991 presented the Wenatchee World with a first-place award for providing carrier recognition via a story about a little girl who invested her earnings in stocks and bonds. This was a team effort with the Circulation Dept.

Retirement Party was Hilarious

Few people got such a funny gift on their retirement as I did as managing editor of the Wenatchee World in 1974.

Chocolate-covered pencils!

They were given to me by Mary Jo Milne, head of The World's women's department at that time. I have had the vile habit of chewing on the end of pens or pencils for many years, including my college days. I have a University of Washington annual that shows me in the section devoted to the U. W. Daily seated at a typewriter with a pencil in my mouth.

I did this not only in the World newsroom but at public functions. A photograph of my standing at the podium after having introduced someone as master of ceremonies at the dedication of Rocky Reach Dam shows me with pencil in mouth.

With Dick Larsen, a key reporter on my staff, as the master of ceremonies there was one laugh after another for me and my family and a couple hundred or so people who had gathered at the Elks Club.

One bit of fun involved the bulky old Underwood typewriter I had used all my years on the paper. I had asked Jack Watkins, general manager, if I could take it with me when I retired. He said he'd determine how much he had to charge me for it. Personally, I thought that was kind of "chintzy."

During the program, Dave Kraft wheeled in a cart with a covering on it. Beneath it I was sure sat my typewriter. He gave some kind of a speech and then pulled the cover back. The typewriter crashed to the floor! I shouted "Oh, my God, my typewriter!" But it proved a hoax. Later they wheeled in the real one with a brass plate on it that read "Hu Blonk's One And Only Typewriter, Presented March 9, 1974."

At my home it joined a similar Underwood that I had used in covering the construction of the Coulee Dam. Later, I was to get another one like it when M.C.-ing a Columbia Basin Development League annual banquet in Moses Lake. It was given to me so that I could continue to write about the project which the league was trying to enlarge.

Key reporter Ray Schrick presented me with a piece of carpet because I was so fidgety at my desk that I twice wore a hole in the linoleum.

A sign on the speaker's stand added merriment. It read "Please limit comments to two minutes . . . . Abusive remarks may run a little longer!"

There were serious moments, too. George Richardson, my city editor, read a telegram from President Nixon which he had gotten through a congressman, I think. The message, printed on a Western Union form read "As so many of your fellow citizens and friends gather in tribute to your distinguished career, I want you to know that I fully share their appreciation of your accomplishments. In your two decades as managing editor of the Wenatchee World, you have displayed qualities of professional leadership, integrity and responsibility that are a credit to the fourth estate and an example of the most inspiring adherence to the traditions of our cherished freedom of the press. You have my very best wishes for every satisfaction and happiness in your retirement." — Richard Nixon.

Probably the most distinguished persons in the audience were four justices of the State Supreme Court, Robert Hunter, Robert Finley, Hugh Rosellini and Robert Utter. I had gotten acquainted with them during my years on the State Bench-Bar-Press Committee. They presented me with a large framed scroll which carried the wording of a resolution that the entire court had passed. It thanked me for services rendered.

George Richardson, my city editor, took over as managing editor and handled the complicated change-over from typewriter to computer and the use of other electronic gear. He performed this task and other difficult management problems very well, I think.

Retirement Led To Humorous APME Incidents

On my retirement as managing editor two humorous APME-related incidents occurred.

At the 1974 convention in Orlando, Florida, a spotlight was turned on Martha and me at the closing banquet. The members were asked to join in singing the following song (to the tune of "You") as written by Dick Smyser of the "Oakridger" in Tennessee:

> Hu!
> Gee, but you're wonderful, Hu.
> Faithful Hu.
> You completey satisfy
> Every need of FOI
> There's nobody like Hu.
>
> To find what's true,
> Many a fight's been seen through,
> Thanks to Hu.
> Blocks to information, Zonk!
> Thanks to zeal by our man Blonk
> There's nobody like Hu.
>
> When fat cats turn the latch key,
> To thwart our search for the facts
> Our hero from Wenatchee
> Has always been there to give 'em the axe.
>
> Incomparable Hu!
> What in the world will we do
> Without you!
>
> Guardian of freedom's fire,
> Here's to you as you retire,
> Let's hear it for Hu.

The second humorous incident was the aftermath of the appearance of President Richard Nixon to the convention. I had come in late to hear his press conference remarks and was surprised to see a vacant seat in the front row. This was the occasion when he said in relation to Watergate "I am not a crook". The minute I heard Nixon say that I knew I had been in on something historic.

The day after the session, I saw an AP photo that showed the President pointing to the audience with his arm outstretched. It looked like he was pointing directly at me. Of course, I got a copy of it.

Clever associates on the Wenatchee World used it as the front cover of the program for my retirement banquet. They had drawn on it a balloon coming out of Nixon's mouth saying "What's this I hear about you retiring, Hu?"

Martha Passes Away

Sadness followed my retirement.

Six years after I retired, Martha passed away. She died in our home in East Wenatchee, not having been in the best of health for a number of years.

She contributed much to my accomplishments. As I said earlier we moved so many times during the Bureau of Reclamation days, but she never objected. I was away so much that I feel she almost raised our daughter alone. I have a somewhat guilty conscience about that.

She was a wonderful person.

With Three Generations of Woods

I have a distinction among the many employees the World has had over the years. I worked under three generations of Woods — Rufus Woods, the original publisher; Wilfred Woods, his son who followed him as publisher; and Rufus Woods, Wilfred's son, who became a most capable managing editor in the early 1990's. Robert Woods, associate publisher, who is Wilfred's second cousin, was another Woods I was closely linked with as he held various key positions.

He was a most talented writer and always provided sound advice, valued ideas and a much appreciated friendship over many years.

Rufus' enthusiasm knew no bounds, particularly where Grand Coulee Dam was involved. He was a key figure in bringing it about. Whenever he gave a talk on the dam project, he'd wave his arms around in excitement and shout out what he had to say. At times he'd get so excited about what he was saying that he wouldn't finish the sentence.

I think the conclusion of the talk he gave at the 1942 commencement of Grand Coulee High School reveals the enthusic way he spoke. He said:

"So there it stands, a monument to the idea and the power of an idea; a monument to organization; a monument to cooperation; a monument to the United States Bureau of Reclamation; a monument to the magic spirit of willing men which accomplishes more than the might of money or the marvels of machinery; a monument to the brains, the intellect of great engineers — and you, class of 1942, could you come back here a thousand years hence or, could your spirit hover around this place ten thousand years hence, you would hear the sojourners talking as they behold this "slab of concrete," and you would hear them say, "Here in 1942, indeed there once lived a great people."

Only Rufus could talk this way.

Thanks to the Woods

All of the Woods had high principles. While managing editor under Wilf, I found his code of ethics the highest. I never had to slant the news in favor of certain interests. To have it otherwise would have greatly disturbed me.

Wilfred was a considerate person and seldom criticized anyone. Several times I asked him if there wasn't something I was doing that he didn't want done. He rarely mentioned a thing. He made suggestions in the course of management, naturally.

While I carried on most of my people's right-to-know activities on my own time I am indebted to him for looking kindly on the expense I incurred and what company time I expended.

I thank all the Woods for a most exciting life of newspapering. Few journalists have been as lucky.